The Fall and Rise of Tyler Johnson

The Fall and Rise of Tyler Johnson

BASED ON THE JOURNALS AND ACTUAL EVENTS OF A YOUNG MAN TURNED FUGITIVE

• • •

Patrice Johnson

Cover background adapted from a photo taken by Tyler Johnson

ISBN: 1542610680
ISBN 13: 9781542610681
Library of Congress Control Number: 2017900754
CreateSpace Independent Publishing Platform
North Charleston, South Carolina

Dedication

To Tyler and to all the happy moments we shared.
Also in grateful appreciation to those special people and families who showed compassion to Tyler and Yuki. The names and locations have often been changed to protect the innocent, so many—if not most—kind acts of selflessness have gone untold in these pages. The food, shelter, transportation, counsel, and friendship of many generous souls transformed the lives of two lost and desperate young people from hopelessness to hope, from tears of sorrow to tears of laughter. No words can express their families' gratitude.

Contents

Map of Corsica

• • •

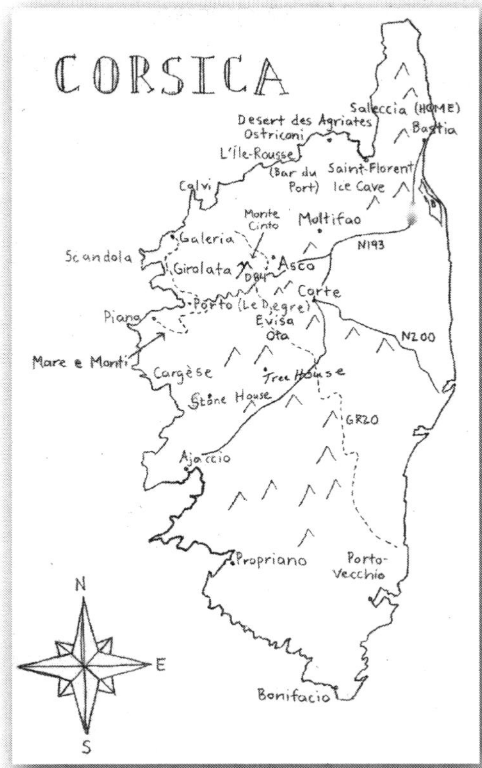

Map handcrafted by Allison McClain (allisoncmcclain@gmail.com)

Foreword

• • •

THE YOUNG MAN I GREW up with was charismatic, kind, fearless, disciplined, optimistic, creative, athletic, handsome, curious, restless, rigorous, driven, naive, funny, irreverent, and honest. Tyler took care of me as an older brother; was my friend and hero. Our judicial system narrowed him to a single word: Terrorist.

Tyler's journals arrived like a treasure chest to our family, an intimate gift. Their contents need not be shared. They hold value without others' knowledge, understanding or approval. For years I objected to my mother's desire to share Tyler's innermost thoughts, struggles and successes with anyone outside our nuclear family. Yet my mother persevered for countless hundreds of hours, alone at the computer, usually in the dark early-morning hours, editing her son's scribbles into a format that could be meaningful to outsiders. The journals contain Tyler's voice, and I suppose she needed to hear it to carry on in present tense.

Now I wholeheartedly agree with publishing this book, not for people's approval of Tyler or to absolve his reputation. I am proud of the person I knew as my brother. We offer the story as a gift to others, as an introduction to a complex human spirit who dared, and struggled, to survive true to his values.

I imagine the tragic turning point when Tyler saw no means of reconciliation and decided to flee. He probably thought *My life is over.* To all of us who have made mistakes that seem irreversible, let us trust that repair is always an option. While we cannot take back our mistakes, we *can* mend the harms, and all parties may heal. No matter how badly we might mess up, potential for repair *always* exists. Like refuse composting and transforming into healthy soil that nourishes new life, our mistakes may fuel deep learning and relationships and wisdom.

Welcome to the nuanced journey of a good man facing impossible moral, physical and emotional conditions. We hope that Tyler's story may nurture a deeper understanding of conflict, powerlessness, loss and redemption. May none of us respond to a mistake thinking *My life is over.*

–Kelsey Johnson
Tyler's sister
M.S., M.S.Ed.

Preface

• • •

February winds were howling outside when the phone rang. "Yes, I am calling from the French consulate," a heavily accented male voice said. "We think we have found your son's body. He was killed by an avalanche." Could we please send Tyler's dental records?

It was the call every parent fears, and one that had haunted my nightmares ever since an FBI agent had pulled me aside and said, "Things like this don't usually end well." Tyler had gone missing six years before that notification from France. A year after his disappearance, we had received what were to become annual letters in which he told us he was okay, and, please, not to worry about him. But they provided no clue about his whereabouts or activities, and last year's letter had carried an undertone of desperation. We had no way to reach him, no way to help—and now the voice on the phone was saying Tyler was dead.

So daughter Kelsey, husband Jim, and I traveled to France to claim the body of our beloved brother and son and to gain a sense of his fugitive life. Among Tyler's final effects, we discovered his journals. In them, Tyler wrote that he was documenting his life "to fill in the canyon of silence."

> The idea is to write everything, I mean everything that has happened during these missing years. Plus of course my usual rambling and maybe a good dose of dreamy mathematics. I'll get it to you as soon as it's done, or rather as soon as the first part is completed.

But this book is not about Tyler's death. That occurs two years later. Rather, it explores an idealistic young man's struggle to overcome the crushing consequences of a night of college binge drinking in a post-9/11 world. *The Fall and Rise of Tyler Johnson* is a story of a resilient young man's struggle to reassemble the shards of his shattered life. Based on actual events as chronicled in his journals and letters, the book is intended to serve as a warning flag to others who may feel tempted to cross over to the wrong side of the law.

Introduction

• • •

Two major science journals have published Tyler Johnson's research in both quantum physics and artificial intelligence. He graduates Caltech at the top of his game, on track to leave his mark on the field of physics, maybe even to change the world. Then, in August 2003 he leaves his family home in Pennsylvania to head for the University of New Mexico and start work toward a PhD. But he diverts for a quick return visit to California.

After a few glorious days of exploring the Channel Islands with his Japanese girlfriend, Yuki, the two venture to Caltech to celebrate with Tyler's wild-genius mentor, doctoral candidate Daniel "Danny" Blair. Tonight, instead of pasting their usual Go Metric bumper stickers in Pasadena's hard-to-reach places, he and Danny plan to affix SUVs = Terrorism stickers to the bumpers of gas-guzzling SUVs.

But the stickers have arrived misspelled, and binge drinking inspires the suggestion to use spray paint instead. They pile into Danny's car, and he drives to a dealership in Arcadia where they tag monster chrome bumpers with environmental slogans such as I ♥ Pollution and Killer. A cruise to Duarte, and Tyler scrawls *Polluter* on a Hummer. Then they roll to a dealership in West Covina, and a Hummer erupts in flames. Fire everywhere. An outbuilding blazes.

Next morning, Tyler and Yuki awake to television broadcasts of charred vehicles and a zoomed-in image of a scorched door panel bearing the letters ELF. "The FBI is treating the case as domestic terrorism," a reporter announces. "The bureau has launched a nationwide manhunt for activists of the Earth Liberation Front, which they consider to be one of the nation's most dangerous extremist movements."

Pursued as a domestic terrorist and facing a mandatory sentence of up to life in prison, Tyler must decide: come forward and risk spending the rest of his life in prison—and expose Yuki to possible imprisonment in Guantanamo—or take a chance at eluding the FBI. Trying to focus through a rising swell of panic, he pulls out his journal and writes:

> All scenarios indicate school out, nearly every way impossible.[1]

Tyler is twenty-four. He will remember this as the moment when he decides to flee and become a fugitive. He cannot foresee how this decision will lead to battles against starvation, thirst and exposure in the deserts and mountains of Corsica, France. Nor can he imagine the human and creature assaults that await him in the urban jungles of Marseilles and Paris. He gives no thought to the degradations of homelessness or to the havoc that

1 Excerpt from Tyler's journal around 3 February 2004.

living an underground life will wreak on his relationship with the woman he loves. All Tyler knows in the fog of distress is that if he hopes to have a shot at freedom, then he must leave behind his life, his dreams, his country, and all he holds dear.

Stress. Falling.

• • •

Tyler shivered in the chill of what he knew could be his last Albuquerque sunset. His fingers inserted the key in the Cavalier's ignition. Then he stared across the lot until the parking stripes stretched and slumped like jaundiced hands on a Salvador Dalí clock. Tick. Tock. The FBI had probably arrested Danny by now. They'd come for him next. He had to leave this life behind, not sit here like a damned short-circuited robot. But what if none of this was real?

Tyler recalled the Altoids-scented breath of the kindly registrar. He pictured her blue-haired halo and the worry lines creasing her face. Again, her chubby index finger guided his pen to a form's signature line, the header reading *Withdrawal Form, University of New Mexico.* Just as had happened then, his eyes filled with tears. Yes, his withdrawal was real: the hardest thing he'd ever done, until now.

If—when—he drove off this lot, he was going to cross another line of no return. His mind flashed on the unchecked arrogance and anger in Danny's voice, the irresistible taste of strawberry gloss on Yuki's lips, the relentless lap of hungry flames. Then a blizzard of sensations skittered like mice through his brain. No. He had to push down the panic. Had to write his few remaining options in his journal and choose one.

Tyler let go the key and reached across the red vinyl seat to his backpack. Inside, he felt the smooth cardboard cover of his comp book. He propped it against the steering wheel and let the black-and-white pattern swirl him into an alternate dimension in which heavy muons spun in short-lived orbits around their protons. He exhaled into a wave of nausea and cracked open the pages to his pencil bookmark. He willed his shaking fingers to grip his chewed #2. Then he wrote.

EMOTIONS.

What the hell are they?
Possibly just a trap.
If you escape, then here do you go?
The trap is necessary context.
Without it we have no meaning;
With it we are burdened.
Tragic dependencies.[2]

He needed to hold his emotions in check, to clear his mind, to think. The snapping of graphite broke what was left of his

2 Excerpts from Tyler Johnson's journals are depicted in a different font and have been edited very slightly, mainly for punctuation and spelling.

concentration. Searching for guidance, he scanned the entry he'd scribbled after Danny's phone call last night.

> All scenarios indicate school out, nearly every way impossible.

Yes, he knew what he must do. There was really only one choice, and its chance of success was next to zero. Could he do it? Could he flee? Stalling, he let his gaze shift to a prior entry.

> 27 January 2004. Tragedy is a state of mind. Life is awareness of mind, or rather that mind has states... Tyler has a beginning, and Tyler has an end. In between is a game played by two adversaries. Death is the opponent, and he always wins. The goal is not to play the longest game but to play the most skillfully. The process of playing is precisely what we call life.

If he pretended that the FBI manhunt was a game of hide and seek, if he acted fast and drove straight to the Las Vegas airport without stopping in Flagstaff to see Yuki, then maybe, just maybe, he might escape. The stage was set, the play in motion. How dumb to promise to see her for one last good-bye. Making and keeping a promise was what had landed him in this nightmare in the first place.

"Hey, dog," Danny had said. "I'll order stickers from my mom's print shop. Us guys'll rally for one last ninja night to celebrate your going to grad school. It'll be a blast. You'll come, right, dog?"

"Sure," Tyler had replied. An off-the-cuff answer, one word, and his world had shifted on its axis. What he wouldn't give to tesseract back in time and renege on that promise. If only he'd come straight here to grad school instead of diverting to Pasadena. If Danny's bumper stickers hadn't arrived misspelled or if no one had spray-painted ELF—just three lousy letters. If Danny hadn't filled that empty Corona bottle with gasoline and smashed it on a Hummer. If. If. If.

An oval on the bottom right of his comp book's cover read No boundaries™. They could trademark two absurd words? Every physical object had boundaries—space, these pages, a photon. He had a boundary, and if by some miracle he managed to escape across the US border, then more boundaries were sure to rear their heads. He'd cross into a shadowy, underground realm where people skulked on the wrong side of the law. If he was lucky enough to survive there—and after all this blew over—then he'd still have to find a way to cross back home, to return to everyone and everything he loved.

How could he get by without his best friends Steve and Cam? A year older than he was, they had been there for each other since junior high school. The three of them had learned to skateboard together. He and Steve had teamed up to film their first movie—a school project about the French Resistance during World War II. Together, they'd founded the Physics Club, making geekhood cool—or so they liked to joke with each other. Hell, this was Steve's car. And how could he live without *MeiMei* Kelsey[3] or

---

3 Tyler often refers to his sister Kelsey using pet names such as *MeiMei* (the Mandarin word for sister), Keystone, the Keys, and Keez.

Mom and Dad? Without Grandma J., Grandma and Grandpa W., without his cousins? And Yuki: What to do about Yuki?

A fly buzzed into Tyler's hair, then hurled itself against the windshield. It crawled upside down on the tempered glass and took flight again. Desperate to wing toward blue skies and freedom, it slammed into the unflinching barrier. *Smack. Smack.* Tyler lowered his window and flushed the poor creature out.

Across the lot, the angular brick Physics and Astronomy Building looked plain, even stark, yet inside had felt so right. It was home to his hopes and dreams. On an evening like this last fall, Kevin Morsi had tipped back his Stetson hat and tapped the toe of his cowboy boot.

"Want you boys to meet Tyler Johnson," the professor had drawled to his peers, all world-renowned physicists like him. "This young man's the most promising grad student I've had the privilege to advise, graduated near the top of his class at Caltech with perfect math scores on his SATs and GREs." Then Kevin had passed around printouts of "Evolution of Resource Competition between Mutually Dependent Digital Organisms" and "Continuous-Variable Quantum Teleportation of Entanglement," forever burning the title pages of Tyler's published research into his memory.

"Over a period of thirteen months, Tyler here was the first author of research published in two damned prestigious science journals," Kevin had said, "*Artificial Intelligence* and *Physical Review*."

Evolution of Resource Competition Between Mutually Dependent Digital Organisms

Tyler J. Johnson*
California Institute of Technology, Pasadena, CA 91125
tyler@ugcs.caltech.edu

Claus O. Wilke
Digital Life Laboratory 136-93
California Institute of Technology, Pasadena, CA 91125
wilke@caltech.edu

November 17, 2003

Tyler's "Evolution of Resource Competition between Mutually Dependent Organisms" or more simply "Digital Darwinism," as *Artificial Intelligence* magazine entitled it.

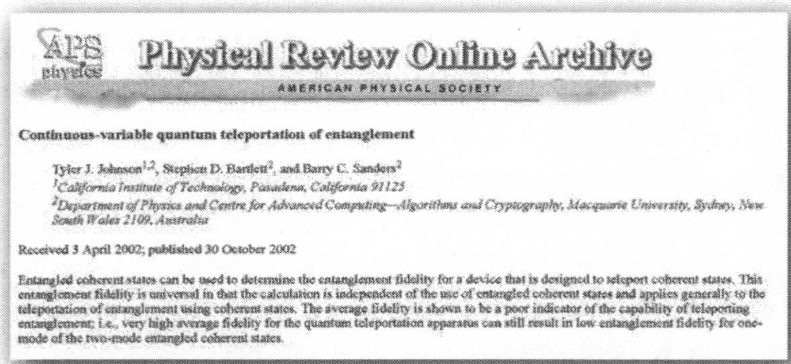

Physical Review Online Archive

AMERICAN PHYSICAL SOCIETY

Continuous-variable quantum teleportation of entanglement

Tyler J. Johnson[1,2], Stephen D. Bartlett[2], and Barry C. Sanders[2]
[1]*California Institute of Technology, Pasadena, California 91125*
[2]*Department of Physics and Centre for Advanced Computing—Algorithms and Cryptography, Macquarie University, Sydney, New South Wales 2109, Australia*

Received 3 April 2002; published 30 October 2002

Entangled coherent states can be used to determine the entanglement fidelity for a device that is designed to teleport coherent states. This entanglement fidelity is universal in that the calculation is independent of the use of entangled coherent states and applies generally to the teleportation of entanglement using coherent states. The average fidelity is shown to be a poor indicator of the capability of teleporting entanglement; i.e., very high average fidelity for the quantum teleportation apparatus can still result in low entanglement fidelity for one-mode of the two-mode entangled coherent states.

Tyler's "Continuous-Variable Quantum Teleportation of Entanglement" research as published in *Physical Review* by the American Physical Society.

Kevin's remarks had made Tyler's cheeks flush, but he had appreciated the professor's welcoming gesture—icing on the cake of a teaching assistantship with free tuition and an annual stipend of $16,000. Yes, five months ago, he had been a rising star with a real chance of leaving his mark on the field of physics, of making the world a better place. Now he was aflame in media catchphrases like "environmental extremism" and "domestic terror."

No way he could shield his friends and family, or Yuki, from the tsunami that was sure to engulf them, but he could do his best to free them from a lifetime of crippling legal fees and heart-wrenching visits to federal prisons. Tyler twisted the key, the engine rumbled, and diesel fumes flooded the musty interior. He willed his right hand to move the gearshift to *D*. His foot eased off the brake, and the car rolled forward, bobbling its dusty white hood onto Lomas Boulevard. The vehicle slowed to a halt under the glow of a stoplight's red eye. Gatekeeper, Tyler thought, between the uni's protective familiarity and a long, dangerous road to nowhere.

The light winked green and dared him to pass. He sat in limbo, observing a car in his rearview mirror. The driver fidgeted before mouthing a one-syllable obscenity and swinging her gray Honda Civic past him through the intersection. Tyler pivoted his foot from brake to accelerator, and the Cavalier glided forward. None of this was real, except that the transformative eye of the gatekeeper and a gram of pressure on a foot pedal were making it real. Like Buddha or God or Zeus, the universe was standing witness in infinite silence, watching him play out his hand, make his choices, and struggle to alter the consequences of one awful, fucked up, and horrible night.

An offhand comment, a stupid remark, had spawned the idea. A week before he was to graduate from Caltech and leave to teach summer school in China, he and Danny were planting Go Metric bumper stickers high on Pasadena's landmarks, a mission they often undertook to refresh their minds before returning to marathon sessions of physics. Tyler had summited the Bank of America building and affixed a sticker for the viewing pleasure of motorists along East Colorado Boulevard.

Rather than congratulating him, however, Danny had snarled, "We should be tagging smog-spewing vehicles." A joke, really, except it conjured up tantalizing possibilities. What better way to raise awareness of the damage that gas-guzzling SUVs were inflicting on the environment than to slap a slogan on their bare-assed chrome bumpers?

As if of its own accord, the 1990-something Cavalier found the entrance to I-25 north and then exited onto I-40 west. Tyler checked the rearview mirror for a tail and watched Albuquerque fade to a speck. Panic was crimping around his chest like barbed wire, so he scanned the red dashboard for a radio button. None. He rolled down the window and let the dry tang of desert air surge into his lungs. *This can't be happening!* He wanted to scream. *I'm a student, a quantum-computational physicist. My life is over!*

The night of 21 August had begun with binge drinking. Who came up with the bright idea to go cruising in Danny's car, anyway? He had spray-painted *Polluter* on a Hummer's door panel. Then all became frenzy. They hit dealership lots from Arcadia to Duarte, tagging monster vehicles with shaggy red slogans. I ♥ POLLUTION. SUVs = TERRORISM. KILLER. In the inebriated fog of early morning, he—or was it Danny?—sprayed Euler's theorem to celebrate its beauty.

Then Danny cruised to Monrovia and Clippinger Hummer in West Covina. Hummers went up in flames. Hell's fire raged up an outbuilding's walls.

Danny was the brightest of the brightest at Caltech, a doctoral candidate in string theory, an awesome TA and friend. No one was ever more built for the role of hero, and Danny knew it. But now the guy had gone off the rails and was making brazen phone calls to the *LA Times*.

Last night, evidently too drunk or stoned to choose his words with care, Danny had slurred to Tyler, "Had to do it. Gotta clear Connole."

Josh Connole, the wrongly arrested, twenty-five-year-old environmental activist from Pomona. "But we agreed," Tyler had choked out through the haze of disbelief. "We'll come forward only if he's unfairly convicted."

"Couldn't wait," Danny had murmured. "But the bastards must have traced my e-mails back to Old Main, 'cause they're interviewing our friends at Caltech. They're asking about me and you both. GR—Not a drill—GR."

Then *click*.

"Damn you, Danny!" Tyler had yelled into the dead connection. "You fuck!" But it was no use. Code "Gotta Run" was in effect. This was all Danny's fault, and the fault of alcohol and bad luck. Great—he was grasping at excuses.

Stars danced on the horizon, and a downdraft of fear swept him deeper toward panic. Yes, Danny was out of control, but face it, code Gotta Run was inevitable. The press was touting the incident as one of the worst acts of environmental extremism in US history. Sure, he'd gone through the motions of a PhD student, attending seminars and fulfilling his responsibilities as a TA, but these days he never sat with his back to the door, and he always, always planned an escape route. Last week an undergrad had dropped a pencil on the tile floor, and the clack had jarred him almost out of his seat.

The desert glided past, juxtaposing its tranquility with Tyler's dry mouth and sweaty palms. The highway's middle line pulsed into the front left side of the car like an intermittent white laser. None of this was real, of course not. What a relief. Any other possibility was unacceptable, unworkable. He started to laugh, an unstoppable, un-Tyler sort of laugh.

A giant green sign loomed ahead: EXIT 198, EAST BUTLER AVENUE, FLAGSTAFF, 2 MILES. He'd been driving for four hours already? Time flew when a person was having fun…or wrestling with a life-shattering problem. He had two minutes to decide. To meet or not to meet Yuki? That was the question.

Sixty seconds. No way. The smart choice was to continue on to McCarran Airport and catch a flight across the border.

Thirty seconds. The silvery lines of Exit 198 peeled off, stretching wide and beckoning. *Two roads diverged in a wood, and I—I took the one less traveled by, and that has made all the difference.* Great. Now Robert Frost was rattling around in his head along with all the other misfires. He'd never questioned the poet's theme that the less-traveled approach offered the superior path. Sure as hell questioned it now.

Two seconds. One. Go straight, he commanded. Straight.

The wheel ticked right, and the Cavalier veered onto East Butler. *Those woods are lovely, dark and deep, but I have promises to keep, and miles to go before I sleep, and miles to go before I sleep.* Yes. His fugitive flight would have to wait. He might be reducing his odds of escape to zero, might be a wanted man, but he was no liar. No promise breaker. Not yet anyway. Come what may, Yuki deserved a face-to-face farewell.

Flagstaff's tiny brick train station materialized before the windshield. Another gatekeeper, this one to the Grand Canyon. Here in the real West, the railroad once meant something. Now its tracks snaked among stoplights, parking lots, and fast-food shops. Add tufts of grass, and this site could pass for any suburban corner of Pennsylvania.

No sign of Yuki. Tyler checked his watch. Definitely the right time. He tensed at what sounded like her whispering his name. No, just the slosh of traffic through wet snow. He pulled to the far side of the tracks and positioned the Cavalier's nose for a quick getaway in case the situation turned sour. Thirty minutes passed. Then he crunched through snow to the station and paced across its beige-and-brown tiles.

No Yuki.

He returned to the car, waited another thirty minutes, and paced through again. An hour past meeting time, and he checked once more. He should leave. Shouldn't have come in the first place. An oncoming pickup drew near, and Tyler's heart crawled into his throat.

The white truck drove east without slowing.

Two hours late. More walking in slush, more gazing at traffic. Three hours. Something was terribly wrong. A police car rolled into the parking lot. Tyler started the engine and hovered his foot over the accelerator. The black-and-white cruised on, riffling a wave of fatigue in its wake. Tyler reclined the bucket seat and tried to ease backward, but a rustle shot him upright. Just his leather jacket. Must close the eyes, only for a minute.

TAP. TAP. TAP. TYLER AWOKE WITH A JOLT, not to cops but to Yuki peering at him through the driver's window. He hopped out and wrapped her in his arms.

> She was all sparkles, the most beautiful little thing. My eyes protested their duty to scan for a tail that might have followed her. Relief poured into our kisses. She seemed out of place here among huge piles of plowed snow, glowing orange under sodium lights, wearing a sleeveless top, high heels that revealed her toenail polish. A fluffy scarf around her neck offered only symbolic warmth. I felt her shivering and instinctively tried to pull her body closer to mine, but we couldn't get any closer.

Parked beside each other, her Corolla and Steve's Cavalier stood out like a pair of white geese on a moonlit lake. "I've been here too long," he said and kissed her again. "We better find a new spot."

She kissed him. "I will follow you."

Neither moved.

At last, they pulled apart. With her car trailing his bumper, he cruised to a corporate complex and parked behind a one-story brick building. Fearing their cars were bugged, they shivered together outside. "It's too cold." Tyler motioned toward the Cavalier. "It's probably safe, or they'd have arrested me by now."

"Okay. Right. Sure."

They climbed inside and locked the doors. Time to say good-bye. "Yuki," he began. Then his carefully planned words churned to mush. She was his world, his everything, and he was hers, too—at least he thought so. Now they'd come to the end, and what could he say? *See you later. Sorry I'm about to be arrested as a domestic terrorist. I'll write you from federal prison, for the rest of my life.* No. There were no words for this sort of thing. None.

Yuki broke the silence. "Don't talk yet. We never know."

"All right." He drove east until Flagstaff's lights were dancing like lightning bugs in the rearview mirror. "Just us and the dark desert sky," he said. They'd been together almost three years now. She'd visited him in Australia. He'd spent time with her family in Japan, and she'd celebrated Christmas with his. Now their moments together were ticking away, and that was the best he could do, blather on about the view?

"Look." She pointed behind them. "Those headlights—I think they're following us."

"Let's hide." Careful not to flare the taillights, he coasted onto a ranch lane. Tires crunched on icy gravel. Then the Cavalier ground to a halt in a depression lined with rocks and scrub brush. Tyler cracked the window, and a silk scarf of cool desert breeze brushed his cheek. "We're out of light shot."

Even so, he and Yuki shrank low in the seat as the suspect vehicle drew near. The headlights curled around a long curve, and the engine's roar faded into the night.

Yuki rubbed two manicured fingers across her forehead. "Guess it was just a semi."

Alone now. Time to try again. "I need to run," Tyler said, and the black abyss swelled toward him. Everything beyond this moment was unimaginable, unfathomable—certainly not part of the present. "It's too hard to say good-bye," he said with a crick in his voice, "so let's not say anything."

She palmed his cheek and turned his face to hers. "No good-byes," she whispered. "My bags are packed. I am coming with you."

Images of them together washed over him, comforting as the switch of a light in a pitch-dark barn. Except that it made no sense for her to abandon her life and join him in his mad, probably futile, rush for freedom. His mind clogged at what might lie ahead: handcuffs, jail cells, and loss so absolute it ground his insides to hamburger. The end could be days, maybe hours away. He took her by the shoulders and pushed her away from him. "You can't come with me. I doubt I'll get far. They're looking for me."

She pressed an index finger across his lips. "I need you. My life is with you."

He gripped the steering wheel with both hands and focused on the graduated spacing between the speedometer lines. "No way. Out of the question."

"You do not understand. I cannot stay. I know too much. They could make me testify against you or send me to Gitmo."

She was right, in part. She couldn't stay in the States. Good chance the FBI didn't know her name yet, but they would learn it soon and come for her, too. "The more distance you put between me and Los Angeles," he said, "the better off you'll be. Maybe you should return home to Japan."

Yuki's face clouded with the same grief-stricken expression he'd seen when she'd received a letter from her mother explaining that their family dog had died. "Please, do not abandon me." Tears brimmed over her lids and trickled down her cheeks.

Time had run out. Decisions had to be made on the fly. Tyler steeled his heart to drive her away, to say false, angry words that would cut so deep she'd hate him forever and never look back. But would she really be better off without him? She didn't deal well with stress or isolation or loneliness. Together, at least they'd have each other's backs. But they'd be more traceable, too. He lost his way in her waiting, pleading brown eyes. "I wish you wouldn't," he said.

She shook her head, and the swish of her silky, black hair filled the compartment with the scent of fresh strawberries. "It's my decision." Barely above a whisper, she jingled, "'I am stuck on Band-Aids, 'cause Band-Aids stuck on me.'"

God, he loved this woman. Like most of her peers, Yuki had studied English for six years before college. But in Japan's shame-based culture, schools discouraged verbalization in class. Mortified of making public mistakes, students prepared for their university entrance exams mostly through written, rote memorization. As a result, many graduated unable to communicate in even basic English. Not Yuki. Having grown up with a passion for American television, both current and past, she could impersonate a wide range of voices and tunes. Whether mimicking James Earl Jones or Miss Piggy, her inflections and gestures mirrored them with near-perfect precision and pitch, despite the occasional wrong word choice.

"What do we do next?" she asked.

He'd already emptied his bank account. His bag was packed and in the trunk. The plan was to bid Yuki a hasty farewell, then tear for the airport. Before boarding a great white bird for parts unknown, he'd call Steve and tell him where to retrieve his car. Now the situation had changed. Yuki needed time to come to her senses: time he didn't have but needed to risk. It was the least, and the most, he could do for her.

"I have to return the Cavalier and pack a few things," he said, a lie of necessity. "How about following me back to Albuquerque?"

She looked skeptical. "My mind is made. I will not change it."

He started the engine and steered back toward her car. "Just think about it. That's all I'm asking."

In no time, he was merging onto I-40 east, headed toward Albuquerque with Yuki's Corolla following two car-lengths behind.

> Like two arrows flying into the color of sunrise, we zoomed through the desert toward Albuquerque. The calm vast sky opened up before us, starting to shed some gray light. Soon pink and peach colored bands succeeded one another. The snow on Arizona mountains cast a modest blessing on two wrecked souls. For a brief moment I felt its intense beauty, and a certain joy for life came back. Sometimes

driving has a magic about it, a trance effect that lets the mind drift. I threw her a warm look. "And you know what? We're gonna make it through this."

The pastels of sunrise gave way to abrasive white light. Yuki sped past and listed onto an exit for Gallup, New Mexico. Tyler trailed her to a truck stop, and they pulled up to the pumps. Pretending not to know her, he watched the meter click higher, as if it were keeping tally of the vehicles that whizzed past along the highway, each potentially loaded with cops or federal agents.

He lifted his gaze to the desert horizon and willed his mouth to stop watering at the aroma of fried chicken wafting from a nearby Popeye's. Yuki had to feel starved, too.

The nozzle clicked off. He caught her eye and motioned toward the restaurant.

She pointed to her car radio and climbed behind the wheel. "It's all over the news. The FBI arrested Daniel Blair," she said, and her car rolled forward.

Too stunned to react, he parked three spaces from Yuki and then trailed her inside to a slow-moving line. He felt afraid to look at anyone, so he stared at the menu board until its images of golden drumsticks and fries swirled to an amber pulp. Two truckers lumbered up behind him. Smelling of chewing tobacco and diesel fuel, the men clapped each other on the shoulders and talked about dumb-shit drivers, crazy girlfriends, and nonsensical road construction. One groused that he was deadheading.

At last, an elderly couple at the counter stepped away with a loaded tray. A mother with a baby on her hip hitched forward to order. Yuki stood next in line.

"You been following those arsons in California?" one of the truckers asked in a heavy Southern accent.

"Yeah," the other trucker said. "I hear they caught one of the bastards because he kept e-mailing the *LA Times*."

"They say some Caltech brainiac did it to make a statement about vehicles burning fossil fuels—something about polluting the air."

"Two million dollars in damages is one hell of a statement. Hope they throw the book at 'em."

"I don't know. I pulled some crazy shit when I was a kid. Guys I knew burned a bunch of school buses, and all they got was damages and community service."

"Yeah, well, it's a different world since 9/11. Rumor has it the FBI put the perps on their Ten Most Wanted list."

"It's not like they killed anybody. Probably just idealistic kids."

"More like they're idiots. The feds caught the one because he kept yapping to a reporter that the FBI doesn't know what the hell they're doing."

"He'll be the lucky one. You watch."

"How's that?"

"You know, first one to talk walks. Guy in jail gives up the others and blames them."

The cash register dissolved into the counter, and time stood still. As if calling a newspaper wasn't foolhardy enough, Danny had to taunt the FBI? That was Danny: belligerent, reckless, attracted to the void. The guy was a black hole, and they were snared in his event horizon, being pulled toward certain annihilation.

Yuki was standing erect as a yardstick, obviously eavesdropping, too. She stepped out of line. No longer hungry, they ducked out of Popeye's.

Early afternoon Tyler wove through an Albuquerque traffic jam. Yuki matched his random turns until they came to the neighborhood where he was renting a room: more specifically, where he was leasing a garage from Cam, who had graduated college two years ahead of Tyler and taken a job with the University of New Mexico's IT department. Cam had bought a house in Albuquerque and rented out rooms to make ends meet. Every nook and cranny was filled with tenants when Tyler relocated to the area, so he and Cam struck a deal: in exchange for a discount, Tyler agreed to remodel the garage and make it his living quarters. And that was what he had done.

The Cavalier and the Corolla circled Casa Gringo like albino ducks on NoDoz. At last, Tyler and Yuki parked a block away. Cloaked behind dark glasses, they charged up the walk and entered by the side door into the brown-carpeted living room. The house smelled of humidity and heat, and an unvented clothes dryer rumbled in the mudroom. Will, the only person home, hunched over a book. Doing his best to appear calm, Tyler snugged Yuki behind him and said, "Hey."

Will glanced up and grinned, apparently unaware that Tyler had even been gone. "Hey."

They hustled across the room, and Tyler swung open the door to his garage bedroom. Clothes lay strewn across the floor. Papers and books dotted the unmade air mattress. Even the carpet samples that dotted across the concrete floor looked tampered with.

"Oh, my God!" Yuki gasped. "The feds were here."

Tyler took her hand to calm her, or maybe himself. In fairness, the room looked only slightly less organized than usual. "It's all right," he said. "I made a mess before I left." What an understatement: a mess of his life, and hers. Four textbooks huddled like abandoned orphans on his pillow, and suddenly the chosen three in his backpack weighed like anvils.

"I should make a quick trip to the library," he croaked. "Need to check flights to Canada."

She eyed him with suspicion. "Promise you'll come back for me?"

Fugitive Flight

• • •

TYLER GLANCED SIDE TO SIDE, SURVEILLING people who had the misfortune to occupy the library at this moment. He pulled out a book and pretended to study its contents. No one appeared to be tailing him, so he hit the computers. An American Airlines flight with a stopover in Phoenix departed from Albuquerque International Sunport for Vancouver in an hour and a half. Seats were available.

Booked. No time to spare.

He returned to find Yuki showered and refreshed. Maybe if he offered her a subtle way out, she wouldn't feel she'd lose face for changing her mind. The Japanese way. "Drop me off at the airport?" He forced a cheerful inflection. "Then you hop a flight to Japan?"

She grabbed her bags and headed for the door. "I come with *you*."

He transferred his bag to her Corolla's back seat, and they each pulled away with maybe enough time to return Steve's car and make it to the airport on time.

Yuki fidgeted at the gate. "Don't look." She angled her head toward two middle-aged guys with briefcases. "Cops!"

Tyler risked a glance. Pinched under one of the men's arms, an unblinking gift-shop teddy bear was fixing an accusatory eye on him. The other fellow looked every bit the rumpled and worn salesman, Willy Loman incarnate. Tyler spoke without moving his lips. "They look like ordinary guys to me."

"Of course they do! That's the point."

In either case, he and Yuki were allowed to board. Tyler rested his head on the seat back, and the half-hour flight to Phoenix passed in what felt like three minutes. Even so, they landed to gut-wrenching delays on the tarmac before disembarking at last.

A gate agent examined his clipboard. "I'm afraid it's too late to make the flight to Vancouver."

Tyler checked the time. In principle they had six minutes. "The plane hasn't left yet," he said. "Has it?"

"No, but it's clear over in Gate 14, Terminal South."

Tyler took off running, weaving among pedestrians with Yuki close behind. Glad for his routine of running ten miles each morning, he pushed faster, harder, his legs burning with fatigue.

"Can't keep up!" Yuki puffed. "You go ahead and convince them to wait for me."

Shouldn't be a problem, if he could manage to reach the gate before the attendants closed the jetway door. "Will do." Keeping left, he charged down the rolling sidewalk, his bags, stuffed with their entire lives, swinging from side to side. "Excuse me," he panted, and pedestrians parted like schools of fish before him. "Coming through."

He thundered past a student with a laptop tucked under an arm and a pack on his back. On the carpet to the right, a lanky, professorial-looking fellow in a tweed jacket was ambling along. A thirty-something man pushed a baby stroller next to a woman speaking with her hands. An elderly couple hugged a bubbling family of four, probably their kids and grandkids, he thought.

Then it struck him. He was witnessing a version of his own life from *A Christmas Carol.* Visualizations of how his days might have unfolded were playing out before his eyes. The student, the professor, the husband and family man, the grandfather—these were lost scenarios, ghosts of Tyler Future, of joys forfeited.

"Last call for passengers departing for Detroit on American Airlines," the intercom rang out. "Flight 412, Gate 12." Another time, another dimension, and he could be boarding that plane for Michigan to visit his grandparents and cousins. Maybe someday he'd take that flight and look back on this mad dash with the cool eye of recollection.

The counter for Gate 14 came into view. Tyler commanded his legs to sprint for the finish, but mind over matter didn't work. His legs collapsed like broken spindles, and he skidded on his knees. He bounded upright and charged full speed to the counter. "Has the plane departed?" he gasped, trembling all over.

Two female personnel, agape at the spectacle, exchanged glances. "No," the brunette said with a giggle. "It's delayed."

The other covered her mouth and tried unsuccessfully to conceal a smile. "No one's boarded yet. Should be about fifteen minutes."

What a relief. A gift from God.

Yuki boarded first, and Tyler lagged behind her. He inched to the back row and settled into the middle seat next to her at the window. She was messing with a bag at her feet as a freckle-faced businessman with red, curly hair dropped into the aisle seat to Tyler's left.

Yuki bobbed a finger at a flight attendant. "She keeps watching us."

"Relax," Tyler said. "She's checking seatbelts."

Yuki pointed her chin toward a passenger who was jamming a bag into an overhead bin. "Who wears blue cardigans? He's a sky marshal."

"My grandpa wears a sweater just like that."

"Oh yeah? Does he have a bump on his waist, too? That is a gun." She rocked forward and back, humming. Then she began to sing, soft and wispy at first but with alarming crescendo. "Ue o muite arukou. Namida ga kobore nai you ni."

What was that tune? Sad and lyrical, like a love song or lullaby, and vaguely familiar. Tyler clasped her hand and tried to sound calm. "We don't know what the situation is."

"Omoidasu haru no hi," she trilled on. "Hitoribotchi no yoru."

He pressed her two palms together. "Do your Buddhist meditation thing."

She blinked as if waking from a dream. "Sure. Right."

Shooting for a pretense of normality, Tyler turned to the businessman and cracked the first stupid joke that came to mind. "These back-row seats have their pros and cons. They don't recline, but at least we get to hear the engines." Before he could tell whether the guy was listening, Yuki's finger jabbed into his ribs.

"What are you doing?" she managed to whisper and yell at the same time. "Don't talk to him."

She was losing it. "Yuki, stop."

The PA clicked on then off. On. Off. On. "This is the captain speaking. Our departure will be delayed fifteen minutes or so. It appears that our scheduled runway is currently inaccessible due to technical problems experienced by another aircraft."

"Don't you see?" Yuki pressed her nose to the window. "Don't you see? It's for us."

Damn. They were so close, but now they were cornered, awaiting checkmate. "There's nothing we can do now," he whispered, and time dissociated from space. Their entire future hung in the balance, and the realness surpassed his ability to process it. His mouth felt parched, every sensation amplified yet stifled. He squeezed his face next to Yuki's, and they peered through the black window. He tried and failed to account for a dozen shifting, colored lights as the cabin grow hotter.

He sat back, inhaled through his nose, and exhaled through his mouth. In with the good, out with the bad. That tune Yuki sang when she was scared—he'd heard it before.

"Listen!" A puff in his ear sent him springing against his seatbelt. Yuki gestured toward the couple seated in front of them. "You hear that?"

"What?"

"They are trying to provoke us!" she whisper-yelled. "It's okay. I don't care. We aren't going to give them it."

"What are you talking about?"

"Never mind, never mind. Better if you don't know. Don't say anything. Just don't say anything."

"You think they're cops, too? You think everybody's a cop. If they are, why don't they just arrest us? Why let us go?"

"Be-cause…" She rolled her eyes in disdain. "They're waiting for a warrant. That is why all this delay, or else they can provoke us to cause problems and…" She was more yelling than whispering now. "So don't do *anything*."

"Ladies and gentlemen." The captain's voice filled the cabin again, seventeen minutes since his last intervention. "We still have not been granted runway access. The other plane will either be repaired or cleared shortly, and we will be on our way." He paused, and his voice took on a comic tone. "A plane has experienced extremely rare technical complications. Flight control informs us that one of its wings fell off."

Gasps echoed through the cabin. Yuki crooked her elbows on her armrests and stretched upward to peer over the seatbacks. "Can you believe that?"

"Great," Tyler groaned. "A clown with a microphone."

"See? I told you." Her eyes jounced to his. "I *told* you."

Desperate, he squeezed her hand and said, "Think positive." How he wished he could heed his own advice. "Tell me about that tune you sing when you're really, really scared."

"What tune?"

"You know." He tried to hum it. She stared at him as if he'd gone Looney Tunes. Hell, maybe he had. Maybe a SWAT team with M16 assault rifles was about to storm the plane and haul them away. Maybe this was all a dream, a horrible, terrible night terror. He reached to adjust the air jet and saw that his hands were jittering like aspen leaves in a September wind, the physiological effect of adrenalin pumping through his muscles. Stale, nauseating air flowed over his face, and white noise hummed through the cabin. Close the eyes. No, open them. Again, he fiddled with the air jet. Again, he pressed his face next to Yuki's, and they stared out the window, searching for something, anything to confirm or allay their suspicions.

By some miracle, the aircraft finally rolled onto the runway. Its engines roared. The cabin vibrated. Inertia pushed them into their seats, and the wings lifted them off toward a new life.

Tyler closed his eyes and drifted in and out of consciousness, neither awake nor asleep, trying to ignore Yuki's incessant chatter. Jumpy as a caged bird in a room full of cats, she chirped about every conversation and clink. Twice he drifted off to sleep. Twice she jolted him awake with a puff of hot alarm in his ear. At last the plane touched down and rolled to the gate.

"Look!" Yuki pointed to crowd-control soldiers filing below the window, their shields reflecting the lights of the night. "Get ready." Her fingers took flight. "They're coming to take us away, ha-haaaa!"

This time she could be right. "Let's just go one step at a time."

The soldiers trooped past.

Then disembarking—slow, cramped, excruciating disembarking. Could a person contract claustrophobia? If so, he was coming down with it. They inched up the airless aisle and at last stepped onto the gangway. They plowed down the terminal toward baggage claim. Tyler retrieved their bags, his head in a fog and legs mired in muck.

Then customs.

They edged toward to a yellow line. A uniformed woman with thin, dyed-black hair waved them forward, then stared through them. "You together or separate?"

Tyler looked at Yuki. "Together." They handed over their passports, but his hesitation must have raised a red flag.

"This way, please." The agent directed them to inspectors who searched their bags for contraband. Of course, they found only Tyler's most cherished textbooks: Larry Grove's *Classical Groups and Geometric Algebra*, David Mackay's *Information Theory, Inference and Learning Algorithms*, and Gregory Naber's yellow *The Geometry of Minkowski Spacetime: An Introduction to the Mathematics of the Special Theory of Relativity.* His wallet, though, bulged with $900 in small bills, and the agents's expressions were clear. They detected something highly suspicious.

To Tyler's surprise, Yuki squared her shoulders. "They have to let us through," she said. "We have nothing illegal on us."

A surge of confidence. "No reason to hold us back," he said. They stepped forward to a short, dark-haired agent and his blond, crew-cut assistant. Both were young and close to Tyler's age.

"What is the reason for your visit to Canada?" Dark Hair asked, and the scene morphed into a weird game of questions and answers.

"Oh, you know," Tyler said. "Just to visit. Check it out."

"Tourism, we'll say. How long do you intend to stay?"

"Like three or four days."

"You students?"

Ask a silly question. Get a silly answer. "Yeah. On vacation."

"You a physics major?"

"Yeah."

Dark Hair focused on Yuki. "And you?"

"International studies." A crick in her voice indicated that her resolve was all but evaporated.

Crew Cut flagged over a female agent.

"Come with me, please." She took Yuki for a private, no doubt intimate, search.

Dark Hair pulled Tyler to a corner. "I was a math major in college," he said in a good-cop, off-the-record tone.

"Oh, yeah?"

"So where's your next destination after Canada?"

Next destination? Should he mention that they weren't planning to return to the United States? If the woman asked Yuki the same question, what would she say? "Don't know yet." Tyler forced a nonchalant shrug. "Gonna play it by ear. They say Vancouver's a beautiful city."

Dark Hair's face brightened. "It certainly is. You'll see what a great place it is."

The agent left Tyler sitting alone in a stark room that smelled of waxed vinyl. Look calm for the cameras, he thought, and slowed his breathing as he crossed his arms. Exhaustion took over, and his eyelids sagged.

A knock, and Dark Hair entered. "All set," he said. "Thank you for your cooperation."

He guided Tyler to Yuki, who sat slumped like a wilted houseplant on a hallway bench. She winced a greeting and rolled to her feet. They passed in silence into the wide-open airport and made a beeline for the nearest exit. The glass doors parted, and they stepped into a chill nighttime breeze. Tyler inhaled and exhaled what felt like his first deep breath in months.

Clean. Everything in Vancouver smelled and looked clean. Tyler and Yuki wobbled under the leaden weight of the bags in their hands and on their backs. All was fiction, nothing quite real. The name Kingston Hotel and images of cirrus clouds swirled among an array of disjointed sensations and colors in Tyler's thoughts.

They labored into the Chinese quarter, and Yuki plunked down her bags to catch her breath. Tyler peered through a restaurant window at a busboy clearing a table. The guy was about his age, height, and weight. In fact, he was Tyler. Tyler was watching Tyler enact a role in a short film. Did Future Tyler speak fluent Mandarin?

"I could use more practice with my Mandarin," he said.

"Yeah." Yuki scrubbed her face with her hands. "Like that is our top priority right now."

They walked on under the cover of darkness, searching for a secluded area to spend the night. Traffic purred to a halt at an intersection, and the scene converted into a spotlighted stage. Unreadable faces stared at them through glinting windshields. Tyler performed his part as a beast of burden and crossed the street. The light turned green. The other players drove on. Then the brief scene passed unremarkably into oblivion.

As they spiraled up a parking garage, the cars thinned. A concrete second-story roof spread before them, barren except for two islands of stalky flowerbeds. Tyler dropped his bags behind the bed farthest from the ramp and turned his face to the open sky. "This will do," he said and helped Yuki out of her backpack.

She stretched and moaned. "I could sleep standing up."

Feeling lighter, or maybe adrift in fatigue, he unfurled their bedroll in the brown, crunchy flowerbed. They climbed inside, sat munching on granola bars, and then flopped onto their backs. Yuki rested her head on his shoulder. "'Winston tastes good,'" she said and blew a frosted stream into the night air. "'Like a cigarette should.'"

Tyler felt the beginnings of a grin, then remembered. "Hey, that tune you sing when you're losing it, it's called 'Sukiyaki,' isn't it?"

"I don't know what you're talking about."

"Sure you do. It's the only Japanese-language song ever to hit the *Billboard* Hot 100 chart in the US." He tried to sing the words, "'It's all because of you, I'm feeling sad and blue. You went away. Now my life is just a rainy day.'"

"Pfft. English words don't come close to the real Japanese."

"What are the lyrics?"

She drew a breath and sighed. "Let us just look at stars."

She didn't want to talk about it right now. He could understand that. "Fair enough." His head lay next to a sprig of fir left over from Christmas. Despite its bleak prospects, the sprig filled the air with the vibrant scent of conifer. Today they were free. Tomorrow, with luck, they would escape to Europe and to who knew where else?

He reached over, and his fingers tingled at the touch of Yuki's bare midriff. She rolled toward him, and they celebrated their existence by making love.

THE FERRY YAWED UNDER THE SLAM of another Mediterranean wave, and Tyler tightened his grip on the deck railing. One month ago today, he and Yuki had set off on their fugitive flight, the airborne portion of which had culminated in Amsterdam. But the city's omnipresent surveillance cameras and police were more than a little alarming, so he and Yuki had caught a train to Paris, only to discover even more watchful eyes there.

No way could they stay in the City of Lights, but where to go? A travel brochure in a bookstore had provided the answer. One look at its photos of an exotic island south of France and captions that promised "remote desert beaches" and "secluded mountains," and Tyler knew they must head for Corsica.

> 3 March 2004. We expected nothing. We sought only a last solace, a temporary refuge before the inevitable *fin*. The plan was simple and unambitious yet embodied our very last grasp at life itself: to frugally survive on remote Mediterranean beaches until we ran out of money. After which, the unspoken assumption was that it would all be over. The house of cards had to fall, so make it last and appreciate every remaining moment of freedom.

But as the ferry approached its port in Bastia, the island's second-largest city, urban lights stretched deep and thick across the horizon in apparent denial of any "solitary nature preserves and backcountry expanses." As if to mock even the pamphlet's claims of a temperate climate, a frigid blast whipped through the layers of Tyler's clothing. A shiver of dread shot up his spine.

The four-story floating casino rumbled under reverse engines. If any armed forces lay in wait, then they would make their move on the docks. In a matter of minutes, Tyler's life with Yuki was either going to take a new tack or crash on the rocks. Tyler slipped into a swirling world of red oil in white paint, and time might have stopped altogether if the laws of physics had so permitted. At the sight of human figures skirting like special forces along the outer deck, he flipped up his hood and inhaled the diesel-thick air. Don't panic—just the crew mooring the boat.

He and Yuki merged into a throng of bag-toting passengers and crossed the ornate-patterned carpet toward open-flung doors. A clack-ata-clack rhythm shot an electric shock down Tyler's legs. Were shells being racked into shotgun chambers? No, just roller bags bumping over the gangway's aluminum treads. He and Yuki joined a procession of souls that shuffled into the moonlit night.

Bulging with baggage and with Yuki at his side, Tyler hustled down a dark street in search of a secluded beach. To the north, blacktop sliced between mountains and sea. Elsewhere, all was city. A gas station sign read SANS PLOMB, and Tyler gave thanks to the periodic table for equipping him to interpret *plomb* to mean lead, Pb. A convex mirror in a store window reflected the perpendicular stripes of the mirror's zebra-like frame onto the street. Tyler stretched out a foot to give himself zebra toes. "Too bad we lost our camera," he said.

"Somebody stole it," Yuki corrected.

"If we're lucky, we'll have plenty of time here to replace it," he said.

Yuki zebra-toed her tiny canvas sneaker beside his. "Perhaps our entire lives."

"No rush."

"None at all."

"We can survive here." Tyler tried to sound reassuring. "We'll just lie low and let the situation blow over. Then we can return to our families and our lives."

Yuki turned away. "So you say."

They pressed on in silence. Twice now he had suggested the blowing-over scenario, and Yuki wasn't buying it. Was she being overly pessimistic? Then again, did he actually believe that the FBI would forget an act of terrorism? Truth was, reality had always felt just beyond his grasp. Mom still teased him about the rice incident.

He was maybe a junior in high school when he had sat at the kitchen table doing calculus. Mom and Dad had said they were going for a walk. Not long after they disappeared out the back door, a pan of rice began to smolder on the stove. The smoke made his eyes tear, but he managed to blink through the burn and continue with his studies.

Mom and Dad re-entered the room just as the smoke alarm started to blast. Mom threw open the windows as Dad doused the charred pan under the faucet. "Didn't you notice the room was billowing smoke?" he bellowed.

"Sure," Tyler had replied, surprised at the absurdity of the question.

"Then why didn't you turn off the burner?"

The answer seemed obvious. "I thought you wanted it that way."

"Why would we want to burn the house down?" Dad had asked. "Think, son. Use your head."

Face it. Common sense was never his strong suit. Given the magnitude of the current problem, the probabilities of its magically fading away approached zero. But for Yuki's sake—and maybe for his own—he needed to go on pretending. He glanced at Yuki, now staring up at him and seeming to probe his thoughts.

On they trooped past characterless buildings and cheap Bastian stores, up one lonely street and down the next. Unfortunately, even their short-term plans to camp on remote sands appeared out of reach because they found no beaches, remote or otherwise. A discarded shopping cart eased the strain on their backs, but its dilapidated steel refused to go quietly into the night and instead screeched and rattled at the turn of its wheels.

They pushed on for two or three more miles. Then exhaustion wore down their standards, and they lugged their bags down a set of scraggy stairs attached to a closed, two-story restaurant. Tyler spread the bedroll beneath the stairwell and gazed over the silver-blue, sea-level landscape. As far as the eye could see, trash and rotting driftwood littered the horizon. Even so, no grimy patch of sand had ever looked so good.

Yuki tugged on his sleeve. "What are we going to do for water?"

His tongue felt cotton-ball dry. "Be right back," he slurred. Leaving Yuki under cover of darkness, he climbed to street level. A light's glow pulled him down an alley and into the doorway of a neighborhood bar. Smoke prickled his nostrils, and the drone of unintelligible conversations clogged his ears. Men in flat tweed caps hunched over five wooden tables. Dark figures with backs of varying widths lined a bar that ran the length of a wall to his right. A busty redhead in a soiled white apron clunked an amber mug on a table. As her eyes cut to him, the room fell silent.

Heads turned and faces went blank. Tyler smelled sweaty wool, stale tobacco, and a hint of gunpowder. The scent of urine emanated from a door marked Toilette. He walked to an open slot at the bar, and a gorilla-size bartender with an offset nose raised a questioning eyebrow at him.

"Water, please," Tyler asked.

The bartender's narrow eyes went blank.

Tyler gripped an imaginary bottle and pretended to sip. "Eau. S'il vous plait."

The man pointed to a chalkboard and read it aloud, "Bière? Du vin? Whisky?"

Soft conversations washed back into the room, and dark frothy mugs migrated to men's lips. To Tyler's left, a hump-backed senior reeked of sinus infection and was angling his head in an obvious attempt to eavesdrop.

"Eau." Tyler walked his fingers over the thick-lacquered bar. "To go. S'il vous plait."

The bartender pursed his lips before digging into a trash bin and extracting an empty liter of wine labeled Mommessin Beaujolais. Without rinsing the bottle, he filled it with tap water and shoved it at Tyler. The bartender's other hand held up five fingers.

"Cinq euro."

"Five euros for nonpotable tap water?" Tyler wanted to ask, but didn't. Instead he paid the man and left.

I had my first encounter with Corsicans. Not exactly a friendly bunch, but I got the water.

Tyler displayed the liter bottle like a proud hunter returning home with a trophy rabbit. "Eau for you," he said.

Yuki, who was sitting cross-legged next to a perfectly symmetrical, miniature teepee of driftwood, broke into a partial grin and stuffed a handful of can labels under her construction. "For a fancy wood fire," she said, and soon they were huddling over a flickering flame.

Tyler put his Boy Scout mess kit to use and boiled the water. Then he filled the sturdy aluminum cup and dropped in a tea bag. They passed the hot metal cup between them, letting its warm, savory contents push the chill out of their hands and their insides.

"Tired?" Tyler asked.

"Yeah."

"Bed?"

"Okay."

He unzipped the sleeping bag and invited her to join him inside its fleece flaps. The odor of sand partly offset the stench of rubbish, and Tyler curled his toes around Yuki's cold feet. Almost at once he felt his warmth join with hers. A barge blew a foghorn in the distance. Car tires screeched on pavement. Thin laughter drifted from the neighborhood bar, and Tyler let go to the whorl of sleep.

At dawn's first light, Tyler studied a map and bus schedule he'd picked up on the ferry. "There's a bus stop in a park not far from here," he said. "If we hurry, we can catch the twelve o'clock and reach Saint Florent before dark. From there we'll hike west along the coastline to the Desert des Agriates. Nobody's going to live there."

"Nobody but us," Yuki said, determination in her voice.

They packed and were about to leave, except there was all this trash. Tyler gathered a few pieces of crumpled plastic and broken glass. "Somebody needs to clean this up," he said and gathered a few more into a pile.

"Stop that," Yuki told him.

"In a minute," he said, and the mound grew.

Yuki locked her thumbs under her pack's shoulder straps and shook her head. "That's a waste of time."

He worked his way down a stretch of multicolored glass, plastic milk jugs, rusted cans, and soiled diapers. "Just a little more!" he called back, and the heap swelled to knee high.

"Let's go."

He should stop, he knew. "Almost done." He had just finished clearing another fifteen square feet when the sight of blood streaming down his thumb stopped him short. "Nasty cut!" He went back to show Yuki the dripping crimson cut.

Sitting on a rock, her knees hugged tight to her chest, Yuki continued to stare out to sea.

He doused the wound in salt water and watched as the red whirl dissipated into the tide. When the bleeding subsided, he elevated his now-throbbing thumb and walked back to Yuki. The sun hovered at eleven o'clock. "Ready?" he asked as if she were keeping him waiting.

Thus they began what became an hour-and-a-half-long march in blazing heat. "Guess my delay earned us an introduction to the hot Bastian sun," Tyler offered by way of apology.

"You think?"

Sweating and hungry, they reached the park and crossed to a signpost with an icon of a bus. An elderly woman with her palm pressed to her jaw sat on a bench underneath the sign. An enviable mustache darkened her upper lip, and a single black hair sprouted from a mole on her cheek. Tyler slid into a space next to her and pointed to Saint Florent on his brochure's map. Between a flourish of her hands and spatters of spittle, he surmised that they had missed the noon bus. Next one, five thirty. He managed to convey that he and Yuki intended to go hiking.

"Acheter maintenantou le maquis impenetrable." She wagged a finger at his feet and pantomimed opening her handbag to shell out money. "Va vous manger tout cru."

The woman clawed at her shoes and re-enunciated each syllable until Tyler managed to deduce that he had better replace his holey skateboarding shoes with leather boots. Otherwise, a fiendish "maquis impenetrable" was going to rip his feet to shreds.

Yuki muttered something about a Super U grocery store that might have air-conditioning, and she strode off in that direction. Tyler decided to take the opportunity to shop for boots. A boutique salesperson convinced him to buy a ninety-seven-euro pair with sturdy soles and leather uppers. He returned to find the curmudgeonly woman gone and Yuki sporting a twenty-four-inch baguette.

They sat on the bench, eating as they scanned for police. A small flock of grackle-like birds pecked at fallen twigs among the sparse grass. One hungry fellow wore a silly-looking beard, so they named him Monkeychin and gave him the last of their baguette, which Yuki explained was called *pain longe*.

At five forty-five, a black-windowed Santini Voyages bus hissed to a stop, its seats loaded with squirming, chatty school kids. Tyler and Yuki squeezed next to an acne-faced teenager with overgelled hair. Yuki breathed through her mouth and blew through rolled lips, her face paling to green.

The passengers thinned at each stop until the bus rolled to its route's end well past midnight with only two wilted fugitives occupying its dimly lit vinyl seats. Tyler gave Yuki a hand descending the bus steps, which felt somehow higher than they had on his entry. Judging from the tremble of her hands, Yuki's muscles were shaking, too, from seven hours of engine rumble and bumpy gravel roads.

The driver, no doubt trying to be helpful, pointed in the direction of what was probably lodging and rattled off a string of instructions. Tyler, too tired to make an effort to understand, simply nodded and forced a grin. The doors closed, and the bus fell dark except for its headlights as they streamed a U-turn. Then driver and bus were gone.

A hundred yards away, the moonlit sea washed ashore, so they lugged their baggage that direction across cold, wet sand to a grove of trees. Since signs clearly forbade camping, they didn't dare pitch their bright-yellow tent. Desperate for sleep, they unfurled the bedroll and dropped to lay on their backs on the chill, twiggy earth. Fingers of a salty, sea-scented breeze combed through Tyler's hair.

"This point at infinity could just as well be any old point," he said, feeling calm now—or too exhausted to feel much of anything. "That's the symmetry of a sphere."

Yuki cradled her head on her palms. "They call this the Pirate Isle. Maybe long ago, other fugitives slept right here on this spot."

To think, rootless exiles throughout time had found comfort in the sea's gentle lap along these shores. Had those people also felt so distant, numb, and forgotten? Tyler gazed into iridescent light as it rippled through a spray of leaves overhead. A vehicle was approaching. He held his breath. Then what sounded like an antiquated truck rattled past. "If they did," Tyler whispered, "they looked up at the same, limitless stars that are smiling down on us."

"What would they say if they could speak?" Yuki asked.

The stars or past fugitives? It didn't matter. She was counting on him to tell her. But how could a guy pretend to know such things? "I don't know," he confessed, and his heart sagged to disappoint her.

We lay down, feet toward the sea, and stared at the joyous stars that had accompanied us this far. Here we were, teetering over the end of the line where the map read in big, bold letters, Desert des Agriates. Inhospitable maquis met blue as far as the eye could see. No towns. No people. Hollow stone ruins, misfit relics of distant times and long-gone civilizations, stood watch over windblown eternity. Ghosts like us.

Home ceased to exist, and nowhere became everywhere. The top of the sphere projected to the point at infinity, completing the plane...suddenly and homeomorphically[4] the surface of a ball. Reliable and true, the earth turned to bring out the stars.

4 Roughly speaking, a topological space is a geometric object, and the homeomorphism is a continuous stretching and bending of the object into a new shape. Mirror images are homeomorphic. Shaping an image of a coffee cup continuously into a donut is homeomorphic.

Geen Doorgang

• • •

Tyler and Yuki provisioned at Saint Florent before beginning their westward trek into the unending wilderness, with no plan to return. Views of the rolling sea, curved beaches, and snowcapped mountains made up for the colorless skies and the discomfort of their cumbersome packs. A small, isolated beach held charm, so they took a break on its fine white sands. Tyler read *Crime and Punishment* until frigid raindrops drove him to erect the tent and climb inside.

Rain and more rain. Wrapped in their crinkly green tarp, he and Yuki stayed dry and reasonably warm. While she sketched plants visible outside the tent flap, he stared at droplets pounding the sand. Say by some miracle they managed to elude the authorities, how safe could they be living in the wild like this? They were undocumented and trespassing. They had few resources, no connections, and a minimal understanding of their surroundings. For all he knew, savage packs of wolves roamed here. Poisonous insects and scorpions—not to mention his personal favorites: snakes and spiders—could be creepy crawling under the tent floor. What about modern-day pirates and gangs?

No way should he alarm Yuki, but the long arm of the law could prove to be the least of their worries.

Tyler pulled out his comp book. He should make a plan, a list of possibilities for building a future. Construction work, he wrote. No tools. Few skills. He drew a line through it. How about teaching high school physics? No, too great a risk of detection. He could teach math or English, but schools were sure to require documentation of legal status or at least a passport for their records. People earned livings by making movies with computers, but that would require investment and take months, even years, before he could turn a profit. The list of rejected options grew.

For the second time, his uncorked, un-Tyler-like laugh erupted from within. "Ah, hahahahaaa!"

Yuki looked up, confused and uncomfortable. Then she donned her television voice and said, "'Celebrate the moments of your life!'" A pause. "'Ask any mermaid you happen to see. What's the best tuna? Chicken of the Sea.'" Then she, too, broke into wild-eyed, un-Yuki-like peals of hysteria.

They doubled over, holding their stomachs and gasping for air between howls. Tears were streaming down Yuki's face, and Tyler realized his cheeks were wet, too. She drew her knees to her chest and threw back her head, wailing in open-mouthed mania. Except a subtle shift was taking place. The corners of her lips were downturned, and her voice now carried a raspy, guttural tone. As Tyler read the changes in Yuki, he felt the changes swell in him as well. Yuki was sobbing, uncontained, sliced through and through.

No. He willed a steel casing around the pressure cooker welling in his chest. No! Yuki would not—must not—see him cry.

She was keening now, wailing and tearing at her hair. He pulled her close and kissed the top of her head. "It'll be okay." He rocked her back and forth. "Shhh, shhh. Everything will be okay." Her fingers dug into his arms, and her hot tears burned through his shirt. He fixed his gaze on a dark cloud rolling in the gray sky. "Shhh." A chill breeze chopped into his lungs and hung there, resisting discharge. "We'll work through this," he said, his voice guttural. "Shhh, shhh."

Yuki fell quiet, and their rocking slowed. Wrung out, they sat motionless, cradled in each other's arms, sheltered in their tent. She pulled away, wiped her face, and blew her nose. A dust devil swirled along the sands, picking up twigs and discarding splinters in its wake.

"Can we have a dog?" she asked, her voice flat.

Tyler put on his scientist voice, his smart, all-knowing, got-it-together voice. "Yeah, we'll definitely get a dog. That's within our space of feasible near-future possibilities with a rather high probability value, especially if we set our intentions toward that subspace." Or something of the sort.

"I don't see why not," she countered. "Just because we are fugitives does not mean we cannot have a dog, does it?"

All this dog talk was triggering thoughts of Cam and Tyler's abandoned garage-room in Albuquerque.

"We need a dog," Cam had insisted to each of his tenants. At every declaration, Tyler had voiced wholehearted agreement. By the time of Tyler's departure, though, no one had acquired a dog.

"We need a dog," Tyler sighed, secretly doubting the wish could come true.

The rain let up, so he and Yuki strolled along a trail that led inland. The violent coast gave way to rolling foothills. Then the trail opened to an expanse of wispy, white flowers dancing atop three-foot stalks.

"Fairy tales," Yuki whispered in awe.

Tyler sniffed a blossom, its scent mild and sweet. "We'll call this Fairy Tale Field," he said. The bleak day darkened, and they made a nest in an alcove of bushes. Rain drummed the tent's roof and confined them inside.

A twenty-minute break gave us the chance to stretch our legs in the sunset. We passed the most magnificent ruins. Two-story buildings built from piled stones had since been reclaimed by local vegetation. Wet plants everywhere burst with color.

We stayed some four or five days in our nest, letting the weather dictate our pace and perhaps also our fates. When the rain let up, we left the tent and wandered toward the sea. First we came across a dense little forest of twisted trees then the longest, deserted, sandy beach I've ever seen. Clean, white, and pure, it soothed the greatness of the sea. Not a soul in sight. There we stayed motionless hours before the expanse, watching the cool rhythm of the waves, listening to its hypnotic chant of freedom in solitude, of hope in the void.

Signage read "Plage de Saleccia / Saleccia Beach." They followed a soggy dirt road across a rushing river to an empty camp office, its doors buttoned shut for the winter. Yuki trooped toward the building. "I'm going to look for fresh water."

Tyler wanted to explore the other side of a hill, so he said, "Meet you back at the river." He made slow progress as he battled through nasty thorns and wet bushes. Probably the "maquis impenetrable" that bristly woman at the bus stop had warned about.

Hungry, itching, and craving a quick dip, he carved his way back toward the river and Yuki. But as the waters came into view, the sight of her stopped him dead in his tracks. Ankle deep in rapids and appearing to grope for a stick, she stooped face to face with a massive, four-legged creature. A wild boar? A bear, perhaps?

Desperate to distract the creature from attacking her, Tyler scooped up a handful of stones and sprinted forward, yelling, "Hey!"

Yuki flailed a mud- or blood-streaked arm, signaling for Tyler to keep his distance. He pulled up at the edge of the riverbank, ten yards from her, within rescue distance. Maybe.

"Got water at the camp offices," Yuki said, her voice slow and steady. "But I failed to pass unnoticed. This big fellow, he trots over and licks me. Then he jumps all over me, and I'm too scared to stop him."

Tyler and the brindle-colored creature locked gazes. Its black eyes, set under protruding brows, seemed to size him up. The boxy head rolled slightly to the side and appeared to rise from a heart-shaped white splotch on its chest. While the dog looked tall and muscular, its ribs were showing. Not a pup, yet young. Maybe a year old. No collar.

Tyler stood stone still and forced a calm tone. "He maul you?"

Yuki splayed her arms. "He was covering me in paw prints, so I climbed a wall where he couldn't jump up anymore. But he wouldn't go away and followed me here…more or less."

"More or less?"

She bent eye level and pulled the giant muzzle to her. "I tried to shoo him away without success." She swung her arms and leaned side to side like the Energizer bunny. "He keeps going and going. Throw something. You'll see."

Tyler ground the stones in his right hand as he picked up a stick with his left. A toss, and the dog tore after it, splashing water high in the air. The dog clamped the stick between his jaws and powered back to drop it at Tyler's feet. "He certainly has a passion for playing fetch."

Yuki giggled. "He has no mean character at all."

A few more tosses. Then they made their way back to camp, dog lagging a few steps behind—or stalking them. Tyler felt uncomfortable at the thought of staying another night in their bush alcove, so he pulled up the tent stakes. "We need to move on."

Dog, now snuffling long-dead coals in the fire ring, lifted his ash-powdered muzzle and tilted his head to listen.

Yuki ducked inside to sweep the tent's floor with a cloth. "What about him?" She handed out the bedroll.

Tyler gave it a shake, folded it lengthwise and began to roll it. "I imagine he'll head home."

"Probably."

They walked on, yet still Dog followed. A few kilometers down the beach, a second set of rectangular roofless ruins outlined what once had probably been a sizable building. Two eight-foot-tall walls stood intact, while fallen stones lay strewn about. Thick maquis overgrew the perimeter of the ruins, but inside Tyler discovered a flat, tent-size clearing, invisible to the outside world.

Here, nested between stones and scrub brush, they set camp. Tyler fired up the camp stove and soon had water bubbling in the pot. Yuki poured in a packet of pasta alfredo, and the scent of cheese and herbs filled the air. Tyler studied the simmering pot, so hungry he could barely wait for the noodles to soften. Dog sat next to Yuki, working his burly jowls and managing to contain quantities of drool. Most of it, anyway.

The food cooked at last, so Tyler filled his and Yuki's bowls. Hoping to dine with a view, he scrambled up a wet, inclined wall. Up top, he turned to look back, but his new boots, while they had demonstrated remarkable traction on dry rock, apparently didn't stick worth spit to slippery rock. His left foot shot downward, then his right.

"Whoooaaa!" Tyler slalomed downhill, accelerating until a boulder clipped his right toe and spun him forty-five degrees. His head felt the slam of a rock, and he lay motionless, unable to draw a breath. Pain stabbed through his hip, up his torso and through his shoulder to his elbow. A blue shroud of unconsciousness began to roll in.

"You okay?"

Yuki was leaning over him. His chest opened at last, and oxygen wheezed into his lungs.

She pointed to his right. "Concerned about your precious pasta?"

Tyler followed her eyes down his outstretched arm. His right hand was still clutching his dinner bowl, right-side up and not a drop spilled. "Damn straight," he groaned and managed to sit up.

Dog pondered the scene, his tail swaying side to side.

Yuki giggled and Tyler joined in. Soon they were curled over laughing, which made up for the throbs in his limbs. Almost.

WRAPPED IN THEIR THOUGHTS, TYLER and Yuki lay awake late into the night. "You hear the dog?" she whispered.

"No."

"Think he went home?"

"Probably."

Silence.

"I'll check." Tyler unzipped the tent flap and poked out his head.

Dog lay on his belly, head erect and watchful as the Sphinx. He swung his muzzle around and his wide, luminous eyes seemed to say, *Sleep safe. I'm on guard.* Then Dog unleashed a burly groan and stretched his muzzle onto his front paws. Feeling sorry for the animal and not realizing the implications of what he was doing—well, maybe not fully realizing—Tyler climbed out and handed him a serving of leftover pasta. Stiff and sore yet feeling protected at last, he ducked into the tent and eased into untroubled sleep.

TYLER WOKE WITH A START in the pitch-darkness. Whatever had jarred him awake felt ominous and threatening. He listened with every fiber of his being, but all he could hear was the thump of his heart. Cold sweat trickled down his armpits. Then it sounded again: a brushing noise, and close. Slowly, Tyler reached out and touched the tent wall. Shit. Something huge and warm was encroaching through the twelve-inch space between the tent and stone wall. The creature, like the alien in Ripley's womb, was stretching their fragile barrier to the ripping point. Less than a millimeter of synthetic polymer was all that separated him and Yuki from bared fangs and slashing claws. Too rounded to be a branch blowing in the wind. No fallen rock would feel this warm.

The massive life form moved. "You hear that?" Tyler whispered.

Yuki lay silent, probably scared stiff.

"It's huge!"

Tyler tried to make no sound as he dug into his pack and felt around for the Leatherman multitool Dad had given him. He found it, pulled it to his chest, and flipped open the blade.

The beast halted its advance. Then its low, prolonged growl filled Tyler's veins with cold slush. Somehow, the tent wall held, and Tyler drew a shallow breath. Wait. He recognized that musky smell, that deep rumble: Dog Bear, and he wasn't growling; he was groaning.

"Ha!" Tyler practically levitated off the ground. "Dog's wedging himself into the narrow space because he wants the comfort and protection of his new group."

Yuki replied with a gentle snore.

Tyler put away his Leatherman and relaxed into the soothing rhythms of deep-sleep breathing—in stereo.

Tyler awoke to the crackle of a campfire and the aroma of toast. He dressed, unzipped the flap, and blinked into a bright, chill morning.

Dog stood at Yuki's side, intent on watching her toss a twig into the flames. "Our friend shows no interest in leaving," she said, breaking into that earnest, carefree smile that had captured Tyler's heart at first sight in an LA nightclub. "He likes us."

Tyler stepped out, grabbed his boots, and tiptoed to a rock chair. Dog sauntered over, and his warm, wet tongue lapped at Tyler's fingertips. A shiver, and he scratched that big, brindled head. "Hey, boy," he said and pulled a pair of socks from his boots. "Is this guy what you had in mind when you said you wanted a dog?"

Yuki flipped a slice of toast on a rock near the fire. "No," she said. "He is much better." She placed slivers of cheddar on the golden tops to make cheesy toast, Tyler's favorite.

The aroma of melting cheese and browning bread set Tyler's mouth to watering. He visited the bushes before trotting to the water's edge and washing his hands. When he returned, Yuki handed him a delightfully crunchy, cheese-laden slice. Tyler took a bite and inhaled a long, slow breath to allow the rich flavor molecules to rise to the back of his nose where his olfactory receptors could better sense them. "It's not like we encouraged him," he said and poured a cup of tea.

"No, not at all." She broke off a piece of *pain longe* and tossed it to Dog, who caught it midair and downed it without chewing. "Well, not much anyway."

A sip, and the tea's warmth radiated through Tyler's chest and belly. "Maybe he needs a name."

"How about Precious?" she suggested without hesitation.

No way was he going to call out, *Here, Precious. Here, Precious.* "Um, remember that Dutch sign we didn't understand in Amsterdam, so we wandered down a dead-end alley?"

"'Geen doorgang.'" Yuki crossed her palm over her chest with a shake of her head. "It meant 'no passageway.' We got trapped. It was terrifying."

"Well." Tyler grinned. "This dog is drawn to narrow places with no exits."

"Ge-en Door-gang?" She crinkled her nose.

Tyler didn't want to worry her, but he also liked the idea of this fellow standing watch over them. They could use a guard dog, and big guy here was a natural for the job. "Geen Doorgang also means 'no entry,'" he said. "There's no way he'll let anybody or anything pass undetected. The name could stand for his role as our security officer, too."

She looked unconvinced. "It's most unusual for dog to have a first and last name."

"Our friend is most unusual. He's a mystery at every corner."

Yuki looked somber. She pulled a tissue from her pocket and fashioned what appeared to be a skullcap with a prong on one side. She set it gently on Dog's head as he peered up at her in pure adoration, his tail wagging. "Ceremonial samurai helmet." Yuki palmed Dog's face between her hands. "You are no longer a stranger. Now, you are a proud warrior. Keeper of small places. Defender of family. You are Geen Doorgang."

Geen Doorgang licked his chops and wiggled his hindquarters forward. *Yes! Yes! I'm Geen Doorgang*, he appeared to say. *What's a Geen Doorgang?*

In the days that followed they grew to know Geen well. Their little group sang into majestic canyons and came to know the stars. They learned to identify bird songs and bathed in clear cascades.

They christened awesome plants and blazed new trails. Geen became a skilled climber, accompanying Tyler and Yuki up and down Monte Geen, Prince Peak, and Stick Mountain. One morning while combing the rocky coast, the trio came upon a digital camera that had fallen off a cruise ship and washed ashore. Kept dry in its waterproof case, it had survived the voyage in perfect working order.

Thus, Geen became their first miracle; the camera, their second. Because of their bony, brindle-haired companion, Tyler and Yuki settled into place and called the desert "Home."

Geen had a fascination for all creatures great and small and an unfortunate penchant for snapping at wasps.

March 2004. It wasn't us who adopted Geen Doorgang as much as he who joined himself to our group, and for his companionship we were grateful. He was always down [up for anything]. At the slightest sign of getting ready to go, he'd be up and on the trail before us.

It must have been hard for him to be with us. We didn't know how to dose his food, and since it needed to be backpacked in and was expensive, we erred on the side of insufficiency. The poor dog was constantly hungry, and this explains somewhat his disobedience when it came to chasing and barking at wild cows. There seemed to be no way to rein him in, and it wasn't for lack of trying. Our obsession with discretion didn't mix well with his silly loud barking at anything that moved. But we loved him anyway.

Geen Doorgang surveys a majestic canyon.

Geen among the "fairy tale" flowers.

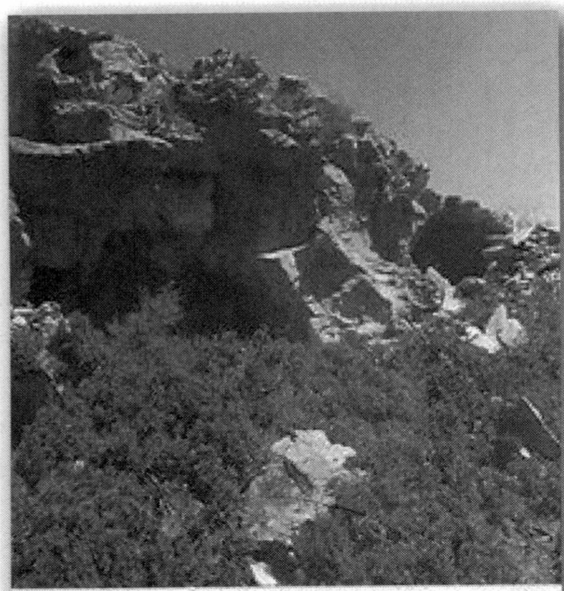

Ice Cave

TYLER AND YUKI WERE CAMPED high in a nook they'd dubbed Ice Cave for its sandy-white color. In a vain attempt to make a softer bed, they fashioned a thick cushion of a leafy plant they called "Miles" for its five-foot height. They sat, hungry and bored, on their newly made mattress.

Yuki scribed 肉 in the cave's sand.

"What's that?" Tyler asked.

"*Niku*," she said with a sigh. "Beef."

He knew how she felt. Noodles and bread and beans were all right, but he craved a juicy hamburger. Hell, he'd settle for a bite of turkey jerky. Ephemeral mists of a memory gathered in his mind's eye, too shy to materialize fully. A seventh-grade book had haunted his nights. What was it called? *The Yearling.* Its premise of a binary world of either survival or death had seemed surreal and heartless at the time. But now he sensed a different side to the story. As with the main character, he had let youthful invincibility blind him to the fragile state of survival. As a kid, the closest he had come to deprivation was the occasional hunger pang. How he'd underestimated his parents' warnings of the paper-thin barrier that shielded today's industrialized world from the jaws of starvation. Yuki's symbol expressed what he now understood at a visceral level: crushing, all-consuming, gut-gnashing *hunger.*

Tyler closed his eyes and could almost taste Mom's tangy, corn-and-pepper chili, rich in *niku.* Then something bumped his elbow, and the dream mists gave way to reality. Geen was whining and squeezing between him and the cave wall. Outside, marble-size hail was pelting the ground like buckshot and terrifying the poor dog. Nothing to do but wait out the storm.

The pummeling eventually stopped, and the "three amigos" raced out to dance like skeleton bones in the strange, chill morning. Geen erupted in raucous blasts and tore after a feral cow. In the silliness of the moment, Tyler sprinted after him, barking also. The terrain sloped downhill toward a flash-flooded stream, and Tyler managed to keep up fairly well. When he reached bottom, he slid across the muddy water into the dreaded maquis. Meanwhile, Geen dodged past the gantlet of thorns and disappeared down a winding cow path. Judging from the barking and baaing, he must have cornered an animal.

Tyler followed the ballyhoo into the flight path of an oncoming calf, no doubt making a mad dash away from Geen and in search of its mother. On seeing Tyler, the calf spun to face

Geen. Barking and snapping his jaws, Geen parried from side to side to obstruct Calf's retreat.

A clatter of hooves, and Mama Cow materialized out of the bushes behind Geen. Geen spun and faced off against her. The dog, crouching and growling; Mama Cow, head low and snorting. She pawed the ground, arcing clogs of mud high behind her, while Geen continued to block her from Calf. Did Geen not realize that Mama was preparing to charge, that he was putting himself in mortal danger?

Tyler read the situation as him and Geen against Mama Cow, so he threw up his arms and roared, "Aarrr!" He stomped toward her, narrowing the distance as much as he dared.

The tactic sent Mama Cow bolting away, but to Tyler's horror, it also emboldened Geen. Teeth bared and snarling, he leaped at the defenseless calf and seized its tender hind leg. Calf bawled and strained to follow its mother. Except the more it kicked and scrambled to escape, the fiercer Geen bit and the deeper his teeth tore into Calf's flesh. Faster and faster, Geen worked his jaws up the flailing leg.

"No!" Tyler screamed, but Geen was wild with the taste of the blood pulsing like a garden hose from the drooping leg. Off. On. Off. On. The air smelled of urine and blood, of sweat and fur and feces. Tyler dove to grab Geen, but his approach sent Calf lurching up the shallow stream, hauling Geen farther away.

"Stop!" Tyler bellowed. "Stop right now!"

Calf shrieked and writhed against Geen's jaws, but they were like vise grips. Calf lowered its chin and stretched its neck forward, as if willing its head to soar free of its body.

Tyler grabbed a deadfall and raced to Calf's defense. He swung the limb like a club and brought it down firmly on Geen's snout. The dog yipped, let go, and retreated a few paces uphill. There Geen stood panting with his tail tucked between his legs, his blazing black eyes fixed on Tyler, and his bloodied tongue lolling out.

Calf wobbled and dropped to its front knees, leaving its haunches raised and pulsating blood. It moaned and lowered its nose inches from the water. Then its hocks buckled and it crumpled into the trickling rivulet. Unblinking and still but for the heave of its chest, Calf gazed up at Tyler.

"Go on," Tyler soothed. "Get up. Go find your mama." He nudged Calf with a shaking foot. No response. He palmed both hands on the soft, wet rump and pushed. The calf's body rocked forward and back, but it made no move to stand. Blood. So much blood. It seeped from Calf's leg and roiled in the muddy waters. It smeared Tyler's hands, hot and sticky and smelling like copper pennies.

He slid his fingers under Calf's bony chest and lifted with all he had. The torso swayed, but instead of using the momentum to stand, the youngster flopped onto its side and lay prone as a fallen log in the cold, shallow rainwater. Only Calf's wild, white-rimmed eye showed life, and it followed Tyler's every move.

Calf was dying, and there was nothing Tyler could do to save the animal. He fought the urge to turn and run and never look back. No. Something was taking place here. Something about overcoming weakness and proving himself, about decency and needing to be brave like Geen in order to survive this new life in the wilderness. Either he had the stuff to show mercy in the face of the natural order of things, or he did not. Either he could perform the wrenching, compassionate act, or he could not. He was standing at a crossroads, and his choice would forever determine the man in the mirror. Only a coward would leave this poor creature to bleed out alone and in agony.

"I'm sorry," Tyler said in a voice not his own. He moved the toe of his boot onto Calf's face. Gently, inexorably, he pressed the little black nose under the surface. The nostrils flared, and murky water rushed inside. Calf thrashed its legs and struggled to lift its head toward life-prolonging oxygen. But Tyler held his boot firm. Raw horror flooded the eye. In the space where eyelid met eyeball, translucent flesh jiggled like a raw oyster. Flailing hooves splashed fluid onto Tyler's legs and chest, into his mouth and up his nose. Still, he pressed down. Calf's mouth opened, and its long, pink tongue extended outward.

"I'm so sorry." Tyler gritted his teeth against the tears flooding his cheeks.

Calf met his regard, and they held each other's gaze. He owed Calf that. Soft black-and-brown hairs flecked the face. The hair was long and curly. Pink lined the nostrils. A teardrop eye socket framed the blue iris. The calf smelled of baby.

The thrashing slowed to involuntary twitches. The baby-blue iris swelled wide, and the black core grew. Tyler's reflection stretched across the convex eye. Moments lasted eons. The open eye pointed up at him. Reproaching. Begging. Confused. Afraid. Resigned. Then a gray, lifeless cloud blocked communications.

Dead.

Calf was soft and brown. The eye, a teardrop. Its iris, milky blue. Tyler lifted his toe, and the nose bobbed upward but remained underwater. Calf's winter coat was long, its hip bony. Burgundy blood swirled in the muddy waters. It seeped from hooves to hips to the underbelly tuft that signified Calf's maleness.

Tyler felt the warmth of Geen's body pressed against his leg. The eye was a blue teardrop. Crimson water washed around Calf's nostrils. Its hooves were mud-brown and burgundy.

Geen's tail slapped Tyler's lower leg. Slap. Slap. Shiny dark skin rimmed the eyelid. Rib lines that should rise and fall lay motionless as sand dunes. Blood oozed from the upper thigh. The smell of blood and manure and urine and mud and Calf.

Geen snugged his muzzle into Tyler's palm, sticky with drying blood.

"You stupid dog!" He drew back a fist to teach Geen a lesson. But he couldn't swing it around. No. He would never beat an animal. Not now, not ever. Tyler lowered his palm to Geen's cowering head and ran his fingers up the warm muzzle, over the cartilage of his low-slung ears. "It's okay, boy."

A wet tongue licked his wrist. The nostrils were pink, the nose dark gray. Tyler lifted his eyes to the maquis, to the thorny, tough, resilient maquis. Feeling nothing—nothing at all—he locked his thoughts on the logic of simple tasks. Drag the body upstream to the stone ruins. Haul it onto a rock. Angle the body to allow the blood to drain. Butcher the meat. Need a tool. Must get a knife.

Tyler pointed at the ground. "Stay, Geen. Eat." He ran full speed to Yuki.

She took one look at him and clasped a hand over her mouth. "What happened?"

"Geen and I killed a calf," he said, his voice breathless and distant. He felt no pride. No remorse. He was a blank page, a robot. The eye was blue. What was he looking for? Yes. Yes. The knife. Tyler rummaged through the pack. "Help me find the Leatherman, will you? We need to convert it to food."

"No way." Yuki glared. "You are stupid."

His trembling fingers found the blade, and he tore off for Calf and Geen. Along the way, he stripped fairy tale flowers off their stalks. On arrival, he layered the tender, white blossoms over Calf's eyes and nose. He stuffed a cupped little ear, but then he ran out of petals. Should he go get more? Then he noticed Geen Doorgang. Instead of devouring a bellyful of meat, the dog sat like a ceramic statue next to the undisturbed body. At Tyler's gaze, Geen licked his lips and looked away.

Tyler decided to think about that later. Right now, he had to figure out how to butcher. As he opened the blade, he took a deep breath and ran the cutting edge below the ribcage. Too light. He applied more pressure, and this time skin parted. Sticky, smelly blood spilled over the stainless steel blade and burned his index finger and thumb. Hot entrails sloughed out of the abdomen and cascaded like snakes over his hands. He jerked back and retched. Then he noticed Geen. Unflinching, he gazed at his master. He was trusting Tyler to do what must be done.

Tyler cut out the liver. "Here you go, boy." He lobbed the floppy, iron-rich organ to Geen. Instead of catching the treat with his characteristic flare, Geen let it tumble to the earth. He gave it a sniff, licked his chops, and returned to watching Tyler.

Trying not to think about the blood smearing his arms and elbows, his shirt and pants and face, Tyler dug high and removed the heart. "You'll like this," he said, and flashed back to Grandpa's gutting a deer.

"High in protein," Grandpa had explained as he flicked a still-warm heart into a galvanized steel bucket for the dogs.

Now Tyler appreciated why Dad wasn't big on hunting. He tossed Geen the hot, no-longer-beating organ. Again, Geen offered only an obligatory sniff and let it fall. Tyler scraped out the ribcage and stomach cavity before angling the body to drain what blood remained. Slicing skin from flesh and muscle from bone, he flicked Geen what looked like the tastiest, most tender morsels. "Eat," he ordered. "Eat!"

Despite his commands, or maybe because of them, shiny red globs of flesh, muscle, and bone mounded at Geen's feet. "Eat! You damned dog."

Geen inched away from the mountain of meat. Something in that canine brain of his had to be interpreting Tyler's behavior as reinforcement of a deep-wired, primordial hierarchy. Hungry and half starved, Geen was insisting on waiting for his master to finish before taking his turn. A saint really. A damned, stubborn, calf-killing saint.

Another trip to Ice Cave. Another frosty nongreeting from Yuki. Tyler returned to the butcher site and loaded garbage bags as full as he dared. He lugged them two at a time to camp and dropped the last bag at Yuki's feet around two o'clock.

"Here's your *niku*," he said. "Eat it, or not. Makes no difference to me." He gathered a towel and fresh clothes, then headed for the river. There he stripped and waded into the waters, swollen with ice melt and rain. The frigid rapids tore at his ankles, knees, and thighs. A fallen tree bobbed partway across the river, so he grabbed one of its leafy branches. An inhale, and he let the raging current pull him under. Clinging to the supple limb, he undulated like a seal against the rocky riverbed until he could hold his breath no longer. Burning with cold, he fought his way to the surface, threw back his head, and let loose a deafening howl.

When his lungs were emptied, he stumbled to shore. There he scrubbed and scrubbed and scrubbed himself dry. *Out, damned spot*, he thought. Who would have thought the calf would be so full of blood? Vaguely aware of his surroundings, Tyler dressed and began the climb to Ice Cave. The effort quelled his shivers and returned sensation to his hands and feet, though it failed to lessen the metallic pong of blood in his nostrils. Ignoring Yuki, he flopped onto their bed of Miles.

She threw wood on the campfire, and Ice Cave warmed to a sleep-inducing cocoon. "It's not right to blame you," she said at last. "I brought this on."

He should probably explain that she bore no responsibility. No word—written or spoken—could have unleashed the day's events. Superstition was a human construct, a product of *Homo sapiens* brain because it was wired to make sense of a mind-boggling world. No. He could barely keep his eyelids open, let alone muster the energy to start a conversation that would challenge Yuki's fundamental beliefs. Besides, she was being nice. Maybe she'd cook some veal. The logic lesson could wait. For now, all he only wanted was for the smoky air to fill his lungs and displace the stench of death.

He closed his eyes, but images of Calf's teardrop eye drove him to open them again. He stretched onto his back and stared at the shale-and-limestone ceiling. He was living in a cave; he was a caveman, and today he had done what cavemen had done since the first hominid walked upright. He had killed a calf, his yearling. In the struggle to survive, he'd crossed from innocence to adulthood, from idealism to realism. Was this a one-way trajectory? He wondered.

The nostrils flared pink.

Tyler rose and carried his boots to the mouth of the cave. They smelled of blood and death, for they, too, had come of age.

Yuki later realized her part and helped me cook the tough meat. It was a pain to eat, boiled meat that chewed like rubber, but we both said it was good, feeling somewhat closer and deserving of this meal. I cut strips, salted and laid them out in the sun to dry, but they were stolen during the night.

Morning dawned to sunshine and vibrant green grass, so Tyler and Yuki went in search of the stolen meat. Movement overhead caught his eye, and there on a rock, a finger-size lizard stood sunning itself. It lifted a front leg, then changed feet in a sort of stop-action dance. "Look." Tyler pointed.

Yuki gasped. "They are all over!"

Dozens of lizards dotted the rocks, each enjoying the sun, each performing the same fancy footwork. "Ninjas," Tyler christened them.

It must be good to be a lizard here, each completely in his element, in the beautiful and complex world filled with brilliant green plants, warm sun and the adventure of life. It's filled with risk as well. Predators are abundant. One day like any other, it could come, and that's it: a swift end without fanfare, yet as painful and real as the end of you or me. No one feels remorse for the passing of a ninja. It's a life pure and free from all the worries of political asylum and arrest warrants.

And impervious to the killing of calves.

Naive Dreams

• • •

Without income, the remainder of Tyler and Yuki's funds were shriveling to dangerous levels. Plus, warm weather was unleashing a deluge of summer ferries and four-wheelers from Saint Florent. Their desert haven was about to crawl with tourists. The time had come to move to the city and rent a cheap apartment. If they could save enough money to hire a lawyer, maybe they could resolve their situation and return home.

Tyler packed for an early-morning departure and then sat down to do math. "One thing about Naber."[5] He traced over a derivative symbol in a differential equation. "The mathematics is standard, but his treatment always keeps an eye on the physics, and he's super clear." How he loved topology[6] and geometry.

"Um hum." Yuki flitted back and forth, busy with one thing or another. "You need to concentrate on all we need to do."

---

5 Gregory Naber, a preeminent mathematician and quantum physicist, author of more than twenty publications.

6 In mathematics, topology analyzes concepts such as space, dimension, and transformation. The field of topology is concerned with the properties of space that are preserved under continuous deformations, such as stretching and bending but not tearing or gluing.

"I am." He could understand her anxiety. The idea of his leaving her and Geen alone and taking the train south to the island's west-coast capital was disconcerting. Tomorrow would be the first night they'd spent apart since they'd arrived on the island. Big changes were afoot. "The first order of business is to gather information and rent an apartment," he said. "With all the tourists coming, it should be a breeze for us to find jobs."

"How do you expect to find an apartment?" Yuki asked. "No one speaks English."

"Got it covered." He grinned. "I haven't just been doing math, you know."

"Oh, yeah?" She pasted an imaginary phone to her ear. "I'm the landlady. You're calling on an ad. Bonjour?"

"Bonjour. Je vous appelle au sujet de la chambre, vous avez à louer," he replied. "That's 'Hello, I'm calling about the room you have for rent.'"

Yuki raised a finger. "'Oui. It is available and cheap—very, very cheap.'"

"Nous aimerions faire un rendez-vous pour le voir," he said, as French as a Frenchman, maybe. "That's 'We would like to make an appointment to see it.'"

"Fine. I will show to you two at o'clock." She hung up her imaginary phone and tapped his sternum. "You are ready."

"That's right." He went back to his math, and Yuki's flitting dissolved into the background noise. "Until now," he said, "I never really understood the origin of the Yang-Mills-Higgs field or its significance in physics." A clacking sound forced him to raise his eyes. Yuki stood in front of him, working a pair of scissors.

"You need to understand this." She bobbed the shears at his nose.

"What are you doing?"

Rather than answering, she circled behind him and yanked a comb through his snarled hair.

"Ouch." He reached for her hand, but she moved it away. "That hurts!"

Snip. Snip. "Stop wiggling."

Clumps of dark-brown mats were patting Tyler's shoulders and drifting onto the sand at his feet. "Is this necessary?"

"Necessary is as necessary does."

What was that supposed to mean? "Do you have any clue how to cut hair?"

A tug on a strand shot pain through his scalp. "Beggars cannot be losers."

"Choosers." He corrected. "Don't try to fight my cowlick."

She grabbed his shoulders and squared them. "Sit still."

"Not too short."

Scissors snapped all too close to his eyeball. Maybe he should keep quiet. At last, Yuki handed him a cosmetic mirror. "Handsome man."

Almost two months had passed since he'd seen his reflection or given thought to his appearance. The face looking back at him resembled the Tyler he remembered. More tanned. Thinner. His expression carried a depth he didn't recognize—serious, maybe even solemn. "Not bad," he said.

"Proper appearance is most important," she said. "No one is going to rent to a stinky, stained, long-haired bum."

Tyler examined his T-shirt and khakis. Sure, they had a few stains. The knees were threadbare, the pant legs frayed. So what? Trying not to sound dismissive, he said, "This is France. Nobody here's fussy about clothes or body hair."

She jabbed her index finger at him, the one that allowed no further discussion. "Landlords care. If you to want get us an apartment, these clothes need hot water. You go to the laundromat now."

The nearest *laverie automatique* was in L'Île-Rousse, seven hours away by foot. "You're kidding?" He checked the sky, and the overcast sun hung well past ninety degrees. "It's after one o'clock."

Geen stood equidistant between them, a neutral third point in their family triangle. His eyes cut back and forth to each speaker and his tail marked time like an intermittent windshield wiper. Yuki jammed a bulbous black plastic bag into Tyler's hands. "You wash clothes tonight. Catch train to Ajaccio tomorrow, first thing."

"But—"

"No buts." She wagged a finger. "'I don't like big butts, and I cannot lie.' Go now."

"Fine." He sighed. "Better give me your dirty stuff, too. I'll wash it and bury it in a bag to keep it safe from thievery. Then we won't have to pack so much out when we leave."

Before Tyler could prepare a set of math problems to occupy any downtime that he might encounter, Yuki had stuffed nearly all of her clothes into another garbage bag. She ushered him on his way, and seven hours later, with his back aching under the rolling weight of the dirty clothes bags, he strode onto a beach outside L'Île-Rousse. It was too late to do laundry now, so in the blue light of a waning gibbous moon, he spread his bedroll between clumps of maquis at the edge of the shoreline. After downing a can of cold chili, he crawled between the sleeping bag's flannel-lined panels.

Splats of rain forced Tyler awake in the darkness of early morning. Then the clouds let loose. He gathered his bags in the downpour, sloshed into town past unlit shops, and turned onto allée Charles de Gaulle. Subcompact cars nested like sleeping manatees next to the trunks of grand trees that lined the boulevard.

The laverie automatique's doors were locked, and a sign read Ouvert 7 à 7. His pocket clock put the time at 5:03 a.m., so he made his way back to the beach and took a seat under a closed café's beige awning. From his aluminum chair at a bistro table, he watched umbrellaed workers arrive and disappear into the café. Rain continued to hammer craters into the sand as the sky lightened from black to gray. Since no one seemed to mind his presence, he opened a paperback to review his French. Odd that the café would be this active, this early.

Rats. Today was Sunday, 28 March: Daylight Saving Time. He reset his clock for ten minutes to eight and returned to the laverie to find the narrow, three-washer joint open and empty. Too bad he lacked the enormous quantity of coins required to run a washer. Besides, he needed to find a restroom. Hoping to remedy both needs at the nearby Supermarché Casino, he jogged the block there and bought a loaf of bread.

The checkout clerk didn't seem to mind giving him his change in coinage, but when he asked about restrooms, she shook her head and replied curtly, "No toilettes."

All right, he could look for facilities on his way back to the laundromat. But he found none. The washing machine's cryptic and misleading diagrams put him on guard for shenanigans, so he wasn't surprised when the soap dispenser refused to release its contents into the load. A little tweaking and he managed to bypass the mechanism altogether. While the agitator was obediently sudsing, he calculated that his funds would run short, so he made a second trip, this time buying a newspaper and still failing to locate a restroom.

On his return, the washing machine had skipped a cycle and failed to rinse, so it had managed to win this round. Tyler rinsed the clothes by hand in a tub and wrung them out to dry. The dryer took three iterations before it began to roll.

His need for a bathroom now pressing, Tyler headed back into the rain. A pizzeria, a souvenir shop, a café—all refused him the use of their facilities and directed him elsewhere. A café worker jabbed a finger westward. "Just go to the public toilets."

Tyler searched for the alleged facilities in vain before checking on his laundry and resuming the hunt. Yes! An unmarked door down an alley opened to three pay stalls. Damn. Each required small change, and he had only a two-euro coin. Sweating now, he plunked it in.

Nothing. The damned device refused to release the door, let alone return his money. Desperate, he retrieved his laundry and endured a thirty-minute slog to the train station.

"No toilettes," a male clerk declared.

I asked politely where the nearest one was, and the man laughed, "About a kilometer that way."

I shit behind a train car.

Tyler's insides were quivering in humiliation as he made his way toward his campsite in the pouring rain. How could a fellow human being deny a person a crap? Or rip off someone's belongings simply because their items were left unattended? Hell, people wanted to catch him and throw him in a cage. Fine. From now on, he was done with his species. He was going to shun *Homo sapiens* just as they shunned him. They would be but ghosts, strange humanoid creatures like those Yuki said Japanese fishermen sometimes encountered at sea. What did she call them? *Ningens.* Yes, humans were ningens to him.

Tyler jammed what he needed into his packs and buried the rest before catching the train out of L'Île-Rousse for Ajaccio to the southwest. Through his window, he watched a hard rain slap the opaque, white-capped face of the Mediterranean.

Standing on a corner in the glow of a streetlight, Tyler listened to the *dong* of an ornate clock atop Ajaccio's white, two-story train station. 8:30 p.m. Gulls cawed as they circled a ten-story, blue-and-white SNCM cruise ship in the port across the street. West winds carried scents of motor fuel with a hint of bilge water. The name N193 topped a street sign. Below, green arrows all pointed the same direction to strange places called Calvi, Bonifacio, Sartène, Campo dell Oro, Marconajo, and Port Charles Ornano.

On principle, Tyler felt inclined to walk in the opposite direction, but the sign for Campo dell Oro sported an icon of a beach umbrella. Assuming *campo* to mean campsite, he headed that way in search of a secluded spot to spend the night.

Unfortunately, Campo dell Oro was a hotel. It had a beach behind it, though, so he set camp between bushes and pulled out his journal. In the reflective glow of the moon, he wrote.

> I realized today how lonely it is to be without Yuki and Geen. I'm so grateful to have her with me because it makes life so much more enjoyable. I don't know how I would keep sane without her.

Rising early, Tyler bought a current issue of *Corse Matin*, Ajaccio's newspaper. The classifieds brimmed with ads for pricy apartments. Only single-room flats—whatever they were—looked the least bit affordable. He rang the first number.

"Bonjour."

Mustering his most friendly French, Tyler did his best to say, "Hello, I'm calling about the room for rent. Is it still available, and do you allow pets?"

The lilting response might as well have been Martian.

"Pardon?" he asked.

Slower, the voice articulated in French, "Yes, it is available. No landlords allow pets. Where do you work?"

"Oh, uh, we only just arrived," Tyler managed. "We expect to find jobs soon."

"Call back when you have work." Click.

He tried a second number.

"Oh, no pets! Show me your work contract, and I will show you the room."

"We'll be getting jobs right away."

Click.

Third number: "No pets, of course. No apartment without a job contract." Click.

Fourth and final possibilities: click and click.

Tyler expanded his search area to include a northern suburb called Mezzavia. Rents looked cheaper there, probably because of its distance from the central city. Sadly, though, his conversations ended the same way as the others: click, click, and click. Discouraged, he punched in the last number.

"Oui. How may I help you?" The voice sounded like that little exorcist woman in *Poltergeist.*

A prank? He almost hung up. "I'm interested in the room you have advertised," he said, "if it's available and you allow pets, that is."

"I have one room left in a third-floor flat," the cheery voice squeaked. "But no pets. I'm sorry, but you'll find no one allows pets, my dear."

No mention of requiring proof of employment. "I'll take it," Tyler said.

One hour later, he handed a month's rent to a little woman named Rosine, occupancy to begin 1 May.

On his return to the desert, Tyler told Yuki the good and bad news. "We have a room, but we can't bring Geen."

She looked more pained than surprised, as if her fears were coming true. "You tell him," she said and stepped away.

Tyler cupped Geen's head in his hands and stroked his ears. "Leaving you is the right thing to do," he said. "Has to be this way if we're ever going to find a way out of this situation and get home."

Yuki, who was sitting on a rock, rolled onto her back and gazed up at the sky. "Has to be this way."

Geen fixed an unusually intense and trusting gaze on Tyler.

"Shit," Tyler said. "We have a cheap, safe place to live. We're comfortable and could survive here a long time, enjoying this life."

Yuki examined the clouds. "We run out of money, and we starve."

"We'll work the summer and come back for you this fall," he told Geen. But the words sounded flat, like saying "See you later" to someone he never expected to meet again.

Geen rested his muzzle on Tyler's knee and appeared to listen with his whole being. Tyler sat mute, scratching the brown-and-black hairs on Geen's neck.

THE NEXT FEW DAYS were filled with preparation. Tyler contacted a friendly fellow named Neru who had taken a liking to Geen at Ostriconi Beach. Neru jumped at the chance to take Geen and promised to give him a good home. Then departure. Geen trotted merrily ahead, unwittingly leading their five-hour trek from Saleccia toward his new home. Along the way, they took pictures of Geen and recorded the sound of his flapping his ears in a tunnel.

The campground office came into view, and they lingered outside. Tyler threw a stick for Geen, and his buddy dutifully returned it, though he acted subdued and carried his head low. Tyler couldn't bring himself to look at Yuki, but he could feel her gaze.

L'Île-Rousse lay two hours farther southeast. If they were going to catch the train to Ajaccio, they had to leave soon. "It's time," Tyler said.

Tears were streaming down Yuki's cheeks as she knelt and wrapped her arms around Geen's neck. "We will come back for you," she whimpered, "and I hope you will be here." She stood and turned away. "I can't watch." Then she slumped toward the beach.

With worn steps in tired boots, Tyler led Geen to the shoddy office. The only pay phone within three miles clung to a wall like a black-hooded assassin. Tyler made the call and then turned to the receptionist. "This is Geen," he choked. "His new owner promises to pick him up right away."

"Will he bite?" the woman asked.

Unable to speak and trying to contain welling tears that threatened to spill over his eyelids, Tyler shook his head. He turned away and left Geen with his long tail wagging and his eyes brimming in trust.

"It's done," Tyler told Yuki. They walked along the beach before cutting inland over rolling terrain.

"He'll be okay," Yuki said at last.

"Yeah." Tyler nodded. "Neru's a decent guy." They wended among rounded stones lining a dry riverbed. A furry creature skittered into a hole along the bank.

"Did you tell the receptionist to tell Neru that Geen like lots of water?" Yuki asked.

"He'll give him water."

Yuki pointed to a wasp nest high in a beech tree. "Geen is allergic to wasps," she said.

"If he doesn't snap at them, they'll leave him alone." They heard the clatter of hooves, and a brown cow disappeared into the maquis.

"You think Neru will hit him for barking?"

"Doubt it." A cow pie looked dry, but Tyler's foot squished into it. The stench of manure accompanied him for half a mile. At the base of a ravine, they dropped their packs on the shady north side of a boulder and shared a crusty baguette. Yuki stretched out for a nap while Tyler washed down the heel of the loaf with warm water. He pulled out his journal.

> Today begins a new chapter in our lives. We lost our best friend today, and he characterized the prior chapter, a transition from stressful misery to pleasant optimism. We are moving on to an apartment in Ajaccio, so we had to say good-bye. Even when reading a book, it's sad to leave the last chapter behind, but we rarely notice because our attention shifts to the upcoming chapter. It's somewhat different when you are living the story, but the dichotomy still exists.
>
> I'm looking forward to what lies ahead: comfort, ningen community, and business. But I hate to think about what had to be left behind: the beauty, the freedom, the plants and most of all Geen.

Who was he kidding?

> Leaving Geen was one of the hardest things I've ever done. A real test of severity. This action illustrates

> the iron and concrete state of mind we are in, the will to survive vetoing any desire for happiness, luxury or niceties.
>
> So we have moved off in search of a sustainable situation, jobs, the clandestine underground work you find in the din and rattle of smoky bars and dim-lit kitchens everywhere in the world.

Yes, he expected long hours of busing tables. What he hadn't expected was this haunting sense that in leaving Geen, they were betraying a sacred trust.

"It was the right thing to do," he whispered to Yuki, curled on her side and sound asleep—or pretending to be. "Had to be done."

They hitched a ride to L'Île-Rousse, arriving too late to catch a bus or train to Ajaccio. An awning outside a closed travel agency offered shelter, although the pounding droplets made staying dry difficult. They bedded down, and Yuki curled into a cocoon. Tyler kept watch, writing into the night.

> Life seems to set up little transitions to give us a chance to reflect, to see ourselves from a new perspective and, more importantly, to appreciate the essence of it all. Present and future chapters meet, merge and blend together. There is a theorem in vector calculus that for any two functions defined or nearly defined, there exists a continuous joining of them as long as one is an epsilon between the

domains to round the corners off. That is exactly what these two days are. The transition could be shorter, but that might mean I have to reflect at a rate beyond my capacity. So on into the night. Wet streets and neon lights paint a dreamy sleeplessness.

Ten more hours until the train came; eight for the bus, or so people claimed. Tomorrow would usher in either a long, nauseating, early-morning bus ride or smooth locomotion in a standing-room-only passenger car. He hadn't bothered to find out the relative prices. No matter. One way or another, they would reach their destination and spend another homeless night before they could move into their room.

I'm looking at a superposition of future states. Unfortunately, I can't skip ahead without breaking the superposition. I mean, if it happened that I were in Ajaccio right now, but I had no memory of how I got there, I would have a superposition of states, but that doesn't really happen since I'm going to pass through it and measure it. Anyway...

Looking back can be a dangerous activity. I've done a lot of odd things, and I think I've been lucky enough to appreciate them along the way. That's the most important part, to appreciate life along the way. The road trip to Wyoming with Grandma J. and Kelsey...what a beautiful experience.

Now I'm leaning against a transition door with my head feeling the rainy night. Rain can bring out the best of a bad situation, but often it's also the reason the situation is bad in the first place. So bad is all a state of mind, a judgment passed by someone who bothered to stop and pass judgment. If you feel it, it's a lot more than good or bad. If you don't bother to feel it, then why pass judgment? Such things reflect only on the passer, not on the situation. Now the two sides are mixed, bland and mildly unpleasant. Must sleep.

As it turned out, they missed the six o'clock bus and caught the standing-room-only, seven-thirty train instead. Tyler dropped his bags at his feet and gripped an overhead bar. Letting his eyes fall closed, he relaxed into the sway of the passenger car. Eight stops and one-and-a-half hours later, the train glided into Ponte Leccia. There they changed trains and were lucky to find seats.

Mountains peaked upward like sharks' teeth to the left and the right as the train rocked southward through the center of the island. The steel rollers screeched to a halt at Corte, Vizzavona, and wherever else passengers pulled their cords, and that was fine with Tyler. He had a seat next to Yuki and a terrific view out her window. Plus, the citrus-scented woman across the aisle didn't seem to mind sharing her newspaper.

Around noon, they chugged into a sea of sidewalks, shops, and traffic. Yuki was gawking like a kid in a video-game parlor. "It's a real city!" she chimed.

Tyler squeezed her hand. "Half the equation's in place. We have a room within walking distance of the central city." He pointed to yet another bar. "They're all over the place. We'll have our pick of jobs."

They disembarked and hauled their belongings to a phone booth. He dialed Rosine, and the landlady's childlike voice squeaked a warm greeting. Communicating with her proved harder than Tyler remembered, but she seemed to understand what he was trying to ask, and he caught the gist of her responses: Why no, it was no problem that they had arrived a day early. No need to wait until tomorrow to move in.

"I shall pick you up in five minutes," she said.

Fifteen minutes passed. Then a worn, canary-yellow Peugeot bumped a front wheel over the curb and rocked to a halt. The vehicle appeared driverless except for a telltale tuft of gray hair that spiked above the steering wheel. A plump hand waved hello, and Tyler recognized Rosine's trill voice. He made introductions before stuffing their bags under the hatch and into a backseat cluttered with old newspapers, McDonald's wrappers, and a pair of lace-less tennis shoes. He squeezed next to a framed poster of a big-eyed girl with parrots perched on her white-gloved arms. Yuki sat up front with Rosine.

Immersed in the woman's birdlike chatter, they listed along the center line as traffic backed up behind them. An oncoming Mercedes jounced up on a curb to avoid colliding with them head-on. At last, Rosine's car bobbled up a driveway next to the rental house. She slammed on the brakes, and Tyler leaped out as the car ground to a standstill.

Trailing Rosine up two flights of stairs was like forwarding frame by frame through a video. At last they came to the chalk-yellow door, and she swung it open, saying, "Voici." Here you go.

"Merci." Tyler watched her sway along the hallway and disappear down the stairs. Then he and Yuki stepped into the flat. He had forewarned her about the room's small size and orange-pink color, so this came as no shock to her, but the twenty-inch television was a different story. She made a beeline for it and spun its knobs.

"You never told me it came with TV!"

Tyler felt himself grin as he swished open a dust-scented curtain. "I was saving that as a surprise." He looked into a back-alley trash container three stories below. "Not much of a view, but we have a window."

She swung open a door to a two-foot-wide closet and nodded approval. "Enough hangers for all our clothes!"

Vacillating between hope and concern for what was to come, Tyler ran a hand over the room's only table, drop leaf and pine. Its two chairs wobbled on the irregular plank floor. "We're not used to this sort of luxury," he said. "We've forgotten what's normal."

Yuki eased onto the mattress, and the box springs creaked. She pinched a pillow. "'It's squeezably soft. It's irresistible.'"

He flopped down beside her and pulled her close. "Please," he said. "Squeeze the Charmin."

After midnight, they turned on the TV and discovered the Arte channel. Reclining in bed, they lost themselves in a short film featuring a fictitious underworld of Europeans. "Art meets adventure," Tyler said with a yawn when it ended. Yuki was sleeping, so he turned off the tube closed his eyes, too. But the characters haunted his thoughts. He rolled onto his side and dug his notepad from the pocket of his cargo pants.

Bewildering and soft images echoed the same vibes as our little corner here, quiet and dark, lost somewhere on the inside of this vast, twitching world.

THE NEXT DAY, EAGER TO SHOP for the best-paying job he could find, Tyler rose before sunrise. Moving quietly so as not to disturb Yuki, he gathered a clean set of clothes, his Nalgene bottle, half a baguette, and Naber, of course—in case he had time between interviews. Then he stepped into the hallway.

The house lay still as a snapshot, its boarders asleep behind locked doors. The floorboards complained of his passage, and he had the eye-poppingly green community restroom all to himself. Once Tyler was showered and shaved, he creaked downstairs and stepped under a lettered awning that long ago may have been burgundy. Weeds sprouted between a yellow-trimmed curb and the sidewalk. Across the narrow street, a footpath cut a diagonal through an empty lot.

Tyler paused to appreciate two tall, street-side sycamores. The fresh scent of their hand-size leaves offset, in part, a whiff of raw sewage drifting from a nearby steam grate. The trees took him back to his childhood home in Glenmoore, Pennsylvania. He was maybe twelve—half his lifetime ago—when he and Dad had pruned and preserved a monarch sycamore beside the pool. And now he was here.

Tyler turned right and struck a long stride. At this pace, he stood a chance of trimming his walk to an hour.

AJACCIO PROPER WASN'T LARGE. More long than deep, it faced south into the Mediterranean and hugged two hundred degrees of a moon-shaped bay. Its name, derived from the Roman *adjacium*, meant place of rest. During the summer, the city's leeside harbor served as a popular destination for the rich, and Tyler could see why shepherds would guide their flocks down from the mountains to winter in safety here.

Avenue Napoléon, rue Bonaparte, College Laetitia Bonaparte, Aéroport d'Ajaccio Napoléon Bonaparte—a person couldn't throw a stick without hitting a sign that laid claim to Ajaccio's favorite son. Tyler angled left toward a bar. Le Capitole looked promising but was yet to open. Continuing along boulevard Charles Bonaparte, he came to a strip mall of dark-windowed bars and restaurants. Signs promised ten o'clock openings, so he took up residence on a white concrete traffic barrier and delved into Naber.

Doors started to open, so Tyler entered a restaurant called L'Amirauté. Since the place shared a crescent-shaped blue-gray sign with an adjacent pizzeria, maybe he could double his chances of a job offer. A lanky, white-shirted manager greeted him at the entrance. The smiling, thirty-something fellow dipped his head, probably hoping for his first customer of the day. "Bonjour."

L'Amirauté gleamed with white wicker chairs, and the dining room featured a picture-perfect view of yachts and blue sea. It smelled of fresh linens and butter. "I'm looking for work," Tyler said in his friendliest French. "Washing dishes, busing tables—anything really."

The manager eyed him up and down, and suddenly Tyler felt acutely aware of the fray along the hemline of his khakis. "You're not French," the man huffed. "Our customers prefer authentic French."

"Je comprends. J'apprends à parler," Tyler said. I understand. I'm learning to speak.

The manager sighed and held out his hand. "Papers?"

Tyler left the palm empty. "I was hoping to work for cash."

"Oh no!" The man turned and straightened a place setting. "Pas de travail." No work.

"Merci quand meme." Thanks anyway, Tyler said, and beat an awkward retreat. No worries. He looped past three decorative shrubs and stepped into Bar Le Yacht.

An assistant manager listened patiently to his spiel before flicking her wrist. "Pas de travail."

Coté Port and Le Grill brushed him off with the same curt response. One manager upturned his nose and added, "When we hire, we look for Corsicans or people with papers."

Tyler strode into Old Town. At place Foch he found a medieval gate and, not surprisingly, a statue of the Little Corporal, Bonaparte. More importantly, terra-cotta-roofed cafés and restaurants lined the center square. Some of them had to need a dishwasher or busboy, albeit nonnative or fluent in French.

"Pas de travail." "Pas de travail." "Pas de travail." To no avail.

Hungry and on edge, Tyler stepped into Restaurant les Palmiers and asked for nondocumented work. The gray-haired lug in charge deepened his scowl and opened his mouth to speak. Before he could utter the tired refrain, Tyler raised an open palm to stop him and vented in English, "I get that you Corsicans have a deep-rooted resistance to the outside world, and believe me, I don't like this influx of tourists any more than you do. But for Christ's sake, even a foreigner has to eat!" He instantly regretted his outburst.

Thankfully, the manager gave no indication that he had understood a word and said simply, "Pas de travail." But then the salty local flicked his fingertips under his chin and turned away saying, "Vous baiseur fou."

Yes, Tyler guessed he deserved that. Maybe he was a crazy fucker. What did he expect, that employers would fall over themselves to hire an applicant who sounded foreign, who had no papers, and who conveyed the social guardedness of a fugitive? He slumped to a seaside mooring and took a seat. Chewing on his stale baguette, he watched a ship's mate hose down a shiny white yacht. Then he walked to the bus stop. Saturated in diesel fumes and body odor mostly from his own armpits, he boarded and rode back to Mezzavia.

Yuki wasn't home, so he showered and tried to read on the bed with his back to the wall. Maybe she was having better luck. Right. Compared to her, he was fluent, and he didn't *look* foreign. An Asian woman was practically a circus oddity in these parts. His stomach knotted at the thought of the receptions Yuki was likely enduring.

The door clicked. Footsteps. Yuki flopped facedown beside him. She smelled of cigarette smoke, fish, and more than a little perspiration. Judging from her sigh, no point asking if she'd found work.

She plopped a loose fist on the mattress. "I learned some French today."

"Let me guess. 'Pas de travail'?"

"You got it."

"We're fresh from the wilderness and late for the hiring season." He took a deep breath and released. "Maybe we should try to relax and go with the flow."

"How?"

One word, yet it carried a boatload of sarcasm. They were so accustomed to struggle that the notion of kicking back no longer existed in their thought processes. Every action needed to advance their situation, not trigger an equal and opposite reaction. "You're right," he said. "We have no margin of error. It's flawless or the floor."

"'Flawless or the floor,'" she said with a sigh. "What do we do?"

"All right," he said and the sheer act of planning felt oddly fortifying. "Rent averages thirteen euros a day. We need to keep food and other expenses to three euros. No more riding the bus. We'll walk an hour each way and keep looking for work. We'll persevere."

She inhaled an imaginary cigarette and blew imaginary smoke into the air. "'I'd walk a mile for a Camel,' or a job."

"We need to learn the language and find work," he continued, "so we should talk with people. But we also have to remain anonymous and change identities every so often." He rolled onto his side and gazed into her eyes. "We're caught between two opposing forces."

She pressed her hips to his. "Between rocks and hard places."

He kissed her. "Flawless or the floor."

Pas Bonne Manger (Not Good Eating)

• • •

When they weren't trodding to Ajaccio in search of ever-elusive work, he and Yuki kept to themselves. They settled into long hours of learning French from magazines, television, and their dictionary. Tyler found a tape recorder in a trash bin and restored it to working order. This came in handy for practicing pronunciation and for recording and deciphering television dialog.

One morning, he was in the flat's green community bathroom preparing to leave for another day of job hunting. As he shaved, he stopped and started the tape recorder, replaying last night's local news.

"You are from Canada, right?" a throaty voice resonated from inside the drumming shower.

Jacques. That smiley, out-of-work truck driver who lived alone across the hall. The guy always wore shorts and a T-shirt that exposed tattoos of a guitar, an eyeball, and entangled, KISS-like spears. "Yeah." Tyler rinsed the shaving cream off his face and proceeded to brush his teeth.

Jacques stepped naked and dripping wet from the shower amid a roll of steam. When dressed, he gave the appearance of stockiness. In the buff, his round belly balanced on spindly legs. And he was hairy. Dark, thick curlies sprouted everywhere, and not just in the predictable places. Tyler averted his gaze to the rim of his sink.

"I think I haul off to Quebec and find a job," Jacques said as he rubbed his balding head with a dingy towel. "But first I must speak the good anglais."

Was this some sort of test? Tyler paused from brushing his teeth. "They speak both French and English there."

Jacques stepped into view. "But women, they like the smooth-talking anglais." He toweled off his flapping penis before spreading his legs and scrubbing his crack. Last, he wiped his face and a moustache that connected to a furry goatee. "I tell you what. I teach you French. You teach me anglais."

Tyler returned his toothbrush to its plastic baggie and slid it into his pants pocket. Jacques spoke Corse, that unique blend of Italian, French, Genoese, and pirate. He'd make an ideal subject. "Sure." Tyler handed Jacques the tape recorder and dug into his back pocket for the day's vocabulary list: animal names, P through S. "Mind reading these in?"

Jacques turned the recorder on and off. He appeared to study the list and its sample sentences. "I sing at family weddings," he said. "My dream, it is to be a pop singer. You like me to sing these?"

"Reading them will do just fine."

"My wife." Jacques swung his instep forward as if driving a soccer ball. "She kick me out of our house in Alata."

"Sorry to hear that."

Jacques rolled his hairy shoulders. "Better than having cancer."

"Oui." Tyler nodded. Yes, he guessed all misery was relative.

THAT NIGHT, TYLER AND YUKI were making dinner in the community kitchen when Jacques joined them. He held out the tape recorder to return it to Yuki. "Here you go," he said.

Yuki was stirring a pot of beans and rice, so Tyler took the machine and set it on the counter. "Thanks," he said. "Care to join us?"

Jacques inhaled deeply and waved off the offer. "Merci, but I eat only one meal a day to lose weight." Then he lowered his voice to speak confidentially to Tyler. "And to better seduce the women."

Judging from that sheepish grin, he'd already eaten today.

Jacques rubbed his chin. "What's the English phrase you say to convince a girl to sleep with you?"

No wonder his wife had thrown him out. At a loss to come up with a catchphrase, Tyler confessed, "Not sure there is one."

The rice simmered, no longer in need of stirring. Yuki bobbled her spoon at Tyler and instructed, "Translate pheasant, peacock, pig, prawn."

"*Faison*, *paon*, *cochon*, and *crevette*," he replied, pleased with himself.

Jacques rolled his eyes and kissed his fingertips. "*Faison* all dark meat. *Paon* taste like chicken. *Cochon* so sweet and juicy. Prawns in sauce to die for!"

Yuki appeared not to hear Jacques's culinary assessment and instead pointed at Tyler. "Partridge."

"*Perdrix.*"

Jacques closed his eyes and smacked his lips. "Oula la la!"

Tyler, inspired by a love for animals, had survived long patches of vegetarianism, as had Yuki. Actually, he'd never known anyone to have a softer heart for creatures than she had, so he knew exactly what lay behind her frustrated expression. She turned to him and said, "Porcupine."

What was that word?

Jacques stuck out his lower lip and waved his hands side to side. "Pas bonne manger," he said. "Not good eating."

"*Porc-épic!*" Tyler blurted out. Then, hoping to help Jacques overcome his prejudice against porcupines, he volunteered some factoids he'd learned from Yuki's zoology book. "You know, as many as thirty thousand quills cover every part of a porcupine's body, except its stomach. It's an amazing defensive adaptation."

"Old World porcupines live in southern Europe," Yuki added, "and have quills as long as twenty inches."

Jacques looked as though he were sucking a lemon. "Pas bonne manger."

"They can live fifteen years in their natural habitats." She punctuated her syllables with bobs of her spoon. "These include wooded areas, prairies, mountains, rain forests, and deserts."

Tyler recognized the passages. She was reciting them verbatim. "That's right." He grinned by way of support.

Jacques looked at them as if they were dullards and repeated louder, "Pas bonne manger!"

There was no budging him.

The beans and rice were soft and blended, so Tyler and Yuki bade Jacques good night and returned to their room. Tyler turned on the recorder, hoping to listen to Corsican pronunciations as they ate. Wispy and sensual, Jacque's voice modulated from the machine.

Yuki scrunched her nose. "Porn."

Tyler pressed the off button. "No career for him in voice-overs." Then he added, "Well, maybe in X-rated ones."

For a free night on the town, he and Yuki liked to dress up and set out to roam the hot, deserted streets with camera in hand. Tonight, a buzzing sodium streetlamp cast an orange pool of light, and Tyler flashed on an idea for shooting another slideshow for Mom and Dad. Memories resurfaced of filming with Steve, and limitless future possibilities opened to fill the void of a future erased and re-erased. For a fleeting moment the world felt almost normal again, as if the adventure had tamed to a controllable level, as if he had his life back.

He and Yuki ambled along an empty sidewalk and took turns viewing the city through the camera lens. Wooden scaffolding blocked their progress, so they snapped shots of its gray timbers sprouting like crystal formations up the side of a building. Stark angles and shadows cut across the pavement and lured him and Yuki to dip underneath the scaffolding's bony frame.

Then Tyler saw him. Hunched in shimmering light between black lines, a wary porcupine eyed them.

He didn't run, just curled up into a protective ball of spikes like a sea urchin tossed to dry on the sidewalk. "Pas bonne manger," we told him, and he probably figured that's why we left him alone to go about his peaceful night.

How odd to encounter the very creature they'd just discussed and defended. Maybe that was the essence of opportunity: What a person sought, he noticed. What he noticed, he might someday seek. Conversely, would unnamed dreams lie forever beyond reach and be unattainable? And what about dreams a person sought with all his heart, but were simply too hard to attain?

The days stretched and time battered on. It was a kind of relentless obstacle course that is common in university life, where you never get a moment off because there is always more to learn and do. Sometimes though, to change the atmosphere, we would walk over to an ancient aqueduct and sit on the arches high above the grass below. Watching the grazing sheep inspired me to bust out the computer and write a simulation of swarming behavior. "Swarm, simple laws complex intelligent phenomena" displayed on the command line.

It seemed important at the time.

We had only one reviving dose of our Saint Nature. We met some turtles and took a new path, starting from some houses below the cliffs of Mt. Gozzi. It was hot and a long uphill battle with the maquis. Near the top, we needed to cut horizontally over to the trail, and it should have been easy, but I kept stumbling as gravelly rocks rolled out from under my feet. Getting fed up, I shouted angrily, "Can I just walk please?" which pleased Yuki very much.

19 May 2004. I feel I have been destined for this. It's like my whole life has been in preparation. Not that it's any less painful, but if it were any other way, I would have some uncomfortable feeling that I had missed it, betrayed myself. For the first time in my life, I fall asleep easily. What does that mean?

There were times when I had a glimpse of this, long ago when I was roaming around China. It was all about being *real*. That was as far as I got. I was always a bit shy of it. I'd think it would be real if there were no turning back, if the past was locked away and the future unknown. As much as I tried, I could never deceive myself into thinking I wouldn't return. Those times when I imagined circumstances not unlike now, then I'd shudder, sometimes almost break down and cry, console myself with how glad I was that it was all only imaginary.

THEIR TWENTY-EIGHT-DAY RENTAL CONTRACT ended on 1 June 2004. Tyler and Yuki had to move out, so they spent the evening on the street, waiting and watching, debating their next course of action. Around midnight they wandered to the flat of a guy they'd met on the streets.

Strung up and out, Little Bear, or "Petit Ours" as he was known in French, was indeed little. Whether engaging in open-bottled philosophy or telling raunchy jokes over beach campfires, he spasmed with eagerness for life, because Little Bear hated life as much as he loved it.

"That Rosine is a bitch, yeah," Little Bear said, but he didn't just speak. He spat his words hard and fast. "How dare she give you the boot?"

Raised in an intellectual left-wing family, Little Bear was born on track for higher education, but during puberty he realized that academic geekhood wouldn't win him girls. This led him to drop out of college and take up alcohol consumption as his outstanding personal characteristic. Indeed, Little Bear's capacity for drink earned him respect and standing among the unrespected, young, street-dwelling, party-going punks of Ajaccio. His pad served as a gathering spot and point of departure for rambunctious nights that generally culminated with vomit-stained clothing and hoarse voices hurtled through the steamy summer streets.

"It's not really her fault." Tyler tried to explain. "Our lease ran out."

"Fuck her. Fuck that bitch." Little Bear jabbed a beer into Tyler's palm before bowing to Yuki and kissing the back of her hand. "Yuki, my beautiful." He pressed her palm to his heart. "Dump Marco and please to come to me. I beg you."

Tyler felt a nervous jolt at the mention of his alias, Marco, even though this Thursday would make five months since he and Yuki had fled the States. He'd chosen the name Marco because, at the time of his exit, he could barely run a search for the latest quantum research without coming across breakthroughs from Marco Someones or Someones Marco. He'd opted to go by the name for the anonymity it seemed to offer, and yes, he supposed, to retain a vicarious connection with the group.

Yuki, who seldom spoke French and never chanced to do so in public, yanked her arm back and asked, "'How about a nice Hawaiian Punch?'"

Everyone laughed.

Now apartmentless, Yuki and Tyler threw themselves into drinking and at some point engaged a man named Milos in conversation. A regular for the hopping nights that originated from Little Bear's, Milos was also there late mornings and afternoons, smoking hash until the night bore out its adventures. Whereas Bear seemed content to stay forever in Corsica, Milos talked of travels to China. He professed to have studied kung fu at Shaolin and spoke of hundreds of other potential adventures. These, of course, took precedence over and ruled out both school and work. In contrast to jumpy, quick-witted Little Bear, Milos was dull and confident. He had everything easy that Little Bear had rough, especially his effortless success with women.

"You need a room?" Milos asked when the topic arose.

"Yeah." Tyler downed the dregs of his third beer. "But two people without jobs can't afford four hundred euros a month."

Milos spread his arms wide. "Move in with me! I live in my grandmother's apartments and manage them in my off hours. I have an empty room."

If only. "Thanks, but I doubt we could afford it."

"Sixty euros a month and it's yours. With the rent you pay, I'll be free of the usual worries about money."

Tyler read cautious hope on Yuki's face. "Mind if we take a look?"

Milos was already on his feet. A short walk and they were stepping into a bright-blue stucco apartment building. At the end of a yellow-walled first floor and past a trashcan ripe with empty wine bottles, they climbed a set of stairs to an enchanting red floor. A flight higher and they reached the apex, floor three. Here, a brilliant-purple hallway terminated at an equally purple door.

Inside, a shadowy cubicle lay covered in wallpaper straight from a Wong Kar-Wai film. Thin pink curtains dangled over a window draped in an unplugged string of flower-shaped Christmas lights. A blue two-person table stood like a headless stick horse in the far corner next to a bare twin bed.

"We'll take it," Tyler and Yuki blurted out in unison.

July 2004. The month passed and we had only one lead for a job, but that was all we needed.

Tyler sank into the wobbly wooden chair and scooped Yuki a spoonful of spreadable Speculoos from their half-empty jar. The substance resembled peanut butter in both color and consistency, but its slightly caramelized, almost-but-not-quite-gingerbread flavor tickled his nostrils. "There's no use walking to Ajaccio anymore," he said. "If a job opens, managers just call applicants they have on file."

Yuki took the spoon and indulged in a measured nibble. "Documented applicants with phones that work."

He dipped a spoonful for himself. "Time to change our strategy. Maybe we can find jobs through people we know."

She closed her eyes and savored the taste before sipping her chipped cup of tea. "How? Our group values freedom and fun, not work."

Tyler couldn't stop himself from sliding half his scoop onto his tongue, but he managed to hold off swallowing and let the Belgian cookie delight dissolve in his mouth. "We'll have to keep our priorities to ourselves, or they won't be our friends," he said. "Except we need to reach out—to network." A sip of tea, then he licked his spoon. One more dip and he'd have his two-hundred-calorie ration for the meal.

Yuki took another nibble and sighed. "You want us to stay away from ningens. You want us to network with ningens. 'What do you want, good grammar or good taste?'"

He could understand her frustration. "You know that John Marshall, the one who speaks English and works at the ferry docks?" Yes, he was grasping at straws, but he needed to give Yuki something to hope for—maybe himself, too.

"The quiet one with the ironed pants?"

"Yup."

She puckered her lips and smacked a kissing sound. "He is always smooching with his girlfriend."

"He invited me to his house. Maybe I'll go and see where it leads."

Tyler and John stepped into the kitchen of a roomy two-story condo that smelled of dish soap. A tall, slender woman in pressed khaki shorts and a sleeveless yellow top turned toward them from a white-enameled sink. Her wavy auburn hair hung to her shoulders and was clipped away from her face. Short bangs.

"Hey, Mum!" John called as he dug into his pocket to retrieve a ringing flip phone. *My girlfriend*, he mouthed to Tyler before disappearing into what was probably his bedroom.

Mrs. Marshall propped a dripping china plate upright in a green dish drainer. Wiping her hands on a towel and shaking her head, she turned toward Tyler. "My John," she lilted in flowing British English, "when he falls, he falls hard. I'm Helen Marshall."

The woman's English words resonated like musical notes in Tyler's ears. She didn't come at him to kiss his cheek, but neither did she extend an arm for a handshake. Unsure what to do, he stood like a tree stump with his arms limp at his side. "Nice to meet you," he said. "I'm Marco."

She broke into a cool, relaxed smile that revealed a small mouth and proportionately small, straight teeth. "Care for a spot of tea?"

Tyler sensed this was hardly the first time the gracious woman had gotten stuck with entertaining a guest of John's. "I'm good," he said, as a whiff of her lavender bath powder washed over him. A linen dishtowel hung over the oven-door handle, so he scooped it up and stepped forward to the dish drainer. "Mind if I dry, Mrs. Marshall?"

"Be my guest, but you must call me Helen." She returned to washing. "Tell me how it is you know John."

No way he could call John's mother Helen. He set about wiping a wet china plate. Rimmed with pink-and-green flowers, the porcelain felt warm and smooth to the touch. To think that he used to balk at washing dishes because food scraps gave him the willies. Now he'd give a big toe for a dishwashing job—or any job for that matter. He set the plate on the counter and reached for a slick bowl. "Through mutual friends," he replied. Eager to hear her speak again, he asked, "So what brings you to Corsica?"

She'd met John's father, she said, at a youth hostel in Spain. Marrying him had transplanted her to mainland France and ultimately here to Corsica. "I miss London," she said, "especially the Natural History Museum and the Old Vic Theatre."

Their conversation settled into a comfortable rhythm. Yes, he and his girlfriend, Yuki, were enjoying their stay in Corsica. The Ajaccio ports were amazing; the sunsets, out of this world. After months of struggling to communicate in French, this free-flowing exchange lifted barbells off his shoulders, or maybe this light-headedness was coming from starvation. Regardless, the easy conversation was making colors more vibrant, the air richer with oxygen.

"Listen to me prattle on," Mrs. M. chirped. "It's simply delightful to speak English with someone."

"I agree one-hundred percent." He felt the beginnings of a grin, and his long-dormant facial muscles thanked him for the stretch.

"Are you American?"

"Canadian," he lied, a necessary untruth, except it pinched like shoes one size too small. "From Vancouver."

She dropped a handful of shiny silverware into the drain basket. "A lovely country. I've never had the pleasure to visit, but my husband's cousin works in insurance there. I don't suppose you know Tony Marshall?"

"Sorry." A flash of dread. More questions and she might expose him for the fraud he was. The thought of her catching him in a lie made his jaw clench. Something about her parent-ness made him desperate to avoid reading disappointment in her eyes. He was thankful that she fell silent as she drained the dishwater and swabbed the enamel sink until it gleamed. "So what are you and Yuki doing here?" she asked at last.

"An extended stay." He dried a handful of spoons, forks, and knives and set them on the counter. "Looking for work."

"How's that going?"

A block of ice hardened in his chest. *Horrible. Without documentation, we can't get jobs to save for a lawyer to help us untangle this mess, or lease an apartment, or even buy food. Yuki's losing her mind, and maybe I am, too!* He could say none of this, of course, and he wasn't about to deceive her again, so he just shook his head. She pointed to a drawer. He opened it to an organized wire rack. There he placed spoons with spoons, forks with forks, and knives with knives.

Moving with the ease that comes of familiarity, Mrs. Marshall put clean plates and salad bowls in a cabinet to her left. "I'll get these." She waved him to an aluminum-legged table with a pearl-gray top. "You take a seat. Keep me company."

Tyler felt grateful for a chance to calm the porcupine quills that had begun to spike into his Adam's apple. "Okay," he said and settled into a captain's chair.

She opened another cabinet to put away clean cups and a platter. Then she swung open the refrigerator door, uncapped a liter of milk, and filled a tall, leaded-crystal glass. She removed a small china plate, reached into a jar, and produced a stack of cookies. To stop his mouth from watering, Tyler tried to focus on a framed wall picture of a still life of a fruit bowl. Van Gogh–ish. Consistent shadowing. Good use of size to convey depth and dimension.

The sound of cookies skidding across a china plate seemed to fill the room, and the sweet aroma of shortbread made his head spin. Now he knew how Geen Doorgang must have felt that night of ski-falling down Pasta Rock. Mrs. Marshall plunked the plate of cookies in front of him. Probably in wait for John or a church bake sale or evening guests. Tyler braced his hands under the table to steady a wave of tipsiness.

"Eat." She produced the glass of milk and slid it under his nose. "You're skin and bones."

These were for him! John's mother was offering him milk and cookies. Tyler's eyes flushed, and he attempted to protest. "You don't have to feed me."

"I want to."

He clamped his right hand around the chill glass to refrain from stuffing all five cookies into his mouth. It had been weeks, maybe months, since he and Yuki had splurged for milk. Odd that he'd never noticed its incredible creamy scent. Using his left hand, he lifted a cookie and bit it in half—only half. Buttery, sugary flavor exploded on his tongue, and he could feel the calories rush into his veins and malnourished muscles. He forced himself to stop guzzling the milk.

"Delicious!" Bite. Sip. Chew. Bite. Chew. Sip. "Thank you." He drained the last drops. Foregoing manners, he pressed his index finger onto crumbs that flecked the plate and sucked them onto his tongue. Now he felt starved: hunger-crazed, calf-killing ravenous. "These were amazing," he said.

John's mother took the plate, reloaded it with Gournay cheese on table crackers, and slid it back to him. Tyler's nose tingled at the peppercorns and garlic as he popped a cracker into his mouth. Savory, creamy cheese softened and charged his taste buds. As soon as his mouth was empty, he would thank her again. Tell her how delicious this was. He nodded and moaned, "Umm."

She rinsed his glass and filled it with ice water. "John mentioned you and Yuki are on your own," she said. "Do you have family?"

The question solidified the cheese and crackers to thick paste. He took a sip of water, shook his head, and forced a swallow. "No family," he said, trying for nonchalant. "We'll be fine, soon as I get a job. Things are just a little tight right now."

"These Corsicans." She bubbled a motherly chuckle. "I saw a sign in a bar that read, 'If it's tourist season, why can't we shoot them?'"

What he wouldn't give to hear Mom laugh like that, to feel her warm palm on his shoulder, to tell her he loved her. John had no idea how lucky he was. Tyler glanced up to two penetrating green eyes.

"You're bright, articulate, and personable," she said. "If you like, I could speak to my friend Myrna. She runs Ajaccio Vision, and she's always looking for good tour guides. Unless I'm overstepping?"

Tyler couldn't believe his ears. "Yes," he stammered. "I mean no, you're not overstepping at all. I'd appreciate your help, very much."

John emerged and downed a cheesy cracker. "Mum, are you boring Marco?"

Mrs. Marshall looked as if she might reply. Instead she picked up her black handbag and headed for the door. "I'm off to see Myrna right this instant. Check back with me tomorrow, Marco, if you will." Then she was gone.

Short and no-nonsense, Myrna Sikorski terminated the interview after ten minutes of casual conversation. "We need an English-speaking guide," she said and handed Tyler a script, "if you can start tomorrow and if ten percent of your daily revenues is satisfactory?"

He almost jumped out of his seat. "Sure! Absolutely!"

Tyler arrived at Place Foch twenty minutes early. Clutching the memorized script and reciting it under his breath, he passed the town hall and the four-lion statue. The small, white ticket office stood before a row of double-decker buses lining one side of the square, like yellow welcome wagons—or maybe warning signs. What if a tourist turned out to be a person from the past or somehow recognized him from newspaper photos? A US cop on vacation? An FBI agent? More scary was the small matter that his and Yuki's survival depended on his doing well. Tyler inhaled deeply and stepped through the office door.

A brunette with a lazy eye looked up from her computer screen and smiled. "You must be Marco," she said in broken English. "I am Delia."

He returned a sheepish smile and reached out to shake, then yanked back his hand. Rubbing his sweaty palm on his pant leg, he said, "Hi."

"Don't worry," she giggled. "I take it easy on you…your… um…day one and all. I give you city tour. Only five passengers."

At seven euros per person, his take would be 3.5 euros. Easy, glorious money and a job he'd enjoy. "Thanks." His voice cracked. "I'm a little nervous."

"You have bus four." She leaned toward him and whispered. "Do not mind the Rudolfo. He want very much the job, but he speak the English more bad than me. Remember, read the script and just keep talking."

"Okay. Thanks," he said, wondering about this Rudolfo.

The bus was boarding, and a tanned, fortyish driver with clipped, curly black hair sat behind the wheel. He smelled of aftershave and wore a silk tie. The tour company's embroidered yellow logo blazed proudly on the shoulder of his blue, short-sleeved shirt. The flap over a breast pocket read *Rudolfo.* Tyler dipped his head and smiled. "Hi, I'm Marco."

Rudolfo's hands continued to grip the steering wheel, and he stared straight ahead.

Maybe the guy was hard-of-hearing, Tyler decided, and that could be a good thing. He wished he'd bought a logo patch and a tie like Rudolfo's. Relax. He was clean and shaved. Yes, his shirt was faded, but it still had all its buttons, thanks to Yuki. Besides, the passengers would be listening to his voice and watching his face. They'd hardly notice her repairs to his pants pocket. Maybe.

He clipped the mic to his shirt and helped aboard a gray-haired, grandmotherly woman with swollen knees and clumpy brown shoes. According to the roster, she was his fifth and final passenger. He smiled, and three faces grinned back at him. Two invisible guests must have seated themselves up top on the open-aired deck. No doubt, they'd hang on his every word.

Rudolfo closed the doors, and the bus rolled forward.

"Welcome to Ajaccio Vision—the best way to discover Ajaccio," Tyler said, without need of his notes. "I'm Marco, and I'm grateful to be your guide. Over the next forty-five minutes, we'll see the sights of the city and make four stops. If you don't speak English and didn't intend to take the English-speaking tour, please raise your hands." Wait. That made no sense. If passengers didn't speak English, how would they know he had just asked them to raise their hands? Quick. He translated to French. "Si vous ne parlez pas anglais, s'il vous plaît se laver les mains."

Crap. He had asked them to wash their hands if they didn't speak English. "Augmenter," he corrected. "Haut les mains."

A wide-eyed blonde in a straw hat swung her arms into the air like two goal posts.

"Do you speak English?" he asked her.

"Yes." She lowered a palm and gripped her hat brim. "But you told us to wash our hands. Then you yelled at us to raise them. Is this a stickup?"

"No. Sorry. It's okay. I shouldn't try to speak French. We're good." But they weren't good. He looked out the windows and had no idea where the bus was. He was completely lost. He looked to Rudolfo for guidance, but the driver was busy nosing the bus into oncoming traffic. Tyler thought he recognized a landmark. "To your left, you see the Fesch Museum." Or was that the Bonaparte Museum? The passengers gazed out their windows, their expressions blank yet seemingly content.

Tyler turned to Rudolfo and whispered, "Where the hell are we?" Crap. His mic was on. Three pairs of curious eyes settled on him. Desperate for something to say, he read shop signs. "And off to your left is a Super U, a popular grocery store." Delia had stressed that he should keep talking. But what to say? "Corsica sprang into being about 250 million years ago when geological upheavals threw up the mass of granite that forms the backbone of the island."

Transfixed faces gazed out the windows. "So if you pilfer stones, you'll leave with a piece of the rock. Of course, if everybody did that, with three million visitors a year, it wouldn't be long before Corsica shriveled to sea level, so please, just leave the stones alone, all right?" Oh boy.

Deaf and mute, Rudolfo drove on to who knew where.

"The palm trees you see are trimmed every year. Otherwise, they'd look like giant wookies."

Myrna let him go at the end of the day.

I managed to fuck up royally, missing the schedule, running out of things to say, even getting the names wrong. The tourists didn't notice or care, but the bus driver did.

July 2004. The very reason we had left our paradise in the desert was to get a job and work out

> a plan of long-term survival. The tourist season had already started without us. We were stuck paying rent, spending money and not even being happy. We learned, or should have learned, how to socialize, but it didn't work out so well. Yuki started passing more and more time in our room all alone, and I turned back to my math books. Thin hope weakened but hung on and would have snapped if not for an idea. Internet was too expensive, but by saving web pages onto disks, lengthy examination would be free afterwards. The computer could become a means of living and took on added importance. Our last hope.

Website design and management. Yes. He could do that. Piece of cake. The problem was the computer. Given its elevated importance, that constant whir of its fan was no longer just cause for concern. Now, it was all-out alarming. Dust was probably clogging the ventilation system and threatening to overheat the unit. He had never tinkered with the insides of a computer before, but how hard could it be to clean a fan?

Tyler turned the machine upside down and examined it for a latch or release button. Tiny screws appeared to be sealing the chassis tight. Fine. He made a trip to a local computer store and coughed up the euros necessary to buy a set of mini screwdrivers.

Using his new tools, he carefully removed all of the screws. But the exterior casing refused to pop off. Probably just stuck. He pulled and pushed. Cursed and pried. He could practically smell the dust bunnies knitting like felt around the fan and plugging the air supply. They would melt the circuits and fry his precious microprocessors! Tyler blew into the vents and snarled at the dusty air. "You damned shell!" he yelled. Yet still it would not open.

Okay. Fine. He counted to ten. Better take a break. He'd program the epsilons to process more variables and then come back to this. He opened the laptop and pushed its on button. Nothing. Another press. Again nothing. He held the button for thirty seconds. Still nothing. Again and again he tapped. No response. The power cord was plugged in. The chassis's alignment looked fine. He disconnected and reconnected the battery.

Dead.

The laptop refused to turn on. I had missed a screw and broken the motherboard. I had snapped our thousand-dollar laptop-our final avenue out of this hieroglyphic maze of stress and fear and poverty-into a dead chunk of inert matter.

Crashing

• • •

Street sounds filtered through the room's drawn curtains and mixed with static-riddled music from a radio. The constant background *shhrtchsh* made Tyler wish he'd never retrieved the thing from a trashcan and restored it to basic functionality.

Yuki jostled his shoulder. "We need to get out."

"I'm figuring out a cool example of a homotopy invariant," he explained.

"No, not cool." She fanned her face. "It's hot in here."

He continued to delve into quantum field theory and topology and then, "Ha! The final and initial points are the vector, so it'll finish in the same point as it started."

Yuki swirled a finger beside her head. "Oot-fray, Oops-lay." She threw open the pink curtains and stared outside. "I bet Carrefour carries Froot Loops."

He wrote.

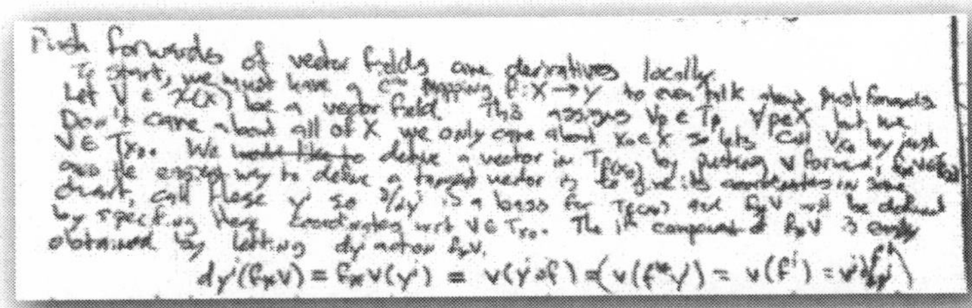

Push forwards of vector fields are derivatives locally....

"Mezzaluna Bar a Vin has new owner," she interrupted again. "Maybe he would hire you."

"You gotta see this." Tyler ran his pen over the paper to guide her through what he had learned:

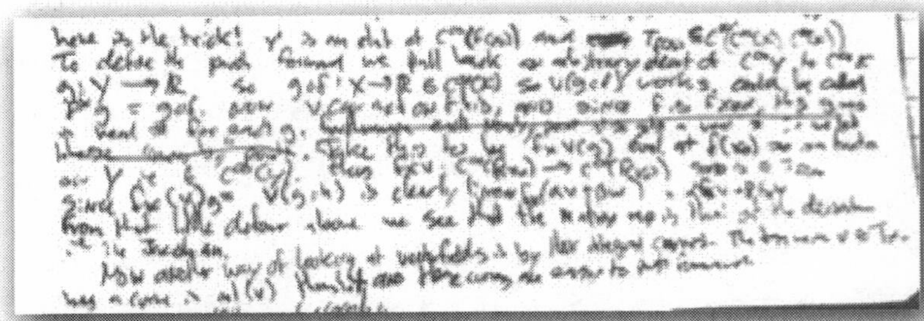

Here is the trick!

"Pfft." She pointed a stiff arm at the clock. "How much math did you do today?"

"Um." Tyler force ed a glance at the ticking travel alarm. "Fourteen hours, oh yeah." This tracking of each day in terms of hours devoted to math, this valuing his life according to the math learned and applied—by these measures he was living the productive life, achieving prolificacy, like Paul Erdős, his hero. Tyler pictured the gray-haired Hungarian who took speed into his eighties so that he could do math nineteen hours a day.

"'You deserve a break today.'" Yuki rocked back and forth, hugging herself, on the covers. "'So get up and get away to McDonald's'—or anywhere." She swayed faster, creaking the bedsprings louder until the room resonated like a Pennsylvania woodland at dusk in August.

Despite the dim overhead light, Tyler wrote as fast as his fingers could go. "Schwartz gets the Klein-Gordon equation."

No reply.

Something caught his eye, and he glanced up to see Yuki standing on a chair. She was taking down the curtains again. "You washed those a couple of days ago," he said and his helpful reminder prompted a furious flap of crimson cotton material toward his face. He raised a quick forearm and blocked getting snapped. "Hey!"

"Dusty." She stepped to the floor and crawled into bed.

Peace at last. He hunched over his notebook and looked into vector fields by their tangential integral curves. Then his vision clouded, and he blinked into early morning streams of sunlight. Yuki was yelling at him again, her voice tinny, as if calling to him from inside a drainage culvert.

"You hear me?" She knocked his shoulder with the heel of her palm. "We cannot live like this!"

"Sure we can," he said, surprised at the illogic of her statement and the frogginess in his voice. "We *are* living like this."

Yuki pinched his earlobe. "This is not living."

"Cut it out!" He brushed her hand away. "That hurts."

She spun the radio's dial to pure static, lofted both arms over her head, and swayed from side to side. "*Tay ina win*," she sing-songed, modeling Jodie Foster in *Nell*. "*Trouble goes away at night, and Nell calls May—and Nell and May—yes, Nell and May are tay ina win*." She laughed, more like shrieked, then flopped face down onto the bedcover. "Midnight!" she bellowed, her voice muffled and cottony. "Night mid. Night night."

The unwashed pink curtain mounded on the floor like discarded afterbirth. Yuki was probably going to sleep again. Come to think of it, she was always in bed of late, taking long naps, blasting that damned radio. He unplugged the contraption and stretched out beside her. "What's the matter?"

"I'm fine," she mumbled into her pillow.

"Let's go buy a baguette."

She rolled away from him. "No."

"We'll go for a walk. Have a picnic."

She slapped the sheets. "Go if you want to!"

"What's your problem?"

"Nothing."

A pause. "I know there's something bothering you."

"*You* are what's bothering me. Leave me alone!"

"No need to get nasty." He left to make tea in the kitchenette down the hall. On his return, he washed down the last of a stale baguette and rehung the pink curtain. Then he studied prime ideals and quotient rings.

It was dark outside, and Yuki was fiddling with a burned-out bulb on the window's string of flower-shaped lights. She climbed in bed and curled into a fetal position. Tyler tried to chew his thumbnail, but there was nothing left to chew, so he tried for his index fingernail. Nothing there to bite either. Hell, he'd chewed all his nails to the quick. On a whim, he flipped through his journal in search of a page that bore none of his mathematical scribbling. He had to go all the way back to April 2004.

> I delved into topology, really learning it for the first time. Continuity real continuity. It all made so much beautiful sense. Countless hours lying about, yellow Naber in my hands. Sometimes I even studied by firelight, but that wasn't really enough light. Yuki-her sweet little heart-would throw one little stick on after another that burned a short-lived bright flame, so I could read.

Beneath the entry Tyler added:

> We both still believed in my potential as a physicist.

Then the context of the entry struck him. How could his and Yuki's relationship have cooled to such an extent in just three months? He turned to a new page, dated it 20 July 2004, and began to write.

> For what? For what? Why do we struggle for air in this tale told by an idiot? ...I measure the days only in terms of how many hours are devoted to math, and life itself only in terms of the math learned. Occasionally the real world taxes a portion of my concentration to manage our life, but

> my calculations invariably conflict with the self-destructive urges of my only companion. Regrettably, [Yuki's] diplomacy has failed to earn any share of the energy devoted to math, and her emotionally backed arguments for reclusion don't appear even worth the time to debate. Pushing and pulling, irritation and frustration have become so typical that they cease to be bothersome. Not exactly the ideal environment to foster love and passion.[7]

How had he and Yuki sunk so low? Then it dawned on him. When they were living in the desert and on the streets, their daily struggle to survive, while agonizing and difficult, had commanded their attention. Now, without enough distractions to keep their losses bottled up, the truth was bubbling to the surface, rotting and fermenting like the refuse that burned his nostrils from the trash bin below. Worse, his actions were what had brought them here.

Tyler flooded with regret for the LA incident and for migrating them to Ajaccio where they were constantly bombarded with unintelligible tongues—or Babylon as he and Yuki referred to cities in general. He was sorry for leaving Geen Doorgang, for hiding behind math, and for finding no resolution to their situation and no way home. Most of all, he wished he'd never dragged Yuki down with him. He pictured Geen next to the red tree with the word *Wrongdoer* carved in its trunk, and he knew, just as he'd known the moment he'd read that word. Though some stranger

7 Passage, actually written at a later date about this period, has been converted to present tense for readability.

had etched it into the bark years earlier, it applied to him. Calf killer. Geen leaver. Future annihilator. Yuki crusher.

Tyler swallowed a jagged marble in his throat and dropped onto the bed. Yuki lay facedown on her stomach, resting her forehead on her fists. "I'm sorry we left Geen," he choked. "Sorry I brought us here."

"Me, too."

"We could return to the desert," he said. "But our euros will tick away to an unforgiving fate. Once they're gone, we won't be able to feed ourselves, let alone find a way to go home."

"So we go broke and starve." She rolled over and sat up, rubbing her eyes. "What's new?"

No discussion? No disagreement? Either her spirit was completely broken, or she had already come to the same conclusion. He stood and put on his optimistic voice. "We would have a stretch of time before our funds run out."

Yuki grabbed her knapsack. "At least we will have Home and Geen."

"Oh, fuck it." Tyler strapped their bedroll to his pack. "Let's be at peace in nature."

In thirty minutes they were sitting on their rucksacks at a palm-shaded bus stop. The five o'clock wheezed up, spewing muffler exhaust into the air. Its doors swung open, and they climbed aboard, exiting north along the same route by which they had entered. Only difference was that, this time, light beams were lancing through the smudged windows of a bus instead of a train.

He counted thirty-three stops. Then the bus gasped to a halt just past their orange-pink Rosine room. Disembarking.

Grocery shopping. Then they shuffled to the side of the road to thumb their way out of town. Ten or twenty drivers whizzed past, their eyes fixed straight ahead as if Tyler and Yuki were fence posts. Then a familiar yellow Peugeot wobbled to a halt.

"Hop in, you two," Rosine chirped from below a rolled-down window.

As before, the car brimmed with clutter, but today it smelled as if a stray orange had rolled under a seat and lay moldering away. Two bags of groceries topped a pile of yellowed newspapers in the backseat. The framed poster of the big-eyed girl was still wedged behind the driver seat, except this time she and her parrots appeared to glower unspoken accusations at him.

Tyler crammed what he could of their worldly belongings into the hatchback. Then he settled in among the debris in the backseat. Yuki squeezed into the death seat up front with Rosine, and the Peugeot edged forward in the direction of Mount Gozzi along dry N194. The little landlady chatted merrily as she steered straight through a fork and veered left to avoid a roadside bush.

"You can drop us off here!" Tyler yelped, then added apologetically, "We appreciate your giving us a ride…and your renting to us."

"Oh, posh." Rosine pulled to a stop in the middle of the road. "Glad to help," she said in French. "You two coming back soon?"

Tyler grabbed their bags and climbed out, avoiding eye contact. "Not sure."

"Well, you were good tenants. I'd rent to you any time."

Yuki, standing at his side, slung her pack onto her back and said, "Thank you."

They exchanged good-byes, and Rosine tootled down the road, her battered car drifting from side to side like a yellow ball caught in the on-off pull of an electromagnet. Tyler stuck out a thumb, and a silver Renault with a college-age driver pulled over.

The anthropology major dropped them off in the vicinity of the entrance to the Mare e Monti Trail. "That's 'Sea and Mountain,'" Tyler explained to Yuki. "Soon as we are on the trail, we'll find an inconspicuous spot to camp."

They walked on, searching every critter path and gap between bushes for the trailhead.

"Tired," Yuki said with a sigh.

"Can't be far now." He checked the map again but was unable to read it in the dim light. No matter. He knew where they were, approximately. "Trailhead has to be close." Mosquitos whined in his ears. They stabbed at his cheeks and neck, at his arms and back.

Yuki fanned her arms in front of her face. "Um hum."

Exhausted dusk gave way to starry night, and they slogged on. Their zombie feet crunched on gravel and still no trail or trailhead. Was that a swish of reeds in the hot breeze or just the rustle of his khakis? Tyler stopped to listen.

Yuki pulled up beside him, and the whine of mosquitos rose to a fevered pitch. "What's wrong?" she asked as she flailed her arms in front of her face.

Tyler pointed to the right. "That little swamp can't be more than thirty feet long, but it'd provide cover." Cover *from* cops and hoodlums and territorial landowners; cover *for* snakes and spiders and creepy-crawlies. "Could be dry this time of year."

"Where? I don't see anything." Nevertheless, she followed him toward the rustle of weeds.

Tyler pushed aside six-foot-tall swamp grasses to clear a path to the interior. The area smelled of bog, but his footsteps were falling on firm, dry ground.

"Bugs are terrible in here." Yuki's voice carried her about-to-cry pitch.

Tyler stomped fronds flat between two sedge mounds. "This is probably the best we can do," he said and spread the bedroll onto a cushion of reeds.

Yuki dropped prone beside him and snugged a sheet under their feet. "Hungry." She sounded exhausted and discouraged.

Tyler tucked the sheet over their heads and combed a strand of hair off her face with his fingers. "Me, too," he slurred with fatigue. Something bit his neck, and he crushed a plump, squirming insect. "Probably not safe for a campfire," he said, and tried not to picture the hairy, eight-legged arachnid that had just sunk its fangs into the soft tissue of his neck. Then sleep enveloped him in its blanket.

A NUDGE JARRED TYLER AWAKE, and he opened his eyes to Yuki standing over him. Her toe rocked his upper arm. "Let's go," she said. "Need water."

He listed upright, and her face caught his attention. Her eyes were swollen near shut. Red bumps dotted her cheeks and forehead like measles. "Whoa!" He plucked a dried stem from her matted hair.

Her eyes narrowed even further. "You look just as bad."

He touched his face and what felt like pimples flamed and itched. He dug out the map. "The trailhead starts at some stone ruins. They're right here somewhere." Seeing no blue squiggles that might indicate a river, he tapped an index finger on a little green cabin. "We're bound to cross an unmarked stream, but worse-case scenario, this refuge'll have water. It can't be more than seven miles as the crow flies."

They found two ancient walls nearby. Unfortunately, the area also served as a dumpsite for locals and passing motorists. Plastic bottles, beer cans, and treadless tires marred the flat trail. Half a mile in, Tyler veered onto a goat path, and the two wended their way between blackberry brambles.

They allowed themselves two sips of water every hour as blazing morning sun turned to sweltering afternoon. Tyler's head was throbbing. His mouth felt like parchment paper. Pausing to take a sip from his Nalgene, he noticed Yuki looking on in crack-lipped silence, her water bottle bone dry. "Here." He handed her his last few drops. "You take it."

She upended the bottle and successfully captured maybe a teaspoonful. "Thanks," she rasped, her voice like gravel.

They walked on with the sun easing past three o'clock. "Between turns and switchbacks," Yuki groaned, "that stupid crow is making us go fifteen miles."

He should probably clarify the expression to prevent Yuki from developing a profound dislike of crows, but talking would evaporate what little moisture remained in his throat. Instead, he shook his head and croaked. "Damn crows."

Late afternoon, a log-built refuge shimmered like a chimera on the horizon. They stepped up their pace. "Go knock," Yuki managed. "Get water."

"It's late. The keeper'll know we're planning to camp."

"Let him call the cops. It's better to die in jail than die of thirst."

Tyler took off his hat and ran his fingers through his matted hair. "Stand in front of me," he said. "The sight of me would scare the guy."

Yuki shuffled to the wooden door and rapped twice.

No answer.

Tyler reached around her to knock hard, three times.

"Qu'est-ce?" Who is it? A voice snarled from within.

Yuki wouldn't speak French, so Tyler said, "Randonneurs. Besoin d'eau. S'il vous plait" Hikers. Need water. If you please.

Silence while the keeper probably checked a peephole. At last the door grated half open, and a thin, hunched man who smelled of fireplace smoke peeked out. "You can't sleep here."

"Just need to fill our bottles," Tyler rasped, too dehydrated to lick his chapped lips. "Then we'll be on our way."

Keeper glared at Tyler. "Against the law to camp," he declared in French.

"Yes, sir."

Keeper studied them a long moment before jutting his stubby chin forward and cracking the door open enough for them to squeeze in. The room looked to be twelve by twelve. A rusted white refrigerator hummed on the right. To the left, a worn cloth recliner hunkered before a muted TV that was flashing images of John Wayne in a bar fight. Straight ahead, a hand-crank pump extended its spout over a mound of dirty dishes. Tyler made a beeline for the sink and pumped the curved metal handle until precious clear liquid gushed out.

He and Yuki took turns gulping from their palms. They scrubbed their faces and arms, cooling the sting out of their bug bites. Tyler dunked his head under the stream and held his breath against the stench of a slimy charred pot as cool water streamed through his hair.

"Hrrruck." Keeper cleared his throat. He stood rigid and scowling.

Ignoring the hint, Tyler worked the handle while Yuki refilled their bottles. Then, under the burn of Keeper's withering gaze, they slipped across the wooden planks and onto the stoop. "Thank you," Tyler said.

The door slammed shut. A deadbolt clicked.

"What'd we do to him?" Tyler asked under his breath.

"Bitter old man." Yuki's voice sounded pinched.

Unable to bear the pain in her eyes, Tyler turned back to the trail. Rocks and scrub brush mounded ahead like malevolent poltergeists. He wanted to yell *fuck you* at them, to throw stones at stones, to stomp the hard-packed ground that slapped at his throbbing feet. Left. Right. Ten steps. Twenty. Keeper had no right to treat Yuki like that, or him either. No right at all. One hundred steps, and he realized his jaw was aching because it was clenched. Who gave a shit what that keeper thought, anyway? But what if these feelings weren't all about the old man? What if this was about rejection and isolation, about being shunned?

He used to like people, and they liked him, too. Those teen years spent behind braces and retainers were awkward, sure. But he was sociable enough. Teachers and other students usually greeted him warmly. He used to feel happy and welcomed when he entered a roomful of family and friends. Now all that had changed. Somewhere along the line, he had become a threat, the enemy, and the rejection cut even deeper because he knew Yuki was suffering the brunt of it, too.

> We were at the end of our limits, tormented by thirst, heat, insects and the suspicious eyes of our own species exiling us; a forced march of rites through physical obloquy. Numb. Tired and worn to indifference
>
> Reality beyond our salty eyes began to be sculpted. Canyons started to rise from the landscape, and the trail hugged steep rock walls. As the first stars made their appearance, we found ourselves in steep rugged terrain with nowhere flat enough to lie down. We continued on anyway, rising steadily from a dark green creek in the center of a ravine. Just before breaking over the ridge, when visibility had reached prohibitive levels, out of the steep side appeared a small flat spot just large enough for the tent! The first such spot we had seen in hours.

Tyler headed for the outstretched palm of rock, saying, "This could work."

"No way." Yuki's tone registered absurdity at his suggestion.

But he had already dropped onto the jutting rock and was erecting the tent, though he had to avoid looking down the precipitous drop or he might freeze up and cling to the mountainside. "Tent only hangs over a couple of inches!" he called out.

Yuki crab-walked down the cliff and crawled inside the tent. "Not a smart choice for unlucky people."

Tyler stretched out along the outer edge. "Maybe our luck has changed its cap."

She leaned across him and patted the ten inches that separated his body from a vertical drop to certain death. "We better hope so," she said. "You fall, and you're taking the tent and me with you."

To give luck a hand, Tyler wedged his pack between his back and the nylon barrier.

Tyler woke to the chilling realization that his knees were extending over the brink. A roll and he lay facing Yuki. But his attempts to wake her triggered a disconcerting body flop and several unnerving arm flaps. Eventually, she blinked awake, and he convinced her to rise slowly and watch her footing as she climbed to the safety of the ridge. With the added room to maneuver, he was able to take down the tent, and soon they were tramping across another ridge.

As if in answer to the rumble of their stomachs, they came to a tree loaded with low-hanging black cherries. They devoured a succulent breakfast and sat gazing across an expanse of red granite peaks.

"They look as if they're superintending the region," Tyler observed, "like Rodin's *Burghers of Calais*."

"So how do they feel about us?" Yuki asked.

Inanimate objects didn't *feel* anything. Sure, natural processes had led to the emergence of the earth's biodiversity, so all living beings shared many of the same molecules as those peaks, including hydrogen, water, nitrogen, and carbon. But mountains were hardly alive or sentient. Still, way back on the molecular clock, in the distant evolutionary past, the first single-celled life had drawn its DNA from the planet's primordial soup. Generations of mutations and adaptations had sprouted from that simple evolutionary ancestor, giving rise in time to him and Yuki.

No, the mountain was unlikely to feel anything toward him, but he felt a great deal toward it: Awe at its majesty, humility in its immutable presence, and reverence. Hard-wired within him was a deep-rooted connection to all things Earth. Maybe these mountain peaks struck him as paternal, maybe he felt an instinctive connection to them because that was as it should be, because these peaks were part of his heritage, the building blocks of his existence. Far below, at the confluence of two sheer gorges, the River Tavulella and its tributaries converged like bulging blue veins. How apt.

"Maybe those peaks are our welcoming committee," he mused. Tyler led the way downhill to the mighty Pontu du Zaglia Bridge. Here in 1797, Antonio Bensa had labored to span two gorges in order to allow transient shepherds and villagers to escape one crisis or another. The master mason must have witnessed spring runoff, because he sculpted his mystical stone arches to span high and wide so that torrents of ice-melt could rage uncontested beneath.

But this was 22 July, and summer's waters flowed low and bucolic. Serenaded by the splash and babble of children at play, Tyler clasped Yuki's hand and the two inched across the stone abutment onto the high, narrowing neck of the arch. A white-bellied swift careened overhead in the cloudless sky.

"How many before us have crossed this bridge," Tyler wondered, "fleeing known threats to unknown ones and seeking only reprieve?"

They left Pontu du Zaglia behind and turned into a soft breeze. Coming to a rocky meadow, they dropped to the ground in the shade of a pine tree. A swallowtail butterfly was fluttering among thistle blooms. "The flap of a butterfly's wings," Tyler whispered, and the gentle press of Yuki's shoulder confirmed that she was watching, too.

Attracted perhaps to the sheen of Yuki's hair, the creature flitted toward them and lighted on Yuki's bangs. Confident and content, it fanned its yellow-striped, rice-paper wings. Sky-blue speckles flanked a crimson dot on the base of its back—a female perhaps, decked out to impress a mate.

Yuki sat motionless except for the barely perceptible scrunch of her shoulders. Then she began to sing, "'*Everybody doesn't like something…*'"

Tyler eased his index finger up and offered the butterfly a perch. It crawled aboard, tickling his knuckle with the clamp of its suction-cup toes. "'*But nobody doesn't like Sara Lee*,'" he breathed, more off-key than he liked. He raised the creature to eye level between them. "Nice to meet you, Miss Sara."

Miss Sara lingered a moment before lifting off. She fluttered toward the river and lit on a purple blossom, perhaps to enjoy a reviving meal of nectar.

No road passed here. A little venturing upstream, and we were alone with the turquoise waters under the shade of pines. A lightness we hadn't seen in months returned to our spirits, and slowly we let go the headaches of Babylon.

Settling down to make love in the sands of eternity, we realized we had been set free.

Lord of the Flies Arrives by Yacht

• • •

Tyler and Yuki lingered at their riverside refuge until their food supplies dwindled to two packs of ramen noodles and a bag of stale GORP, as Kelsey called the mixture of granola, oatmeal, raisins, and peanuts. Hoping to explore a remote area and, yes, maybe procrastinating for fear of not finding Geen Doorgang, Tyler suggested, "Girolata's along our route. Why not take a spur there to see what it's all about?"

"*Why not*?" Yuki leveled a sardonic gaze at him. "How much difference can a day or two make?"

Sarcasm. A diversion to Pasadena, a misspelled bumper sticker, three letters of the alphabet—the slightest shift in the space-time continuum could trigger massive, unintended consequences. She had said *sure*, though. No point probing. He nodded in the direction of Girolata. "We can resupply there, too."

They walked along tar-smelling blacktop before swerving onto a pathway with orange paint blazed on scrub trees. A patch of brambles begrudgingly gave up the largest blackberries Tyler had ever eaten. He and Yuki packed a Tupperware dish full and continued on.

Late afternoon, and smooth, round pebbles were crunching underfoot. Bussaglia Beach spread out before them. Sitting on the unusually clean beach, Tyler and Yuki watched the sun set over the horizon. Then they bedded down in a thirty-foot-wide, wind-carved amphitheater and fell asleep to the lullaby song of waves splashing off cupped walls.

Rising early, they trekked on and soon reached the illustrious Girolata. Contrary to the beach's idyllic portrayal in travel brochures, however, burnt-skinned tourists swarmed its trash-strewn shores. Those who weren't sunning themselves on the sands milled about commercial shacks, snapping photos and shopping for knickknacks. Tyler and Yuki resupplied and beat a hasty retreat along the cove.

They arrived at a solitary pebble beach overlooking Scandola Nature Reserve. Yuki set down her pack and read from the brochure, "'The UNESCO World Heritage site is an unmissable experience. The cliffs and grottos are magical. Fishing is forbidden in the reserve, where exotic sea life teems in abundance.'" Disrobing to her bikini, she folded her top, shorts, and socks and set them neatly on her backpack.

Tyler dug out their goggles and handed her a pair. "Let's test that hypothesis."

With her black goggles snugged to her face, Yuki looked part beetle, part Martian. "Race you!" her nasal voice called as she bolted toward the sea.

Tyler sprinted after her, tossing off his shirt as he ran. They splashed hip deep in clear waters, and soon, tall, flat fishes were nibbling on their knees and toes. Yuki giggled and bounced like a pogo stick. Tyler tried to stand still. Then he took a deep breath and dove underwater. A school of bright-yellow fish materialized among his bubbles, and the creatures wiggled just beyond his reach.

After a long swim, tired and refreshed, he and Yuki retreated to the shade of their tarp to escape the sun and snack on shelled peanuts. "Look." Yuki was pointing toward the sand on Tyler's left.

Peanut skins and husks were lined up and moving as if of their own volition, but miniscule legs were squiggling underneath. Ants. Determined to salvage their legume delights, the tiny creatures were hefting crumbs two or three times their own size onto their tight-waisted bodies and then trooping away in a winding processional.

A gecko-like creature darted onto the scene, obviously hungry for the tasty ants but wary of Tyler and Yuki.

"Long-tailed, brown-spotted Tyrrhenian lizard," Yuki whispered. "Native only to Corsica and Italy's Sardinia."

Lizard moved into position at the far end of the peanut-toting caravan and braced himself upright on bony, ET-like fingers. He cocked his head and waited.

Lead ant marched toward Lizard, and when it came within twice the length of the lizard's body, out lashed a sliver of a tongue to lap up ant and all. The new grand-marshal ant, ignorant of the fate that awaited it, tromped into harm's way, and he, too disappeared with the snap of a tongue.

A dinghy from a sparkling white yacht nosed onto the beach, and a barefoot teenage couple stepped off. The boy, more squat and darker-skinned than the girl, looked comfortable in his tight green swim briefs. His companion, a paper-thin brunette in a pink polka-dot bikini, strode on athletic legs that bowed slightly at the knees. Her top rode high on two still-developing breasts as the pair flitted along the water's edge, moving with the fluid intensity of young lovers.

They stopped to peer into a tidal pool. Boy inched his hand down Girl's spine and dipped his fingertips inside the back of her bikini bottom. She curled a loose strand of hair behind her ear and appeared to be looking around for something. She pointed to a pair of goggles that Tyler had inadvertently left on the beach, and she said something to Boy.

He scooped them up and trotted over. "Sono questi il vostro?" Are these yours? He asked in Italian.

Boy's puppy-like manner reminded Tyler of himself as a teen. No, he'd never had the baby fat that this kid had, and he hadn't been raised wealthy as this kid obviously had been, but he had never lacked for basics like food or shelter—until now, anyway. He used to play like this, carefree and happy, his biggest worry being what to say to silky-haired Marcia. Tyler nodded and accepted the goggles. "Grazie."

Boy crosscut one finger over another. "Coltello?"

Tyler dug into his pack and offered a stainless-steel dinner knife. "This?"

The dull blade seemed to satisfy the ruddy-cheeked teen, who jogged back to his date. The two skittered to the dinghy, stooped over its sides, and emerged brandishing a homemade harpoon. Racing like kids playing tag, they tore back to the tidal pool. Boy and Girl pumped their knees in the air while taking turns hurtling the spear into the water.

Then, like a gladiator piking a severed head, Boy lofted a skewered eel into the air. Brown with yellow spots, its mouth wide and screaming, the creature writhed on the spear tip. Or maybe that hissing sound was coming from Girl. She was bouncing and clapping like a prize winner on *The Price Is Right*. Grabbing hold of the spear, she lowered the flopping eel to the ground and, laughing, pressed her foot to its head.

Boy unstrapped the blade and shoved it through and out the other side of the eel's body. He and Girl took turns stabbing the eel as if they were chipping at a block of ice. The hapless creature continued to flail, unwilling to die without protest. Boy swung it onto the rocks like a wet towel, yet still it squirmed. Girl bellowed, wild and untamed.

Yuki covered her mouth and eyes. "Think about how much suffering is going on," she said, sounding breathless.

"And how do you think they fished it?" He never should have lent them the damned knife.

Boy fisted a beach stone and slammed it down hard on the eel's head. Finally, it lay limp. Boy jabbed the knife into the sand, and its dark red hilt angled upward like a sundial, matching a bulge in Boy's shiny green trunks. Girl, appearing to take no notice of her boyfriend's erection, adjusted her polka-dot bottom. She retrieved the knife and knelt at the water's edge, washing her bloodied hands and the blade in a dreamlike motion.

Moments passed. Then Girl stood tall, and Boy clasped her hand. Taking long, synchronized strides, the couple approached Tyler and Yuki. Their gaits seemed different somehow—their shoulders tighter; muscles that once looked soft were now hard. The effervescence was gone, as was the flirtatious giggling.

Splattered in blood and smelling of eel, Boy handed Tyler the knife. "Grazie."

Tyler remained seated and glared into Boy's opaque Gucci sunglasses.

Girl removed her dark glasses and said, "Grazie." Her eyes glowed green, her lips half parted.

Silence stretched thin between them. Then the pair strode to the dinghy and zipped away to Daddy's yacht.

Tyler set the knife on the rounded pebbles where the ants and Lizard had enacted their life-and-death drama. But cruelty had played no role with those creatures. They had simply done what they needed to do in order to survive. Boy and Girl, though, had performed a scene from *Lord of the Flies*. Junior-high literature again—so many lessons of survival his curriculum had tried to forewarn him about. Sure, he had gotten the idea that animal spirits and evil exist within human nature. What he'd missed were the additional themes about impulse and choice, about the influence of circumstance and perspective, about the results of lack of empathy…and the drawbacks to feeling it.

Freedom comes at a price. Being free means free to lose yourself to a fall, to drown a calf, to be harpooned or to harpoon, to steal rum and Coke from hotel receptions, to get sacked.

The bald, shiny forehead of Oppression is behind every mask, behind the ubiquitous cameras that enhance his eight-eyed vision. He casts his web

> through the streets and across the sky. The more you struggle to get out, the more entangled you become, all the while vibrating signals of your location. Trapped. Freedomless.

Perhaps freedom meant not recognizing Oppression's presence, not seeing it coming. Like all illusions, maybe freedom existed solely in a person's mind. But even if only a state of mind, was freedom not a person's greatest, most precious possession? Maybe feeling free meant believing one's self to be free. Therefore feeling free equated to freedom. When a person knew that he must go to work tomorrow, he might realize that he wasn't free. Then again, if he believed he had a choice—that he could accept the financial repercussions of abandoning his bullshit job—was he not free, no matter the choice he'd made? But what if a person couldn't find a job, bullshit or otherwise? What freedom did a person have when he couldn't sustain himself, let alone the person he loved?

By definition, the ability to decide between options formed the basis of freewill. Otherwise, a probabilistic Turing machine would qualify as possessing free will, as would a trapped eel or fly inside a windshield. The game was set, no point playing. So where did fate step into the mix? Maybe the age-old enemy of freewill was an illusion, too. Maybe fate was equal to and the opposite of the illusion of freedom.

> We never could wash the smell of fish off the knife.

Forest fires blocked the last two days' worth of trail to Ostriconi Beach, so Tyler and Yuki hitched into L'Île-Rousse to stock up on provisions. He complained that she spent too many euros on nuts and juice. She complained that he was an ass.

"Fine." She walked away. "I will go on my own."

"I'll rendezvous with you at Home!" Tyler called to her back.

She flicked a confirming thumb in the air and yelled, "We find Geen together."

Tyler strode along the trail, and nature's numbering system, the Fibonacci sequence, seemed to be on display everywhere he looked: 1, 1, 2, 3, 5. The series of numbers in which each number was the sum of the two preceding numbers accounted for a conch shell's strong, versatile shape. That flower over there—its florets applied the golden ratio to maximize their capture of light. He picked up a pinecone, and its bracts clearly optimized the distribution and survivability of its seeds. Even the barbs on the cursed impenetrable maquis arced at 137.5 degrees, the golden ratio, 1.61803. Phi.

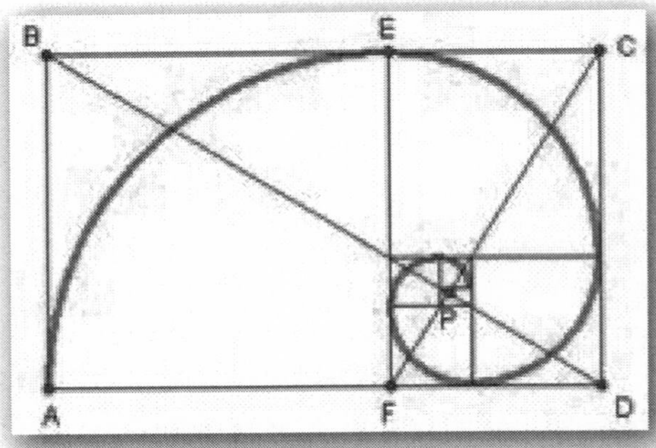

The Fibonacci Sequence, or the Golden Ratio, in graphic display.

It's things like this that you always pay attention to, once you notice them. But the catch is that it's surprisingly difficult to notice them in the first place for lots of reasons. First off, humans often aren't interested in anything outside the ningen community, including remoteness from so many things that appear as if they were allergic to ningens.

As a consequence, we tend to feel remote from untold life forms that behave as though they are allergic to us. If we chance to notice them, it becomes clear that the world is filled with amazing creations and once observed, always observed.

Compare Geen Doorgang to ningen. Yes, GDG is cooler than most people, but maybe that's because we have developed criteria to fail humans. We don't apply these criteria to Geen. If we did, he might fail, too. How does he view the world? Would he not litter and profit as much as he could? The only thing limiting his destruction is his own incapability. At least with the humans, you can try to talk them out of it. Some of them are civilizable.

Tyler took a path that ran parallel to a chicken-wire fence. His thoughts returned, as they often did, to his research on digital evolution. What did it mean to be *civilized*, really?

Could it be defined as working together as a society? No, too anthropocentric. Ants worked together, and no one would consider them civilized. *Civilized* was the opposite of *savage*, which was the natural world. To survive, creatures had to fight with all they had. Death to the losers. More struggle ahead for the victors. Stop fighting, and most organisms faced certain death. Therefore, a necessary condition to becoming civilized had to involve succeeding enough to transcend the survival game. The state of becoming civilized had to capture the notion of freedom from the life-or-death struggle.

But success did not stop a creature from destroying its habitat or killing others. Cats toyed with mice, and humans slaughtered eels for the fun of it. Without competition, bacteria in a petri dish went exponential and eradicated their food sources to the point of dying off. Unchecked by predators, all creatures—whether flies, spiders, birds, cats, foxes, or coyotes—overran their habitats. Safe at the top of the food chain, human tribes were overpopulating and depleting their environment on a path toward self-extinction. Of late, though, due to the availability of effective birth control, the populations of industrialized nations were stabilizing. Free will was playing its hand.

> Clearly, the success condition is insufficient to create a civilizable state. Further criteria are required to determine which evolutionary systems may produce civilization. The really fundamental change is to break away from savage habits, to view the external world in a way other than as something to conquer. It is this non-adversarial outlook toward the environment that makes for the true definition of civilized.

On reaching Ostriconi Beach, Tyler savored a can of cheap beer in the tunnel where he had rubbed Geen's flappy ears and bid him good-bye. He found Yuki sitting on the beach, and they united in their mission. Geen Doorgang was close. Tyler could feel it.

Memories of a few short months ago flooded back. Except that summer's reality bore little resemblance to what he recalled. The chill deserted waters were gone, and in their place spread a sea of human bodies. The hot, tourist-packed sand had forgotten the frosted wind that once caressed it. Instead, heat rippled off oiled, topless bodies. Parents called to kids, paddleballs whacked, and glee-filled whoops joined in cacophony.

Tyler and Yuki plodded on, their boots dirty and their packs weighing heavier with every stride. "I feel like an alien elephant," he observed, "walking through my occupied homeland."

Yuki jammed her thumbs through her shoulder straps and quickened her pace. "No matter. We know this place."

"And we know a spot where quiet turquoise waters wash across fine sands."

"That's right." She pointed her head to a clump of maquis. "Wasps stung Geen Doorgang over there."

They passed a depression that once was mud. "I buried wrinkled potatoes to germinate over there," Tyler said. How foolish he had been to think he could eke a harvest from the now parched earth.

For two days they cooled in limpid waters and collected shells among pebbles, making their way east and north along the rocky, sun-scorched coast. Nearly every rock and bush triggered a memory. Then at last, the Desert des Agriates's coastline stretched to Plage de Saleccia with its smooth half mile of sand. Not six months ago, they were its only human inhabitants. At this beach, baptized in March rains, they had felt the stirrings of their new life together. Now, despite access solely via a twelve-mile dirt road, the beach squirmed with sunbathers and swimmers.

They pitched their yellow two-person tent where they had once hid it among sagging, twisted pines. As if to ridicule their former discretion, colorful canopies, umbrellas, and tents populated the entire length of the beach. A great bonfire roared at the far end.

Geen Doorgang's new owner, Neru, sometimes worked nearby at a seasonally closed campground, so Tyler and Yuki walked the sand, searching every face in the hope of spotting the man. Tyler's heart leapt at the sight of a large, brindled dog plowing through the shallows. But it wasn't Geen.

They donned their goggles and dove after minnows in the calm morning waters. They pretended to be sunbathers. They faked long, leisurely naps. Anything to avoid the inevitable. At last, Tyler turned to Yuki. "It's time."

"I guess so."

They walked in silence to the campground's office and launched their investigatory mission. Under cover of playing Ping-Pong, they scanned every nook. "Geen!" Yuki called out covertly. "Here, Geen."

No response.

The pit in Tyler's stomach knotted to a fist, and from Yuki's expression, her heart was breaking, too. Then certainty set in. Geen was not here.

We slooped back to the shade under our sad tree and quietly traced fingers in the sand. Not knowing what to say, we waited for dusk's mosquitos to chase us into the tent.

STRANGERS EVERYWHERE. GEEN NOWHERE. "Saleccia doesn't fee like Home anymore," Yuki said.

Tyler shook his head. "No reason to stay."

They set out and in two days returned to Ostriconi and the tunnel where Geen had flapped his ears. Time to leave for good, but Tyler's curiosity pushed him to the camp's reception booth where he had entrusted the woman with Geen three months ago.

"Bonjour." The matronly woman smiled at the sight of him. She smelled of plastic wrap from a box she was unpacking. "I remember you," she said. "You're the English-speaking chap who dropped off the dog."

"Oh, oui." He flooded with mixed emotions—discomfort at being memorable and hope that she might offer good news.

She rubbed the small of her back. "The dog's owner came and claimed him."

"He promised he would," Tyler said, his spirits rising.

She ran a palm over her dewy forehead. "But a few days later, don't you know, that dog showed up here again, nothing but skin and bones." She looked to Tyler for comment, but a belt was squeezing the air out of his chest. "So we gave his owner a call, and he drove over and picked him up again. Haven't seen that dog or heard anything from the owner since. He isn't at Saleccia?"

"No." A jagged clog blocked Tyler's throat. "Didn't see either of them."

"I'm sorry." She tilted her head and studied him. "I can see that dog meant a great deal to you."

He managed a nod and left.

What a soldier. Geen had made the choice to be with us. He had abandoned his full food dish and comfortable life on the beach to hike alone to our shared spots in the desert where he once was hungry but loved. He was truly part of us. The story brought tears to Yuki's eyes. Geen had come back for us as we had for him. As in his case, ours was a trip with a hollow ending.

So there we have it. Our first and possibly only friend, Geen Doorgang, is no longer with us, and it's not within our power to re-join him. Sad, but maybe it's better this way because we really can't keep him. He was the most important element in our lives for one of the most difficult stages. For that he will always have a special place in our hearts. He can never be replaced.

THEY WANDERED BACK TO L'ÎLE-ROUSSE and set camp next to the train tracks where the homeless sometimes flopped. Too hot for a fire, so they sat in silence as late dusk descended over them.

"Shalom aleikhem."

The male voice shot Tyler to his feet, and he stepped between Yuki and a stranger whose face lay shadowed under a head of spiky, dark hair. "Hold it right there!" Tyler warned, thinking Geen Doorgang would never have let an intruder get the drop on them like this.

The man halted and lowered an oversize knapsack to the ground, freeing a hand to brush aside his locks. "Sorry, Marco, I did not mean to startle you."

Tyler squinted in the dim light. He could make out a close-shaved mug of a man who appeared to be in his thirties. One eyebrow rode ride high, the other low. The features were so asymmetrical that if either half were mirrored, then two distinct faces would emerge. Yes, this was the guy he used to meet for language lessons when he came to L'Île-Rousse to buy provisions and dog food. "Ouni?" Tyler asked.

A laugh confirmed Ouni's identity. "I see my *goyim* friends waited until the last minute."

Friendly, enthusiastic Ouni used to make Tyler laugh. Not today. He forced a grin. "Last minute for what?"

Beaming a slanted smile through stained and crooked teeth, Ouni strode toward them and greeted them French style. "For bon voyages, of course. I take a boat home in two hours."

Tyler felt dumbfounded. "You're sailing for Tunisia tonight?"

"Aye. I'm crewing for fare," Ouni tee-heed. "The poor boat."

Considering what he'd witnessed of Ouni's mechanical skills, Tyler shared the guy's concern. He pictured the sad, precious pink bicycle with the loose chain, dry-rotted tires, and broken spokes that Ouni had so generously lent to him. "I'm really sorry about losing your bike," he said. "I should've bought a lock."

Ouni laughed, merry as ever. "Not your fault someone stole it. Now come. We go to a café for a *chagiga* of sorts." He looked around. "Where's Geen Doorgang?"

Tyler turned away to grab his pack and help Yuki with hers. "Gone," he croaked. He led the way downtown, on to another farewell, permanent as Geen Doorgang's yet with fewer pangs to the heart.

Minutes later, they slipped into chairs at a sticky bistro table outside a crowded café. While they waited for Ouni's flatmate to join them, a young waitress with pink-streaked hair and a navel ring brought them orange juice. A hot thread of breeze wisped between babbling, scented pedestrians as they strode toward live rock music streaming from next door. Bass rhythms pulsated through Tyler's chest to his backbone and made his toes wiggle.

"You said that Jews are less than three percent of the population in Tunisia," Tyler said, "and that you are persona non grata. Is it safe for you there?"

Ouni lifted a shoulder. "Yahweh provides. We Jews are used to being odd ducks. We all migrate home eventually."

"I can relate," Tyler said, and the words came out a whisper.

"Tunisia needs me." Ouni explained that the Mustapha Ben Jafar, the leader of the Democratic Forum for Labor and Liberties needed him. "Defenders of human rights are calling for the unification of democratic forces. We have *tikvah* that there will be transparency in government." He raised his glass in toast to the center-left secularist party. "L'cayim."

They tapped plastic cups, and Tyler took a sip, hoping to stretch the delicious, tangy pulp through the evening. The level of Yuki's juice dropped barely a centimeter.

"Aahhh." Ouni smacked his empty glass on the table as though he'd downed a shot of vodka. "Know anybody who wants my job? I leave a vacancy."

Oxygen drained from the area. "An undocumented job?" Tyler asked.

Ouni showed his stained teeth, minus one incisor. "Bar du Port, but I warn you: the boss man is *meshugah*."

"I'm all about *meshugah*s." Tyler tried to make light.

Ouni spun a finger beside his ear. "I'm telling you he's crazy." A sage nod. "Ezeh bassa. Probably best not to mention my name. I gave somewhat short notice."

"How short?"

Ouni broke into his roguish, lopsided grin. "Tonight when Boss hand me my pay, I say, 'Good night. Peace out. I quit. Bye-bye.'"

They all *l'cayim*ed. "It's after two," Tyler said, his feet dancing to tear for the bar. "Any chance the boss is still there?"

Ouni nodded and stood. "Yahweh willing, with no Ouni to kick around, Boss will work very, very late. Now I must be off, my friends."

They repeated shaloms. Then Ouni slipped like a cat into the night and out of their lives.

Tyler downed his drink and dug his plaid shirt from his pack. A few wrinkles but it had all its buttons. "Can you believe that?" he asked Yuki as he stripped off his T-shirt and threw on his job-hunting shirt.

She held up crossed fingers. "I'll wait here."

"Shouldn't be long." He buttoned as he jogged toward Bar du Port.

The two-story restaurant and a tiny customs office sat alone on a long pier of rocks and pavement. Purple awnings extended over glowing, first-floor windows that looked into a large dining area. Inside, white-shirted waiters were hustling here and there, setting tables for the next day. Tyler tried a door. Unlocked. He stepped into a room that smelled of rum, bleach, and body odor. A large, ruddy-complexioned man was flailing his arms and barking commands in French. Had to be the boss.

"We're closed!" he roared at Tyler.

Unfazed, Tyler walked straight up to the man and extended a hand. Boss pursed his lips and turned away, thrusting his weight onto pigeon-toed, grease-splotted black shoes that looked about to pop their seams. Apparently he wasn't one to burden himself with pleasantries.

Tyler stepped into the man's line of sight and applied his well-rehearsed French. "I'm looking for cash work in the kitchen or busing tables," he said, trying not to sound desperate. No point revealing that a reliable source had told him of a fresh opening.

Boss hiked up a belt that was showing signs of strain. "Nommer?"

"Marco, sir. Marco Sosson." Tyler felt a warm glow at speaking his alias surname. When he and Yuki first fled to France, he'd chosen Sosson because, if spoken with a French accent, *Johnson* sounded like *Sosson*. Silly, but in this small way he had hoped to hang onto an integral piece of his identity. Maybe, he had speculated, whenever he heard Sosson spoken aloud, it might remind him of who he actually was. And that had just happened.

"Toutes les maladies?" Any diseases, Boss asked, overly loud, as if he were repeating the question.

"Uh, no. No, sir."

"Ever serve jail time?"

"No."

"Will you thieve from me?"

"No, sir. I will not."

"Forty-five euros a day." Boss turned up a burn-scarred palm. "Start the afternoon shift tomorrow. Five o'clock sharp."

He must have heard wrong. "I have the job?"

"Work lasts until the place is cleaned and reset, usually around three in the morning, three days a week—maybe more if you work hard and business goes well."

Tyler extended a hand to seal the deal. "See you tomorrow at five." Instead of shaking, Boss unleashed a curse at a slow-moving female employee and tore after her like a rabid raccoon.

Tyler took a moment to absorb the scene. White linen tablecloths and glass centerpieces glinted in wait for tomorrow's customers. Outside, lights illuminated gently rolling whitecaps on both sides of the pier. Bar du Port was heaven on earth. He practically floated out. When he was well beyond hearing distance, he let loose a whoop that would have parted the clouds if there had been any.

> Can't believe it. I am ecstatic. This abandoned dream of finding work has come true after all. Seems like so much money. Well below minimum wage, but we are desperate. I would have accepted much less.

Tyler found Yuki sitting in the shadows of the bar with the live music. He gave her two thumbs up and shared the details as they made their way back to the tracks. "We can't live here beside the tracks," he said, pacing back and forth, looking in vain for twigs to build a campfire. "It's too dangerous and well traveled. Need to find someplace secluded."

Yuki stretched out on the sleeping bag and tucked her hands behind her head. "I keep thinking about Geen Doorgang. What if he returns and we're not there?"

"We'll have to find a spot to flop that's walking distance from the bar. I can't show up for work all sweaty."

"I have this feeling. He could come back any day."

Tyler's khakis were stained. He sniffed his armpits. Oh boy. "We need to do laundry tomorrow and find some beach showers."

"I'm going back to Ostriconi and Saleccia, first thing tomorrow."

"What?" Tyler recognized that determined tone. "For how long?"

Silence.

Alarm bells clanged in his head. Was she using Geen's loss as an excuse to leave him? "How about three days?" he asked. "That'll give me time to find us a place to live, and I'll have my first pay by then."

"Four days." She rolled onto her side and turned her back to him.

He felt nauseated at losing Geen, too, but now he had to prepare for a job. Wasn't she glad for him? For them? Maybe part of her felt sad because he had gotten a job and she hadn't. He dropped cross-legged onto the bedroll next to her. "I'll make enough to tide us over while you look for a job, too," he offered by way of consolation.

No answer.

"Things will work out." He almost added *I promise*, but how could a guy promise something he had no control over? Then again, with a job, maybe he could have some control, finally. Maybe he could make things work out. "Everything's going to get better now," he said. "You'll see."

Yuki had to have heard him. He could tell by her breathing that she wasn't asleep. He stretched out on his back next to her and looked up at the stars. So much needed to be done to live here in L'Île-Rousse as a working man, as their bread winner.

The next morning dawned to clear skies, and they located unattended beach showers farther south of town. Neither he nor Yuki dawdled in the cold showers, but they both emerged clean. Yuki, who had already packed her bag, gave Tyler a hug and said, "This time I will find him."

Tyler watched her troop off, her hair wet and her stride determined. "Be careful," he called out. "I'll put together some group-theory exercises for you to practice when you come back in four days."

She flagged a comb overhead and kept walking.

The Age of (False) Optimism

• • •

Tyler showed up for work five minutes early, smiling and ignorant. No one offered to train him, so he bumbled through moments of confusion, but within an hour he was busing tables like a pro. By three-o'clock closing, though, his feet were spear tips; his eyelids, boat anchors. Covered in sweat yet satisfied to have earned income, he stumbled along the starlit beach in search of a spot to flop.

Three empty white chairs nestled between leggy shrubs outside a yellow two-story hotel. Tyler approached, and no lights flashed on. No voice in the shadows warned him away. He set his backpack on a smooth metal seat, aligned the chairs, and slid under their curved armrests. With mild adjustment, his pack made a decent pillow, and the beachy scent of sand and salt and seaweed cleansed the smell of restaurant grease from his nose. A flex of his throbbing feet set all three chairs into motion, so he flexed and rocked to the rhythm of the waves patting the shoreline. Must get up early in order to avoid notice, he thought, as sleep drifted over him.

Tyler awoke to the chatter of a pair of early-morning joggers. He hobbled on bruised feet to the beach showers, and then, clean and clearheaded, he explored inland in search of a secluded site for a residence.

Too populated.

Too well patrolled.

Too open.

Nothing showed promise.

Work, sleep, and showers passed as before, and the next morning he hugged the coastline south. Still, no location offered safety or privacy.

Day three, Tyler walked the shoreline north. A secluded little promontory jutted into the sea, and to his surprise, its sheer red cliffs hid an isolated stretch of seashore. No houses, no trail, just wild plants and an amazing, sheltered view of the sea. When—if—Yuki returned, they could live in peace, invisible to all but the great Mediterranean. He set camp and then put in a long night at the restaurant.

Before wending his way back to his rocky point, Tyler sat under a beech tree in the glow of a streetlight. As he stared over the glistening waters, his thoughts turned to his family so far away. This past Christmas in Pennsylvania, the 'rents had said they planned to move back to Michigan to be near his grandparents who needed more help. They might all be together now. It was a little after 9:30 p.m. there. Could they be thinking of him, too?

Across the sea, yet not so far away, trees like these probably witness a campfire accompanied by drinking, laughter and the sharing of stories.

Tyler's feet began to adjust to long hours on concrete. Still, work passed in misery. He found several potential improvements to his routine, but Boss wouldn't hear of them. Incapable or unwilling to understand Tyler's well-reasoned suggestions, Boss shook his head and restated the routine, louder and firmer each time. On the bright side, work was taking Tyler's mind off Yuki, gone six days now. Where the hell was she? What if she never returned? What if she had sprained an ankle or was ill or had been accosted?

He was at work, on his hands and knees scrubbing under the kitchen sink when Boss lumbered past. "Clean under the sink," he commanded.

Tyler bit his lip. So far this shift, Boss had told him to take out garbage that he was already carrying toward the door, yelled for him to put away clean dishes that he was putting away, and commanded him to help a customer whom he was in the process of assisting. Tyler returned a bucket of supplies to the now-tidy sink base. Then he headed to check for tables in need of busing.

"Bus tables!" Boss called from behind the bar.

Tyler released a slow exhale.

"Hey." Yuki lifted a drink in greeting from a barstool. A sparse-haired man to her right scowled and adjusted his comb-over. Then he skulked to the end of the bar.

Yuki looked thinner than usual, and she carried a somber air. Tyler stepped near and asked, "Making friends?"

"It's a curse," she said without brightening. "No Geen."

"I'm sorry." His heart would have sunk if he weren't so happy to see her. "We'll check again."

She studied her drink and rolled its straw. No umbrella, probably a cola. Boss issued an "Eh hem."

"Gotta get back to work," Tyler said, "but I got paid 180 euros already, and I can't wait to show you the place I found for us."

Yuki downed her drink. "I wait for you on the pier."

TYLER FOUND YUKI SITTING IN THE DARK. He pulled her to her feet, and they shared a long, slow kiss. "You'll love our new place." He pointed north, so eager to show her—and his legs aching so badly—that he could barely stand still. "It has an oceanfront view with rocks for chairs."

No answer.

"I made up a bunch of practice exercises for you." He steered her off the pier. "You can't see our place from here, but it's not far."

Silence.

They crossed the railroad tracks. "See that fat peninsula with a rocky corner that rises to a wide tip?"

"Uh huh."

"It falls away without warning, so be careful."

"Okay."

They climbed the narrow band of steep rocks, now so familiar that Tyler no longer needed to watch his footing. "Rocks surround us on three sides, so we're invisible from land with an open view to the sea."

Yuki stood at the unlit, stone-ringed fire pit and rotated fifteen degrees, then fifteen more and more until she came full circle. "Invisible?"

"Yup. We can sleep under the stars if we want, and nobody's going to see us."

She looked up at the sky.

He followed her gaze to the Big Dipper. Its handle stood upright. As ever, the two stars at the base of its ladle were pointing to Polaris, steady and true. "Great view of the North Star from here," he added.

She lowered her chin and appeared to contemplate the sea. "Hmm."

Hard to tell what she was thinking. "We have swimming pools, right off our front porch," he said, "and amazing snorkeling."

She set down her pack and untied the sleeping bag, which she then clutched to her chest.

"The place even comes furnished with a community of crabs," he said and wondered if he should consider a career in used-car sales.

She unfurled the sleeping bag, folded into lotus position on top of it, and sat facing out to sea.

Tyler walked among a cluster of shiny-leaved bushes. "We'll have time and freedom to draw all the plants growing around us, if we like."

She pressed her palms together under her chin and closed her eyes. Then she looked up at him and smiled. "This point, it is paradise."

Yuki was back, and this was their new home, Point Paradise.

Each night after finishing, nothing in the world feels better than my quiet walk home in the cool night. The empty streets are all peace, and I have them all to myself. Sometimes I sit under the street lamp and read Spivak's *Calculus on Manifolds* (for I always bring Spivak with me to work).

My bar and a little customs office hug the base of the pier. There are no other buildings. On the other extremity, a red beacon dutifully decorates the night, reflecting across placid waters. Nocturnal fishermen gather like moths about this red light. They post their poles and sit back to enjoy the tranquility of the night. Just like me.

This whole deal–the pier, parking lot, bar, mountains and old stone tower–sits on a little red island, the largest of several red rocks that stick out of the sea. A flat bridge with calm salt water on both sides is the only way out.

Each night on my way home, I cross it. Then just before a train station, I cut through a residential neighborhood and join the railroad tracks on their way out of town. They run between big rock walls. Good graffiti at the beginning. Then that gives way to chiseled rock, crumbly and decorated by ambitious little plants.

I carry no light. I know all the steps along the way, and they know me. A few hundred meters further, one of the walls drops away, leaving a straight-vertical precipice to rumbling green waters. This opens the view and reveals a small peninsula, rounding out into the sea. No houses, not even any real trails, just wild plants and open space. This is our home.

My flip-flops carry me across the dusty surface, and the Big Dipper announces the hour of the late night.

I have five hours a day in paradise, ten in hell. Better than life in prison.

Yuki had prepared a plastic container of rice and beans to satisfy Tyler's late-night appetite. He downed the snack and polished off one of their bottles of water. The remaining bottle, he propped between stones. He eased next to Yuki's softly breathing form, cozy in the L. L. Bean sleeping bag that Mom and Dad had given him last Christmas. He shivered and could feel the cold seeping into his legs, but he could hold off awhile longer before nudging her awake to take his turn in the bag.

Huge Waves to Small Waves

Not even huge waves, just relatively big waves impact the shore. If the gulf is not accustomed to such waves, the tidal ecosystem will have evolved to deal with only the occasional huge wave. The introduction of motor boats could increase the number of big waves by many times, and this would significantly change the coastal fitness landscape. The menagerie of species will correspondingly be altered. Some species specific to the gulf will go extinct, and new species, from elsewhere or not, will take up residence. This would be serious ecosystem change and entirely man-made.

The question I am looking at for the moment is, "Is the original preferable to the new?" In one sense, yes, because humans simultaneously disrupt nearly every ecosystem, which causes further damage as would-be stabilizing factors, too, undergo chaotic turbulence. But that is a separate issue, and even now we can re-pose the question in a broader context and replace "gulf coastline" with "earth ecosystem."

Is the original earth ecosystem preferable to the new ecosystem? In some sense, no. Ecosystems change over time. Humans perturb things and maybe even change the future history entirely. But a future history is just a future history.

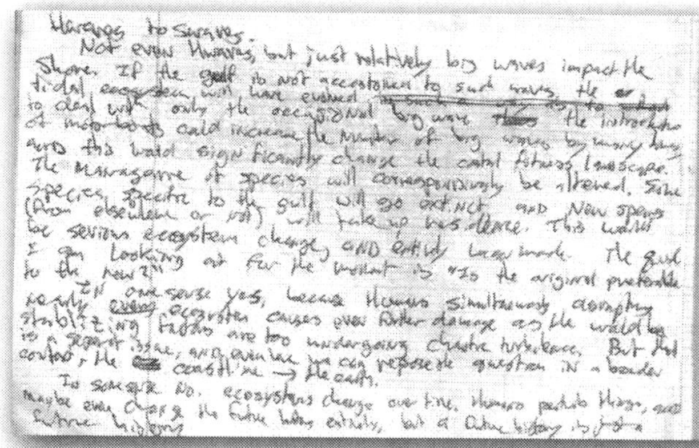

Huge waves to small waves original text.

1 SEPTEMBER 2004. I never thought knowing more would take something away, but it kind of does. It's hard to play the game seriously when you know it's only a game. Those guys who don't know any better than to think it's real look pretty stupid from this perspective, as if they are missing the whole

lot. And that's true. But it's also true that they have something that the thinker has lost. They can put themselves fully into it, lose themselves in the game. The thinker has a hard time abandoning himself like that. If he succeeds, then he isn't a thinker anymore. The thinker can't really escape. He enters a deeper or more abstract and general sort of game, but he can't ever make more than a game of it.

WITH ITS MODERN ARCHITECTURE AND AURA OF INTELLECTUALISM, the University of Corsica might have passed for a school of higher education anywhere. Feeling at home in the airy library, especially since he'd visited twice before, Tyler took a seat next to a stoop-shouldered, boyish-looking student. Their computer stations were situated behind a newly erected bookshelf that probably—hopefully—was blocking the view of the zone's surveillance camera.

Tyler unzipped his backpack and pulled out *The Geometry of Minkowski Spacetime: An Introduction to the Mathematics of the Special Theory of Relativity.* His old friend's bindings were cracked, its pages feathered—the price for accompanying him on this journey to nowhere and a stark reminder of entropy. The gradual decline into disorder wasn't just wearing at the textbook. He felt its downdraft, too, in the fading of key memories, and, perhaps, in the fraying of his own bindings.

Tyler squirmed and patted his pockets until he succeeded in attracting a glance from the student. "Must have left my ID in my room." He shook his head as if to say this wasn't the first time he'd forgotten the bugger.

"Use mine." The pale-skinned guy dipped two fingers into his shirt pocket and produced a student ID that he handed to Tyler.

A swipe and Tyler was in the library system. "Thanks," he said and returned the card. A google of "Gregory Naber" produced the regular list of the professor's publications, plus a new one appeared in the *Journal of Geometry and Symmetry in Physics*, pages 27 through 123. Feeling strangely unrushed, or maybe too curious to care, Tyler opened "Topology, Geometry and Physics: Background for the Witten Conjecture I." Almost at once, he needed to take notes, so he riffled through his textbook in search of scrap paper.

Three neatly creased sheets bearing his handwriting and two photos sloughed onto the desk. One bore a rough edge where Yuki had torn off her image during some long-ago spat. The other showed him lying on his Dabney House bed. How contented he looked, and carefree.

Tyler at Caltech

He recognized these pages—some of his first attempts at journal writing. Pre-Yuki. Just after his first year at Caltech.

> June 1999. It was a sparkly year. Lots of frustration, not from studying, but from the challenges of trying to get the most out of life in an environment that stifled all but academic activities.

In the margin, Tyler Present wrote an annotation.

> I thought I had it all figured out. All the pieces fit together; every piece into its position. Or at least I thought so. Either the things changed, or else I did. But that's a different story.

He read on to see what Tyler Past had to say:

> Physics, yeah, that's what I'm here for. That's the real goal, the end. I'm on the right track, taking care of things. That's all set. Time to focus on the rest, to learn about culture, the interaction of culture with philosophy. People in the world have something to teach. So many girls in clubs to meet-or try to meet. The challenges lie in overcoming a lack of automobile in Los Angeles and in penetrating the real-world social scene and meeting "outside" girls.
>
> A rave this weekend, Monterey Park for Chinese food. Chinese class at the normal university. So many flyers to choose from. I love the smell of the

> flyers. Korean-pop, what horrible irresistible catchy K-pop. We have our own video to film. Problem set due tomorrow.

Back then the enormous world had thrummed with excitement and fascination. Its magnetic pull had never ceded to the fatigue of classwork, so with summer break upon him, he had felt driven to cram his whole postponed life into it. Last year, before coming to Caltech, he and Cam had explored China on a scholarship from the University of Pittsburgh. But he had lined up no such scholarship for this three-month period.

Asia was where things were changing, where he couldn't escape a junkie's fix of adventure. On a whim, he had typed "Jobs in China," and the Internet search popped with help-wanted ads, among them a position for an English teacher in Suzhou. He applied, and within the hour his e-mail returned a job offer.

"I accept," he wrote. "I will arrive before the semester starts." He hit send, and his mind flashed to practical matters, such as how to stretch his scanty funds to cover airfare. How would he get to the school, if it even existed? What made him think he could teach, and English no less? Those were details—no way would he get bogged down in details.

> Life needs to be a constantly stimulating succession of images, sounds and feelings. If things get slow, it's your obligation to stir things up. Under this philosophy I found myself passing the night, walking in gardens, on grass and in closed campus buildings. Not my campus, a much cooler one. I'd just met this girl, but the others I knew well.

Some people have lived twice their age, experienced more than what seems their fair share of both light and heavy experiences. Sandy was one of these people: Living on her own in Florida until moving to California, going to school, dealing with shit like her friends who had her car in Florida. They consistently parked on the wrong side of the street on the biweekly day when that side of the street was due for cleaning, each time earning a thirty-five dollar fine, which over the course of two years came to a bill of over a thousand bucks.

"Fuck that." I offered my advice. "It's not your obligation to pay."

"Yeah, but it's my car, so I'm the one who has to pay. I'm legally responsible."

"But you aren't responsible at all. You had nothing to do with it. It's just stupid."

"That's the world. It doesn't matter at all what you did or why, all that matters is how they interpret it. Whoever they are anyway."

Yes, Tyler Past had understood that the world improperly affixed blame. General knowledge dictated that a person was not allowed to fight. Fighting was bad, seriously bad. But if a person gave up the struggle, was he not expressing tacit approval of injustice? On principle, he felt it better to fight than to submit.

"Just don't accept improper blame," he had told Sandy, thinking that advice should keep her, or anyone, clear of the wrong side.

Tyler studied his entry and noted in the margin:

> There are a lot of reasons not to fight. I wasn't so familiar with them back then.

So absorbing was the conversation with Sandy and others like it that he had passed the next thirty hours awake, entirely neglecting to prepare for his departure to China. He had drifted through the Los Angeles airport, boarded, and settled into a seat that was to serve as his entire personal space for the next fifteen hours.

> This is going to be good. I can feel it, and it's this excitement that makes life worth living. I don't know what's going to happen next, and the suspense keeps me trained on the moment. That's really living. A whole life to live and this is just the first summer. Four years of suffering, but it's worth it. Physics is the priority, but then freedom, that is to say, NOW freedom because it's summer break. I wonder what will happen when I land. No time to think about that now, I've got to get some sleep.
>
> Do I speak enough Chinese? I don't know. It wouldn't be fair if I did know. That would spoil the realness of the moment. If I knew, then it would just be a routine exercise of verification, and that's not what life is about. Life is about taking the most out of each moment, not watering it down with shit you already know. I don't know where I'm going, and that's the beauty of the passage.

> The wall shows a giant TV screen with a map of the earth depicted. Our path, traced in red, tells everybody on board where we are going. The banal verification of routine.
>
> This must be what it's like to wander, to float on the wind. What is this emotion? Adrenalin and fatigue–a blend of anticipation and the kind of euphoria that appears when something long awaited finally arrives. Readiness for any and everything, like the beginning of a movie that you know is going to be good. Did Kerouac feel this way?
>
> This is a beautiful moment, so the longer it lasts the better, for it does not come at the expense of the future. The future will arrive and with it, the unknown. So many unfathomable possibilities, but only one will be chosen to exist in the past tense.

No, he hadn't really believed that he had the world figured out. He just found it sad always to try yet never arrive, to feel on the verge of lucidity yet to be continually confused. Tyler Present added:

> I didn't have any idea of the scope of this set of possibilities, and I didn't have any information to speculate. All I knew was that it couldn't go wrong.

Baggage claim in Shanghai. Customs. Then a glass membrane rendered itself permeable, and he had stepped outside the terminal onto a wet sidewalk. An inventory of his billfold confirmed that he had only fifty-two dollars. He pulled out a business card and an e-mail from the alleged school administrator who claimed to need an English teacher. Suzhou was located near Shanghai and a tenth its size at 1.5 million people. How expensive could it be to take a cab to the school?

Tyler approached a beckoning driver and summoned his best Mandarin. "Suzhou?" he asked. On receiving only a blank stare, he handed over the precious business card and added, "In Jiangsu?"

The thin, well-aged driver studied the card and bobbed his head. "Yes. Yes."

In contrast to his glum mug shot on the dashboard and despite a mouthful of misaligned teeth, driver Li wore a friendly smile. Apparently, he spoke no English other than *yes*, so he used his hands to fill in the blanks. This left the steering wheel disconcertingly unattended—and he had plenty to say. They mimed their way through the standard where-are-you-from and what's-your-name exchange. Then Li pointed to the red tassels and ornaments that dangled from his rearview mirror. "For good luck," he said in Mandarin.

Tyler felt a zing of elation at deciphering the phrase. They drove past red neon lights, and he recognized the word for hotel. Li remembered the "ABC" song, which he sang to completion minus the letter *P*. Tyler corrected him. After all, he was here to teach English. Li laughed with his entire body.

The conversation progressed as much in tacitly forgiven misunderstanding as in real communication. But it didn't matter how inefficient communication was. Simply the fact that it was all taking place in Chinese made it good.

The meter's bright-red numbers ticked higher as Tyler balanced between awe at being in a bizarre foreign land and his struggle to communicate in the native tongue. Then Li threw his arms high and wide, abdicating the wheel yet again.

"Suzhou," he announced, as they cruised into a section of city where neon signs and brightly colored Chinese characters stood watch over black-windowed storefronts. Tyler caught a whiff of what brought to mind an overcrowded chicken coop in the heat of summer.

Li slapped the meter, and its numbers vanished. He rolled to a stop at a place that looked no different from any other. He pointed to a string of characters on a triangular, concrete-block building. "Yes, yes!" he said with a giggle.

The currency-exchange counters at the airport had been closed when Tyler arrived. "Sorry," he said. "I only have US money."

"Okay," Li said with a nod. "One hundred dollar, US."

A few blocks ago, Tyler had converted the yuan shown on the meter to thirty dollars. Knowing better than to start there, he offered twenty. Li appeared to suffer severe neck pain, and price negotiations commenced.

"Eighty dollar. Very reasonable."

"Thirty-five."

"Ohhh! Gas very expensive. Sixty dollar."

"Thirty-eight's the best I can do."

They settled at forty.

Twelve dollars in his pocket. One o'clock in the morning. Alone and stranded on a deserted street corner in a city the size of Philadelphia. Despite the illusion of cleanliness, a layer of grime coated the building blocks. Cars lined the street, and scooters lay scattered across the sidewalk. Orange streetlights spilled their haze over monochrome spots, leaving much of the area pitch-dark. Music whined from a nearby bar.

The five-story building stood not so much on a corner as at a promontory between two tributary streets that intersected at an acute angle. Its entry door gaped open like a mouth at the base of a pointed nose. Unable to resist the allure of an open door, Tyler lugged his suitcase inside.

The first floor consisted almost entirely of a locked steel door covered in flyers and an unlit stairwell. The dark second floor presented another locked steel door, also pasted with flyers, though bearing different images and writings. As Tyler proceeded toward the third floor, stray bands of light lit his way, and the off-key singing grew louder. Reaching a landing, he peered through a glass door into a small office. Inside walls displayed attractive posters. Yes! One featured the school's English name, plus a few Chinese characters that he recognized. He was where he needed to be, so he made his way up two more flights toward the source of the bass rhythms and singing.

A landing opened to a wide-slung door. Inside, pink-and-purple throw rugs warmed a tile floor. Loud-talking families reclined on couches and sat around tables. At the opposite end of the room, a floppy-haired guy throttled a microphone and belted out lyrics as they scrolled across a karaoke screen on the wall. A sign to the left of the entry door read Bar. Inaccurate, but that was its nomenclature.

"Nín hǎo." Two twenty-something guys at the counter flagged Tyler to a barstool and engaged him in conversation. The novelty of his recently bleached hair attracted one of the young men to touch his head. Tyler dug for words to explain that the blond streaks came from a bottle. They all laughed.

A fortyish man with one of the clientele families joined the gathering crowd. "Where are you staying?" he asked. "What hotel?"

"A hotel? I only have twelve dollars US. Don't think…" Tyler took care to put the right tones[8] on the words and to avoid grammatical errors.

"No. Not with that. Some can be inexpensive, but not that inexpensive. It's too late anyway."

"Yeah, it's late."

I patted myself on the back for successfully communicating. They seemed as impressed with my Chinese as I was. Standards for foreigners speaking Chinese were low. In English I'm always confounded at selecting words and sentences from the sea of possibilities. In this case, no problem.

Someone gave me a beer, my first taste of alcohol in many months...I don't remember much, but

8 Tone is the use of pitch in language. Mandarin words may convey entirely different meanings depending on the tones used to inflect their syllables (much like inválid versus ínvalid in English).

> I do recall the view of the room from the perspective of that microphone, and I remember being convinced that if I tried hard enough, I'd be able to read the lyrics in Chinese.
>
> The bar closed around three or four a.m. My suitcase became a mattress on the third-floor landing-not so bad with a sweatshirt for a pillow and skateboard under the thighs. Darkness welcomed sleep, and I dreamed about being awake on a grand adventure.

Immersed in a swirl of emotions, Tyler picked up his pen and wrote in an empty space at the end of the page.

> Reality is a very personal thing, and that night in my reality everything was perfect. I hadn't yet figured things out, but I knew I would someday, and there was no rush. I hadn't acquired a taste for alcohol yet. I hadn't seen *Litter on the Breeze*[9]. I was all dreams and spirit.

Those were good times then when he thought, someday, he'd get life all figured out.

The library's printer had finished spewing out Naber's research, so Tyler paid a student-clerk and exited the building. That night, in the dark early morning hours after work at Bar du

9 *First Love: The Litter on the Breeze*, a 1998 drama film by Tyler's favorite Chinese film producer, Wong Kar-Wai.

Port, Tyler looked to Naber to reveal a glimmer of mathematical clarity, and in those moments of revelation, he felt almost himself again: growing and fulfilled, sheltered from the amorphous fog that so often woke him choking for air.

To Every Thing There Is a Season

• • •

THE APPROACH OF FALL WAS TRIGGERING a mass exodus of Corsica's three million annual tourists. The island's population was about to shrink elevenfold to a mere 275,000 residents, and as the visitors evacuated in droves, they took with them the jobs. Bar du Port closed for the season.

> October 2004. To summarize the events of the past thirty-two days would be impossible, too numerable and dramatic. The period was stained with violence...My boss was so ordinary, but not really mean deep down. Working every day in this kind of modern slavery wore away at everyone's humanity and made their behavior indistinguishable from the case where they were, in fact, mean and devoid of appreciation.
>
> I finished Spivak and advanced myself through another hundred pages of Naber, enriching incalculably my life. Saw some huge waves, learned a bit

> of bartending and recycled two-dozen big garbage bags of glass. We learned something about seafaring folk and their ways that may figure in later stages. We left 1,400 euros richer than [when] we arrived.
>
> We seem to have stepped back from the world and detached, always the goal, but habit or fear for survival had until now been insurmountable obstacles. Everything remains unknown as before, but now I'm capable of answering what I want from life. For most people, that may be the hardest step. For us, there may be harder ones to come. I want Math. I want to see my friends and family again, and I want to sail into atolls and uninhabited islands to watch the sunset and to hear the waves.

Tyler used part of his and Yuki's savings to buy a used laptop. No software to speak of, but he could download Linux and basic programs. Whatever he couldn't download he'd code on his own. But how to support himself and Yuki through the winter? A dull-eyed street person who smelled of BO and rum provided the answer.

"There's migrant work in Moltifao." The man spat as if to cleanse his pallet of the vulgar term. "If you don't mind harvesting crops and sleeping outside and slaving like donkeys for shit pay."

Tyler recalled seeing the village on a map. "Moltifao's inland and north-central," he told Yuki, "an hour or so away."

Understanding and hope flooded her expression. "We sleep outside already. Food there will grow on trees."

That night at Paradise Point, with their bags packed and Yuki asleep, Tyler pulled out his journal and wrote in the light of the campfire.

> We are off to work a nearly dream job picking fruit. We will live in the beautiful countryside, pitch our tent in orchards and spend all day surrounded by green leaves and sweet, delicious smells. No doubt it's strenuous and hard work, but we have been ready for that all along. With the money we make, we will even be able to afford to buy vegetables. What a treat that will be!

Moltifao spread along a rocky crest, and its streets wound down the hillside. The village opened to magnificent views of the Asco Valley, with mountains rising on all sides. Judging from the sundials built into the walls of the fifteenth-century Church of the Annunciation, Tyler put the time at four o'clock. Then four resonant chimes rang confirmation, and an ornate, five-story clock tower drew his eyes skyward to a cross. Fingers of white clouds were caressing the towering spike and creating the illusion that it was soaring through space and carrying Tyler along with it.

He and Yuki passed through town and followed a winding road to a migrant-worker camp. There, they pitched their tent among rubbish and abandoned cars. Other campfires were flickering nearby, so he and Yuki built one, too. They warmed themselves in front of its flames as an unseen Spanish guitar accompanied a doleful male voice, singing of heartache and woe.

Early next morning, they followed a stream of twenty or more Hispanic-looking people to a gathering along a dirt road. Almost at once, a rusted red pickup pulled up, and the throng of hopefuls crowded around. A field boss emerged from the driver's door and stood on the running board.

"Aqui!" The churning crowd called out. "Recogerme!" "Fredriko!" "Oye!"

Tyler hung back, too polite to push, confident that he and Yuki would be selected for their cheery smiles and athletic builds. Instead, the foreman pointed to three weathered men and two hump-shouldered women who scrambled into the truck bed. Then the vehicle rumbled down the road. One after another, foremen drove up, and the process repeated itself.

The next day, Tyler pushed and called out and prostrated himself with the best of them. A gap-toothed foreman pointed straight at him, so he clamored into back of the truck. A glance at the other chosen workers, and Tyler realized that they were all carrying lunchboxes and water bottles. Oh, boy. Then he saw Yuki gazing up at him. Frail and forlorn, she stood like a marble statue among the milling crowd of unwashed rejects. He raised a palm in farewell and rolled down the dusty road to a clementine grove.

Yuki quit trying after a week and redirected her efforts to keeping the two of them fed, clean, and clothed—no easy task, considering the absence of showers and laundry facilities. Plus, food was available only from the local, outrageously expensive grocery store.

Most days, Tyler stooped from sunup to sundown over rows of onions. Other days, he balanced on a ladder to pick clementines. Gradually his muscles toned to the backbreaking monotony. He practiced his Spanish and felt grateful to be working outside. Still, he and Yuki were living as outcasts. The other workers viewed him as unwelcomed competition, and they shunned Yuki as if she were a two-headed witch.

Barely breaking even and itching from bug bites but otherwise healthy, they survived from day to day. Except the temperatures were dropping lower each night. Fewer foremen were cruising up in their pickups. Migrant families were breaking camp in the pitch-darkness and dissipating into the void.

By mid-November, it was clear: the full force of winter was about to bear down on Corsica. Where he and Yuki chose to take shelter was rapidly becoming an issue of survival. Lacking a viable alternative, the two trekked back to Mezzavia and to the confines of Milos's room—back to the downward spiral of joblessness and resource-sucking hedonism.

Two days later, in the wee hours of the morning, Tyler and Milos were stumbling back from Little Bear's. Milos draped an arm over Tyler's shoulders and slurred, "I don't get it, Marco. You are brilliant and well educated, yet you work the harvests with the migrants."

For a brief moment, Mom's voice sounded in Tyler's head, and he channeled her words, saying, "There's dignity in all work." He missed the way she used to pat the back of his hand, how she always expressed confidence in him. Hell, he even missed her dumb puns.

"You watch the skies for Black Hawks, and you never talk about your past. What is it with you?"

"It's private."

"Whatever you tell me, it stays between us."

Usually, Tyler's secret loomed like a hairy, fetid monster between him and others. It compelled him to dodge personal topics, to deflect dangerous questions. He knew the creature fed on his pushing others away because the more he turned inward and the greater his isolation, the stronger the creature grew. Now, under Milos's gaze, he felt the fiend's fangs gnash at his insides.

How he longed to let down his shields and be himself again, to share with a friend. Milos had taken him and Yuki in twice now, and he still charged a pittance for rent. So what if they didn't share the same work ethic? This guy was kind and good-natured and generous. Yes, Milos had proven himself trustworthy, and now he was reaching out. The guy deserved the truth.

Tyler fumbled for the right words, unsure where to begin. At first, his story dribbled out. Then it gushed forth like uncorked champagne. They stood under a streetlight, Milos listening and interrupting only with an occasional epithet; Tyler talking about the incident, about the FBI classifying it as domestic terrorism, about mandatory sentencing and his persistent nightmares. He described how it was corroding his and Yuki's relationship.

Usually the slightest flashback to the situation set Tyler on edge. Tonight, as he poured out his story, his loss and grief swelled in his throat. Even as he stood there and choked out words, the problem somehow felt less overwhelming, less out of control and hopeless. Monster Fear loosened its stranglehold. Almost. Tyler gasped a shaky breath.

"Is Marco Sosson your real name?" Milos asked.

"No."

"What is it?"

Too dangerous. "You're better off not knowing."

"What are you going to do?"

"We're saving up to hire a lawyer who speaks English and specializes in extradition law. We want to clear this up, contact our families, and go home."

Milos swung both arms wide. "My uncle in Marseille will help. He's a journalist with all kinds of connections. Trust me."

"I—I guess that might be all right."

And so it was arranged. Tyler and Yuki were to meet Vincente Benevento at noon in Marseille on Tuesday, 30 November. On the assumption that they would stay in the city until they found a lawyer and resolved their situation, they packed all their possessions for the journey.

"You can store your bags at my uncle's," Milos suggested. "He has a big pad and lots of space."

One thing was odd, though. Tyler asked three times for Monsieur Benevento's address. At each request, Milos seemed to fish for an excuse not to provide it.

"He'll meet you at the train station," Milos assured them. Then, "You can call him," and "He'll be waiting for your call."

Cloudy-eyed and sore from carrying all their worldly belongings on their backs and in their arms, they arrived in Marseille in the sickly early morning. A black suitcase, made of shoddy materials by exploited Chinese mothers, bulged among their array of baggage. The wheel-less canvas bag had been built for an ephemeral existence and bounced across continents only to land in a Corsican dump, where he and Yuki had salvaged it.

> In it we carried our slowly growing collection of appurtenances, not giving much thought at the time to how much it had in common with our own life stories.

In an attempt to avoid the public exit surveillance cameras and officers, they slogged through the darkness along a chain-link fence that enclosed the port. Chill gusts sliced through their jackets, and a locked-down loading dock loomed to their right. Yuki looked discouraged as she snugged her zipper under her chin. Tyler was about to suggest that they take their chances on the requisite exit when he spotted a gap under the fence a few feet ahead.

With a bit of tugging and pushing, he squeezed his backpack underneath. Then he lifted the fence for Yuki. She shinnied under and dragged the rest of their bags through. Then she held the fence for him.

> We moved without destination, full of innocent hopes and naive dreams of rebuilding. All we longed for was a normal existence, to disappear into the crowd and make our way. We were ready to face the cold world along an unknown path, our burden heavy. But we no longer had any choice.

A dirty sidewalk led under a concrete overpass. There, massive support pillars arced to earth like titanic mastodon legs. Exhaust fumes rode the hammering wind and gave the scene a nauseating déjà-vu quality.

"We need a country to grant us asylum," Tyler said as he watched a pair of headlights weave through a desolate lot. "Then we can find real jobs and earn incomes above subsistence level."

Yuki nodded slowly. "A country that will not extradite to the US or Japan."

"Cuba or Tunisia, or maybe China or Iceland or Venezuela might work, but all of those places would make it hard for you to visit Japan."

She waved off his concern. "At least we would have roof over our heads."

"Maybe the lawyer will negotiate for us to stay in France," he said. "I could teach either physics or math. Maybe I could get a research job at a university or even at CERN[10]."

"I could take my last class and get my bachelor's degree," Yuki said. While she didn't exactly sound hopeful, she sounded more optimistic than she had in months.

They trod uphill to an open-air square under wide skies. A commuter charged past, his arm swinging a briefcase. On the far side of the square, they came to a black sign with white letters that read METRO STOP. Its stairs dropped to a well-lit tunnel, frigid but sheltered from the gusts. A handful of business

10 The European Organization for Nuclear Research, known as CERN, operates the largest particle physics laboratory in the world. It is located in Geneva, Switzerland.

travelers milled about the subterranean realm, and Tyler pointed out the slick red bricks that lined the floor. "Polished smooth under the shuffle of soles and souls," he said, trying to make light of the situation.

Yuki shivered and raised a warning eyebrow.

He guessed homophones weren't her thing. At this early hour, they were hardly his thing, either. He set down his bags to study a giant wall map. Yuki plopped her bags onto a bench and slumped next to them. The day was beginning to begin, and the map crawled with tiny lines and street names.

"Someday, maybe we'll know these," Tyler said. "But right now they're intriguing gibberish."

Yuki rubbed the small of her back and stretched. "We should look for a place to stay."

Once he'd pinpointed their current location, Tyler ran his index finger along boulevard de Paris. "Train station looks like it's about thirty minutes away," he said. "Might as well walk."

Yuki reloaded. "Mr. Benevento comes for us at noon. We must not miss him." They ascended the stairs together. Then Yuki strode off in the wrong direction.

Tyler waited for it to dawn on her that he wasn't following. After fifteen steps or so, she turned to look back. He head-nodded in the correct direction and tried not to grin.

The sun came out, and five- and six-story French terraces rose above them on both sides of the street. Blended odors flowed from brightly colored Arabic and Indo-Chinese shops. Tables of baked goods and glassy-eyed fish obstructed the walkway. An elderly man in a fez toted a plastic bag covered with red Arabic characters. Beyond a Chinese supermarket, they came to a swap meet with hundreds of Arabs hawking plastic-wrapped sugar candies, woodcrafts, and jewelry. A group stood chatting and rubbing their palms to keep warm. Tyler approached and inquired about finding an apartment.

"Look for *Le 13*," a fortyish man replied. "Free newspaper."

Tyler nodded in appreciation and said, "Bonjour." He and Yuki slogged up a small hill until they came to a series of elegant granite or marble steps.

"'Le Grand Escalier,'" Yuki read from a sign with arrows. "'Gare de Marseille Saint-Charles.'"

"'Steps to the train station,'" Tyler interpreted.

"The French sounds better," she said, and they began their long ascent.

Up top, they entered through giant doors into a high-ceilinged station. People in business suits and backpacks were swarming all directions. A cadre of machine gun–toting soldiers in berets and military fatigues made Tyler more than a little uncomfortable. He scanned the soldiers who in turn were scanning the crowd. They appeared to be paying attention to no one in particular yet everyone in general. "It's close enough to noon," Tyler said. "We should call Milos's uncle."

Yuki found an opening on a bench and shrunk into it. "I'll stay here."

Tyler left his bags with her and bought a phone card. A pay phone sat vacant just outside the station. Six rings, and a curt, throaty voice answered. "Bonjour."

"Bonjour. I'm Milos's friend."

A pause. Then Monsieur Benevento replied in slow, soft French, "I have spoken with Milos."

"Great. He said you might be okay with us stashing our stuff at your place for a couple of days?"

"Uh huh," he said, sounding hurried or perhaps distracted.

"And he thought you might be able to recommend a lawyer?"

"Look. You caught me at a bad time. Give me your number. I'll call you back."

Tyler read the digits on the pay phone aloud, and Monsieur Benevento repeated them back.

"Call you in a minute," he said. Then click.

Tyler returned and picked up his bags. Yuki hefted her bulging black carry-on and winced, obviously from sore muscles. "Where are we going?" she asked. "Did you talk to him?"

Tyler reached for her carry-on, saying, "Here, I'll give you a hand."

"What did he say?"

"Yeah, uh, he promised to call in a minute. We need to stay close to that outside phone, so we can answer it when it rings."

A flush of worry. "He is our only contact. He has to come through."

"Milos says we can count on him."

Yuki's posture became rigid. "Why do you say it like that? What is wrong?"

Tyler shook his head. "Just a feeling I got. I'm sure everything's fine." The place was crawling like an ant farm, people moving every direction. "Let's get outside." They relocated to the top of the Grand Escalier and sat under the watchful eyes of a pair of white marble lions.

Twenty minutes ticked past as the pay phone maintained its stubborn silence. The steps dropped to a great avenue that stretched as far as the eye could see. "To someone on the far end looking this direction," Tyler said, "these steps probably look like a waterfall at the source of a mighty river." He pictured the two of them floating on a raft. The current was sweeping them toward freedom and family and a normal life. *Easy*, he thought. *Keep the dreams in check.*

Yuki eyed the clock tower. "We have been waiting forty-seven minutes."

Tyler's stomach rumbled again. "You okay with answering the phone if I go find us some bread and a copy of *Le 13*?"

She nodded. "Bring me hot water for tea, okay?"

Keeping an eye out for the newspaper, Tyler followed his nose to a bakery and stood in line. Brief as his conversation with Monsieur Benevento had been, it had taken place in French. What if he called and Yuki answered? She'd have a hell of a time communicating.

The line inched forward. At last he stepped up to the counter and said, "Eaux chaudes." Two hot waters. He also pointed to a loaf of cheesy bread topped with sesame seeds. The clerk seemed to operate in one gear: slow. But at last Tyler was running up the steps with the loaf under an arm and two paper cups of scalding water in his palms.

"Any calls?" he panted, as he handed Yuki the bread and set down the cups.

Her face fell. "No." She broke the loaf in two and handed Tyler the larger portion.

A glance at the clock and he realized an hour and four minutes had passed since Mr. Benevento had promised to call him right back.

Yuki dipped her used tea bag into her cup, and the soothing scent of her Darjeeling made Tyler's nose tingle. He dunked his used chai bag into his cup. Then, just as he took an oversize bite, he realized that his mouth could be full when the phone rang. He chewed fast and washed down the glob with weak tea.

No ring.

He took another bite and slogged it down. Then another and another until his portion was gone, and his belly felt full. He surveyed the incredible view. "Nice morning—if only Mr. Benevento would call."

Yuki looked on the verge of tears. She offered him half her chunk, and when he shook his head, she zipped it into her pack. Ten more minutes ticked past. Yuki adjusted her ponytail and heaved a sigh.

"I'm going to call Milos and find out what's going on." Tyler returned to the pay phone and dialed. No answer, so he left a message.

Call two. No answer. Left another message. He returned to Yuki, and they sat warming in the sun. He was doing his best to sound upbeat—and he could tell she was, too—but he could almost feel the sands of time slipping through the hourglass of their lives. Two hours. He placed another call to Milos. No answer.

"Mr. Benevento could call and hear busy signal."

That was Tyler's fear, too, so he scribbled an out-of-order note and slipped it under the handset. Using an adjacent phone, he called Little Bear, who answered on the first ring.

"Thank God!" Tyler blurted. "Milos isn't picking up. Can you find him for me?"

Long pause. "No," Little Bear said. "I am so sorry."

"What do you mean?"

"I do not want I should be the one to tell you."

Tyler's ribcage compressed. "Tell me what?"

"Milos, well, he does not have the balls to say." Little Bear blew out a sigh. "Before you leave, his uncle, he freak out. He tell Milos to stay away from you. He say he won't meet you, man. Milos doesn't want to speak with you or see you anymore. He's afraid of the US government, man. We all are."

Little Bear had said *we all*. "Who else did Milos tell?"

"Everyone," Little Bear whispered. "He tell us all everything. We are scared for you and for ourselves, oh yeah."

The pit in Tyler's stomach solidified to clay. Different as the Ajaccio crowd was from Yuki and him, they were their only friends. He had trusted Milos, trusted them. Now they would tell their friends and families, and those people would tell others in their circles. "Whisper down the lane" at its worst. Law enforcement was bound to get wind of the story and come after them. Hell, they could be in pursuit right now.

"Thanks for taking my call," Tyler croaked. "Good-bye, Little Bear." He hung up the phone and swallowed the urge to vomit before returning to Yuki. "Corsica is dead to us," he said and recounted the conversation to her.

Yuki's face puckered, and she dropped her head into her hands. "What are we going to do?"

"We find a lawyer." He breathed. "We find jobs and a place to live."

She wiped a tear and stared down the steps. "Nowhere is safe."

Tyler fished for something positive to say. "Maybe Milos's big mouth did us a favor. Now our ties to Corsica are cut. We're free to work as hard as we please and pursue our new lives."

"They are all just a bunch of drunkies and potheads." She mimed cracking an egg and dropping it into a frying pan. "This is their brain. This is their brain on drugs." The trail of a dried tear lined her cheek. "We are better off without those assholes."

He reached for her hand, but she pulled it away. "I better go find that newspaper," he said and tore down the steps, nearly tripping over his feet.

A short, hairy hoodlum with an equally short, hairy pit bull sidled out of an alley and offered him hashish. He declined on the excuse that cops were patrolling nearby, which they were. Cops were everywhere.

A corner grocery store offered plenty of fish odor but no *Le 13*. A café with a red-striped awning featured a rack of travel brochures, absent *Le 13*. A row of newspaper dispensers brimmed with titles, minus the one he sought. Tyler returned to Yuki and said, "*Le 13* gave me the slip again." He told her about the hashish offer, plus the legions of cops he'd seen on patrol.

Yuki splayed her fingers as if over a hot stove. "What if they catch us?"

They'd had months to polish their cover stories, yet here they sat, a confused mess when it came to the past. He took a swig of water from his Nalgene. "Let's get our stories straight, once and for all, just in case."

"The most important thing." She bobbed a finger at him. "Is to never contradict each other."

"I'll say I'm Canadian, raised in Vancouver, birthdate 30 June 1980."

The rat-a-tat of what sounded like an automatic weapon jarred Tyler to sit rigid—only a woman's spiked heels clicking down the steps. The long-skirted female swerved and continued past, leaving behind a familiar aroma. Grandmother W. used to smell like that when she was dressed to the nines. He wondered how Grandma was, and what the perfumed woman would think if she had overheard the two of them planning their cover stories.

Yuki closed her eyes and inhaled. "Chanel Number 5. 'Share the fantasy!'" Then she added, "We shouldn't talk about this here."

"Aww." He waved her off. "Nobody speaks English."

She covered her mouth and directed her words for his ears only. "I cannot hide that I am Japanese. I'll say I am from Kyoto."

"Your education?"

"I went to Gaidai Nishi High School. College at Kyoto University." She punctuated each syllable with rhythmic nods of her head. "I know the schools. Visited friends there."

"Good. The best lie contains elements of truth. We'll say we met while hiking Mount Fuji in 2002—which we did hike then. We just didn't meet there."

Yuki's face softened at hearing the name of her country's most revered mountain. "Fuji-san," she sighed, attaching the *san* term of endearment. Then her eyes flooded with something else: grief, maybe. "My nephew, Shin, he hiked with us when you visited. He gave you GORP because you were hungry."

Tyler grinned at the recollection. "Always am."

"Shin is crazy for you."

"He's a special kid."

"I miss him."

Tyler let his mind drift to bittersweet memories of tossing a baseball with Shin and eating home-cooked meals with Yuki's mother. His thoughts whisked to splashing in Lake Michigan's blue waters and to walking the sands of the Sleeping Bear Dunes as a child. He recalled his family's move to Mt. Vernon, D.C. and his jaw-dropping discoveries at the Smithsonian museums of natural history, and air and space. Before sixth grade they'd moved again. This time to Pennsylvania where the fam had traipsed around mystical places like Independence Hall and Marsh Creek State Park and Hawk Mountain. Happy years passed until he and Kelsey graduated from high school. Then each had trooped off for their higher educations.

"I grew up richy rich." Yuki's voice drew Tyler's thoughts back to the business at hand. "My father is this great success. We have the perfect family." She was chattering like a kid.

"I suppose if you have to manufacture a story, might as well be a whopper, eh?"

"You got that right." Her eyes flashed. "I'll say my parents never divorced. Nobody ever..." Her voice trailed off.

"You speak English?" A male voice interrupted their awkward pause.

Tyler froze and felt Yuki go rigid beside him.

"Eh, mate. I asked if you speak English."

Seated three steps lower and to the left, a Rasta man was waving at them. Next to him, a skinny guy was flailing both arms like windshield wipers at high speed. Undercover cops, maybe? How much had they heard?

"I'm Dino." The Rasta man pointed a thumb at himself and then rotated it toward the still-waving man. "This here's George. He's a corker."

The man looked Rasta but sounded Australian, and everything about him pronged outward: his arms, his facial hair, and especially his dishwater-blond dreadlocks, which spiked like thistles from under his hat. George twitched with excess energy, and his off-kilter baseball cap rode high over his narrow face, adding to his goofy appearance. "Anchorage Buccaneers," along with an eye-patched pirate on a baseball diamond had been embroidered above the cap's brim. Both men's smiles carried the worn look of street people—in their late thirties, maybe.

"I'm Marco," Tyler said, his mind racing. "This is Yuki."

George smiled through crooked yellow teeth and flagged them over. "I'm from Alaska. Dino here's a Kiwi from New Zealand."

Dino cupped a palm. "Come here and have a yack with us in good old anglais."

Yuki hugged her backpack to her chest. "I'll stay with our bags."

"If you hear me cough twice," Tyler whispered, "leave everything and run." He eased down the step to sit next to George. The guy's brown bomber jacket smelled of leather and perspiration. He didn't look healthy enough to work as a cop. "Hey."

Dino rubbed his bearded chin and lowered his voice. "Ow man, you trying to put on a false identity or something?"

What to say? Maybe he could overwrite their suspicions with a more reasonable story. Tyler forced a smile and shook his head. "We're just joking around."

Dino rolled what looked like a cigarette, though it probably was not. "You sound like a yank."

"No, Canadian. Looking for a place to stay."

He recommended *Le 13*, of course.

George dug into his jacket pocket and handed Dino a green lighter. "Not easy to rent," George said in a high-pitched voice with his hands punctuating each syllable. "You need a contract stating you have a job. Otherwise, landlords won't rent to you."

Dino flamed the lighter and lit the maybe cigarette. He closed his eyes, drew a long pull, and the tip flared. The hand-rolled stub jutted like a thorn between his bristly mustache and wild beard. "It's so pissing hard to evict people," he rasped before spewing smoke from his nose. "They want to know you're not a dole bludger."

"A what?"

"Proof you can pay, mate. That you've got yourself a job."

"What about cheap hotels?" Tyler asked.

Dino shook his head. "The cheapest will cost you fourteen euros a night, maybe twelve if you negotiate to stay for a while." He jabbed his cigarette in the direction of the bus station. "They're over there."

"Oh, yeah." Tyler nodded. "We saw some Arab hotels that way."

Dino returned the lighter to George. "*Bidons*, man, little tin cans." He told Tyler about a squat where he and his girlfriend were staying. "We're going to rattle our dags soon," he claimed. "We're moving to Israel."

"Food is cheap, man," George added. "Have you seen the prices?"

"Yeah." Tyler sniffed at the aura of smoke. "We bought a can of ravioli for less than fifty cents."

Dino's smile broadened. "I know the one, man. Isn't very good, but you can survive eating it."

Out of nowhere, three uniformed cops stepped in front of them. "What are you guys doing here?" a muscular officer with thick eyebrows asked in French. Behind him, a hard-looking female cop and a bland younger cop were looking on.

Tyler sat paralyzed as George flung his hands up in surrender and screeched, "We're just smoking a cigarette." The guy snapped his arms down and hugged himself, turtling his head so that only his black cap and a tuft of oily brown hair bumped up on his shoulders.

Play it cool, Tyler thought. Look relaxed. He studied the cops' faces. Boss Cop didn't look convinced. "What about you?" the cop asked Dino. "What are you smoking?"

"*Tabac*, man. Just *tabac*." Dino sounded believable. Almost.

Leader Cop took the joint and brought it to his nose. It was over. Questions. Jail. Extradition. A prison cell. A procession of calamities paraded through Tyler's brain. His instincts told him to cough twice or yell *Run, Yuki! Run!* But logic dictated that if she moved, she would expose herself.

Leader Cop sniffed again, then gave a slight nod.

Dino bobbed his head, the picture of innocence. "Just *tabac*."

Boss Cop stretched a finger toward Tyler's hands. "What about you? What are you holding?"

He splayed his empty palms. "Rien!" Nothing.

The three cops exchanged doubtful looks. Then Boss Cop grunted, "Have a nice day." The trio sidled off to harass other step-dwellers.

Everyone agreed that was too close. Yuki and Tyler wished Dino and George luck before hauling their bulky baggage down the steps and to the Arab section. They checked into a *bidon* as a brassy Islamic call to worship warbled from a mosque's minaret.

The bidon's greatest distinction was possibly that it was the shittiest hotel in the world. Patches of mold spread around a cracked and sagging sink in the corner. Paint peeled off the ceiling, and dirty remarks squiggled like worms down the walls. The bed's linens smelled of cigarettes; the once-beige carpet of urine. They slept in their sleeping bag on the bedcover.

Rising early, Tyler slipped out and at last located the elusive *Le 13.* On his return, he found Yuki stooped over the sink and washing her hair under the tap.

"No hot water," she said, and her voice sounded pinched.

Tyler crawled onto the bed and sat cross-legged on the sleeping bag. Pen in hand, he folded the newspaper across his lap. Eight classifieds showed promise, so he ranked them according to priority. "I'm afraid it'll be the same as in Corsica," he said.

Yuki shunned the stained towel to wring out her hair with her hands. "No job," she said. "No rent."

"That's right."

She hunched over the sink, ran a comb through her hair, and pulled it into a ponytail. "Maybe they would like better a woman's voice?"

"Worth a try."

They checked out and made their way to a pay phone. Tyler pressed in the digits while Yuki held the handset so it wouldn't touch her ear.

Two rings. "Bonjour?"

"Uh, oui," Yuki said. Wide-eyed, she jammed the handset into Tyler's palm. Unfortunately, the call unfolded as feared. No job contract. No lease.

Calls two, three, four, and five yielded the same results. "You know," Tyler said, "Einstein never actually defined insanity as doing something over and over and expecting a different result."

"Just because he did not say it does not make it not true," Yuki said.

Tyler nodded understanding as he pressed in another number. "Time for a change of technique," he whispered,

Then came the inevitable question. "Do you have a job?"

"Oui," he responded. After all, his job was to find a job, right?

"Good. Just need to see your contract."

Tyler hung up.

Nowhere to go. Nowhere to stay. They sat on their bags until one of Marseille's finest rounded the corner.

"Pas flânage," the officer said in a tired voice, sounding more interested in shooing them along than in arresting them, maybe.

They moved on as directed. "French lesson for today: 'Pas flânage,'" Tyler said.

Yuki dropped both her arms and looked toward the heavens. "'No loitering.'"

They paused for a break on a different block, and another patrolman approached. "Pas flânage," Tyler said without moving his lips, and they hauled their possessions onward, pre-empting the officer.

There was always so much to do. We were constantly busy, carrying things, moving, waiting and worrying. Nothing seemed to work out. It was a constant and tiring struggle that brought us in ever tighter circles, ever more frustrated and worn out.

After the first night in the *bidon,* we sought a cheaper solution. We lugged everything to an abandoned lot, fenced off as a construction site just across the street. Here we set up the tent and got out a plastic liter and a half of wine and saluted the sad city from our perch on the cold, crumbly earth waiting to be covered by concrete like its neighbors. That night we found laughter, we found the stars, and we realized that we, too, were beautiful.

Chez Dino (House of Dino)

• • •

THE RUMBLE OF NEARBY BULLDOZERS alerted Tyler to the hard reality that he and Yuki had better wake up and get the hell out. Towing their stuffed, flimsy suitcase through dustless brown dirt, they walked past a congregation of sleepy-eyed workers at the lot's only exit. Then, the day's activities consisted of lurking in and out of shops, cybercafés, and public parks. Even at half a euro, the cost of ravioli was cutting into their meager resources.

Darkness fell, and they migrated back to the construction site, only to find the gate locked. The powers that be didn't want them back. In all fairness, Tyler could understand their perspective.

Another *bidon* stood next door to the Arab hotel where they'd stayed the night before.

"Fourteen euros." The keeper extended an open palm.

"We'll take it." Tyler handed over the money and turned to Yuki, saying, "We can use the euro we saved to buy wine."

They slogged toward the room, and Yuki dropped her bag outside the door. "I'll wait for you here."

Tyler returned in less than five minutes with a fresh plastic bottle.

Yuki used a tissue to touch the doorknob, and we just sat on the bed, our little island of freedom for a few hours. So boxed in by dirty walls, we passed the sorrow of the day into a joyful night.

In the days that followed, they packed and hauled their stuff from one spot to the next, trying to look legitimate so as not to raise suspicions. Always they searched for a job, a better place to live, and a lawyer.

One after another, wide-eyed owners scowled at Tyler. "No, no!" They flapped their jowls. "To hire undocumented workers is illegal."

Yuki's job search was faring no better. Male hotel owners shook their heads and huffed. "Too little. You wouldn't last a day," or "My wife would have my head." Alternatively, women brushed her off with a flourish of their hands. "Too pretty. Nothing but trouble."

No restaurant, bar, or hotel in Marseille seemed willing to hire an undocumented laborer. Tyler had never imagined how nerve-racking and uncomfortable it would feel to be rootless. He felt ungrounded—and he was.

One day, a Sudanese woman was catching a smoke behind the bar where she apparently worked. "Just go on in," she said and waved Tyler through the back door into the kitchen.

Tyler approached a one-eyed, freckle-faced cook and put on his best French. "I'm not documented, and I'm looking to wash dishes or bus tables."

The poor cook threw his hands in the air as if Tyler were aiming a gun at his nose. "You American? You with the government or undercover CIA or something?"

So that explained these knee-jerk responses! His French sounded too American.

At least their quest for a lawyer was progressing with more variety. In a city thick with *avocats*, most employed ardent gatekeepers. "I will have him call you," the administrative assistants crooned into Tyler's ear. "What is the number where monsieur may reach you?"

A reasonable request, except that Tyler and Yuki had no phone, no friends, and no contacts where a caller might reach them.

A cherished few lawyers answered their own phones. Even fewer spoke English. Three conversations held promise at first. One started, "So how may I help you?"

No way could Tyler explain over the phone. "I was wondering if you have expertise in extradition law?"

"I'm in art recovery, so I can help you extradite a stolen Monet," the male voice chortled.

A Greek-accented gentleman answered with honey in his voice. "Yes, I will gladly represent you," he drawled. "Of course, there is a small matter of a five-thousand-euro retainer, payable in advance."

A chipper, British woman showed the most potential. She would need to meet with Tyler, she explained, before she could decide whether to take his case. "How does your schedule look after the holidays? I have an opening on Friday, 28 January."

Oh boy. That was over a month away. "Thanks," he said, "but I need something sooner."

Two weeks passed, and these slum hotels were costing them a fortune. A cheap apartment would be infinitely more comfortable at half the price. Tyler commenced another round of inquiries with each new edition of *Le 13*. Whether calling about an apartment, job, or lawyer, he might as well have prerecorded the responses.

"No work contract? No room for rent."

"No documentation? No job for you."

"No phone number or retainer?" No legal counselor.

To top matters off, Mom's birthday was fast approaching and Christmas was around the corner. Birthdays and holidays were a big deal to his family. Face it. They were a big deal to him, too, and here he was, gone missing without a trace. For all his loved ones knew, he was dead or injured or suffering torture in a four-by-four Chinese prison cell. But he could think of no safe way to contact them and put their fears to rest.

15 November 2004. Present Tense in a Shell.

I'm not sure where I am anymore. All that's left is an empty shell following orders prescribed in the distant past. Sometimes if I watch closely, I can see what's happening, but mostly I just let it pass unnoticed, forgotten and forever discarded.

It's probably past the end, which was never any specific part like I'd always expected, but instead a rather fuzzy business. Tyler died in a slow process of decay, eventually descending below some vaguely defined threshold into non-existence. I, writing this, am merely a shell holding onto some of the last memories in existence of Tyler.

When I pass away, Tyler will be gone forever. It would happen soon, a happy drug overdose to celebrate the finish, but one thing holds me back. I feel I owe it to him to carry out his last wish. You see, Tyler had a sister and a family he loved very dearly, and he never had the chance to say good-bye.

One of my most serious prescribed instructions is to remedy this and put final farewells into place. Perhaps I can find adequate drugs to patch together a decent suicide in Michigan, or perhaps worst of all, even this final gesture will result in failure, too. How much can we really expect from a shell?

LATE INTO AN EVENING, TYLER AND YUKI climbed a graffiti-decorated stairwell to their favorite neighborhood square in the heart district. Cours Julien, as it was called, pulsated with artists, street musicians, and left-wing bobos, short for bourgeois bohemians. Last Thursday morning, he and Yuki had arrived early enough at the Plaine market to negotiate decent deals on coats that, as people said in Marseille, had "tombé du camion," fallen off the truck. Tonight, even though their outdoor terraces were closed for the winter, the area restaurants and hip bars emanated the buttery aromas of tapas, swordfish carpaccio, and pastries.

Tyler's favorite busker was occupying his regular street corner as they approached. Hair long and unkempt, shoes unglued at the toes, Soul Man stood silent, erect, and proud. When he saw Tyler and Yuki join his small audience, he raised a tattooed arm and smiled. "'Caprice in A Minor' for my favorite couple." He snugged his violin under his chin and glided his bow over the strings as if touching a Fabergé egg. The violin began to sing with the spirit of all creation.

As Soul Man swayed side to side playing composer Ernest Guiraud's romantic gift to the world, his buttonless woolen coat fell open. As usual, he was wearing his black T-shirt with LEGEND imprinted above an image of Bob Marley. Strands of Soul Man's slicked-back hair toppled over his vacant, blue eyes, and he stared into the distance as if watching a ghost ship sail over the horizon.

The notes lifted Tyler's hunger and awoke dormant spirits in his heart. He pulled Yuki close and felt the heat of her breast through his new coat. The operatic masterpiece wound to a close, and without losing a beat, Soul Man launched into a slow, aching tune.

"Too sad," Yuki whispered.

They turned to move on to a square where more upbeat rhythms were drifting from a café. But as they stepped away from Soul Man's crowd, a figure slipped from the shadows and gripped Tyler's arm. Out of reflex, Tyler spun to face his attacker and collected into a tang soo do fighting stance.

A short, dark figure flailed his arms and jounced backward. "Marco? Yuki?"

The male voice, the blended odor of leather, *tabac*, and perspiration—all struck Tyler as vaguely familiar. Then he noticed the Anchorage Buccaneers logo on the man's cap.

"George!" He relaxed his hands. "How you doing?"

"Still kicking." A mouthful of misaligned teeth came to light, and George pointed to a nearby steam grate. "And keeping warm."

"I thought you had a squat?"

George nodded with his entire bony frame. "I do, but a man's gotta get out. Where's your flop?"

Tyler met Yuki's gaze. "We move around."

George looked perplexed. "Why didn't you take Dino's squat?"

Yes, the Rasta man had said something about rattling his dags, which Tyler had assumed to mean he was preparing to move. But street people made lots of empty claims—he'd learned all too well—and moving to greener pastures topped the list. "We don't know where it is," Tyler said.

George's arms flapped as if he were doing the wave at a football game. "Come. I'll show you." With that, he bounded like a white-tail deer toward an alley.

Tyler turned to Yuki. "Shall we?"

She shrugged. "Why not?"

A few turns and they were striding southwest along rue Canebière. "It's not the most convenient location, oh no," George said and lengthened in stride. "But it's roomy and homey, yes, and near the sea, and the price is right." The faster he walked, the faster he talked; and the faster he talked, the faster his pace.

Tyler stepped over an inlaid tram track and realized it was his turn to insert a word. "Sounds good," he said. Yuki was trotting to keep up, so he reached out and gave her a steadying hand.

The streets widened and ran straight, drawing ever farther from the central districts. Steel bars encased doors, and businesses bore names like Credit Agricole and CC.

"La Canebière is nice, yes, but it's mostly urban sprawl with little charm." George whirred on, self-propelled by his own running commentary. The street dead-ended at a barrier made of ship moorings. A metro stop gaped empty. "This is quite a ways out," Tyler said, feeling an uncanny sense of uncertainty.

"This way. Oh yeah, smell that? Bouillabaisse—it's a fish stew, you know, a national treasure. Originated right here in Marseille. It's on all the menus."

From the looks of him, George dined in restaurants about as often as he and Yuki did, which was never. Tyler's elbow felt the pinch of Yuki's fingers. A glance, and he recognized her *This guy is a nutcase* expression. George steered them down a marina, past slipways. Tyler counted twenty-one docks, each mooring an assortment of sleepy sailboats, yachts, and fishing boats.

George ticked his right arm out straight. "Over there is Palais du Pharo. Not open at this hour, of course, but something to see in the summer."

No more streetlights. Relying on moonlight now, they strode between two-story warehouses abandoned to wrack and ruin. Right turn. Left. Left. Right. Tyler lost track. He smelled petroleum. Then, moonlit beaches stretched before them, and an enormous abandoned complex flanked them on both sides. Tyler scooped up a rusted plumbing pipe and tapped it on the hard-packed ground. Yuki shivered from cold or fear; he couldn't tell which.

George cut through a trash-littered lot that reeked of urine and rotten potatoes. Sirens wailed, and Tyler saw why. He pointed to a police station and said, "I'm not liking that."

"Yeah, yeah," George bobbed a nod. "Dino and his girlfriend, they only came in and out at night, you see. Dino's girlfriend, she was African. They met in Israel, oh yeah."

A ramp dropped into the shadows. If George was planning an ambush, then this would make an ideal spot. Yuki dug her fingernails into Tyler's bicep and broke into a nervous giggle. "'Never let them see you sweat.'" Then, "'Ban won't wear off as the day wears on.'" She drew a shaky breath, probably readying herself to unleash that Japanese love song.

Tyler tunked the pipe into his open fist and kept his eyes locked on George. "I can take this guy if I have to," he whispered to Yuki—if he wasn't caught off guard and if George didn't have a gang of thugs lying in wait. "Yuki's big on television commercials," he explained with a forced grin.

George pointed to a shambolic bank of battered, unhinged doors to their left. "Two wino bums live there," he whispered, his hot breath stinking of stomach acid. "They are nice guys, yeah, but they drink too much and do bad things. Best to leave them alone."

Tyler widened his line of sight to include both the wino doors and George. "All right."

George wagged an arm toward a scramble of pallets that looked as if a horde of mad beavers had constructed a dam. "All that's just for show," he said, and he tramped down a springboard to a thick chain and oversize lock. Relieved to have some distance from George, Tyler hesitated with Yuki at the top of the ramp.

George gripped a partial sheet of green-stamped plywood. "Move one easy board," he sniggered, "and the whole thing swings free. See?" A doorway opened, and he waved them through ahead of him.

Dino had said he was leaving a squat. There were two of them against one miniature, albeit wiry, George. Besides, what could the guy hope to gain by rolling two other bums? Then again, George had joked, "I'm from Alaska, where the odds are good, but the goods are odd." Tyler turned to Yuki before they headed down the ramp. "You familiar with the phrase 'bum rush'?"

She shook her head. Then recognition crossed her face, and she pointed a finger skyward, striking her Samuel L. Jackson pose. "'What's in your wallet?'"

"You got it." They reached the bottom of the ramp and stepped through the door well.

"'Time to make the doughnuts,'" she whispered. "'Sometimes you feel like a nut.'"

"'Sometimes you don't,'" Tyler replied, and right now, he didn't. He could smell humidity and mold, and as his eyes adjusted to the dim light, he saw that they were standing in a rectangular, tent-covered cavern. Two walls were constructed of rotted lumber; two of cut-granite stone. Flakes of mortar dotted the floor, but in a testament to the skills of long-dead stonemasons, the stone walls stood plumb and true.

George flicked his lighter and illuminated a makeshift table with a stubby white candle at its center. He lit the candle, and the room flickered in a vanilla-scented glow. He flopped down into a rusted metal chair and rocked back and forth to a locust-like *crick-creak.* He pointed toward a junk pile in a shadowy corner. "That's where Dino hid his important stuff like his passport, oh yeah."

Yuki, who had been working her way around the perimeter, lifted a cast-iron skillet off a nail on a wooden wall. "It's like exploring a castle!"

Creak. Creak. "A man's home is his castle." George rocked on, his head thrown back, his teeth glowing like the Cheshire Cat.

Tyler propped the pipe in an empty corner and whispered in a code that Yuki alone would understand, "'Energizer!'" he said. "'It'll surprise you!'"

Mom's birthday:

> For good or bad, I find myself unable to let go of the past. I see the past everywhere, even in the future. While at first I was really living in the present, now I am almost blind to the present. Dreams of the past or a past-like future act like a cage for my mind.
>
> Perhaps by letting go, I could free myself. Am I afraid to let go? Maybe. Or perhaps the path to fulfillment would set me free. I don't know anymore. Uncertainty is heavy. If I could stop and see the present, I would notice the splash of the waves, occasionally a seagull, and the beautiful pattern of flickering issued by the candles in our granite, cold, cave-like squat.
>
> Being jammed into a forgotten corner of the ningen community has much to offer. We can observe from both close up and from a distance at the

same time. We have magazines and wine. The table is covered with pages of text, many decorated with equations from homotopy theory or by Japanese calligraphy. Textbooks open and book-marked. Stacks of images sampled from boxes of magazines. It is tidy, comfortable.

Like most underground mathematicians, staying alive doesn't matter. What matters is being alive to do math. If you dig it, the art is always with you. If you love it, it loves you back. The people around us remind us of how much we had, how much we've lost.

I wish I were surrounded by plants again. I can't offer a rigorous explanation, but the beauty found in the cold concrete of [an] urban setting can never surpass the wet green walls of the forest. As uncompromising as they both are, in nature I feel a brotherhood with the surrounding life. They are struggling to survive, just as I am. Here, the buses and cinderblocks are ghosts who have given up the struggle. I'm somewhere in between.

Meetings and Chance Encounters

• • •

The days were filled with refuse and dreary occupation. Like prisoners, Tyler and Yuki paced back and forth, expending effort without gaining ground. Then, one night as they stood on Soul Man's street corner, waiting for him to begin his next set, Tyler caught a whiff of what smelled like Easter lilies. He turned into the low-lashed gaze of a strikingly gorgeous woman.

French plaits of auburn hair wound across her tanned forehead. She wore an emerald-green silk suit, hemmed midthigh and snugged tight at the waist. Hints of freckles accentuated her moist, tanned complexion. Taller than Yuki yet shorter than he was, she carried a few extra pounds in all the right places.

"Ah, mon cher," she said and unleashed an ear-pleasing string of unintelligible French.

Tyler tried unsuccessfully to process her words, distracted in part by a spray of silver earrings that fluttered like butterflies along the curve of her shapely neck.

"I am Lilou." She converted to flowing English. "I know everyone who is anyone in Paris, and yet I know almost no one here in Marseille. Perhaps you could direct me to La Cantinetta?" She raised a jeweled finger and wrapped her full, red lips around a thin cigarette. She took a drag, then turned her coifed head to stream out a long exhale. "I'm told it is a fine Italian restaurant, and I am to meet a friend there."

Over the course of Lilou's week-long visit, she and Yuki became inseparable. They window-shopped, sipped wine in cafés, and went sightseeing—all compliments of Lilou. Something about her struck Tyler as too generous, too engaging. French people in general and Parisians in particular were hardly known for their friendly natures. Then again, maybe he was just jealous, as Yuki liked to point out.

Then came time for Lilou to return to Paris. He and Yuki accompanied her to the train station. Tears. Hugs. But before Lilou moved toward the car's opened doors, she turned and pressed a folded paper into Tyler's palm. "I have never met this lawyer, but everyone says he is a man of integrity and skill. A friend of a friend has arranged for you to meet at this address tomorrow at ten o'clock. "*Bonne chance*. Good luck."

A glance at Yuki, and Tyler could see that she had spilled all of their secrets. This woman knew everything. He couldn't breathe. Couldn't move. Unable to wave good-bye, he watched Lilou board. The doors closed. The train rolled away.

As if reading his mind, Yuki opened her arms wide in protest. "See? No one's coning to arrest us. We can trust her."

Too upset to speak, he plowed out of the station, down a street, and into an alley. There he paused to open his palm and unfold the paper, blank but for a single name and address: Antoine Prevot of Fabre, Proulx & Prevot, 266 Avenue du Prado.

A lot depended on this day and the meeting that hadn't yet happened. A lot could go wrong. Naturally, my paranoia was inflating reasonable caution into irrational fears. If our phones had been tapped, they could know everything and be waiting for me in front. I almost took the bus, but didn't because in my anxious state of mind, sitting still at the bus stop was just intolerable. So I walked and walked, marching as a kind of therapy.

Tyler arrived in what he hoped was a nearby neighborhood an hour and a half early. Hopelessly scrutinizing a map and unsure of his location or where to go, he wavered toward the idea of abandoning the meeting that an acquaintance of an acquaintance had supposedly arranged for him. Most likely the attorney would turn him down, just as all the others had. Why take the risk? He was circling the block to return along a different route than he had come when a street sign caught his eye: Avenue du Prado. The law office, street number 266, was across the street. With no time to eat and too nervous to feel hungry, he ducked into a potpourri-scented clothing boutique.

On entering the shop, the tinkle of a bell over the white-and-gold painted door fired all of Tyler's hyperacute senses. He shot behind a clothing rack and then pretended to shop for dress slacks, while he staked out the four-story office building through the shop's picture window.

The limestone structure might have passed for any in the central city of Marseille. Other than two suspicious-looking men in black suits lingering next door, all appeared normal. The men disappeared into a cab and sped away, or so it appeared, so

Tyler rehung a pair of gray merino wool slacks and nodded his appreciation to the storekeeper on his way out.

Feigning casual strides, he crossed the street and ducked through the building's oak-trimmed, plate-glass door. He decided to forego the elevator and, instead, took a set of marble stairs. The higher he climbed, the darker the stairwell became. All he could hear was the shuffle of his own footsteps, so maybe no one was following him. Or maybe his pursuers intended to nab him on a higher floor or in the lawyer's office or…

He charged to a door on the second-floor landing and patted the jamb like a blind man in search of a braille inscription. His fingers found a metal plate, but between the dim light and the French script he managed only to make out the letters *v* and *s*. Maybe the law offices were down on the ground floor? But now footsteps were padding on the tiles below. Ahead, a glow was radiating brighter. He ascended to a third-floor landing and plowed past a guy on a stepladder. Ladder Guy was holding a lit flashlight in his mouth and using both hands to unscrew a spent bulb, or so it appeared.

Up and up Tyler climbed to a locked fourth-floor door with no nameplate. Trapped. No choice but to turn and go back down. He returned to Ladder Guy and squeezed between the ladder legs to the third-floor door. Again, he could feel a doorplate. Again, the letters were too dark to read. Below he heard someone climbing the stairs! Three people occupied the stairwell now. Two against one.

A shifting glow from Ladder Guy's flashlight illuminated the doorplate: HENRI'S COMPTABLES FISCALISTES. "Henry-something fiscal": probably an accountant. Wrong door. Counting on the advantage of momentum and elevation, Tyler sped downward toward the second floor. If the approaching person tried to grab him, he'd ram his shoulder into him and hurl himself down the rest of the stairs. From there he could try to run for the street.

The footsteps were closing fast and only a few yards away.

A Sikh in a turban rounded the stairwell. He looked to be clutching a flashlight in one hand and a bulb in the other as he trudged upward toward Tyler. Could the guy hear his heart pounding? Tyler wondered. Ten feet. Five.

"Bonjour," Sikh said.

"Bonjour," Tyler replied, and they passed like two ships in the night.

Sikh and Ladder Guy launched into the babble of conversation. Then Tyler remembered his headlamp. Duh. He dug it out of his backpack and floodlit the second-floor doorplate: AVOCATS. Yes! Advocates, lawyers. He pressed the button. Almost at once, an entry buzzer rasped, and he experienced firsthand what it felt like to jump out of his skin.

He eased through the unlocked door and stepped into a brightly lit hallway. A few steps to the right, an enormous double door swung open, and a rosy-cheeked, cinnamon-smelling woman with a headful of red hair flagged him inside. A dark-haired thirty-something man who was plowing toward a copy machine halted midstride. Papers in hand, cuffs rolled to his elbows, the guy could have passed for Tyler's older, shorter brother. He took a read on Tyler, inside and out.

"Marco Sosson?"

"Yes," Tyler croaked and, out of reflex, offered to shake hands. "Oui."

The man gazed at Tyler's outstretched fingers and administered a quick, reluctant clamp. "I see you've met Cheri. I'm Antoine Prevot," he spoke slowly, articulating careful English with a hint of a French accent. "Call me Antoine, but you should know that I'm meeting with you only as a courtesy to a friend."

Tyler followed Antoine to an office that was lined floor to ceiling with gold-embossed law journals. A blue, pinstriped suit jacket hung on a filigreed brass coat tree in the far-left corner. Strewn papers crested an empire-style desk on a Persian rug in front of a leaded-glass window. Masculine smells of old books, leather, and a hint of aftershave triggered a Proustian moment in which Past Tyler might have crossed over to mainstream stodginess.

Antoine slapped a yellow notepad onto a round, four-chair conference table, conspicuous for its absence of clutter. "Take a seat," he said.

Tyler slid into an oak chair with his back to the shelved books. He sat facing the door, the barrister seated across from him. "Impressive." Tyler nodded at an array of unpronounceable diplomas and awards on the wall behind Antoine's head.

"That's the point of an ego wall," the man said dismissively. "So you're American?"

"Yes. We spent some time in Corsica before moving here." Great. One question, and he had already blown his Canadian cover. Antoine would make a formidable force in a courtroom.

A rap on the door, and Cheri carried in a silver tea set. Antoine appeared not to notice her and continued to stare at Tyler with a blank poker face. The admin rested the service on the conference table as she unfolded a walnut, Victorian tray table between them. She relocated the tea service onto the tray table and poured two cups three-quarters full. Then she exited without a word, closing the door behind her.

Antoine loaded a cup with cream and sugar. "Help yourself."

"Thanks." Tyler dropped in two cubes of sugar, inadvertently splashing a white linen doily. The scrape of his spoon sliced the silence like a violin bow cutting a sour note.

Antoine savored a slow sip, his gaze unflinching. Eventually, he drummed a gold pen on his notepad and said, "I represented an American five years ago, and the CIA, FBI, NSA—a whole alphabet soup of US agencies—is still crawling through my underwear. Took me six months to claw my way off the no-fly list. Been audited twice. I think they freeze my credit cards every couple of months just for shits and grins. I sure as hell don't need more trouble."

Tyler lifted the cup to wet the desert dunes that were parching his mouth. "Thank you for seeing me."

Antoine pinched his pen upright, and his expression read *Let's get this over with.* "Date of birth?"

This was going just super. A complete waste of time. He should probably leave, except something about the man's question would not be denied. Tyler tried to overlook an itch in his lower back. "2 June 1979," he said.

"Full name?"

Why was everyone so damned determined to learn his name? He could say Engelbert Humperdinck for all it mattered, but he doubted he could pull off lying to this guy. Still, crap was crap, and this meeting was a pile of it. The guy didn't like him and didn't want his case. Trusting Antoine with his real name would put his life and Yuki's in jeopardy. Case in point: Milos. No, he should refuse to answer and put this meeting out of its misery. Except this was the closest he'd come to a living, breathing lawyer. Maybe he could learn some things. Besides, this could be his last chance.

"You do have a name, don't you?" Antoine's expectant gaze demanded a reply.

"Tyler James Johnson." The words hung in the air, shrouded and charged, just out of reach, as if he'd summoned a spirit from a once-familiar book. If he had uttered Sal Paradise or Jack Sawyer or Roland Deschain, would they rattle around the room like shackled ghosts, too? Tyler pressed his backbone into his chair to quiet that damned itch.

"So what is your problem, exactly?" Antoine asked.

Where to start? "I'm a fugitive from the FBI, and I want to go home." There it was. Out in the open. Tyler could almost smell the ectoplasm sliming down the man's ego wall. "I'm willing to serve time in prison, just not my whole life."

Antoine clinked his cup down so hard on his saucer that a porcelain chink skittered across the silver tray. "How did you get yourself into this situation?"

A question he'd considered a time or two. "I came to the California Institute of Technology to major in theoretical physics." Tyler almost blabbed that he had started dating Yuki. No, the plan was to hold off and not mention her unless he felt confident that this guy was safe. "I decided to focus on quantum computation, and my TA in string theory became a good friend."

"His name?"

"Danny Blair. I mean Daniel."

Antoine wrote the name, and his severe eyes coaxed more information from him. "And?"

"Danny's the smartest guy I've ever met. He was a PhD student when I was a freshman, but he skipped several grades in elementary or high school, so we're about the same age."

"Tell me about this Danny."

"Well, he's a real bad ass. Considered the Einstein of our generation."

"So Danny's your teacher and mentor? You look up to him like a hero?"

Where was this going? He appreciated Antoine's pretense at thoroughness, but this game of twenty questions was making him feel itchy. Tyler scratched a thumbnail up and down his spine. "I guess. In our spare time, we used to do physics together, plus we ran long-distance and climbed boulders in the desert."

"So you two shared similar interests?"

Great. Now his heel was bobbing like it had climber's disco leg.[11] "Yes, and we could builder with the best of them."

"'Builder'?"

"Urban climbing. We used to plaster Go Metric stickers all over town to create awareness that America needs to convert to the metric system."

Antoine looked up from his notes, and his dark brows furrowed. "So you two failed to see the merit of measuring distance based on the length of a British king's foot?"

11 A rock climber's term referring to the uncontrollable shaking of the leg(s) while climbing. It occurs as the result of tired leg muscles.

Sarcasm. But humor could be a good sign, right? That sounded almost supportive. Tyler repositioned in his chair to suppress the raging nerve endings in his back and legs.

"Vandalism." Antoine took notes. "Misdemeanor, at worst. Any other run-ins with the law?"

"No." Then Tyler remembered. "Well, yes, my friends and I got busted for swimming in a gravel pit on the last day of seventh grade. The fine for trespassing cost me my savings for a bicycle that summer. Does that count? And then there's the incident."

Antoine scrubbed his face and muttered what sounded like a curse. "Tell me about the incident."

The dreaded, inevitable question. No way this guy was taking his case. Probably looking for fodder to share with his poker buddies—or worse, the cops. The sad truth was that Tyler could barely bring himself to think about that night, let alone talk about it. Except that he'd given Antoine reams of incriminating evidence already. Call or fold, as Grandma J. used to say. "Before I started grad school in New Mexico," Tyler said, "Danny invited me back to Caltech for a sort of good-bye celebration."

"The date?"

"Um, 21 August 2003," he said. "I arrived at his apartment around one o'clock in the morning."

Antoine was writing. "What do you mean by 'sort of good-bye celebration'?"

"Because Danny would have done it anyway—the buildering and stickering, I mean. Calling it a celebration just made it more of a party. Our plan was to use stickers to convince Californians to stop driving their gas-guzzling, air-polluting SUVs."

Antoine's neck craned toward his notes like a dentist honing in on a cavity. "You were going to use more Go Metric stickers?"

"No. Danny's mom works in a print shop, so I gave him two hundred dollars for bumper stickers that read SUVs = Terrorism. The sale of oil finances terrorist activities, you know."

"No, I don't know." Antoine sounded even more annoyed, if that were possible. "You paid for these stickers?"

"Yeah. Danny's always broke. He sent out e-mails inviting friends to his place that night to go buildering and tag SUVs. But the stickers had a typo, so we couldn't use them."

Antoine combed his fingers through his head of dark, bushy hair. "So you became a fugitive as the result of misspelled bumper stickers?"

The thought had crossed his mind. "While we were waiting for other people to arrive, Danny's girlfriend brought out a case of beer, and we started drinking."

"Let me guess. You got drunk."

Tyler nodded. Antoine was clearly a busy man, which was probably a sign of competence. Maybe he was asking questions so that they would run into a second billing hour. "Nobody else showed up. Danny had some spray-paint cans, so we grabbed them and drove around in his car."

"Whose idea was that?"

"Could have been mine. Don't remember. We were drunk and joking around." Tyler's leg was pumping like a jumping bean now, and the arch of his back itched as if it were covered in poison ivy. "Things spiraled out of control, and by three in the morning, we were wasted. Danny went ballistic and threw a

Molotov cocktail through a parked SUV's side window. I went off on him, and he gave me his word he wouldn't do it again."

"When you two were joking around ahead of time, did anybody talk about burning vehicles?" Antoine asked. "If so, prosecutors could argue that it was conspiring."

"No way. Absolutely not. We conspired to paste bumper stickers on SUVs."

Antoine dropped his pencil on the notepad and sat back. "It didn't occur to you to get away from a crazy asshole who was throwing bombs?"

"Maybe. But as I said, I was drunk and he was driving. We ended up at another dealership, where he pulled that stunt again on SUVs and an empty outbuilding."

"How many SUVs?"

"Four were burned. They say we spray-painted 125."

"Jesus." He bit his lower lip. "Anyone hurt?"

"No."

"What were the damages?"

The more they talked, the more growly Antoine's voice became. A couple more questions and Tyler expected the guy might start lobbing loose objects at him. Tyler eyed an etched paperweight and said, "The *LA Times* put the number at between two-and-a-half and five-million dollars."

The muscles in Antoine's jaws rippled. "What you're telling me sounds like a California case. Why did you claim to be a fugitive from the FBI?"

"The SUVs were made in Detroit and crossed state lines to reach California." Tyler was full-out trembling now. Even his voice was shaking. He folded his hands under the table and took a deep breath. "The FBI maintains that damaging the vehicles interfered with interstate commerce."

Antoine shot to his feet, and his poker face cracked as he stormed around the room. "Christ. That's a stretch." He arced an arm. "Why would the Federal Bureau of Investigation want to involve itself in a state's vandalism-and-arson case?"

Inhale. Exhale. "Reports focused on a vehicle sprayed with the letters ELF. I hear the US government considers the Earth Liberation Front one of the top domestic terrorist movements."

The color drained from Antoine's face. "You painted 'ELF'?"

"Danny must have." Tyler was covered in sweat and shaking like a Parkinson's sufferer now. "He's always talking about them. I painted Euler's formula."

Antoine braced his arms on the table and leaned in three inches from Tyler's nose. "Why the...why would you do that?"

Tyler smelled Antoine's hair gel and his tea breath. He wished he'd stayed in Chez Dino. Should have kept doing his math. "Because it's the most remarkable formula in mathematics," he said, then added, "and I was plastered."

Antoine returned to patrolling the room. "You mentioned Molotov cocktails."

"Danny's gas gauge is broken, so he always carries this plastic Tide bottle filled with gasoline in the back of his car." Tyler pressed the weight of his right leg onto his toes, which only succeeded in giving more height to each leg bounce. "He filled an empty beer bottle and yelled that he was going to recycle it. I was too drunk and too stupid to realize what he was talking about."

A knock, and the admin eased herself halfway through the doorway. "Your two o'clock is waiting."

Antoine gave her a blank stare. "If I take this case, the entire US government is going to climb between my sheets."

Cheri settled a knowing gaze on Antoine.

"I'm telling you, no lawyer in his right mind is going to bite into this shit sandwich."

Here it came, the "This isn't a good fit for me" line. Tyler reached for his pack in preparation for Cheri to offer to show him out. No. He sat back. Why make it easy for them?

"What am I supposed to do?" Antoine asked Cheri. "Throw this kid to the wolves?"

Cheri raised her eyebrows and broke into a Mona Lisa grin or smirk or wince. What was going on here? Tyler held his breath for fear of disturbing the superposition.

Antoine plowed his fingers through his hair. "Shit. Block out the afternoon of the ninth for Mr. Sosson." He looked at Tyler. "Will that work for you?"

Did he just hear him correctly? Was Antoine going to help him? "Uh, absolutely," he stammered. "That'll be great."

"Very well." As Cheri pulled the door closed, she dipped her chin and covered her face under a thick spray of red curls, but not before Tyler detected a hint of a grin.

Was he misreading the situation? To confirm, Tyler asked, "So you're taking my case?"

Antoine rolled an acquiescent palm. "What the hell." He rose, signaling an end to the meeting.

"Uh." Tyler stayed seated. "There's another issue we should discuss."

Antoine walked to the window and stared out its leaded panes. "Let me guess: you can't pay me. May not be a damned rocket scientist like you, but I sure as hell saw that coming."

Quantum computational physicist, Tyler wanted to correct him but didn't. "I'll pay you back somehow. Can we run a tab?"

"Right. Of course." Antoine turned to him and flagged his arm at the door. "Now get the hell out of here before I change my mind. I need a couple of days to look into this and brush up on US law. In the meantime, jot down ideas about a resolution you'd like—an agenda, if you will."

Tyler stood. "Thank you." He hesitated again.

Antoine looked about to blow a valve. "What is it now?"

"When you check into stuff, I need your word that you won't research my name or the incident. Internet searches and phone calls would raise red flags to the NSA."

A pained look. Then Antoine blew out a sigh. "Jesus, I hit the trifecta. I take on a client who's in a hell of a mess, flat broke, and trying to outwit the most powerful government in the world."

"Everything electronic is traceable," Tyler said, "and, believe me, the NSA traces it. They tried to recruit me as a code breaker. Snagged my roommate."

This time when Antoine combed his fingers through his hair, tufts remained standing on end, creating a striking resemblance to that poor urban *porc-épic*. "Fine," he snarled. "You're the client. You have my word."

Tyler practically floated out of the building, so light-footed he might have been walking on the moon.

9 December 2004, Meeting two. Once again, Tyler staked out the limestone office building from the boutique across the street, just in case Antoine had changed his mind and alerted the authorities. Feigning interest in his favorite pair of merino wool slacks, Tyler watched a stout man in a rump-hugging trench coat enter the building. An elderly couple and a mail carrier were approaching from the east. The postman took purposeful-looking long strides. The couple held hands, steadying each other. None of them cast furtive glances or bulged in places that might conceal firearms. The wise choice would be to reschedule or cancel, except that Antoine was the only hope, and he was amazing.

"I can give you a good price on those slacks," the straight-backed clerk said, his eyes reading, *Shit or get off the pot.*

Tyler returned the slacks to their spot on the rack and shook his head. "Thanks. Guess not." The tinkling doorbell announced his exit, and he ducked into a stiff breeze. Flipping up his hoodie, he crossed behind a passing delivery truck that smelled of onions. No one approached, so he swung open the heavy glass door. Inside, stale air hung silent. To avoid a repeat of the stairwell fiasco, he slipped into an elevator capsule and pushed the second-floor button. Built to ferry no more than three people and smelling of hydraulic grease, the brass-lined cage clanged upward in slow motion. At last it bumped to a halt. A terrifying pause and the door glided open.

Tyler strode to the dark double doors and pressed the ringer. One, two, three, four, five seconds passed before cinnamon-scented Cheri greeted him with a sisterly smile and led him to Antoine's doorway.

Hunched over his desk, Antoine was scribbling on a ruled yellow notepad atop a six-inch stack of papers. His rolled shirt sleeves indicated that he had been at work since early morning. Cheri rapped a knuckle on the open door, and Antoine continued to write. Another knock and he raised a blank gaze. Recognition filtered in, and he sprang to his feet.

"Marco! Come in." Unsmiling yet perhaps not antagonistic, Antoine tucked the notepad and a file folder under an arm. He migrated to the clear-topped conference table and dropped into his chair. There he opened the file and fanned the corners of twenty or so printouts slathered with handwritten notes. "I looked into extradition," he said, "and tried to find if there are warrants out for you."

Tyler's chest clenched, and he realized how a defendant awaiting a jury verdict must feel. "Any luck?"

"Well, I was somewhat hampered in my efforts."

"Hampered?"

"I respected your request not to conduct any searches that might alert the FBI to your whereabouts." He shrugged. "Didn't really matter. Anything classified as terrorism, they keep very secret—hearings, warrants, investigations, everything."

"There's no way to tell if there are warrants for my arrest, here or in the States?"

"No." Antoine drummed his fingers. "Just so you know, if there are warrants, they never expire."

"So much for deluding myself that this will blow over."

Antoine pursed his lips. "The FBI will make the case that your fleeing the country is an admission of guilt. Even if you could prove Danny instigated the incident, that still would not exonerate you."

"Oh."

"There could be warrants for you in the US but not in France. No way to tell. I suggest we err on the side of caution and assume that there are warrants everywhere."

We. Antoine had said *we.* They were in this together. What a relief. "Makes sense."

"What's on your agenda?"

Tyler dug out his scrap of paper. A glance, and he noticed he'd used the plural, "for both of us." Too risky. He refolded his agenda and clasped it in his palm.

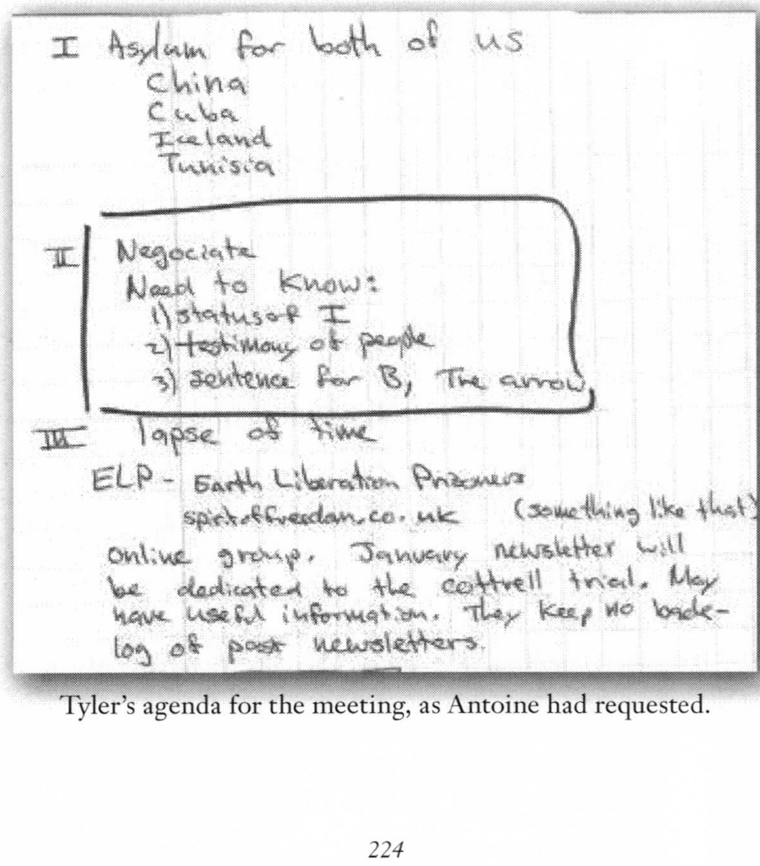

I Asylum for both of us
China
Cuba
Iceland
Tunisia

II Negociate
Need to know:
1) status of I
2) testimony of people
3) sentence for B, The arrow

III lapse of time
ELP - Earth Liberation Prisoners
spiritoffreedom.co.uk (something like that)
online group. January newsletter will be dedicated to the cottrell trial. May have useful information. They keep no back-log of past newsletters.

Tyler's agenda for the meeting, as Antoine had requested.

"I was wondering," he said, "about the possibilities of asylum in other countries, plea agreements, and maybe turning myself in."

Antoine jotted notes. "Your timing couldn't be worse," he said. "After 9/11, charges related to domestic terrorism carry minimum penalties." He pulled a printout from the file folder. "I found a press release from the US Department of Justice on another domestic terrorism case." He read aloud: "'Each count of arson and attempted arson carries a mandatory minimum term of five years in prison, up to a maximum of twenty years. Use of a destructive device in relation to a crime of violence carries a mandatory consecutive sentence of thirty years in prison. Conspiracy carries a maximum sentence of five years. Each count carries a potential fine of up to $250,000.'"

Five years. Twenty years. Thirty-five years in prison. "Consecutive. That means one sentence after another?"

Antoine held his gaze. "Yes."

"What's a count?"

"Each damaged vehicle could be one count. You could be looking at thirty-five years without the possibility of parole and millions of dollars in damages."

Antoine's lips continued to move, but a hum in Tyler's ears drowned out the words. The room faded to musty gray, and his lungs contracted shut. Still, knowing had to be better than not knowing, right? "I can't spend the rest of my life in prison," he managed to choke.

Antoine stabbed his pencil into his pad. "Here in France that offense carries a maximum penalty of three years."

Tyler drew a shallow breath. "I could handle three years."

"It's possible you could be tried here, but the US will take steps to extradite you." Antoine pushed back his chair and strode to the window. Hands on his hips, he stared through the leaded glass. "Your best option for now is to stay in France while I work out a plan to fight extradition when the request comes."

Antoine knew what to do. He had it all figured out. "Whatever you suggest," Tyler said.

Antoine examined a row of gold-embossed law books. Then he paced back and forth in front of the diploma wall. "You can't stay in the city. You'll be caught and extradited."

Tyler couldn't bear to sit, so he stood, too. His knees wobbled as if they might crumple, so he braced himself on the back of his chair. He and Yuki had discussed how they dreaded the idea of spending the holidays caged in Chez Dino, but the prospect of venturing onto the streets felt even more distressing. The colored lights, the ringing bells, Christmas music—all were painful reminders of the family time they were missing and how they were trapped in a world not their own.

Thinking out loud, Tyler said, "We were tossing around the idea of spending Christmas in Paris."

Antoine snapped to a halt. "We?"

Shit. Should he do this, expose Yuki? She had said to lay it all out if he trusted this guy. "Yuki," he said. "She's Japanese. She fled the States with me."

"Japanese?" Antoine scrubbed his chin. "Any chance she has dual citizenship? She American also?"

A deadbolt twisted in Tyler's gut. "No."

Antoine blew through his lips and picked up his pace. "Foreigners aren't subject to US protections. At the very least, they'll consider her guilty of aiding and abetting. They could ship her off to Guantanamo Bay as an enemy combatant. You wouldn't be able to verify she's there, let alone get her out."

"We figured," Tyler said, his voice half whisper, half squeak. He cleared his throat. "That's the main reason why I let her come with me." As he uttered the words, he felt the truth leak into his consciousness. Central to his decision to flee the country was his need to protect Yuki. Innocent as she was, her affiliation with him put her at the greatest risk of harsh repercussions. This monster threat of Guantanamo had turned the tide against his coming forward. It had washed away all options but one: to become a fugitive.

Antoine circled around and took Tyler by the shoulders. "Spending the holidays in the City of Lights, that's a good choice. They are used to tourists there."

"Paris it is, then," Tyler said, unsure how to respond to Antoine's grip.

Antoine released him to lean over the conference table and take pencil in hand. "Give me your address, phone number, and e-mail. I'll contact you when I learn something."

Well schooled in evading this sort of request, Tyler trained his gaze on the window and said, "I'll give you a call."

Antoine appeared to lose himself in his notes. "If I need to contact you or if there's trouble, we'll use a code name for you. How does Mario sound?"

He liked this guy more and more. "Good. Sounds good."

"After Paris, it's best if you return to Corsica." An amused grin, maybe fondness, crossed Antoine's face. "People in that region take a relaxed approach to the law. They'll ask few questions."

Return to Corsica? The thought of a chance encounter with Milos or Little Bear twisted Tyler's gut into a knot. He put on his scientist voice. "It's a small island. I get the feeling word travels fast there."

"Ah, true!" Antoine's chuckle warmed the room. "Still, it's the best place in France for you."

Antoine looked as if he were about to cue him to leave, so Tyler gestured toward the desktop computer on the hand-carved desk. "I don't want to trouble you, but do you have an online account for ordering books?"

Antoine grinned and bobbed an index finger at his pregnant shelves. "My wife calls it *la compte plus regrettable*—the 'most regrettable account.'"

Tyler heard himself chuckle: a sound from the past. "Would you mind ordering a few books? I'll reimburse you."

Suspicion crossed Antoine's face. "Books?"

He dug out his list and handed it over. "Algebra and chemistry mostly, and a biology book for Yuki."

Antoine studied the titles before walking to his computer and tapping a few keys. He waved Tyler over and stepped aside. "Put whatever you like in my cart, but brace yourself. Shipping may cost more than the books themselves."

It took only a moment to locate the titles: *Probability Theory: The Logic of Science* by Jaynes, Szabo's *Modern Quantum Chemistry*, and Miller's *Biology*. Antoine was right about the shipping. Tyler counted out four-hundred-dollars worth of euros and offered them to Antoine. "Merci beaucoup. This means a lot me."

Antoine waved him off. "You keep that."

"I want to pay you."

He smiled. "Consider it a gift."

"I'd like to pay. Really."

"Please." Antoine's voice turned firm and inarguable. "I insist. You mentioned that your grandfather served in France during World War II. Consider it a token of appreciation for the immense debt we owe him and your family."

Family. Tyler bit his lower lip to stem an emotional tide. Failing to think of a better word, he ground out, "Merci."

Antoine leaned over his appointment book. "Let's meet again before you go to Paris. How's the twenty-second work for you, say, ten a.m.?"

Tyler felt sheepish, ashamed. "My calendar's open."

"Okay. I'll see you then, and bring Yuki. I'd like to meet her." Antoine studied him. "You look starved and sleep deprived."

Tyler reached out a moist, trembling hand to shake goodbye. "I'm fine."

Antoine brushed it aside to grip Tyler's shoulders and peck both cheeks. "In France we bid hello and adieu like this."

Overwhelmed, Tyler moved toward the door. "The twenty-second it is. Ten o'clock." He turned to Antoine. "I don't know how to thank you."

"You can do that after we get you through this." Antoine looked somber. "For now, just take care of yourself and Yuki."

What unworldly forces had led him to Antoine? Tyler could only guess. But he felt grateful with all his heart.

Tree Alone in the Forest

• • •

Tyler and Yuki slipped out of Chez Dino under cover of predawn darkness. Yuki applied bright-red nail polish under a streetlight. Then Tyler waited for her outside a McDonald's for forty-five minutes. She emerged wrinkle-free in her red-satin blouse, black slacks, and heels. Her coiffed hair brushed across her shoulders in a shampoo-scented swish. Tasteful makeup accentuated her enormous brown eyes, and she walked with a spring in her step. Pale, yes, too thin, yes—and drop-dead gorgeous.

"You sparkle like a Christmas angel," he told her.

She put on a pair of sunglasses and rocked her head backward, pretending to play piano. "'Oh yeah,'" she sang. "'She's irrepressibly lovable, unsurpassably colorful and intimately soulful. You've got the right one, baby.'"

"'Oh yeah,'" he Ray-Charlesed back at her.

She pulled off her shades, and her brow wrinkled. "What if he does not like me?"

"Not a chance."

ANTOINE'S OFFICE FELT LIKE HOW A SAFE HOUSE probably felt to a spy coming in from the cold. Antoine gaped at Yuki then recovered with friendly two-cheekers. "Thank you for coming."

"Nice to meet you," Yuki replied, barely audible.

Antoine handed Tyler a box labeled LIVRES. "Merry Christmas," he said, revealing a set of straight white teeth. "Judging from its weight, they filled your whole order."

Unable to wipe away a goofy grin, Tyler hugged the treasure box to his chest. "Thanks."

Antoine led them to the conference table and motioned for them to sit. "What do you know about Daniel Blair's situation?" he asked.

Tyler shook his head and set the box on the floor between his feet. "Nothing, really. We're afraid to run any searches. We know he talked to the press until he signaled for me to run. Then he got caught."

"Well, a friend of a friend found some information on him. Did you know he's serving an eight-year sentence for conspiracy to commit domestic terrorism?"

Tyler felt a wave of relief. "That's a long time, but he'll have his life ahead of him when he gets out. Maybe they couldn't make the charges stick."

Antoine knitted his fingers on the table. "Danny got off light because he laid the blame on you."

Tyler shot back so hard in his chair that it rocked onto two legs. "No way. He wouldn't do that."

Antoine rolled his tongue under his lips. "Danny's attorneys are appealing the case," he said. "They claim he has Asperger's syndrome."

Tyler looked at Yuki, and she shook her head. "We…we don't know what that is."

"It's a form of autism that makes people unable to read social cues. The attorneys claim you manipulated him into committing the arsons."

Tyler felt the room close in. "I don't know about Asperger's, but it's nuts to think I manipulated Danny. Nobody manipulates that guy."

Antoine paused. "You were free. He was stuck in jail and facing life in prison. It's not uncommon to blame the party who's at large."

Tyler's heart sank. "This means if I come forward with the truth, it'll show that Danny perjured himself."

Antoine nodded. "That's right. Your word against his."

"If I prove I'm right, then I'll be responsible for sending one of my best friends—and the Einstein of our generation—to prison for life."

"I wouldn't look at it that way if I were you. He shouldn't have lied."

Tyler thought he might vomit.

Antoine broke the silence. "After Paris, where are you planning to stay in Corsica?"

This sounded like a meeting's-over signal. Tyler scooped up the box and stood. "I'll check my e-mail once a week in case you contact us."

Yuki slipped a warm palm under Tyler's arm and said, "Nice meeting you."

"We'll be in touch." Tyler couldn't stop cradling the box like a baby, so he reached around it, unsure how to initiate this cheek-pecking procedure. "Thank you, again."

Antoine moved his eyes from Tyler to Yuki and back. "My family's ancestral home is in a village on the western side of Corsica," he said. "I ran the idea past my brothers and father, and we would like you two to stay there through the winter."

A glance at Yuki, and Tyler realized his jaw had gone slack, too. "Oh, uh." No way they could afford a whole house. "Thanks, but no. We appreciate the offer, though."

"No charge." Antoine held up a picture of a two-story stone home that might have served as a set for *Braveheart*. "You'll be doing us a favor. It's empty all winter, and we could use house sitters. My father's place is next door, so he'd like you to keep an eye on that, too, if you don't mind. He moves in first during the spring, and our whole family joins him in June. We spend summers there."

"Uh...um," Tyler said, dumbstruck. "I...I suppose we could."

"Good," Antoine said. He jotted something down on his notepad. "After Paris I suggest you take the ferry from Nice to Ajaccio on New Year's Eve. Staffing will be minimal then. You can take a bus to Porto where I've arranged for my friend to pick you up at the bus station." He tore off the sheet and handed it to Yuki as a doctor might pass a prescription to a patient. "It's all there—the address, the dates and contact information."

Visibly shaken, Yuki held out the paper for Tyler to see. He grasped it with both hands. In addition to an address, dates and times, it contained a name, Jean.

Antoine lifted his suit jacket off the hall tree's curled brass hook. "You hungry?"

The question shot hunger pangs through Tyler's belly. "We're good," he said, and he caught a whiff of strawberry scent as Yuki's hair swayed side to side.

"No," she declined. "But thank you very much."

Already at the door, Antoine appeared not to hear them. "Well, I'm starving. I hope you won't make me dine alone. My treat."

Speechless, Tyler returned the precious paper to Yuki for safekeeping. They trailed Antoine to the elevator, to lunch, and someday, maybe, to a new life.

Christmas in Paris.

> 25 December 2004. We nest in the heart of the colony, in the so-called capital, with a most up-close and personal view of the ningens. They live in a dirty and noisy world, but for all that can be said against it, it has something very magical about it. It glows in the dark, and what magnificent colors!
>
> The ningens organize their colony much like their own bodies. There is a small but important nervous system that dictates the operation. This central nervous system has a large brain, where most of the computation takes place. But unlike the body, the capital is also a center of most functions of the superorganism.

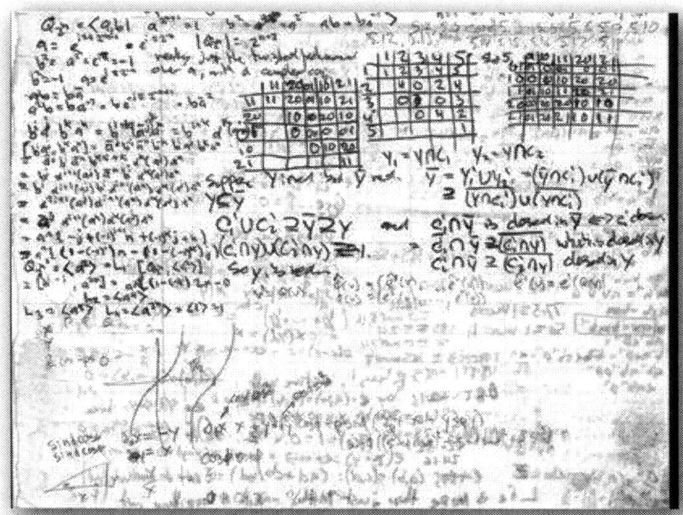

While he and Yuki nested in the heart of the human colony in Paris, "with a most up-close and personal view of the ningens," Tyler occupied himself with math.

28 DECEMBER 2004. THE BRIGHT LIGHTS were supposed to be cheery, the hubbub exciting. But Tyler had never felt more alone and isolated, so distant from his family. One way or another, before leaving Paris tomorrow, he had to find a way to let his family know that he was all right—well, alive anyway. But how to contact them without arousing the attention of the FBI and revealing his location? He had an idea.

Last Christmas at home—an unfathomable thirteen months ago—Kelsey had rattled off three grad schools where she had applied. He couldn't recall the universities, but she had been debating whether to specialize in oceanography, volcanology or geology. Given her stellar grades and GRE scores, she would have had her pick of schools. When he'd joined the physics department at the University of New Mexico, they had issued him an email and website address, plus a physical mailbox for snail mail. Good chance other departments in other universities would do the same.

Tyler purchased an envelope from a tourist shop. He slipped into an Internet café, reserved an hour, and took seat at a quiet corner table. If Kelsey had decided to pursue oceanography, she would have gone to the Massachusetts Institute of Technology. He Googled "MIT Woods Hole." No reference to Kelsey. Arizona State led the field of volcanology. No Kelsey there. That left geology. Penn State was the leader in that field, but that wouldn't work: she got her B.S. degree there. Running out of time and losing hope, he keyed in "University of Michigan Geology Department."

Bingo! "The Department of Earth and Environmental Sciences is pleased to welcome Kelsey Johnson." Her name, underlined in blue, indicated she had a website. He moved the cursor to click on it but stopped. No, better to wait and do that just before exiting the café.

Fingers trembling, he scrolled to the department's contact-information page and addressed his envelope: Department of Earth and Environmental Sciences, c/o Kelsey Johnson, University of Michigan, 2534 C. C. Little Building, 1100 North University Ave., Ann Arbor, MI 48109.

Toggling back to Kelsey's website address, he clicked on it and counted the seconds as it downloaded onto his flash drive.

Must leave now. Right now. Except a photo caught his eye. His extended family, gathered at the homestead farm, held aloft a giant poster board with messages handwritten to him.

"We love you and miss you. Please take care of yourself and come home soon. Love, Grandma."

"Every day we think of you and miss you. Love you. Amy and Terry."

"Love you always and totally. Be good to yourself. Love, Mom and Dad."

"Take care of yourself, bro. Love you, Kelsey."

Cousins Bryan, Kimmy, Dane, Randi, Mallory, and Alaina wrote, "You're in our hearts." "Come home! We miss you and love you. Be safe." "Miss you, Tyler." "Thinking of you! Much love!" "Miss you, and we'll always be praying for you."

Blinking back tears, he scrolled to a picture of Kelsey shouldering a bear rifle atop an Alaskan mountain. She had summered in the Alaskan backcountry, helping with another PhD student's structural-geology research. What was this? On 4 September 2004, while sitting on a cabin porch in Cantwell, she had written him a poem.

Ode to Tyler

...I thank you for existing,
for being someone I can defenseless-
ly love so thoroughly that your
loss caused me to suffer.
Both my respect and suffering for you
have catalyzed enormous growth in me.

You inspire and prompt me to realize my own passions,
to become aware of my strength,
resilience and character.
You are my greatest teacher, of the highest caliber.
You are my greatest friend.
I thank you.
I remember you.

A wetness in his eyes was fuzzing out the letters, and the website had finished downloading. Tyler pocketed the flash drive and stepped onto the lonely street. Trying to pull himself together, he stumbled to a park where he drafted a letter. In the hope of conveying a thousand inexpressible sentiments, he enclosed a photo of him and Geen Doorgang. Then he headed for Paris's Charles de Gaulle Airport.

In the hope of conveying a thousand inexpressible
sentiments in his letter home, Tyler enclosed
a photo of him and Geen Doorgang.

Light was the word to describe Terminal 1. Skylights honeycombed the ceiling and framed sunlight into parallelograms that stretched like liquid pools across the marble floor. Invisible cameras were no doubt tracking his every movement, and software was trying to pinpoint his facial markers. Tyler snugged his baseball cap low and made his way toward a wall of glass on the far end of the terminal. An arriving passenger enfolded what Tyler assumed to be her parents in a tight farewell hug. Squeals of delight echoed all around as sons and daughters, mothers and fathers, grandmothers and grandfathers filled separation's holes with details of their lives.

Dear Kelsey, Mom & Dad,

Sorry to miss your graduation, Kelsey, but so happy to see how well you are doing. You really make me proud. It wouldn't be possible to ask for a better little sister. I wanted to say Merry Christmas to you, Mom & Dad, and the whole family. It would be nice to have some news from you. I'm doing fine, good health and all that. Please don't worry about me. That goes especially for you, Mom. I'm sure I've put you through more than anyone could deserve to endure. Sorry wouldn't be enough, but I'll say it anyway. I'm sorry. You all are forever on my mind, and I look forward to the day when we can be reunited as a family again. I wish I could be there to spend the holidays with you. Nowadays, all I've got are tears that can't dry and wishes that can't come true. I love you all very, very much.

Love,
Tyler

Outside the envelope in the spot where a return address should go but could not, Tyler wrote the symbol for *Tree Alone in the Forest*:  If the FBI intercepted the letter, the symbol might prompt them to hunt for him in China. Kelsey, Mom, and Dad wouldn't be able to write back, of course, but they were sure to find someone to translate the Mandarin. They'd want to understand his state of mind, and this symbol captured the heart of it.

Tyler found a college student standing in a café line. Charming Yanna with his smile—and five euros—he elicited her promise to mail his letter when she landed home in Belgium.

On his return to Chez Dino, Tyler shared his joys with Yuki and showed her the pages of Kelsey's website. Out of curiosity and aching to reach through time and connect with his sister, he checked his journals for the date Kelsey had posted her ode. To his surprise, he had also made an entry on 4 September 2004:

> Our mountain path lasted a fortnight and passed through a number of forests, separated from one another by sterile rocky landscapes typical of the high altitudes. Despite the season, patches of snow lingered on, slowly changing color under the action of living microorganisms. The only real colors that managed to break from the bland silence of this space came from a deep, purifying lake. We passed a quiet day along its cliff-lined shores, absorbing the water's cold reflection.
>
> The lake, maybe younger than the mountains, seemed more willing to speak its wisdom to patient, chap-lipped vagabonds:

Stillness and Silence.

Cool ripples pass on their own.
They aren't pushed.
The past is real.
The future doesn't always begin in the present.

I couldn't tell if the cliff was waiting to fall, but it certainly wasn't in a hurry. That night the stars glowed and danced as if stolen from the New Mexico night.

Then came the storms.
Then passed the storms.

He, too, had written poems, perhaps at that very moment as Kelsey was writing *Ode*. He wrote in the margins of his journal.

On the same day, Yuki and I were setting off on foot toward the mountains, leaving behind a village of stress and exploitation. The road started with a steep uphill climb to a sunset over the valley. We dined on lentils from a can, potato chips, beer and fresh air. Sunsets frequently stand for the end, but this one marked the beginning of what I later called the Age of Optimism.

Yes, he remembered the day. The skies were clear overhead, so he and Yuki had pressed on, replenishing their provisions in Corté and following the River Restonica up a long, winding ascent. Standing above the swaying pine tops near Mount Rotondo, he had listened to the river's meandering headwaters burble through scrub brush and over scattered rocks. Canyon walls varied in steepness and height, sometimes stretching to sharp spikes or towers. As if unwrapping a surprise gift, the walls had pulled away to expose a giant bowl of grassy plains.

As Tyler read on, he saw that he, too, had been thinking about Kelsey and the family:

> The stream lost its way on the equipotential[12] and dizzily wandered about. We named this wonderful place, the Palace.
>
> It's hard to say when,
> and maybe when doesn't matter.
> But I can see the fam here
> with picnic tables filled with food,
> lawn chairs and well-told stories.
>
> I can see the happiness on their faces
> and hear the laughter, theirs and mine.
> Dad's smile, Kelsey's laugh, Mom's
> bellowing war cry-
> all real,
> only a little misplaced in time and space.

12 In the field of hyperphysics, equipotential lines are like contour lines on a map that trace lines of equal altitude. Equipotential lines always run perpendicular to the electric field. In three dimensions, the lines form equipotential surfaces.

A broom can't sweep dust out of the air.

Shaking and about to break down, he noted in his journal:

> It had been a long time since I'd lost communication with loved ones, but the desire to express moments and places doesn't fade fast. When things are hard, the mind can busy itself in the struggle for survival, a technique which proves its worth in terms of practicality but cannot be considered more than a temporary solution. Constructing and persisting in illusions inescapably produces long-term discontinuities, and I had heaps. Sifting through the strings in my head was about as productive as cleaning one tar-covered chopstick with the aid of another.
>
> Uncertainty from lack of information is a curious form of torture. I hated not knowing what was happening back home. Helpless in all respects except to imagine, deaf and blind to the passings of the world where I belonged. Yet worst of all, I was dependent on my torturer for protection. It was the uncertainty that saved me from the most painful news. As cruel or unforgiving as my speculation could be, it didn't have the power to kill. Holding it back was its inability to CONVINCE. Like waking up from a nightmare, one can argue it away as not real. But this last resort, my final defense of ignorance, could evaporate as fast as the hated uncertainty could collapse.
>
> A circular business.

Tyler and Yuki bid farewell to Paris, took a train to Nice, and boarded the sunset ferry. On 31 December 2004, it glided into Port of Corsica-Ajaccio and docked, three hours late. Tyler locked his jaw to suppress a yawn as he schlepped the flimsy suitcase down the gangplank behind Yuki. They headed for an open-air bus station about a hundred feet away. "The morning bus to L'Abri is long gone," Tyler said. "Next one departs in six hours."

Yuki sagged. "We will never catch Antoine's friend now. He'll think we're big flakes."

They had walked only a few steps when a grainy voice to Tyler's right asked, "Marco? Yuki?"

Tyler turned and came nose to nose with a face full of salt-and-pepper whiskers. "I thought you might take this ferry." The man's lips parted to an engaging smile. "I'm Jean, your ride."

The two-story, Old-World manor resembled an overexposed photo—drained of color, monotonic except for dark-purple shadows that cupped like black eyes under its windows. Tyler felt all too close to the Ajaccio crowd, which probably explained why he imagined the mortar between the fieldstone walls changing to slime and oozing into the home's interior. He surged with guilt. He should feel grateful for a roof over their heads. Yes, he was grateful. Enough of this silly sense of dread. He unlocked the door and put on a smile.

"Peace at last," he said and gripped the patinaed brass handle to swing open the oak door for Yuki. "No more lugging our stuff all over." He followed her inside and dropped their bags, allowing a moment for his eyes to adjust.

Meanwhile, Yuki darted across the living room and turned on the lights. "Ooh, electricity! Beautiful fireplace!" She flitted into the kitchen and whooshed curtains open over a sink. Tyler heard a splash. "Hot water!" She ran upstairs and called down, "Three bedrooms! A shower!" A door thunked closed, and Yuki materialized at the head of the stairs. She held up a vacuum cleaner like fisherman displaying a trophy marlin. "No more dirt!"

The front and back doors rattled under a wintry blast. Window jambs tunked back and forth, and a frigid gust washed over Tyler's cheeks. He nudged a throw rug under the door sweep with his foot, yet a fresh blast swayed the room's brass chandelier. Shivering now, he checked the perimeter. No heat registers. Behind an interior door, he found only a closet—no furnace.

No problem. The massive fieldstone fireplace that adorned most of the living room's north wall could easily heat the whole house. He opened a cabinet door to a built-in woodbox. Odd, it sat empty except for a few cobwebs. Tyler ran his fingers inside the hearth and found the damper's lever. It wouldn't budge, so he slid out the firewood grate and scooched on his back to look up the chimney. Yes, light was shining down the flue through a grapefruit-size opening, so the damper was open. He reached up and touched thick, black soot.

Yuki returned rubbing her upper arms. "Stop playing with the fireplace. We need to turn on the heat. It is freezing in here."

Tyler slid out and stood upright. "I don't think anyone's wintered here in years," he said and smudged soot between his index finger and thumb. "Place isn't weatherized for year-round use."

Her eyes scanned the perimeter. "Where is the thermostat?"

He head-pointed to the fireplace. "Right here."

She ran a hand over its stately, cream-colored mantel and jabbed a finger into the hearth. "Okay. 'We bring good things to life.' Now."

Tyler understood her eagerness. Two days of travel on scant food and sleep, and now the cold was making their teeth chatter. But she had no clue about the care and feeding of a fireplace. "The thing about chimneys"—he moved his fingers apart, like pulling taffy—"is that they use the fire's heat to draw out smoky air. They have to be kept clean, or soot builds up and chokes off the draw. A clogged fireplace can fill a house with smoke in minutes."

"I am cold and tired. Do not lecture me about stuff." She marched into the kitchen, and Tyler heard the roll of one drawer opening after another. Yuki emerged with a faded newspaper. She smacked a packet of matches into his palm.

He showed her his soot-covered fingers. "This stuff's highly flammable. It can turn a chimney into a giant torch."

She yanked a used tissue from her pink jacket pocket and covered his fingertips. "Good." She retrieved the newspaper and began to tear its pages into strips. "More heat. Start fire, will you?"

Careful not to touch his fingers to her jacket, Tyler braced the heels of his palms on her shoulders and forced eye contact. "Yuki, a chimney fire can reach enormous temperatures in a flash. It sounds like a tornado and can burn a house to the ground."

She threw off his hands and flopped into a high-backed rocking chair, pumping it back and forth like a marathon bicyclist nearing a finish line. "Are you telling me no fire?"

He hesitated. "You don't want us to burn down Antoine's ancestral home, do you?"

She rocketed to her feet and planted her arms akimbo. "You're so smart. How do you plan to keep us from waking up frozen?"

He drew a breath to explain that if they died of hypothermia, neither of them would wake up, frozen or otherwise. Maybe this wasn't the time. Instead, he said, "We'll have to block off as much outside air as we can and maximize the thermal and solar heat."

She hugged herself and paced to the kitchen and back. "This is no stupid theory of thermal physics. This is real—real, real cold."

He found a sheet in an upstairs linen closet and tacked it over the stairwell to block warm air from rising. An oak harvest table stretched almost the length of the kitchen, so he pulled out a chair and sat down to write out a list. "You interested in making a trip to the store? We need a roll of plastic, toilet paper, thumb tacks, and painter's tape."

She snatched the paper. "And food. We need food."

The door slammed, and she was gone. He stared after her for a moment and then fiddled with the flue until it finally scraped closed. By draping a blanket from the mantel he slowed the draft, and toilet paper served well to plug gaps around the front door.

Yuki returned and set two bags on the counter. Together they cut pieces from the plastic roll and covered the windows. Unfortunately, the wrap also blocked a good share of sunlight and solar heat, plus any view of approaching lawmen.

"No good," Yuki said, her words slow and slurred.

Hypothermia was setting in. Desperate, Tyler turned on the electric oven and opened its door. "Just for a few minutes," he said, "to take the edge off."

The room warmed and grew dark, so they turned on a kitchen light. Yuki set about putting away the groceries. "To celebrate New Year's," she said, lofting a bottle of wine for Tyler to see.

THE HANDS ON THE GRANDFATHER CLOCK in the living room were ticking toward eleven o'clock when Tyler had an idea. He dug two blankets from a closet and handed them to Yuki. "Drape these over the harvest table so they hang to the floor, okay? I'm going to grab us some rocks."

"Why?" she asked, unfurling a blanket. "What are you doing?"

"You'll see." He darted out the front door and, next to the road, found a couple of flat, plate-size stones. These he carried inside and washed clean. He turned the oven on and placed the rocks on a low rack. "Soap stones," he explained. "My grandmas used to warm their beds with these when they were little girls." In a few minutes, the stones felt hot to the touch, so he wrapped them in towels and placed them inside their makeshift hut. He climbed underneath and lit a candle.

"Come on in," he said.

Yuki crawled into their flickering abode, and they sat basking in radiant heat as the clock chimed twelve times. Then they shared a long kiss, and Yuki raised her glass in a toast. "To Antoine and his family."

"And to hope for the upcoming year." Tyler pulled her close, and she rested her head on his shoulder. Warm and content, Tyler closed his eyes and felt Yuki fall slack with sleep. Thus, they welcomed in 2005.

THIS JANUARY COLD SNAP was feeling more like an ice age. Tyler pushed away from the table and dropped to do another thirty pushups. Once he felt somewhat warmer, he re-draped a blanket over his head and shoulders and returned to his math. Yuki was kneading bread dough on the counter behind him. Kneading and kneading.

"Yeast must have warm air to rise," she muttered. "This is going to freeze to an ice cube."

A rap on the front door shot an electric charge down Tyler's spine. "Go! Go! Go!" he rasped as he grabbed their packs and ripped the plastic off the back door in preparation for making a mad dash to the mountains. Yuki peeled up a corner of the front window's plastic to peek outside. If she nodded, he'd open the door. If she bolted toward the back exit, then he'd shove the sofa to block anyone's entry and follow her out.

Yuki rubbed at the window and whispered, "Too frosty."

Great. After all their practice drills, when it came to the real thing, they fell apart. "Who's out there?"

"Nobody," she whispered, "but I think they left something."

Tyler knelt next to her and cleared a patch on the frosted glass with his thumbnail. There on the doorstep like the proverbial baby in a basket sat a giant black trash bag. A bomb? A Trojan horse? Or, sometimes a trash bag was just a trash bag. Minutes ticked past, and the bag neither wiggled nor exploded. Tyler eased himself outside and untwisted the tie. Then he felt his face flush. "It's loaded with old clothes."

Yuki joined him in rummaging through the sack. Then she stood upright. "The villagers must have noticed our shivering." She raised a hand in thanks to unseen and, no doubt, watching eyes. "They took pity on us."

Tyler slung the bag over his shoulder and faced the gravel road. He wanted to heave the sack onto the frozen gravel, to stomp on it and strew it across the road. He fought an urge to howl *Fuck you!* at the top of his lungs and to drive a fist into Stone House. Instead he stood there, just stood like some damned deranged Santa Claus carrying a shiny black bag on his back. He felt the burn of the neighbors' judgment, heard the slap of their wagging tongues. *That poor, destitute couple*, they were probably gossiping. *They can't even clothe themselves.*

"They think we're a damned charity case," he said, loud enough for any listening ears.

Yuki smiled through gritted teeth. "Don't be an asshole." She held open the door. "Come inside."

Bag on back, Tyler stood firm, searching for hidden, judgmental faces. He thought he saw a curtain move. Then he dropped the bag on the stoop and walked inside. Yuki followed, toting the bag.

The rest of January passed colder and darker. Twice, Tyler picked up his journal. He ought to write something, he knew, but no words came. Cloaked under layers of secondhand clothing, itching in humiliation and nervous energy, he sat and did math or slipped unseen from Stone House to explore the terrain around L'Abri.

At a later date with clear-eyed hindsight bolstering his spirits, Tyler wrote of this period as an introduction to his journals, or "Tome," as he had begun to call them.

> It doesn't really matter why I write. All that is supposed to count is what I write, and there are a lot of worthy things to be written. I'm not gifted in the art of making up stories, so I will stick with what I know, just tell it how it is, what I've seen, experienced and done.
>
> Theorems. Probably the worthiest of all expressions, I've written many a theorem. There was a time when that was all I did, theorems, exercises and math. I wrote so much, and we were so poor that there wasn't enough paper. I covered the insides of all the cardboard food packaging, mostly from cheap cookies, and filled a stack of neatly unfolded boxes with tiny mathematical scribbling.
>
> These were the good old sad times, back when I was still myself, the me from before, more or less unchanged. In a way I lived the ideal then, my time free and dedicated to math. Great nature

exploration hikes started just outside the door. I'd trot off to climb around in the woods, mountains and valleys, wearing my gray wool V-neck woman's sweater, found in a Marseille squat we named Chez Dino. Dino was a Kiwi Rasta man, living on the streets with his African girlfriend he'd met in Israel.

I had all this with my cheap cookies, calculated as the best calorie to cent ratio, other than pure colza[13] oil. We lived, or at least let the time pass, alone in a giant stone house. Miserable, especially for her. I could escape into my world of mathematics where painful matters couldn't touch pure abstraction. Concentrating for hours every day without stopping, I explored a fantasy world of ring theory, Galois fields, R-Modules and Abelian groups.

Yuki sat thinking about all we had lost, about our lives, dreams, family and friends lost, our future a dark horror. She slowly starved herself on specialized diets, based on her food allergies. We didn't talk much. Fought often. Would pass weeks or months without making love.

I can't remember.

Relentless and obstinate, I required myself to finish every exercise at the end of each chapter in my *Abstract Algebra* book. Most problems were easy, but sometimes I couldn't find the solution. I

13 Colza is a comparatively nonodoriferous, yellow and nondrying oil obtained from the seeds of Rapeseed. In France, especially, its extraction is an important industry.

once spent nineteen days stuck on a problem. From morning until night it migrated in my mind. I worked on it in my dreams, trying and retrying different approaches.

Then victory.

I was so happy to finally break it that I wanted to spin in delight, to shout the solution to the whole world.

Yuki glared at me disdainfully.

These were the times when I held the ideals, the dreams and passions from before. I had lost much on the outside, but I was still the same Tyler on the inside.

Thus, the winter curled into the fetal position and slipped into hibernation.

Construction

• • •

Yes, Yuki's idea to build a tree house was a fine idea—a place of their own, away from ningens in a wilderness watchtower. But where could Tyler build a livable home in a tree in a safe and invisible location? What design should it take? No way could they afford to buy construction materials or tools. First things first: must find a location.

For nearly all of February, Tyler examined a map and conducted reconnaissance. At last, he narrowed the options to three sites. The first and closest would be fairly easy to show Yuki, except her extreme diet and allergies had left her frail, without energy, and in a constant state of apathy.

Finally, one drab day, she threw up her arms and said, "Fine. No more nag-nag-nagging. Let's go."

They began a modest climb into the forest and followed a trail of dark, soft soil along a babbling creek. The beauty of the site appeared to impress her, at least moderately. Then she waved a dismissive hand. "Too close. Too well traveled."

His thoughts exactly. "Want to go to Potential Site Two?"

She shrugged. "If you want to."

"I do," he said, and soon they were walking along a horizontal trail at a canyon's *bocca*, its mouth. A climb up a steep hill and they reached Site Two. Tyler put on his sales voice. "You can't see L'Abri from here."

She pointed in its general direction, off by sixty degrees. "It's too close."

"Yeah, but we could create secret access, so it has both positive and negative characteristics."

She swiped a raised thumb sideways like a baseball umpire calling an out. "No water. No good." Then she added softly, "I guess we can spend the night if you want to."

She was open to camping. That had to be progress. Maybe. Tyler threw up the tent and gathered fallen sticks and limbs for a fire. The sun eased toward the horizon, and they sat on a silent peak, watching the sky turn orange and pink. The evening passed wordlessly as Tyler tossed branches onto the ever-waning flames.

Tyler woke to blue skies and the scent of bread toasting on campfire rocks. He sat down to enjoy the toast with hot tea as Yuki moved about packing, obviously in preparation for heading back to Stone House.

"You know," he ventured, "I could show you Site Three today."

"We need to get back."

"Why?"

She spread the dusty white coals with a twig before rendering the campfire lifeless with sand and stones.

"Site Three's a full day from here," Tyler pressed her. "The hike could be fun."

"All right." She shrugged, anything but all right.

Before she could change her mind, Tyler lifted her pack as well as his onto his back. As before, they powered up a steep climb. By taking breaks every few hours, they managed to hike all day. Dusk was settling like a silken web over the area when they followed a path to its end and cut across steep, dangerous terrain. Before them a flat, grassy area nestled among an array of rocks.

"These could be chairs." Tyler sat to demonstrate. "This could be our patio."

Tired and no doubt hungry, Yuki rolled a shoulder.

The splash of an invisible waterfall serenaded the scene. "Hear that?"

"Water," she said, her voice flat as a Euclidean plane.

Tyler stood to point out a noble ridge. "Look up there."

Jutting from rocky crags on the side of the mountain—in defiance of wind, rain, and gravity—a mighty oak stretched toward the skies.

Yuki stared in silence.

Tyler pointed across the canyon. "On my first exploratory mission, I crossed the creek and observed that tree from the almost-inaccessible cliffs on the other side. Then I checked from below, and it's only visible from the top of a big rock, deep in the maquis."

She ran her eyes over the terrain, thinking, maybe even intrigued.

"The last time I was here," he added, "the air filled with light snowflakes and a magical drizzle. Even with just my sweater from Chez Dino, I didn't feel cold." He opened his mouth to explain how the angle of the canyon must have served as a windbreak from a northwesterly wind. No. If she wanted to know why, she would ask.

She turned ninety degrees and studied the landscape. She rotated another ninety and another and another until she came full circle. "This amazing place fights cold," she whispered, awe in her voice. Then she broke into a winsome smile. "Yeah, we could live here."

Tyler tucked an arm around her waist, and together they surveyed the scene.

First priority: Create secret access. From L'Abri, a narrow, abandoned-looking path led partway to Future Site of Tree House. To verify its privacy, Tyler hid in a patch of bushes before sunrise like a deer hunter on opening day. At 9:15 a.m. a shepherd, called a berger in French, herded a flock of sheep onto the path and trekked upward. Come four thirty and the woolly mammals clattered back down, their berger in tow. Next day, same pattern. Alternative access required.

Across the river, jagged terrain and thick, spiky bushes discouraged traffic of any sort. No one would discover a secret trail there, so Tyler and Yuki set about moving rocks and hacking through the impenetrable maquis. At the end of the day, with their long sleeves in tatters and their hats rimmed in sweat, they congratulated themselves on carving fifteen feet of secret trail, complete with an invisible entrance. They christened the section "Beginning."

They cleared fifteen or twenty feet each day, before the underbrush thinned. Where they spooked a wild horse, the segment became Horse. A dusty goat path became Dirt. Only Wall, which ran along an ancient stone barrier, welcomed them with minimal angry thorns and passable ground. Thus, their project evolved into seven phases:

1. Beginning
2. Horse
3. Dirt
4. Wall
5. Field
6. Pipe
7. High

TODAY, AFTER LONG HOURS OF TRAIL-BREAKING across Field, Tyler and Yuki were making their way down the mountainside toward Stone House. As usual, they varied their route to avoid attracting attention and to increase their odds of coming across construction materials. Fast-food wrappers, bottles, soiled diapers, magazines, tires, and tin cans lined the road, but they managed to scrounge a few scraps of wire, an empty milk container, and twenty feet of cracked hose. Too bad that lumber was conspicuously absent because lumber was what they needed most.

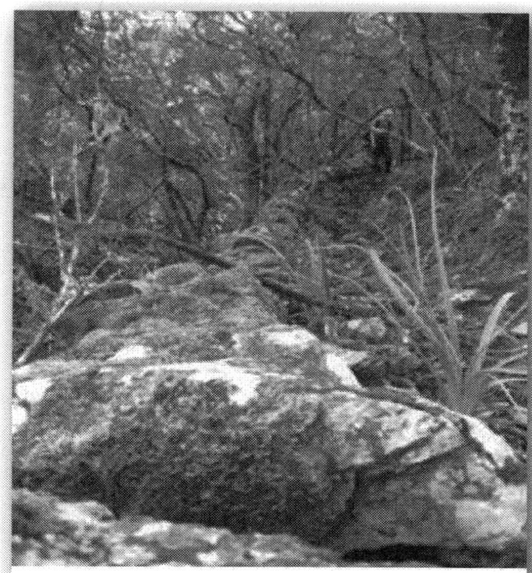

Tyler along "Wall"

They decided to head for Stone House to shower away their itches and layer on clean clothes, so they bore left at the outskirts of L'Abri. Just past the trailhead to the berger's path, they cut through a vacant, overgrown lot that would have been totally flat but for a cluster of weeds that mounded upward like a hairy brown mole.

"That's odd." Tyler pointed to the weedy bump. "The rest of the area lies flat."

"Um hum." Yuki trudged on.

He angled over and poked his foot into the knotted mass. His toe struck something hard, and he recoiled at something long and gray. A snake? No, the thing wasn't slithering away. Tyler leaned in and touched a woody object. He wedged his fingers underneath it. "A board!" he called, lifting. Reedy foliage was binding it to the ground, so he gave it two hard yanks. A plank swiveled upward, bringing with it a wall of boards and plant life. The air filled with the scent of soil and roots. "It's a whole pallet!" he called to Yuki, now standing just outside the mound.

"Is it any good?"

He brushed off the dirt and debris. "No sign of rot. Looks like solid oak!" Another foot probe, and he found a two-pallet stack. "Jackpot!" he called as he tipped one on end.

"I found one, too!"

Yuki, surrounded by tall weeds, stood with her arm raised like the Statue of Liberty. Instead of holding a torch, she was pointing skyward.

Walking one corner forward and then the next, Tyler moved a pallet to a clearing of sandy soil. "Four for the floor," he said, practically giddy.

Yuki sidled up and nodded toward a row of buildings. "Careful. People can see us."

Rats. Commercial buildings with second- and third-story apartments faced them on two sides. Tyler detected an aroma of chai and honey. Residents were returning home from work and relaxing over hot cups of tea. Barely moving his lips, he ground out, "We can't leave this pallet exposed. Someone will take it."

Yuki's shoulders curled inward. "What do we do?"

He nodded toward a clump of bushes on the far side of the berger's path.

"Let's stash it over there. I'll take the front. You take the back." He gripped the pallet with both hands behind him. Yuki picked up her end, and they marched toward the footpath like two ants toting a precious peanut husk.

With twenty feet to go, the tinkle of a bell stopped them in their tracks. A lead ewe clacked onto the street in front of them. Then the flock followed single file down the berger's path with their knit-capped herdsman bringing up the rear. He fixed a suspicious gaze on Tyler and prodded a straggling lamb with the tip of his shepherd's hook. The spindly-legged creature bleated and jounced forward.

Tyler nodded hello and shifted direction toward a rusted garbage container. If the berger responded, his gesture was too subtle to discern. "We're just good citizens," Tyler said under his breath to Yuki, "disposing of trash."

Berger and his woolly entourage disappeared around a corner, sparing Tyler and Yuki the charade of heaving the pallet into the container and later having to retrieve it.

"The sun is at four thirty." Yuki giggled from behind. "What were we thinking?"

Tyler inhaled the fragrance of rough-hewn oak and chuckled. "A tragic result of overconfidence." They stashed the pallet, then returned under a blanket of darkness to relocate it to Beginning's thicker brush cover.

Early in the morning, they resumed clearing Field. To avoid another chance encounter with Berger and flock, they returned at late dusk. Taking advantage of the dim light, they snatched a second pallet and toted it to safety without incident. By 9:00 p.m., they had liberated all four oak treasures.

Next day, Tyler and Yuki applied their finely honed techniques to rummage through the rubble of a demolished building. Amid broken concrete and drywall, they discovered a trove of oak two-by-fours. The following evening, they rescued a metal cable and a half-dozen boards that had actually fallen off a truck.

> Even the nails were taken from the wood and recycled, plus a half-dozen boards we found one by one along the side of the road-abandoned or just forgotten by construction workers.

Given enough finagling, discarded table forks served to pull nails from scrap wood. Rocks made decent hammers, despite their maddening propensity to smash thumbs. A shredded roadside T-shirt worked well to wipe off dirt and grime. To ensure that the staging pile behind Beginning's bushes remained small and inconspicuous, Tyler and Yuki advanced their payloads upward along each newly cleared section of trail: a long and tedious process.

Then there were the pesky varmints. While most creatures remained at bay during daylight hours, they rallied in force after dark. No matter how high on branches Tyler suspended their food—no matter how large a stone he placed over protective pits—mice, wild boars, and unnamed beasts of the night breached his defenses. What the four-legged marauders missed, spring rains and ice runoff saturated.

One morning, Tyler and Yuki returned to find their precious food stocks both shredded and soaked. "Shroaked," Yuki said in summary.

Did she know that wasn't a word? No matter. "We're shroaked," he agreed.

Next morning, after a night of torrential rain, they were walking parallel to a drainage ditch on their way to Beginning. The rising waterline was about to crest the riverbank, and Tyler saw why. Just ahead, a logjam of tree limbs and rubbish was blocking the flow. Among the hodgepodge, a blue object floated like an oversize fishing bobber.

"Looks like a cooler," he said as he sidestepped down the bank. Almost at once, he lost his footing and slid hip deep into the churning brown gravy. "Cold!" he gasped.

"'Help!" Yuki giggled. "I've fallen and I can't get up.'"

He slogged to the intact-looking container and called back, "Must have rolled off a tourist's tailgate last night." With Yuki's help, they lugged the cooler to the road. Inside, they discovered a loaf of bakery bread, sandwich meat, cheese, and chips. Though half an inch of clear water sloshed on the bottom, the bagged items all rested dry and undamaged atop a jar of Grey Poupon, two apples, and a bottle of expensive-looking red wine.

They drained the water, and Yuki dried off the mustard and apples. As she squared up the bottle's loose label, she read, "Beaujolais. Georges Duboeuf."

Tyler extracted a shrunken, dripping bag labeled *Glace.* "Ice," he said. "Could be the container doesn't leak, and that water's just melted ice."

Yuki tore open the sealed bag of potato chips. "Feel sorry for the people who lost it." She munched a giant, curled chip.

Tyler sank his teeth into a plump, red apple. "Be a shame to let this go to waste."

"That would be wrong." Crunch. Crunch.

"Just wrong." They finished their snack, and Tyler hefted the cooler onto his shoulders. The two strode down the road and turned onto Beginning. On arrival at Future Site in a little over two hours, they feasted on deli-meat sandwiches with cheese. Tyler raised a plastic cup of water in toast. "To present abundance, and in tribute to times of hardship."

Yuki tapped her plastic cup to his. "To abundance."

Full and content, they set about a long day of clearing. When their labor was done, they polished off the last of the container's perishables. Then they selected a pair of west-facing rock chairs and sat down to watch the sunset. Yuki opened the Beaujolais and poured two plastic cups. They sipped the luscious liquid as the sun eased over the horizon.

Moving quickly to take advantage of the remaining light, Tyler transferred their pasta, bread, Speculoos, and, of course, Spirito cookies from his backpack into Blue Cooler. He snapped the lid shut and laid a hand on its white, rippled top.

"Blue Cooler," he said, "tonight you face the test of battle. May you fend off Grendel and nature's brigands."

Yuki patted Blue Cooler as if it were a faithful dog. "'Take a licking and keep on ticking.'"

They headed downhill.

Next morning, they finished the last section of trail and arrived to inspect Blue Cooler. Its plastic lid bore scars of critter teeth, but its contents had survived intact. "I'll haul up the rest of our stuff and make a ladder rope tonight," Tyler said. "Tomorrow we can start building Tree House."

"Then tonight I will finish our lounge," Yuki said and trooped down to the waterfall.

> Below by the waterfall, Yuki constructed a beautiful lounge and kitchen by the fire pit with a view between the pools, the trees and the vines. The sounds of running water and shade made it an ideal place to read.

19 April 2005. Tyler lay awake, vacillating between anticipation and concern. He'd worked out the architectural design and rechecked each of his measurements. All the materials were staged where they needed to be. Yuki worried him, though. While she seemed willing, she possessed neither the strength nor the confidence to scale imposing heights, and he wondered if she understood the risks. He pulled out his journal and wrote.

> An injury in this remote location with our political situation would spell sure disaster.

Yes, he had better caution her. "We need to be *careful*," he emphasized. "If one of us gets hurt, it'll be hard to reach a hospital, and they'll want to see ID's. We should only go if we're on the verge of death."

Yuki pointed toward the granite cliff and Noble Oak that jutted out from it. "One false move and splat." She made a nosedive gesture.

Okay, she got the drift. "Ready to build us a tree house?"

"Of course."

"All righty then." Tyler led the way up the cliff along winding, natural steps. At one point, he and Yuki were almost within arm's reach of the tree's upward-shooting trunk. But as they climbed higher, the gulf between them and the tree grew wider. Soon they came to a giant boulder whose flat edge protruded to within ten feet of a massive near-horizontal limb that was to serve as tree house's main support beam. To Tyler's left, six water jugs and a coiled turquoise hose nestled close to the cliff—right where he had placed them in preparation for today. He picked up a lump of limestone and tapped two pre-marked *X*s on the boulder.

"Our floor joists will span between this rock and that limb," he explained. "I'm going to go back down and carry two-by-fours up the tree. I'll drop an end over to you, and you anchor it to the center of an *X*." He tapped the middle of an *X* where the lines intersected.

Yuki gazed at Tyler's markings. Then she peered out at Noble Oak. A breeze swayed the outstretched limb, and its branches scuffed the rocky mountainside like long-nailed fingertips. "I hope you know what you're doing."

"Me, too." The tree looked to be almost close enough for him to leap out and grab—if not for that pesky twenty-foot abyss between the mountainside and the trunk. Despite telling himself not to look, he risked a downward glance. The jagged rocks below gaped up at him like shark's teeth hungry for his flesh. Yesterday, when his plan was more fantasy than fact, the deadly gap had struck him as intriguing, maybe even exhilarating. Now, with the prospect of implementation at hand, "exhilarating" wasn't exactly the word that came to mind. "Foolhardy" seemed to fit better.

He studied the rope ladder. The contraption he'd braided from scraps of twine and so confidently secured to the main support limb, now dangled limp and puny. It looked about as sturdy as tree moss.

"I'm going down now," he said, sounding far from the nonchalant he'd shot for.

Yuki pursed her lips and shook her head.

"Going to carry the two-by-fours up the ladder," he said, as much to convince himself as her. "You wait here, okay?"

"I do not know about this." She pointed to the tree. "You call that Noble Oak—letters *N.O.* Bad sign."

Tyler left her muttering to herself and wended down the rock steps to the base of the tree. The two-by-fours and metal cable lay exactly where he'd staged them. A finger of breeze swayed the ladder, and its lower rung brushed across his thigh like a spider web luring him to climb aboard.

He draped the looped cable over his shoulder and broke into a nervous chuckle. "Here goes nothing," he called.

"I have a bad feeling about this," she called back, "very bad."

He picked up the longest, straightest two-by and climbed onto the bottom rung. The ladder jittered under his weight but held. With considerable effort, he carried the board up to the support limb where he wedged it and the cable into crooks of the tree. Hopefully, they wouldn't shift loose and clobber him on the head. After descending and hauling up the second two-by-four, he scrambled on top of the limb and clamped his legs tight around it. Panting and wet with sweat, he lifted a board and balanced it vertically.

"Stand back," he called, feeling like a plate juggler.

Yuki stood on the boulder almost eye level with him but twelve feet distant. Her face looked puckered with worry. "Do not drop that thing on me, okay?"

"Remember. Don't reach out. I'll drop it and you can slide it into place."

Yuki ducked behind a rock. "Better not smash into me."

"Here it comes," he called, and let the board tip toward the mountainside. At first, the two-by-four barely moved, but it steadily gained speed and momentum.

"Aahh!" Yuki covered her head.

Whack! The tip slammed onto the boulder, six feet shy of cracking her skull. The whole two-by-four reverberated like a rocker's drumstick and nearly rattled him out of the tree. "You okay?" He called as he rebalanced on his lofty perch.

"You trying to kill me?" She crawled out on her hands and knees and dragged the board's end to the center of the far *X*. "You're one crazy son of a…" Her voice trailed off.

"One more." He hefted the second board to vertical, and this time Yuki disappeared behind a more distant battery of rocks. The board fell hard and bounced almost into place.

Yuki emerged to slide the tip onto the second *X*. "Tie your ends now," she commanded in a shaky yet proud-sounding voice. "Be done with it."

"Not yet," he said. "These are our floor joists. They have to be leveled, or the floors will never lie flat." Those were Dad's words. Tyler recalled them from long ago when he and Dad had built a playhouse. How odd to hear them coming out of his own mouth. "Can you toss me an end of that hose?" he asked.

"Why?"

"I'll show you. Hang onto the other end and be careful not to let the weight knock you off the ledge."

Grousing in Japanese, Yuki hefted the coiled hose hip high and stepped on a loose end. "Get ready." She swung back with her whole body and let fly. The turquoise loops unfurled toward him like a striking rattlesnake. The tip flopped over the joist and began to slither off.

Tyler stretched outward and caught hold of the nozzle. He sat upright and called, "Now, hold your end at the top of the board and fill the hose with water."

Yuki didn't move. "Why?"

"Because water is isotropic."

"What?"

"Water at rest seeks pressure equilibrium," he said, trying to muster the patience to explain the obvious. "In fluid mechanics, the state of an isotropic fluid is defined by its mean mass per unit volume or density, its temperature, and its velocity."

"Dear God."

How could he put this? "Think of the hose as a *U*. The height of the water in each arm of the U depends on the water pressure, so it'll flow from side to side until the pressure equalizes. Water wants to minimize its potential energy."

Still, she didn't move, and she was looking less confused and more annoyed each moment.

"It's a basic principle of statics." He heard condescension in his tone and couldn't help it.

She grabbed a jug and poured the water in. "Can't you just say they will be level?"

An odd question. "You asked me *why*, not *what*." He sensed that she was fighting an urge to yank the hose and topple him out of the tree, so he fell quiet and held his end at a height where he guessed was close to level. "Now hold the nozzle of your hose at the top of the board and fill the hose to overflowing."

"I'm getting all wet."

"This won't take long. That's good. Now fill it to the top. I'll move my end until you tell me your water is resting at the top."

"We could be done by now." She filled the hose again.

He moved his nozzle lower. "Can you see the water?"

"No," she moaned, "and my jug is empty."

He crimped his end. "I'll wait while you refill it."

22 April 2005: Tree house floor made of salvaged pallets and leveled with water in a hose.

She dropped the nozzle, and a stream of water must have doused her feet because she yelled, "Stop it!" She snatched the end and toted it with her to the water jugs. Carrying two milk containers plus the hose, she returned and leaned over to refill the hose. "My knees hurt."

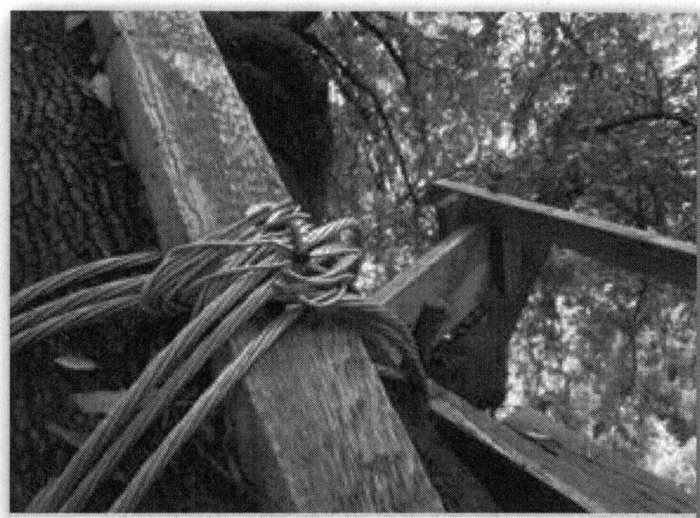

Securing Tree House with scavenged metal cable.

"Almost done." He moved his board higher. "Now you want your water to mound with surface tension."

"No, *you* want tension. This is heavy."

"Do you see any water yet?"

"No." She splashed in nearly the whole gallon.

"Surface tension, not overflowing."

"Stop yelling at me."

"I'm not yelling."

"You are, too."

"Am not."

"Are, too."

By a miracle, the water in both ends reached its mark, and they leveled the two-by-four. Tyler strapped his end to the limb using the cable, and they repeated the bumpy process to level the second joist and all four points of the frame. This brought satisfied smiles to them both.

22 April 2005. The tree house was an evolving project with new additions and plans appearing ad hoc. We were limited by the pallets, which were reconstructed to provide the floor. Additional supports were made from logs lying around and held in place with recycled string.

One edge of Tree House bounced under threat of collapse, and unfortunately, it protruded over the most dangerous drop. Yuki bobbed a warning finger at Tyler. "Stay away from that edge."

Not an option. "I need to slip down there and shore up that floor," Tyler said.

"Right." Yuki rolled her eyes. Then it seemed to dawn on her that he wasn't kidding. "No way."

"If something's worth doing, it's worth doing right." There it sounded again: Dad's voice. He enlisted Yuki's help, and they gathered branches and leafy debris into a pile at the base of the potentially bone-crushing drop.

Yuki assessed their creation with a glow of pride. "Fall now, and you'll land on a soft mat."

The cushion, probably twelve feet thick, would certainly do the trick if it were in the right spot, which it looked like it was. "Sure will," he said and proceeded to fashion a support beam from a freshly fallen, four-inch-thick deadfall. Once he had stripped off its branches, he carried the weighty pole up to Tree House.

"There is no need to do this," Yuki insisted.

"I'll be fine," he said as he knotted a makeshift rope harness under his thighs. He tied a looped rope to his waist and eased under the jouncy floor to hang suspended. "Okay!" he called, smarting under the pinch of the harness.

"Here it comes." As Yuki pushed the knotty support beam across the floor and over the edge, it sprouted over Tyler's head like Pinocchio's elongating nose. "It's very heavy!" she warned.

He swung back and forth, extending his reach and preparing to grab the log that was now slowly pivoting toward him. "Steady," he said softly. "Easy does it."

"Really heavy!" Yuki groaned. "I'm not sure I can hold it."

"Just take 'er easy. Eeeeasy."

"Look out!" she screamed.

The log was swinging downward, whipping toward him. He braced, and saw-toothed knots ripped through his hands and up his arms. Bark dug into the soft tissue of his thighs, and the log whammed into his chest. A high-pitched whine rang in his head. Time slowed. He was swinging and clinging and spinning. Pain: searing, burning, teeth-grinding pain. The log was propelling him toward the rocky cliff under Tree House. Depending on his spin at impact, he was either going to crash backward onto the rocks and sever his spinal cord, or his arms would strike first and snap like twigs. Either way, his weight and momentum would probably break the rope. Thank goodness for the leaf cushion.

A glance and Tyler yelled, "Shit!" The brush pile lay to the right, far short of his trajectory. "Hold, rope. Please hold." Wind thundered in his ears. Blinding pain shot through his head.

Somewhere in the muffled distance, Yuki was screaming, "Tyler!"

Frame by frame, he spun toward the razor-edged rocks. Then his shoulder thwacked, and he jarred to a dead stop. Absolute calm. He hovered weightless, crunched against the rock wall and unable to breathe. Slow as an expanding sponge, he and the pole-log began to swing outward. Then they were sailing away from the cliff. Yes! The ropes were holding.

Whirling, twirling, soaring, he filled his lungs. An unearthly "Aaaahhh" rang in his ears. "Aaaahhh" The howl was coming from within him. He managed a breath and then the involuntary howl resumed. A joyful noise. The taste of blood.

"You okay?" Yuki screamed. "I could not hold it!"

The drop from Tree House.

Tyler clung to the swinging pendulum like a barnacle. Forth and back. Back and forth. "Aaaahhh." He gasped a breath and managed to squelch another howl. Everything burned—his cheeks, his head and hands, his arms and legs.

"You are bleeding!" Yuki cried.

"Bleeding's good!" he gasped. "Means I'm alive." Working through the pain, he maneuvered the deadfall into place and managed to secure it with the rope strapped to his waist.

"Why didn't you let go of that stupid log?" Yuki called down to him as he began to inch upward to safety, his fingers so swollen they were barely able to grip.

"Didn't think of that." He winced.

Yuki helped pull him up top, and Tyler leaned against the tree trunk, his legs too shaky to hold him. She stood staring at him, growing paler by the second. Then he saw why: his hands and knees were oozing blood and swelling to monster proportions. He smelled of sweat and blood.

Yuki head-pointed toward Lounge. "You need to soak those cuts." She wrapped her arms around his waist and helped him hobble down the stone steps to the pool. "Good thing we had that leaf cushion," she said and spread a blanket for him to lie on.

Tyler recalled the woefully inadequate, nowhere-close debris pile, and he imagined him or Yuki asleep and rolling off the floor's edge. "I'm thinking we had better expand that cushion," he groaned, "in case it's ever called on to serve."

Past Meets Present

• • •

24 April 2005. Yuki straightened from her yoga warrior pose. "Tree House would be perfect if we had Geen Doorgang here. He would love it."

Her words took a moment to penetrate the ring theory dancing around in Tyler's head. "My hands and legs are almost healed," he said. "Let's go fetch that dog."

He had seen Yuki in high gear before, but never like this. She had both bags packed and hers snugged to her back before he could put on a clean pair of socks. Since Stone House was on the way, they could check on it and fill up their water bottles before heading out.

They reached Stone House in an hour and a half. "We go in, refill, and leave," Yuki said. "No dilly dilly."

"No dilly." Tyler inserted the key and turned the knob, but as he opened the door, a subtle *swish* made his skin crawl. The fireplace looked fine; the living room and kitchen were unchanged. Yet something was off. A legal-size envelope behind the door caught his eye, and written on it in thick black ink was the word Mario.

Tyler's feet were nailed to the floor. At his side, Yuki stared down at the envelope. It bore no address, no stamp, only one word, Antoine's code name for him, written in Antoine's flowing, hurried hand.

"We shouldn't read too much into this." Tyler stooped to pick it up, vaguely aware that Yuki had closed the front door and was locking the deadbolt.

She bumped him with her elbow. "Are you going to open it?"

He ran an index finger under the flap and removed a single folded sheet of printer paper. *Need to speak with you. Please give me a call.* The room darkened and closed in.

"He's trying to warn us!" Yuki's voice rose to a squeak. "They're coming for us!"

A distinct possibility. "We won't know until we call him." Tyler tried for calm but missed the mark. "We need to get out of here." He strode to the kitchen to fill the water bottles. Think. Must think. "Let's continue on to the Desert des Agriates to find Geen. We can get there on back trails and call Antoine from a pay phone along the way."

Yuki grabbed his now-full Nalgene and tightened the cap. "How many pay phones do you think we'll find along backcountry trails?"

The maleficent, sweaty swamp creature that usually crouched in dark corners and rumbled in thunderclouds was creeping closer, making its move. Tyler felt lost in the tall weeds of a nightmare. He was flailing and running, trying to take flight from the fiend at his heels. Its rank, desiccating breath was frying his brain from the inside out. No, he could hardly blame Yuki for questioning his thought processes.

"I'm just saying." He topped off her water bottle and rummaged in a drawer for matches. "We should keep to the trails and go into towns only to use a pay phone." The coherence of his words surprised him. He let the robot inside take over. "They'll assume two people on the run will head west to a ferry or airport, but we'll go east and circle north. That'll also give us the advantage of knowing the terrain—some of it anyway."

Yuki jammed a book, three calligraphy pens, and a large ceramic ashtray into her backpack. "Oh, God. Not again. I cannot do this again."

The wall clock read 9:48 a.m. "Antoine could be at his desk now. Let's call him from the pay phone at the grocery store before we leave town."

Yuki was trying to squeeze a couch pillow into her pack, but as she pushed in one corner, the other tip popped out. She alternated punches faster, harder. Whack-a-mole. Pound. "Get in there!'" She pounded.

Tyler caught her fist midflight and pressed it to her side. He pulled out the pillow and ashtray and returned them to their rightful places on the end table and sofa. "They like it better here," he said and zipped up her bag. He took her hand and led her out the back door.

They zigzagged down blocks and vacant alleys. The pay phone was empty but in full view of passing motorists—and law enforcement. Tyler dug out his emergency prepaid phone card and pressed the access code.

"Thirty minutes remain on your card," an automated message warned him.

Tyler dialed Antoine.

"Fabre, Proulx & Prevot," the cheery admin said through the handset.

"Hi, Cheri." Tyler cleared his throat to cover the quake in his voice. "This is Mario. Antoine asked me to call."

"Mario?" A pause. "Oh, yes, I'm sorry. He's in court today. May I have him return your call?"

"No, thanks. I'll try later."

Tyler ushered Yuki eastward up a well-traveled shepherd's path. Lost in his own thoughts, he bolted past a flock of grazing sheep. They passed the Fango River and its sequence of pools. Then snowcapped Monte Cinto, the island's tallest mountain, rose to the northeast. As they proceeded north, the mountain appeared to inch south until it towered ninety degrees to their right. By 3:00 p.m., the great mountain stood watching over them from the southeast. They arced northwest, and it disappeared behind them. Still, they pressed on and reached the outskirts of Galeria around five thirty.

In a daze, Tyler turned off the trail into a thicket. He dropped his pack onto a patch of grass. He longed to sit down but felt too tired to risk it. "I'll go find a pay phone," he said, "and bring back some water and food."

Yuki slid out of her pack and crumpled to the ground. "I'll wait," she rasped.

He found a booth on a busy street corner. "Twenty minutes remain on your card," the card's female voice chided.

Five rings, and Cheri answered. "Oh no! You just missed him." She sounded worried, as if she feared the fates were aligning against him. Maybe they were. "Mr. Prevot very much wishes to speak with you," she said.

Tyler bit his lip. To ask would be stupid, really stupid. Cheri might not know to guard her words. She could blurt out anything. But any risk would be more tolerable than this uncertainty. "Do you know," he whisper-croaked, "why he needs to speak with me?"

"No, I'm afraid I do not."

"Think it's urgent?"

"I don't know about urgent, but he's most insistent to speak with you. Would it be possible for you to call back tomorrow? His calendar is open between four and five p.m."

"Insistent," she had said "most insistent." Good news was "exciting," maybe even "eager." It was never "most insistent." Bad news—knife-in-the-gut news—well, that could be insistent. They were screwed. "Uh, sure. I'll call then. Thanks."

Grayish-orange cars streaked past, their engines growling like hounds on the scent of a rabbit. That couple across the street: Were they window shopping or watching his reflection in the glass? Dust choked his windpipe. His lips tasted of chalk. Too bad his Nalgene was bone dry.

Tyler snugged his hoodie around his baseball cap and took a circuitous route to the public fountain. The spigot took its time dribbling fluid into his Nalgene, and he drank it empty as Yuki's red bottle slowly filled. His toes wiggled, anxious to propel him forward, backward, anywhere except town, but he managed to refill his Nalgene. A quick trip to a grocery store, and he bought bread, crackers, and a jar of Speculoos. His feet carried him to the campsite as if of their own accord.

Tyler and Yuki rose in the predawn light and angled north along the trail. One step in front of the other, they walked hour after hour. Tyler lowered his gaze from the skies to the hills to the ground just ahead of each footfall. Though she wasn't complaining, Yuki's blisters had to have blisters, too. A nearby clock tower was chiming three o'clock as they limped to an isolated beach outside Calvi. A phone booth nested under the terra-cotta roof of the Santa Maria hotel, so Tyler lifted the handset. A dial tone buzzed.

"It works," he said, "but we have an hour to kill before I can call Antoine."

"Let's go to the beach," Yuki sighed, and soon they were lying on the sand and soaking their sorry feet in the sea. Yuki flopped onto her back and groaned, "March of the penguins."

He rolled onto his back and let the tide massage the throb out of his legs. "We can't miss this call," he said and drank in the cool, salty air.

"No, we cannot," Yuki slurred.

"Probably okay to rest our eyes," he said, "just for a minute."

"Um hum."

Tyler bolted upright at the touch of a cold, wet nose on his cheek. A rat-size dog tucked a bony tail between its legs and scurried to an elderly woman wearing an oversize, flowered scarf. A full moon was bathing the beach in blue-gray light. Way past five o'clock. "Damn!"

The woman waved her apologies and stooped to collect a seashell. "Bitsy, leave those young people alone," she said in English.

A whiff of lavender bath powder reminded Tyler of Grandmother Johnson. She liked to collect seashells, too. Not long ago, he had walked with her along the sugar-white sands of Florida's Coquina Beach. Together, they had collected tiny pink shells and listened to gentle, Gulf Coast waves just like these. An ocean away, yet worlds distant.

Yuki rubbed her eyes. "What time is it?"

He wouldn't have bothered to answer, but her fingers prodded the sore spot in his shoulder where tungsten pins still smarted from a snowboarding accident, also long ago, also worlds apart. "Too late," he said. "We'll have to try tomorrow."

"Better reach him then." She yawned and fanned sand out of her hair. "Or we will have to wait all weekend."

"I know that," he snapped and regretted his tone at once.

They hustled to a public bathhouse and returned to a pair of rattan chairs outside the Santa Maria. There they feasted on spreadable Belgian-cookie Speculoos on crackers and sat in silent contemplation. Household lights switched off as the moon climbed across the sky.

"It's irrational," Tyler confessed, "but I feel closer to Antoine just being near that pay phone."

Yuki made a face and said, "That's dumb." Then she added softly, "Me, too."

"Can't sleep here."

"No."

"Back to the beach?"

"Okay."

They migrated toward the calming roar of the sea and selected a pair of lounge chairs in a nook outside a sleepy bed-and-breakfast. Tyler stretched out in the dark, while Yuki launched into a rambling tale of how sea-monster tails caused the splash of waves. Somewhere between her description of their blue-black fins and their insatiable hunger for human flesh, a blanket of sleep plugged his ears.

Tyler woke to the chatter of staff arriving for the nine o'clock shift. A few jiggles, and Yuki opened her eyes. They hit the bathhouse and beach. Then he tried the phone again.

"Ten minutes remain on your card."

Tyler punched in the number.

"Antoine Prevot," the voice answered.

Tyler's heart skipped a beat. "Bonjour. This is Mario." His voice sounded gravelly, as if disguised through a voice-changer gadget. "What's up?" he asked. Yuki was pressing in close, so he held the phone for her to hear.

"I hope I didn't worry you," Antoine said, sounding relaxed and friendly.

"Oh, no," Tyler said, all coolness. "No worries."

No worries? Yuki mouthed, then wagged her head. "Really?"

"Well, I was thinking," Antoine said. "Without being able to look into your situation, I've reached a dead end. I was hoping not to show up empty-handed when my family and I arrive on the seventh. Do you have any suggestions as to how we might move forward?"

That was all? No boogeymen around the corner? No CIA or Mossad? No gendarmes in hot pursuit? Antoine just wanted advice on ways to proceed? Tyler wanted to dance and whoop at the top of his lungs. He stared straight ahead and said, "Uh, yeah, sure. Mind if I contact you in a few days?" Antoine would know that by contact, he meant that he would write.

"That'll be great."

"Thanks. Thanks for—"

The line went dead. The card had timed out. Tyler settled the handset onto its hook and joined Yuki in doing their—albeit tender-footed—happy dance. "Come on," he said. "We're buying breakfast. Then we have letters to write and a leisurely walk Home to find Geen Doorgang."

Yuki nodded and then furrowed her brow. "Just because he does not tell us they are after us does not mean they are not after us."

She was right, of course. Nothing about their situation had changed. "No," he said. "We can't let our guard down." Still, he was unable to stop grinning and ate like he had a hollow leg, as Grandpa J. used to say. The beach café offered unlimited toast with coffee and eggs. Later, under a beach umbrella, he drafted the letter to Antoine.

I've written a letter to Norman telling him what we know and asking him to wait until we get the rest of the information before doing anything. I also stated precisely what we ask of him: to assess the feasibility of negotiating. So all we need is a plan to get this information, and fortunately we've got one.

There is a guy I know outside the US who I believe we could ask to look around on the internet and gather information. Since he's already linked to me, it wouldn't be at all odd for him to be reading up on this. However, he's a likely person for me to contact, so we have to be careful. The plan is to mail him a letter and a CD from Nigeria. The letter will ask him to do a little research on our current status, and the CD will provide, (in addition to music) an encryption protocol to be used for his response as well as for further secure communication. He could, perhaps, even mail some printouts directly to Norman.

Letter to Antoine. Norman is a fictitious name of a friend Tyler had made while on a quantum research project in Australia. He must have made the acquaintance of someone who was planning to travel to Nigeria and could mail the letter from there.

11 May 2005. After posting letters to Antoine and others, Tyler and Yuki stuck out their thumbs. A curly-haired driver offered them a ride and dropped them off in L'Île-Rousse. Tyler

found a spot behind rocks that blocked some of the unrelenting winds, so they set camp there, and Yuki drifted off to sleep. The tent's constant flapping grated on his nerves, though, making sleep impossible. He pulled out his journal and stared at its worn green cover. It had been a long while since he'd visited his old friend. He clutched his Bic between finger and thumb.

> The climb out took considerably more time than the descent into the state of mind of panic. Falling in was quick, rapid and even thrilling. Once I got there, I didn't quite realize where I was and, thus unrecognized, didn't even try to climb out. Only after having made it out could I see the process. While I was in the midst of it, it was completely real, too real, so real that it seemed like an illusion.
>
> It feels good to be free from the panic. Ironically, as calm sets in, I feel comfortable, relaxed, completely at odds with the turbulence and struggle that now belongs to the past.
>
> So many directions to go, so many words to throw down that I can't organize anything coherent. The first question is where to start, so to settle it, I'll start with the present, which of course won't be the present anymore when you read this. But it's my present right now as I write, and as the writer I get to decide which present stands.
>
> The sound of the waves on this deserted beach or the turquoise color of the sea, they are embedded in-and each very accurately reflect-my present

state of mind. My legs and shoulders are a little sore from the days of hiking to get here. It was a beautiful walk through snowcapped mountains and pine forests. Now we rest our bodies before continuing on. I wouldn't quite say carefree, but nearly.

There is a garden, a Geen Doorgang and countless pools and cascades to look forward to. The distant future is far enough away to be ignored, and the past grows more distant every day. I'm free enough to let my mind pursue what it wants, math. Everyday worries and obligations are gone. I can finally rest and devote myself fully to the abstract.

The last stage, Village Life at Stone House, turned out to be anything but happiness. Between us there was a lot of hostility. Love stepped into the background and stayed out of view. Yuki was the least happy I've ever seen her, and I have no idea why. Other than our relationship issues, I was quite content. Now our issues are clearing up. Our big hope is to find Geen Doorgang, and then life will be good. It's not likely he will be there, so this will take a lot of work. But this time, from the state of mind of calm, I think we are headed into a harbor of happiness-the forest, the streams, math and good food.

The Stage of Optimism turned out to fulfill itself indeed, though in a completely unexpected way. None of our expectations or ideas panned out, but others, better ones, presented themselves. We ended up coming back to where we started, this time with real prospects and newfound self-confidence. All in all, the stage would be more appropriately named the Age of Exhaustion.

After a week of searching in vain for Geen Doorgang, both Tyler and Yuki were on edge and short-tempered. "Maybe I should check our inland spots on my own," Tyler suggested at last.

Yuki glared at him. "Good idea."

He trooped off to Ice Cave and sat where Geen Doorgang would have liked to have sat. Strange to return to a place so electrically charged with memory and emotion.

This had been their asylum. They called it Home. Tyler remembered the days spent watering their gardens. He recognized the wild plants and recalled climbing over these rocks. Those were exceptional times. There was no future then; the past, completely cut away. All they had was this place, each other, and Geen. Everything was a possibility then, yet nothing seemed possible.

What an indescribable feeling it was to sit here again, to know that he would leave and where he would go, to have some concept of a future, and most powerfully to know that he would—could—never return. Home, their home, was completely different back then. They'd had nothing else. Each moment had lacked a time frame and felt eternal. He had once planned to return and perhaps never leave. How to express the transformation since then? He was looking at the same rocks, the same place, yet all was different, changed.

Life was a nightmare then, though he couldn't help but look back with longing. There was real laughter in those smiles, real pain and fear. Their emotions belonged to no larger picture and felt concrete. He and Yuki had stood alone without the support of greater context, without a vacationer's perspective. These were no mere moments along a path. They shared their realness with no one. The beauty of the mountains and sea had absorbed him, driven every chemical reaction in his body. The canyons, trees, sand, and clouds were all that existed and all that he wanted.

These flat rocks—they had slept outside the tent on them. Over there, Geen had stolen some food. That tree still had WRONGDOER carved into it—haunting, disconcerting WRONGDOER. Here was a stove he'd built out of stones. Most days they'd moved, and each location needed a new stove, so he'd grown proficient at building them. This old stove had survived. It looked operational, as if awaiting his return. Yuki had made him panini here. How he'd loved that. This world had felt wondrous, yet now he could become bored.

"Wake up!" Tyler shouted. He climbed higher, his pack heavy with provisions, the sky so dark he could barely see his way. Over there he had proved theorems, learned about manifolds, and created exercises for Yuki. Here he thought about open covers.[14] No, those eureka moments would never leave him.

Geen Doorgang had eaten his meals from these holes in the rocks. That concave boulder had served as their bed. Tyler had

---

14 In topology, the notion of an open set provides a fundamental way to speak of nearness of points in a topological space without explicitly having a concept of distance defined. Once a choice of open sets is made, the properties of continuity, connectedness, and compactness, which use notions of nearness, can be defined using these open sets.

mixed his baking-soda toothpaste in that cupped stone. They'd pitched the tent over there, though the cheap polyester hadn't blocked much of the wind. These crazy rocks had laughed at him like hallowed skulls.

> I wouldn't wish to go back or to repeat those moments, and things have certainly improved since then. But those times will always have a raw freshness that can never be matched. Emotions like those I feel now are but mere echoes, yet still, if I were a crying man....
> They are the elements that tears are made of.
> Never come back again.
> Never come back again?
> Never come back again!?!
> How can that be possible?
> How?
> Must always return.

In that moment, Tyler realized that no amount of hunting or wishing or willing could transport Geen Doorgang to the present. But Geen lived on in these rocks, in the air that swept over them, in the campfire ash, in a time past. So, too, with his own life.

Tyler Johnson Past could no more transport to Marco Sosson Present than Geen Past could cross over to Geen Present. Tyler Past was gone, relegated to memory, to the biology of chemical communications across the synapses that had connected them. Yet the past lived on as part of Marco Sosson

Present, as part of the changed person who now stood here. He looked back with bittersweet longing to Tyler Johnson Past, and in that moment, as a finger of breeze brushed his cheek, he felt nothing and yet everything; empty yet full. The two phantoms of past and present overlapped and merged. Tyler Sosson became one.

Tyler reunited with Yuki along the River Restonica. They had trekked barely a half mile along its shoreline in the gloom of overcast skies when she threw down the tarp and motioned for Tyler to take a corner and help stretch it out.

"Can't be much past noon," he said and made no move to comply. "We can cover more ground before the rain hits."

"We'll set camp here," she said, and her tone left no room for discussion.

"Fine." Mildly annoyed, he helped erect a lean-to.

Maybe an hour passed before a hard rain beat down on them, and they climbed into their alcove to sit facing the river. Rain splattered the polyester roof, and the roar of white waters reverberated in Tyler's ears. Even so, he kept hearing other noises. Either the Restonica was playing tricks on his ears, or dogs were barking nearby. Yes, definitely the high-pitched yap of a Chihuahua or maybe a Sheltie.

"You hear dogs?" he asked.

The rapt look on Yuki's face was confirmation enough. "I saw a flyer in a grocery store about a dog rescue around here," she said.

"Oh."

She locked a questioning gaze on him. "Maybe we should think about getting a pup."

A peal of deep-throated bays pinged Tyler's heart. He missed Geen, even that incessant barking of his. The thought of adopting a pup triggered a flush of guilt. "Geen can never be replaced."

"He is gone one year now. We will not get him back."

Tyler applied counter pressure to his forehead to suppress the throb of a headache. "Dogs are great, but in the end there's always pain."

A fresh chorus of canines erupted, and Yuki squeezed his arm. "The kennel is for unwanted and abandoned dogs. The flyer read, 'Prendre une maison et sentir l'amour.'"

"Take one home and feel the love," he translated. From her expression, she already knew the meaning. Uh oh. She had not only taken the time to figure that out, but she had also memorized the original French. That couldn't be good. "Look what we did to poor Geen," he protested. "No home. No jobs. We were barely able to feed ourselves, let alone a dog." What he didn't say—what he couldn't say—was that in giving Geen up, he felt they had broken a sacred trust. "Somebody else'll give those dogs better homes."

"So you want to pass the buck and hope somebody else will step forward?"

The walls of the lean-to closed in. "I'm not sure we're ready."

"Ready is as ready does." She leveled a Forrest Gump gaze at him.

She was talking about a flyer, had insisted that they set camp early, and picked this spot. This was a set-up. Even so, Tyler could feel his resolve draining. Yuki didn't take well to the word *no*, and he couldn't bear the thought of reading disappointment on her face. He blew a sigh. "I suppose it wouldn't hurt to look."

As if on cue, the rain let up. Yuki led the way onto a nearby trail that, coincidentally, took them in the direction of the commotion. "Looks like a private residence," Tyler said.

"We will take a look." Yuki trooped toward a shed with a chain-link enclosure that was brimming with furry, yapping dogs.

"We're trespassing." Tyler ground to a halt. "We should leave." But as he stood there, a stout caretaker in coveralls and a shredded straw hat emerged from the shed.

"Bonjour!" she called, waving an empty food dish at them. "Some great pooches here need good homes!" she said, or may have said, in French. Tyler detected the name Marta amid the jumble that followed. Yuki managed the introductions as the caretaker ushered them to a pen roiling with all sorts of canines—big dogs and little, dark and light, old and young. Two pups were separated from the others in a small enclosure.

The long-haired puppy jumped on the fence and knitted its front paws through the woven wires. The other, a short, brindle-haired pup, wore a floppy, rose-colored satellite dish around its neck. It approached more gingerly, remained on all fours, and peered up at them through earnest, piercingly intelligent eyes.

Marta pointed at the cone-wearing pup and said something that sounded like, "That one's fine. He made the mistake of poking his snout into a grown-up's dinner dish. Collar keeps him from scratching at those bites on his neck. Long-hair's his brother."

"Poor baby." Yuki stuck her fingertips through the fence. "Are those big dogs mean to you?"

Injured pup was sniffing her fingertips with its black button nose when Agile Pup knocked it aside to lap feverishly at her hand. Its wild tail whapped Injured Pup's face. But instead of backing away, the smaller brother pressed forward and seemed to grin up at them. It had a Corsinu coat like Geen's, and its expression read of courage in the face of adversity. It appeared to find life amusing, maybe because of the clown collar or maybe because of a bump on its skull that spiked to his own personal mountain peak.

The caretaker swung open the gate for them, so Tyler and Yuki stepped inside and squatted on their heels. Agile Pup jounced onto Tyler's knee and licked his face, engulfing Tyler in that delectable puppy smell. Injured Pup lagged back, wagging a cautious tail and gazing up at Yuki with brown, adoring eyes. Strange, musical notes were emanating from its throat, as if it were intoning a Druid's tale. "Arroo loo lum loo."

"If we decided to take one," Tyler asked Yuki, against his better judgment, "which one would you pick?"

She beamed. "Both are so cute!"

Okay. She wanted him to pick, but she clearly preferred the injured pup. Tyler felt the same way. He stood and turned toward Marta, now sloshing a water bucket toward the larger pen. "We'll take the little guy with the floppy pink halo."

"A fine choice," she called out.

Yuki scooped up the pup, and it yelped. She murmured something in Japanese, and it grew quiet, though was trembling.

Marta led them into the shed and to a rusted metal desk in the corner. Her soiled fingers opened a small wooden box with a broken brass hinge. She pulled out a blank index card. "Have a name in mind?"

Yuki repositioned her grip on the wriggling pup. "He is a singer."

Tyler recalled the word for *he sings* from high-school Spanish class. "How about Canta?"

"Canta Loo because he sings 'loo loo.'"

"That'll work," Tyler told the caretaker.

In a stiff, untrained hand, Marta wrote *Cantalu, 23 May 2005.*

Cantalu was struggling full force now, at risk of breaking free and falling, so Tyler lifted it from Yuki's arms. He cradled the pup to his chest and did his best to comfort it, despite the flip-flopping cone. "I get the feeling our lives are about to change," he said and made a mental note of the date.

They walked toward the river, Tyler petting the pup. "It's okay, little buddy," he repeated. "It's okay." A glance at Yuki's blissful expression, and he felt a surge of happiness. Hoping to avoid dampening the moment, he said, "It probably isn't safe to keep Cantalu as his name."

"'Course not." She smiled. "Anybody who belongs to this crazy family must have an alias."

Family. She called them a family. "*Chiquito* is Spanish for tiny. You like that?"

She leaned in to address the pup nose to nose. "Chiqui-to?" she asked, and his ears perked up.

"Chiquito it is then," Tyler said. By the time they reached the river, the name had shortened to Chiki. "Not the trio we intended," Tyler said as they broke camp, "but a good trio nevertheless." He mulled over an idea. "You know how we came here to find Geen and introduce him to Tree House?"

"Ye-es?"

"Maybe we should introduce Chiki to it?"

She wagged a knowing finger at the pup and sang in perfect-pitch soprano, "'Like a good neighbor,' Tree House is there."

Unfortunately, Chiki refused to follow them, so they took turns carrying him along N200. Tyler set down the wiggle worm to give his aching arms a stretch. "Enough of this," he said and removed Chiki's scratch collar. He snugged the pup's bony rump inside his backpack and eased the pack onto his back. The swaddling seemed to calm Chiki at once, and he settled in for a contented ride.

Tyler carries the pup in his backpack.

In an hour, they passed through a quaint village where Yuki snapped a photo. Two more hours, and they set camp in the dark under a grand oak. Tyler shared his water with the pup. Then dinner. He and Yuki climbed onto their bedrolls and unzipped the sleeping bag to use it as a blanket. Chiki refused to come near and instead curled into a ball next to a fallen branch, his wary eyes watching them from a distance.

"You think it is permanent," Yuki whispered, "the damage from those mean dogs?"

"Too soon to tell." Resting his head on his hands, Tyler watched cirrus clouds wisp across a glowing full moon. The nutty scent of oak blended with a cooling coverlet of dew. "All we can do is give him time and kindness."

THEY MADE GOOD PROGRESS and arrived in the vicinity of Tree House in the gray of dusk. Leaving Chiki on a lower landing, Tyler led the way up the winding rock-steps to the lofty bridge into Tree House. They crossed and unfurled their bedrolls, then returned to Chiki. For his safety and because he didn't seem to care to be near them, they carried him lower to a miniature cave not far from Pool. There they made him a soft bed of fresh grass and leaves.

Tyler put on his headlamp, and he and Yuki trudged back up the rock stairway. Eighteen, nineteen, twenty irregular steps. They were halfway to Tree House when a ghostly moan made the hairs on Tyler's neck stand on end. The wail grew louder and crescendoed to a shriek of agony.

He spun, ready to battle a predator for the life of Chiki. But as the light from his headlamp cascaded over the rocks, he spotted Chiki alone on the landing at the base of the steepest steps. Incapable of following any farther, the poor pup tilted his nose skyward and howled in utter heartbreak.

"It's all right, little buddy." Tyler handed his headlamp to Yuki and clambered down the steps. On reaching Chiki, he wrapped him in a hug, and a warm, wet tongue lapped his chin. "I think Mikey likes us!" he called back.

"Guess he wants to belong to our group after all." Yuki's giggle sounded from behind the headlamp, which was blinding as a Broadway spotlight.

Tyler averted his eyes. "Little buddy's too clumsy to stay in Tree House. Want to pitch the tent at Patio?"

The light pivoted off him like an airport beacon and streamed up the mountainside. "I'll get the bag and bedrolls," Yuki called as her footsteps padded up the rocks.

They all slept together in peace.

Closure

• • •

Summer of 2005 passed with only one major setback. Tyler fell sick at a site they'd christened San Diego and thought he might die.

> Can't move. Can't eat, lying on the ground. Too hot on my face, but shivering. Goose bumps, but I'm radiating heat. Yuki takes good care of me. Just hell lying in the sun, even though this pine forest is beautiful. I ask myself if I'm going to die, seeing the branches, the blue sky and the mountains in brief moments when I manage to open my eyes. Ephemeral glimpses. I ask myself if I'm not already in heaven, and in my delirium, it doesn't even matter. Apricots. Thirsty. But water makes me sick. Apricots save me.

Now the days were growing shorter, the nights colder. Antoine and his family, having summered in Corsica, were soon to leave L'Abri for the mainland. Tyler and Antoine, hoping to avoid the villagers' listening ears, arranged to meet in Ajaccio on the twenty-first. Afterward, Tyler and Yuki could shop in the city and stock up for another long winter at Stone House.

Yuki was on edge of late. Considering how miserably she had passed last winter, Tyler decided to broach the topic with caution. He pulled out a sheet of paper and asked, "What do you say to our buying some items to help us pass the time better?"

"You have your books and all that math," she said flatly.

"Yeah, but I can't sit and stare at a computer all day."

"Yes, you can. You do it all the time."

Ouch. "I was thinking if we replaced our broken camera and added a decent memory card, we could have fun with it this winter."

"You mean *you* could have fun with it."

"I'll share."

"Right." She studied a torn buttonhole on her blue jersey top. "If I had a sewing machine, I could make clothes. That would save money, and maybe I could design new fashions and sell them."

Tyler pictured a fifty-pound sewing machine strapped to his back for the trek back to L'Abri. "Sure," he joked, "and let's buy a lawn roller while we're at it, and maybe an elephant."

Big mistake.

Yuki's face fell before scrunching up in anger. "You carry your stupid books all over."

Uh oh. "I'm just saying we should think about it."

She jammed a pair of socks into her pack. "Forget it. It's stupid."

A sewing machine. Never would have guessed. "No, it's not," he said. "You should get one."

No response.

"I don't want to carry it, but we can have it delivered. It's doable."

"Really?"

"Absolutely."

"It can be a small portable."

He wrote *sewing machine* on the list and underlined it twice. "Done."

Long pause. "You're riding the bike, right?"

He nodded. "I figure we'll take turns. Whoever's walking can hold Chiki's leash. It'll be good exercise for us all."

"I bet we will run into the Ajaccio crowd," she said, her voice barely a wisp.

So that was what was bothering her. She was afraid of seeing those people again. The thought had been bugging him, too. They'd have to camp on the beach, and street people tended to be acutely aware of the comings and goings of other street people. Several of them were part of the Ajaccio crowd who hung out at Little Bear's pad and partied over late-night beach campfires. Tyler recalled Milos's false assurances that his uncle would help them. The recollection of Little Bear's awkward explanation set his molars to grinding.

"I'm thinking we should look them up," he muttered. "Face them straight on."

"No need for closure with those assholes." Yuki bit her lower lip. "You know, with the tourists gone, we will stand out—me Japanese and us with a dog."

He pulled his math book onto his lap. "We'll be careful."

"Without Chiki and me, you could zip all around and be invisible."

Crap. "You trying to wheedle out of going, missy?"

"It is more efficient and less risky if I stay here with Chiki."

Oh no, not the safety-and-efficiency card. She had a point, though. On his own, he could probably knock off their to-do list in a week. Plus, they were together constantly. A break could be healthy. "You really want to stay?"

"Sure!" she brightened. "If you don't mind."

"Of course I mind." No way he wanted to tackle Ajaccio on his own. He took a deep breath and exhaled. Hell, why should they both suffer? Besides, his premonitions about this trip were growing darker and more disturbing each night. No way was he going to tell her about them. She'd worry herself sick. They were probably just byproducts of his paranoia. But if things turned sour, she'd be safe up here—well, safer. "Would you be okay here all alone?" he asked.

"Oh yeah. I will keep quiet as a mouse. No campfires, and Chiki will guard me." She hopped to her feet and sang as she marched a square, '*My dog's bigger than your dog. My dog's bigger than yours.*'" She added, "Don't forget to buy dog food."

"You have to write down and prioritize every feature you want in your machine."

"Easy peasy, lemon squeezy." She cupped her fingers signaling for him to pass her the list. "I know already."

"You promise you won't complain about the one I buy?"

She held up the three-fingered Boy Scout pledge, the one he'd flashed her a time or two and said, "I promise. I will pack all our stuff and meet you at Stone House."

He eyed their assortment of possessions. "That's a lot to carry on your own."

"You pass right by the house, so you can drop off some stuff. I'll bring the rest. No problem."

Today was Monday, 17 October. "If I leave first thing tomorrow morning, I can make it back on the twenty-fifth. You'll meet me at Stone House next Tuesday?"

A vigorous nod. "Tuesday. Absolutely."

So that was that. He was about to undertake a solo expedition into the Valley of Death. Well, into a dreaded coastal city rife with ningen betrayers and predators.

18 OCTOBER 2005. TYLER PAID THE CASHIER for Band-Aids, disinfectant, aspirin, plantar-wart remover, and other must-haves. He strode outside and strapped his bags to his bike. Then he sat on a concrete block under a giant Carrefour sign and wrote.

> I'm sitting in Ajaccio now, seeing the familiar in an unfamiliar way. This place has lots of details that trigger memories.

There was more contrast here than he'd expected. A year ago, a constant background hum had pressured him to find a job and take action to build a future. There had been excitement, too, and naive hopes and ambitions. Anything felt possible, and with so many potentials, he could dream all day about how good the future could be. He and Yuki were really floating then, or falling. Maybe the two were the same, depending on the frame of reference. He needed more time to process the swirl of emotions, all of them strong yet contradictory.

Now the background hung silent. He missed Yuki and Chiki already. Thinking of them made him feel as if he were slipping into a sinkhole, so he pictured Chiki's ears, and the image lifted him up. Almost.

Face it. He was stalling. Three hours of chasing sewing machine ads, and now he stood musing in Mezzavia. He could have started here and ended on the far side of Ajaccio, but no. Had to go for this whole closure thing that Yuki's psych book railed on about. He threw his leg over the nut-cracker seat and wheeled toward Milos's grandmother's apartments.

He found Milos stooped over a fountain in the back courtyard. The guy looked the same, maybe with a bigger paunch. "Hey," Tyler said.

Milos stood upright and turned his head, revealing a scruffy goatee. "Hey, Marco."

Tyler rubbed his chin in acknowledgement of Milos's new look. "Suits you." He stepped under the low-hanging branches of a brown-leaved chestnut tree.

"I'm winterizing." Milos waved a fidgety screwdriver at the fountain. "You back for good?"

"Just visiting." This was the moment when a friend would ask if he had a place to stay and offer the old room if it were still available. Yes, if Milos valued their friendship, then he'd apologize for lying and stranding the two of them in Marseille. He'd at least make excuses for not answering Tyler's calls.

Silence.

"What's new with you?" Tyler asked.

Milos shrugged. "You know…the regular…partying at Little Bear's. Sophie and Jorge went back to the mainland. What's up with you and Yuki?"

Tyler's mind clogged. He could hardly say they lived in a tree like the Swiss Family Robinson, or that their lawyer provided them shelter during the winter months, or that they might have to flee from France to seek asylum in a country that didn't extradite to the States. Should he mention Chiki? No. Better not say he was going to buy Yuki a sewing machine, either. Nothing was safe to tell this guy.

"We're good." Tyler played the dry, personality-less role. "Met some interesting people in Marseille. Saw the sights." Great. The master of spellbinding conversation. Where along the line had he become boring? Extensive and diverse as the list of his negative attributes was, it never used to contain the word *boring*. Now, the incontestable reality was that he simply came up empty during crucial moments like this when he needed to say something, anything, to push a conversation forward.

Milos dug into his pocket and pulled out a pack of cigarettes. "Sorry about my uncle." He rapped the pack against his index finger. A lone cigarette nosed out for Tyler to help himself. "He's one paranoid dude."

"No worries." Tyler waved off the offer. "I wouldn't take your last cig, even if I smoked."

Milos stowed the cancer stick between his lips, crinkled the empty pack, and chucked it against the trunk of the chestnut tree. The cellophane bounced onto a sandy patch before rolling to a stop between green-and-tan tufts of grass. Milos scratched a match and lit the cigarette. He drew a deep pull and flicked his glowing matchstick into a wall of tinder-dry ivy.

Tyler pressed his tongue into his lower cheek and tried not to stare at the litter. Unable to contain himself, he scooped up the cellophane and retrieved the spent match. "Well, I gotta get going."

"Good to see you, man." An obvious lie.

"Yeah, you, too." Another one. Feeling the burn of Milos's gaze, Tyler strolled through the dank, plaster-walled entry and swung onto the bike. Without a glance backward, he cruised to the nearest corner. Yes, he guessed he felt a little disappointed. But did he really expect that after all this time they would have grown closer? Would he have made the trip to Ajaccio just to see Milos? Hardly. Catching up took all of one minute.

So much for closure.

Tyler felt isolated, for sure. Milos had looked uncomfortable to see him, but the guy had made an effort and was friendly enough. Face it. The walls were as much imaginary as real, as self-imposed as they were external. For one thing, he had diverged from the mentality of those who threw trash on the ground. The gap was so wide that he doubted he could overcome it, and because this category of people was vast, he was left alone in this world. This sucked, but at least he wasn't one of them. Get real. Littering was the least of the differences that separated him from others.

Tyler dipped an index finger into his back pants pocket and confirmed the shopping list was still there. He reached his flop spot on the beach and sat in the dark, staring out to sea. *Fear.* That was the word lurking behind all this. Was he really afraid of communication, or did he perceive that others feared him? Probably both. Socialization was a matter of practice. He could make an effort to learn techniques like laughing off awkwardness with a friendly smile. But smiles had to be genuine. Fake ones came across as twisted.

For Yuki the task would prove harder. She needed confidence to make mistakes in order to learn from them and, just as importantly, to unlearn her previous socialization. Changing fundamental aspects of their personalities might prove the hardest task yet—not something he looked forward to. Would he like the person he became? Hell, he didn't care much for Mr. Boring here, and that shift had occurred without his trying or even noticing.

> It's times like this when I wonder where this is all going. The future feels like a gloomy sack of wet beans, something that you'd rather forget about, but it has a nasty penchant for not being forgotten. If only the future didn't smell so bad.

Tyler stepped into the single-story Italian restaurant, and Antoine flagged him to a linen-covered table in the far-left corner. This was a first: Antoine was early. The small, dimly lit room smelled of garlic and marinara sauce, and its ten tables were spaced to allow for private conversations. Three loud-talking, Portuguese-sounding women occupied a table on the right. A big-haired waitress was seating two men in black Italian-leather jackets near Antoine's table. No cameras in the ceiling—at least none that Tyler could see.

An open bottle of wine separated two half-filled, stemmed glasses at Antoine's table. Antoine's dark, wavy hair bordered on windblown and curled below the collar of a green golf shirt. He looked rested and relaxed. Working part-time from Stone House seemed to have smoothed the usual bags under his eyes.

They exchanged French greetings. Then Antoine kept hold of Tyler's shoulders and looked him up and down. "Ah, you're looking tan and muscular, *le frérot*. Much healthier than when I first saw you. And how is *notre cher* Yuki?"

Tyler felt a glow to hear Antoine call him "little brother" and for him to say "our dear Yuki." "Life on the Pirate Island appears to suit you, too." Tyler smiled. "Yuki's good. She said to tell you hello. She's sorry she couldn't make it today."

They brought each other up to speed on their summer's adventures, though Tyler omitted any mention of Tree House. No point burdening Antoine with information that the United States might someday compel him to share.

They toasted to good health and good fortune. Then Antoine murmured, sotto voce, "Bad news first. I've yet to receive a CD from your friend."

Tyler nodded. "Probably afraid to stick his neck out. I can't blame him."

Antoine slow-sipped his wine. "I hope you don't mind, but during one of my travels to the States, I asked a favor of a friend. He, in turn, asked a friend to put out some feelers. The fellow turned up some disturbing news."

The ground shifted under Tyler's chair. "News?"

Antoine reached into a leather satchel on the floor and pulled out a quarter-inch-thick stack of papers. "Apparently, the US attorney in Los Angeles is unwilling to discuss a deal because the case is too high profile. The feds are keeping President Bush briefed."

Tyler forced a breath and made a feeble attempt at humor. "If I'm their biggest threat, then I guess I can rest assured that my homeland is secure."

Antoine raised his glass to Tyler's. "Let's drink to that."

The wine tasted dry, smoky, and out of this world. Tyler tried for calm and collected, except he couldn't pry his focus off the pile of papers. "So what is it you have there?"

Antoine dipped a subtle nod toward the men in leather jackets. Instead of replying, he scribbled on a notepad and slid it to Tyler. "You know anything about this?"

Harried-looking letters spelled out *ELF arson, Operation Backfire, Washington State, 2001.* Tyler strained to recall four years ago—a different life, a different dimension. "No."

"Five ELF/ALF activists," Antoine whispered, "are alleged to have firebombed a horticultural facility and started a six-million-dollar blaze." After a sideways glance at the nearby men, he continued, "I have it on good authority that a federal grand jury in Seattle is going to issue indictments. They may have done so already."

Tyler waved an open palm over the notepad. "I had nothing to do with any of this."

Antoine leaned in close. "Didn't think you did, but it shows how seriously the US agencies are taking any ELF-related actions. One of the alleged perpetrators, Justin Solondz, is now a fugitive."

"Never heard of him."

"They've pursued him like fox hounds across Eastern Europe and into Russia and Central Asia. Word is they're closing in on him in Mongolia."

Tyler clutched his wine glass, but his hand was too shaky to raise it to his lips. He let go and interlaced his fingers under the table. "Go on."

"I'm sorry to tell you this." Antoine cast a furtive glance toward the leather-jacketed men and his voice softened to lip-reading levels. "But you should know: given the priority of your case, if the US learns you're in France, there won't be much I can do to stop them from extraditing you."

The dull hum that had begun to sound in Tyler's ears was growing louder and making it hard for him to concentrate. "Are you saying I should leave France?"

The jacketed men were giving their waitress a hard time. Something about their *stufatu* lacking sufficient flavoring of cloves. *Not right away*, Antoine mouthed. *I doubt the US knows you're here.*

"Because if they knew," Tyler's voice croaked, "they'd have snatched me already?" His fingertips were digging into the flesh of his knuckles, so he pulled his hands apart.

Antoine responded with a subtle nod. "At the very least, they'd ask France to issue an arrest warrant, and I'm fairly certain there isn't one here. But you must keep your head low. If an officer so much as catches you jaywalking, he'll run your prints through the system, and the US will come knocking."

Yes, he must take more care. If the authorities were closing in on this Solondz guy, then there was a good chance they were closing in on him, too. "I'm not breaking any laws. It's just that..."

Too flummoxed to finish his sentence, Tyler let his words trail off. He was saved by the big-haired waitress's interruption. Her toes bulged between slats in worn leather sandals, and her calves popped with varicose veins.

"Votre commande?" Your order, she asked, pad in hand.

"I thought we might go traditional Corsican?" Antoine asked Tyler. "In honor of a great winter of ahead with your watching the house."

More charity under the guise of compensation. Lacking the steam to protest, Tyler did his best to sound lighthearted. "Sounds good to me."

"We'll both have an order of *brocciu*, *pulenda*, and *figatellu*," Antoine said. They watched the waitress walk away. Then Antoine's gaze swung around to Tyler. "Living on the streets exposes you," he said, completing Tyler's unfinishable sentence for him. "You are at risk of arrest for vagrancy."

Tyler felt himself shrink at the word "vagrancy." Of course, Antoine had to know that he and Yuki were homeless, but so far they'd managed to skirt the topic. Now the swamp creature was rising out of the muck. This man who had taken him under his wing, who called him little brother, who had helped him and Yuki beyond measure—this cherished friend must see him as a charity case. It wasn't bad enough that Tyler was a wanted man on the run. No. Now it was obvious that he couldn't feed and clothe himself. Couldn't put a roof over his head or provide for the woman he loved. He was a blazing failure.

Antoine pressed him. "Camping is fine during the summer as long as you always carry a few euros on you. You're housed for the winter. Don't worry about that. But you must take extra care."

Tyler nodded. No words could express his gratitude, or his humiliation. He forced a grin. "So France not having a warrant: That's the good news?"

"Nope." Antoine popped his *p*. "Applying for asylum will take time. I'll need to do some legwork, and you'll have to fill out applications, do interviews—each country has its own lengthy process." He slipped a sheet of paper across the table. "The co-owners of a restaurant in Porto have agreed to hire you and pay you under the table. The job comes with free leftovers, and they'll rent you a bungalow at a reasonable rate. The pay's not great, and the job won't start until tourist season begins in mid-March."

Tyler stared at Antoine's handwriting: *Le Degré, Porto.* He had noticed the western port city on a map, midway between Calvi to the north and Ajaccio to the south. "You found me a job and an affordable place to live?"

Antoine shrugged off his miracle work. "You'll need to interview, of course, and get trained. But the income should tide you and Yuki over until your immigration paperwork comes through."

He had always wondered what it would feel like to have a brother, and now he knew. How could he ever show his appreciation to this man for providing shelter, for helping them live free, for helping him pursue asylum and, now, finding him a job? "I don't know what to say." Tyler's mind fuzzed blank. "Thanks. Thanks a lot."

"Now listen. There are certain countries that do not extradite. You are a brilliant physicist. Any nation with half a brain should wet itself to offer you asylum. You'll lead a decent life, but you'll never be able to reveal your true identity or return to the US or France."

Leave and never come back? The thrumming in Tyler's ears became a pipe-organ blast, stuck on a chord from *Phantom of the Opera*. Antoine was his lifeline, his only true friend in this fugitive life other than Yuki. The possibility of never seeing him again, while ever present in the past, felt as palpable as the jagged icicle that was crystalizing in his throat. He would miss seeing his friend over the next few months. Couldn't imagine losing him forever. Tyler tried to swallow. "Yuki and I have talked about this," his voice cracked. "If we ever have to leave France, we'd like to go to Venezuela. I speak a little Spanish."

Antoine studied him hard. "Did you pick that country so you can slip north to visit your family?"

Tyler studied the tightly woven linen tablecloth, made soft from untold launderings. "It's scary how well you know me."

"I must advise you against such an action. That would be extremely risky."

Tyler gripped his chair's armrests. "Let's take this one step at a time. If I've learned one thing, it's that life rarely turns out as we plan." A person could take steps to improve the odds, though, and over the past year and eight months, he had honed valuable skills. He now knew how to live invisibly on the streets and how to slip like a fox into wilderness brush. He could travel miles without leaving a footprint and eke water out of desert sands. Yes, if he and Yuki made it to Venezuela, then he would journey to Michigan. Maybe he would see his family for only a few days—maybe the reunion would cost him his freedom—but somehow, some way, he was going to get home. He pictured Mom's happy tears. Smelled Dad's Barbasol shaving cream and felt his strong arms hug him in welcome. He heard Kelsey call *Tylie!* and laugh at a *Big Lebowski* joke.

Antoine raised his glass. "To a bright future."

They clinked their goblets, and Tyler managed a swallow.

FIVE DAYS IN AJACCIO WAS LIKE taking a bite of a "shit sandwich," to borrow a phrase from Antoine. Food and sundries were costing an arm and a leg, not to mention gold-nugget pricing for bike tires and sewing machines. He might as well have asked vendors to sail a ship to Jupiter as to ask them to make a delivery to L'Abri. Cops were on patrol everywhere, and to top it off, the beach showers were closed for the season.

> Hating life. Hating walking. Hating Ajaccio. I hate everything. Most of all I hate life, and I hate myself. This whole fucking thing, can I go on like this? Well, I have to. I have to remember Yuki and Chiki are depending on me. I don't hate everything because I love them and my family so far away. As long as they exist, I don't hate everything. Most of all I hate flat bike tires. Damn.
>
> Hate changes to fear via the medicating of the herb. Now it's constant fear. Hate to walk for fear of being stopped. Hate to stop for fear of

looking suspicious. Most of all, hate being in Ajaccio because I fear I will never make it back to see Yuki and Chiki.

Have to be careful. No risks. Not worth it. I wouldn't give a shit if I were alone, but I'm not. I have something to live for, so better play it safe. Sleep with a knife beside me. Walk along the beach, not the road.

22 October 2005. Damn. They burned my stuff. The coals are still hot. My stuff is in them and in the smoke that pollutes the air. I didn't have much. Luckily I brought most with me in the heavy pack. But why'd they have to burn my things? I had been here three nights. People saw me every morning.

This is their way of saying I'm not welcome. Fuck them. I didn't like being here anyway. Fuck them. But better move on. Not very likely, but possible that the next step will be to have the police kick out the vagrant. They don't want people living on the beach. I did leave some shit and piss there, but the spot was hardly clean to begin with.

Better move on.

Here's okay. Can't go any further without passing through a brightly lit restaurant pressed up against the water. Sure as hell don't want to be seen.

Maybe those were the guys who burned my stuff? Don't want them to know where I've gone. Could go along the road, but that means going all the way back to the fire or climbing up a steep bushy slope. I'll just stay right here.

There's someone with a flashlight. What's he doing? He's by the beach where I was, where the coals are still hot. Is he coming this way? Is that a little dog barking? Probably just walking his dog. Okay. I'll watch and wait. Better not wait in the shadows, too obvious I'm hiding. There in the light-but kind of behind a rock from his perspective-I wait and watch, eating Spirito cookies.

Time passes. He goes away, but never leaves the little beach over there. I should just go to bed, wake up early and move on. Don't know if anybody occupies that house next to me. The window has shades drawn now, but maybe an early riser will open it for the sunrise, only to find my blue sleeping bag right below. Probably okay for one night.

I eat some bread and cheese, settle comfortably into my bag, thinking about my bad premonitions before the trip. It's passed okay so far, but it's not over yet. I so want to see Yuki again.

Tyler set down his green notebook and rolled onto his back between a house's stone foundation and a row of bushes. The leaves, though scant, would probably conceal him, if he remained still and if that red squirrel would stop chattering about his presence.

No dog was barking inside—no interior footsteps, no kitchen clangs, no yammer of television—so the house was probably empty. He might be able to pass the night undetected. Hated to trespass, but public areas weren't safe.

Constant uncertainty and fear wore a person down eventually. Not that he was broken already or breaking down. But how would he know if he were? Would he recognize the symptoms? What if thinking about breaking down was a symptom? His subconscious mind could be trying to warn him. Then again, his best defense was probably to stay alert to the risk. Thank goodness he was going back soon. With luck, in seventy-one hours this trip would exist only as memory, as part of Tyler Past.

His stomach rumbled, and it was too early to sleep. On the bright side, the food money he'd used to buy a tire-repair kit was paying dividends. No more leaky inner tube. He trained his thoughts on his happy homecoming. He couldn't wait to kiss Yuki. It had been such a long time since they'd kissed, really kissed. Chiki would be overcome with wiggling. The cute little guy.

Tyler lay on his back and snugged the sleeping bag's flannel liner under his chin. Above in the gutter, a lonesome weed was sprouting next to the downspout. Despite the bad—impossible—place that it had picked to sink its roots, it kept reaching for the light.

23 October 2005. Tyler woke to bright sun and the chimes of a distant church bell. He scrambled to sneak away, grateful that no one had called the cops on him. Nothing would be open on Sunday. People would be less suspicious of a person hanging around the docks, so he cruised to a slip and took a seat next

to a canvas-covered boat. Leaning against a pylon, he munched GORP and listened to waves lap the satiny white stern.

Boredom had never been an issue because he usually had plenty of activities that needed doing, and he always had math. What was he thinking to have only brought twenty-six math problems for the trip? He had polished them off two days ago. Now, all he could do was wait for tomorrow to settle on a sewing machine and coordinate delivery. He probably shouldn't spend the money on a camera. Then again, the situation on his return would be the same as when he left, and at the time, he was convinced he needed one. Yes, he had better get the camera—not the memory card, though.

Pondering hypotheticals was always good for passing the time. What would the world be like if the order of technological development had unfolded differently than it had? Say guns had been invented before money? A conversation with Phil came to mind.

"Capitalism's flawed," Tyler had waxed philosophic with his Caltech roommate. "Left to its own devices, its competition is heartless, and it encourages an insatiable consumption of resources."

"Communism's not perfect, either," Phil had mumbled, his eyes locked as usual on an electrical-engineering textbook.

"But unfettered capitalism devours just about everyone and everything in its path."

"We'd be dead," Phil said with a shrug. "But communism devolves power into the hands of a few and turns corrupt. That's no way to live."

"You're right," Tyler had said, having witnessed firsthand how corruption permeated China's political system. "Communism substitutes an omnipotent government for an omnipotent god and tramples individual rights in the process."

"Its bureaucracy kills innovation and chokes the life out of freedom." Phil had then bobbed his hairless, undershot chin on a thumb and index finger—his tell that he was contemplating something. "How about somewhere in between and we keep the best of both systems?"

"That's socialism," Tyler countered, "and it kills healthy competition and individual freedom. It inevitably accumulates the worst of both, not the best." What were those end results he'd ticked off? Excess consumption, corruption, bureaucracy, and unfettered concentration of power.

Phil's voice stretched drum tight. "Well, I'm not for anarchy."

"Me neither." Tyler had slumped into a tattered, overstuffed chair. "Anarchy has all the problems of capitalism and communism, except guns are its currency of power instead of money or government."

Phil had set down his pencil. "A world with guns and no government would be about the worst imaginable."

An understatement. "Anarchy creates a vacuum, and somebody always fills it—usually the most vicious competitor." Then Tyler had flashed on a scary thought. "The worst-case scenario has to be despots with the ultimate weapons."

"You mean nuclear?"

"Yeah. Could be catastrophic."

The clock tower had donged 3:00 a.m. and cast a pall over the room. "Someone needs to formulate a new political system," Phil had said, as he flopped onto his bed and disappeared under the covers.

Tyler pictured his brass study lamp, a high-school graduation gift from Aunt Phyllis. He recalled the feel of cool tile under his bare feet as he padded to his twin bed on the opposite side of the Spartan but comfortable room. The window had overlooked a terra-cotta roof that he liked to climb onto. And the food. What he wouldn't give to sink his teeth into one of Caltech's hot roast-beef dinners with mashed potatoes smothered in gravy.

"That's right," he had told Phil. Then he'd added, half joking, "I'll take care of that tomorrow." But the next day had been too busy and the next and the next. Delays piled up. Present Tyler was finally getting around to it. His beta version of a refined economic/political system employed capitalism as a tool, not as a moral principle, and his mathematical simulations were showing promise. He wished he hadn't left the computer with Yuki. He would like to write evolution simulations that factored in technological achievements like guns and trade currencies to see how they played out.

A security guard was approaching, so Tyler slid into his backpack and onto his bike. He pedaled to a trash container behind a professional building. No smell of rot, and the container blocked an apartment building's line of sight. He made himself a flop before climbing inside. The contents were mostly crushed boxes and old marketing materials, but then he spotted *Adventure* magazine, the February 2005 edition.

Climbing out and onto his bedroll, he tried not to read too quickly. A particularly interesting feature story, set in Yosemite National Park, told of a ranger operation rescuing hikers off El Capitan. Even so, Tyler checked the time and celebrated the passage of each half hour.

No food. His stomach was chewing on itself. Someone in an apartment was frying chicken, the aroma so delicious it hurt. Continue to go hungry like this, and malnutrition would get the best of him. Good thing he was going back tomorrow. No more worrying about lists and false friends, or cops and pillaging residents, or hunger and boredom. What a fine evening Tuesday would bring.

TUESDAY, 25 OCTOBER 2005. TYLER WRAPPED each brown egg in newspaper and placed all twelve in a cardboard box. Using a bungee cord, he secured the carton behind his bike seat. With one pack strapped to the handlebars and the other on his back, he threw a leg over the bike and set off. Free at last. A photo sequence of Ajaccio fading behind would have been fun to show Yuki. Too bad the sewing machine, groceries and delivery charges had cost more than he had expected. Maybe he could save up for a camera with time-lapse capabilities. Waiting could be a good thing. It'd give him a chance to do more research.

Tyler stood on the pedals and pumped, his heart pounding in anticipation of seeing Yuki and Chiki and from peddling uphill in a buffeting wind. A few hours and two bio-breaks later, he wheeled behind Stone House, propped the bike against a post, and carried the supplies inside. Empty.

No problem. He was early. If he hurried, he might catch Yuki coming down the trail and surprise her. In high gear, he toted the remainder of the bundles inside and unwrapped the eggs, setting each in the refrigerator. Only one casualty, and they'd fry it tonight. Tyler nested the cracked egg in a plastic bowl and refrigerated it alongside its siblings. After locking the bike in the shed, he set, taking Yuki's favorite route through L'Abri.

On reaching Beginning, he ducked under their brushy secret entrance. Here in the shade among earthy aromas, he felt home at last. What if she'd chosen a different path through town? He could have missed her. Relax. She'd see the supplies and know that he'd arrived safely.

The climb past Horse and Dirt smelled of fallen leaves. The temps were warm and comfortable. Feeling fatigued and wishing he'd brought water, he stretched out on Wall for a catnap.

Tap…tap…tap. Tyler bolted upright. Yuki was making her way down the rocky trail with Chiki trotting ahead. With her packs mounded high and wide, and with her walking stick, Shorty, marking the rhythm of her stride, she looked like an elfin princess.

Chiki snapped to a stiff-legged halt and sniffed, sensing Tyler's form yet apparently unable to identify him downwind. Yuki bumped past, so he followed on her heels.

"Helloooo!" Tyler waved.

Yuki raised Shorty in greeting and maintained her pace.

"Woof." Chiki rocketed toward Tyler and slammed into his knees, nearly knocking him over.

Tyler knelt to pet the wiggling mass. "He's bigger," he laughed. "I'm serious—he's grown!"

Yuki was fast approaching under her enormous packs. Thinking it might knock her off balance, Tyler quashed the urge to take her in his arms and kiss her. He wanted to dance and make love, to share all he'd experienced.

"Hey." She swung a leaden tote into his hand.

That was it? No squeal of surprise. Not even a smile. "Wow! This is heavy," he said.

Without breaking stride, Yuki and pack glided past and on down the trail. "While you were playing in the city," she called over her shoulder, "I was stuck packing and lugging all this crap."

Tyler reached down and scratched Chiki's ears.

Eggs were a real treat.

Clouds, Real or Figurative, Have a Tendency to Evaporate

• • •

WHAT WERE HIS GREAT-GREAT-GRANDPARENTS LIKE? Tyler wondered. Did they daydream into sunsets and have laughs that made everyone in a room laugh, too? What were their fears? People always had love stories. Some of them had lived until just a few decades ago, yet today's descendants remembered only their names, if that. Maybe a few photos faded away in drawers. The few who carried a single recollection of these foregone personalities were old and soon to join the ranks of the nearly forgotten. How many generations had passed since his early *Homo sapiens* ancestors walked the earth 150,000 years ago? Assuming a new generation every twenty-five years, six thousand generations had passed before him. And prior to *Homo sapiens*, hominids had experienced great, never-to-be-known adventures, too.

22 November 2005. I've been thinking a lot about the insignificance of life recently. People lived entire lives hundreds of years ago, their dreams and sorrows no less real than mine, their lives no shorter and no less real.

These thoughts struck Tyler as obvious and, yes, a little sad. He realized that he, too, would someday join the parade of forgotten souls. That was simply what life was—or the passing of it, anyway. He could record and store information, try to slow the process, but the erasure would nevertheless occur. Even if detailed CDs or other technology existed to preserve information about the lives and personalities of those in the past, records were unlikely to be read. Besides, what did it matter if the data existed or if anybody viewed the materials? Records were a far cry from existence.

Life unfolded like a film in real time, each scene running for a finite interval. Immortality neither strutted nor fretted its hour upon the stage because it played no role, and that was just as well. Who would want to watch a movie that never ended? A story need not be long or have a happy ending to be a good one. His life was no different. Biology, ecosystems, and life in general joined in a beautiful dance of molecules and energy. He felt proud to have participated. What an experience. He drafted a poem.

I Will Be an Old Man

I will be an old man someday.
I will be the exclusive proprietor
of some real treasures,
and by real I, of course,
mean imaginary.

For these treasures exist
as they are or will be
only as memories,
memories in the mind of an old man

who lived when they were indeed
as real as real can be.

Some of these are already in the past.
Others must wait for some future time
before they can find
their rightful home in the past.

I will have the memory
of glowing particles of dust
swimming about the room
above a red carpet
made bright by the sun
in a house near Chelsea, Michigan.

I will remember periods
spent floating on love,
as one would [on] a cloud or idealism,
at times seeing the world
as it should and could be.

I will remember The Fall,
striking the hard world below
because clouds, real or figurative,
have the tendency to evaporate.

Yes, I will be an old man someday
with these possessions.
But now I am young.
I am the proud governor

of billions of living cells
whose well-being it is my duty to ensure.

I've always been an optimist,
and I hope that despite the cruel beating
that old man will have received,
life will not have succeeded
in robbing him of this trait.

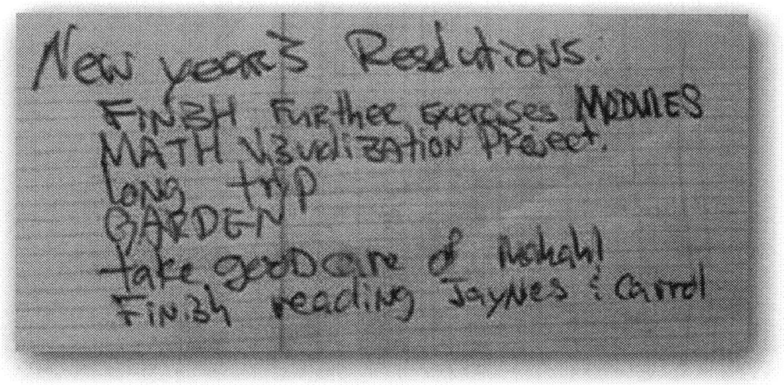
New year's Resolutions:
FINISH Further exercises MODULES
MATH Visualization Project.
long trip
GARDEN
take good care of Mahahl
FINISH reading Jaynes & Carrol

Tyler's New Year's resolutions. "Mahahl" was
his term of endearment for Yuki.

January 2006. Tyler and Yuki again managed to mail letters to their families. This time, in the hopes of establishing communications, Tyler enclosed a decryption key.

January 2006
Dear Mom and Dad and Kelsey,

It's been way too long! How is everyone? Where to begin? I miss you guys so much. Things are just fine on this end of the wire. I'm real sorry for all this being-gone business. It happens, and I don't know what to do besides push on and hope for an improvement. I love you all very deeply and never meant to hurt you guys, but I'm sure you know that already. Through difficult times we find strength, and after all this, at least we can say that we have grown stronger together.

I've been saying it, I'll say it now, and I'll keep on saying it till the end of my days, "I ain't dead yet." And don't you forget it! In fact, I'm fine. The only hard part is being so distant from the fam, missing you guys and regretting that I've caused you analogous suffering. I don't want you worrying about me; it would be a waste of worries that could be better spent elsewhere. Not to say go ahead and forget about me! Just bear in mind that I'm okay, a bit unconventional you could say, but safe, healthy and productive.

Hope all is well at home....

How does it feel to be back in Michigan? In addition to being reunited with many old friends, I'm sure you guys have made tons of new ones. For Mom and Dad, being back home after such a long time away might give a real feeling of peace. Despite the damn cold winters and the straight, flat, very long roads, it must be very comfortable. You've probably rediscovered things that were once so familiar you couldn't have imagined them. Life is filled with all those details you don't pay much attention to. The big things aren't a problem. You notice and therefore hold on to them.

It's the little things that escape our efforts to remember and conserve. They're always hiding in the backgrounds of photos, in wallpaper and especially in smells. It's easy to lose that sort of stuff, despite returning periodically. I've discovered a lot of stuff packed into old memories that I never even noticed over the course of recording these memories. Living in MI must really bring back to life all these neglected treasures. I hope you aren't too busy to enjoy it!

I'm always asking myself the question: What's Kelsey doing right now? What about the 'rents? There's a whole lot I'd like to ask, but I'm not sure how you could answer. Where there's a will, there's a way, as the fella says. Really, in terms of communication, the situation can only improve.

I've got heaps of stories to share with you guys. Some cool adventures, some endurance tests, some downright lousy experiences and some uplifting ones. It's been an eclectic mixture of the best and worst of... well, everything. I've met some really beautiful people and also some real scumbags. Humanity has a lot to be proud of, and in some ways, I feel I've witnessed its greatness like never before. We have our embarrassing points as well, and I've had the honor of seeing some of them rather up close and personal, too....

I look a bit different now. In fact, I'd be surprised if you'd even recognize me anymore. I bear a strikingly strong resemblance to Ray Charles, except I can see just fine. Who'd have known? Not exactly what I would have imagined five years ago.

I hope you are all able to keep moving forward. I sometimes find myself moving in circles, but at least I keep circling in the same direction.

Well, I miss you all tremendously. You are always in my thoughts and dreams, and I know this separation won't last forever. I'm sorry, and I can't say it enough. And don't worry about me, at least not yet. If anything bad happens, you'll be the first to hear.
Lots of love,
-Tyler

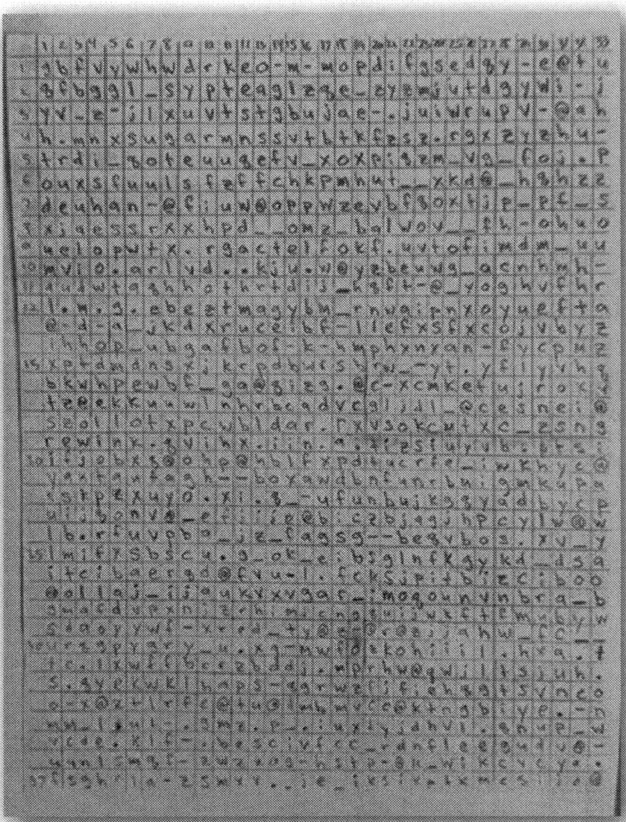

Tyler created and enclosed the above encryption key along with a set of instructions for communicating in secret with his family.

When two parties use the same key, they can exchange messages that are nearly impossible for outsiders to decode. His family worked each night for months in the hope of decrypting an e-mail address or a hidden message in his letters. Applying the key, they posted e-mail addresses on a website for him to contact them anonymously. They checked regularly for his response, but none ever came. Later, when reading his journals, they found an entry describing how a wind had blown his key from the pages of a book that he was reading in the mountains. Without his key, Tyler had no means of decoding their messages to him or of finding the encrypted email addresses that they had posted.

FEBRUARY 2006. LIFE COULD MEAN NOTHING or everything in a place like this. Tyler's toadstool-shaped perch jutted from the mountainside, allowing him just enough room to sit cross-legged and peer over a sea of dancing treetops. A spring breeze, pregnant with the scent of pine sap, was sweeping up from the canyon below. Clouds were playing tricks with the sunlight, swirling rays and shadows over the page of his journal. God, it felt good to be himself again. He turned over another theorem and slapped down an isomorphism.

Yes, the Age of Construction had turned out to be the most pleasant and productive stage so far. Henceforth, he was going to work toward specific goals. He wrote.

A plan for a future still feels more like a dream for the future, but it's at least realistic. It's moved from completely out there string theory to now having some feasibly testable predictions. The experimental results aren't in yet....

First and foremost, he aimed to reconstruct the love between Yuki and him.

Tyler stared over the valley and watched a bird of prey ride the currents. Its wings outstretched, the hawk circled around and around, en route to nowhere. Below, a rabbit was probably minding its own business, munching on a three-leaf clover, oblivious to the flex of talons high above. Maybe it offered its beloved mate a tasty niblet.

Not the rabbit's lucky day.

Yuki could be making panini for dinner. Tyler fantasized about sinking his teeth into pan-seared bread, ham, and gooey cheese. He climbed to safety and made his way toward their forest campsite. A few yards out, he smelled rice and beans.

Yuki looked tired as she handed him a plateful. "Here you go."

"Thanks," he said.

They ate in silence, watching the sun ease below a western peak. Then they cleaned up and sat gazing into the fire.

Yuki's eyes glistened in the reflection of the flames. "If you could go back in time," she asked, "would you do it all over again?"

"Starting before or after The Fall?"

"After."

He opened his mouth to suggest they start before so that he could avoid repeating that horrible mistake. He'd be halfway through his PhD by now. She'd have her bachelor's degree. Maybe they'd have married. More likely they'd have gone their separate ways. But no. This was Yuki's exercise, her rules. "Well, throwing it all away and starting from scratch like we did back then—we would probably be in the same position, except for the knowledge we've gained."

"Would you still flee and become a fugitive?"

All was crisis back then. Now the excitement had faded. The adrenal glands were emptied, and clay-footed reality tramped over their daily lives. "Probably," Tyler said, "but I doubt I could redo all that came after. I'm too exhausted from the fight and the flight—and certainly from the fright."

Silence.

"How about you?" he asked.

"No," she said without hesitation.

No to fleeing the country or to fleeing with him? He wanted to ask, probably should ask, except that he could read the answer in the slump of her shoulders, in the tiny, crescent-shaped wrinkles that creased the corners of her mouth. Regret hung in her downcast eyes, in her terse, one-syllable, negative response. Regret for choosing a life with him—her disappointment in him—radiated from her into the air that he breathed. He didn't dare ask because he couldn't bear to hear the answer, and that stung.

"How are you coming on your goal to design and produce fashionable clothing with your sewing machine?" he asked—a pointed question, intended to jab at the open sore that was her heart.

She looked into the waning fire and blinked slowly. "Clothes came out more in the beginning."

"Guess you made everything you had in mind." The bitterness in his voice took him by surprise.

She obviously heard it, too, and her expression hardened. "That's right."

What was going on here? Was he hurting her because she had hurt him because he had hurt her? Then it dawned on him. Their relationship—everything they did, all they were as individuals and as a couple—revolved around the incident. Unable to move forward along life's natural course to careers, marriage, a home, and children of their own, their relationship was spiraling up and down, going nowhere like that hungry hawk. But the hawk was operating according to the prescribed rhythms for a bird of prey. Not so with the two of them—they were out of sync with life as it was supposed to unfold for humans. They were flapping round and round, caught in the downdrafts of regret and disappointment, of fear and loss and isolation. The Fall's vortex had them in its clutches and was thrashing the tender remnants of their love to pulp.

Tyler wished he could undo his words, but they were out there, fueling the relentless gnaw of the incident. No do-overs. No take-backs. "I haven't done much on my plan to make movies, either," he said, hoping to break the cycle. "All I have are some ideas. I've learned what can be done with the computer, and it's pretty feeble."

"Doesn't matter," she said. "You don't have time because all you do is your computation project."

There it was, the inevitable barbed response, and not unwarranted. "You know that song you sing when you're stressed, the one I mistook for 'Sukiyaki'?"

Her lower jaw edged forward. "What about it?"

"I found it on YouTube, and the title translates to 'I look up as I walk.'"

"So?"

He had committed the words to memory: "'I look up as I walk, so that the tears won't fall, remembering those spring days. But I am all alone tonight.'"

She wore the look of a trapped rabbit. "So now you're an expert on Japanese?"

Ignoring her comment, he recited the second verse:

I look up as I walk,
Counting the stars with tearful eyes,
Remembering those spring days,
But I am all alone tonight.
Happiness lies beyond the clouds.
Happiness lies up above the sky.

She poked a stick at the fire until its tip flared. "You're a poet, and you think you know it."

She was angry. Good. Maybe she'd let her emotions bubble to the surface so they could address them and work them out. He attempted to sing the words. Off-key, but what the hell.

I look up as I walk,
So that the tears won't fall.
Though tears well up as I walk.
For tonight I am all alone.

Remembering those spring days
But I am all alone tonight.
Sadness lies in the shadow of the stars.
Sadness lurks in the shadow of the moon.

Yuki glared at him through glistening eyes, and then her diminutive soprano joined his tenor.

> I look up as I walk,
> So that the tears won't fall.
> Though tears well up as I walk.

They closed out the last verse. "But I am all alone tonight."

Could the human heart actually break? He slipped an arm over her shoulders and tried to pull her close. "You can talk to me." But she stiffened and shot into the bushes.

A minute or two passed before she returned with branches bristling from her arms. She dumped the wood onto the fading fire and sat on a semi-flat rock, her arms crossed. Thick smoke curled into the air and blanketed the campsite.

"How did you first get into your epsilon creatures anyway?" she asked.

She was deflecting again. Mom used to redirect the conversation, too, and it used to work on him when he was ten. Tyler stood and rolled his sit-down rock outward to fresh air. Yuki continued to sit—or hide—in the cloud of smoke. Tyler glimpsed tears streaming down her face. Maybe he shouldn't press her more. He had raised the issue. She'd talk when she was ready.

A twig ignited and flames lapped through the stick pile, effectively clearing the smoke. Tyler leaned into the orange light and absorbed the fire's crackle. Yes. Maybe someday Yuki would let him in. For now, she obviously wanted to—maybe needed to—keep her feelings to herself. "I came up with the idea in Christoph Adami's class," he replied. "Evolution and Biocomplexity."

"That professor who bridged entire scientific disciplines in his lectures?" she asked.

Tyler recognized those words. He had once spoken them to her and long since forgotten them. "Exactly! I used to spend hours hanging around Chris's lab, talking evolutionary theory." It had been a while since he'd thought about the friendly, energetic professor. He missed Chris. "One of his lectures touched on how biologists could simulate the influence of one evolutionary factor, but when it came to simulating the effects of multiple factors, they could only speculate."

"So you decided to solve another world problem, right?"

Bitterness. He could overlook it. "Yup, made it my term project, and for the next few weeks I actually had fun at Caltech. I figured if I could apply group theory to software code, I could simulate multiple competitive factors. I kept hitting dead ends, but then voilà, my program actually worked."

"Sure. Piece of snake."

No way would he correct her. "Instead of eating food, breathing air, and reproducing in the flesh like real life-forms, my digital creatures consumed math in order to exist and propagate their species. Just as water and organic compounds gave rise to life on Earth, but my primordial goo, composed of 1s and math processes, gives rise to epsilons A. Then epsilons A evolve to add 1 + 1 equals 2."

"So 2 is poop. Your epsilons poop numbers."

She was trying to be mean, except he couldn't help but grin. "In a manner of speaking, yes. Flesh forms like us use chemical processes. We convert food to kinetic and thermal energy in order to survive. My epsilons survive by using mathematical functions. They add and subtract to feed on numbers for their calories."

"So math is calories." Staring through him, she added, "You live on math. You are an epsilon."

"Now the primordial mix holds fewer 1s and some 2s. Epsilons pass their designer genes onto their offspring, and pretty soon Epsilon B either mutates or evolves to digest 1 + 2, producing 3s. Eventually, competitive species C mutates or evolves to eat 3s."

"A bunch of poop eaters. No big deal."

"Each species represents a complex algorithm. My program gives epsilons mathematically measurable characteristics, so it can simulate how competitive species thrive or become extinct based on complex conditions. That's why I'm so interested in group theory, open sets and topology."

Her expression softened. "Your digitals 'Simulate conditions in seconds that might otherwise take millions of years to evolve in the real world.'"

Ha! She was quoting his paper. She'd never mentioned that she'd read it. "That's right," he said, recalling the day Chris had called him into the lab. Visibly excited, the professor had tapped a few keys and run Tyler's program.

"This is an elegant solution," Chris had said. "It's breakthrough stuff." He had waved Tyler's term paper at him, saying, "You need to rewrite this and submit it for publication." Then Tyler had noticed the giant red 4.0 on its title page.

Taken by surprise and feeling awkward, Tyler had laughed. "You sound like Barry Sanders. He said the same thing about the quantum-teleportation research I've been working on. Said I should submit to *Physics Review*, and now I'm swamped with putting the finishing touches on that."

"Hmm." Chris's dark head of hair had bobbed in thought. "Physics is your major, so that has to be your priority. You open to collaborating? I know a PhD candidate who might be interested in acting as second author. Maybe he could work with you to write the article."

And that was that. Red-haired, methodical Claus Wilke had come into Tyler's life, and soon they submitted a work that explained Tyler's software program and the mathematics behind it. The prestigious American Physical Society had published Tyler's quantum research first. Then, thirteen months later, the International Society for Artificial Life published his and Claus's research in *Artificial Life*.

Then came The Fall.

Three months after "Digital Darwinism" hit the presses, Tyler had fled, a fugitive. Now he and Yuki were homeless, destitute, and caged like prey rabbits on this rock. No, Yuki's disappointment in him couldn't come close to the disappointment he felt in himself. Maybe that accounted for the sting of her words. Plus, she was right. His digital-evolution project was all consuming. He fed on it. Maybe he *was* an epsilon.

Tyler glanced up to see Yuki staring at him. She made no effort to talk, so he said, "Guess I've been a little preoccupied. All I can think of are algorithms to evolve my epsilons."

She sighed. "And talk about your group-theory magic."

"It's more than magic," he said. "It's mathematics." Images of abelian groups, rings and vector fields flooded his thoughts, and he felt the lure of math's siren song. "Stefan Banach said, 'Mathematicians see analogies between abstract structures. Great mathematicians see analogies between analogies.'"

"Is that what you want to be, a great mathematician?"

Pursuing quantum-computational physics was out of the question. Too traceable to him. Math and Yuki were all he had left, and he could feel them slipping away, too. "I think my little epsilons may be showing real promise," he said, disappointed to hear desperation in his voice. "They could be groundbreaking."

"You talk about them like they are your babies."

Her words still carried a barb, but they no longer sounded openly hostile. He stirred the campfire. "I'm programing the offspring to inherit the needs and wishes of their parents, and that drives supply-demand curves."

Silence.

Tyler tossed his stick onto the coals, and in the quiet of reflection on their conversation, puzzle pieces began to take shape and fall into place.

In the days that followed, Tyler felt the stirrings of a new line of thought.

> I have redirected my expected career from math to Bio, or "computational genetics" as I would call it. The emphasis is on the comp aspect/value of bio-diversity. Along the way I took a tangential-seeming

detour to visit my lifelong friend, quantum mechanics, and with that my understanding of QM into a film.

So off this pleasant diversion stage floated, only to be burst sharply as the ground caught up. The turning point came with a lot of adrenaline, yelling and anger.

C'est Comme Ça. (It Is How It Is.)

• • •

In March 2006, Yuki suggested that they introduce Chiki to Home at Saleccia Beach before Tyler reported for the job that Antoine had arranged for him at *Le Degré* restaurant,. Hitchhiking went well, and in a few days they were walking along the shoreline, teaching the floppy-legged yearling to cool his paws in the salty sea. Chiki slumbered to the splash of waves on sand. He sniffed hoof prints and scat in the Desert des Agriates. Outside Ice Cave, Chiki dropped his nose onto his oversize paws and bumped his rump in the air to bark at ninja lizards.

Then it was time to depart. The three of them made their way to Ostriconi Beach where a pock-faced Hungarian driver gave them a ride along the coast to L'Île-Rousse. He dropped them off only a couple of miles from the station. Since the train to Porto wasn't scheduled to depart for another two hours, they lugged their packs about halfway and took a roadside break.

Across the street at a public campground, two teenage guys were taking turns kicking a soccer ball into a net. To their right, seated at picnic table, a couple of senior citizens were engaged in a board game, probably chess. The air smelled of fresh-mown grass until a white pickup truck skidded to a halt on the gravel shoulder and rolled a plume of dust into the air. License number 3875GC2B.

The gray-haired driver cranked down his window as a teenage version of him eyed Tyler from the passenger side. "What are you doing?" Elder asked in French.

If Tyler weren't holding his breath to avoid inhaling quantities of dust particles, he might have joked, *We're off to catch Thomas the Train.* No, a stranger might not take kindly to a foreigner poking fun at Corsica's antiquated, single-gauge railroad. Instead, Tyler referred to the regional rail network by its name, saying, "We're on our way to Chemins de Fer."

Neither courteous nor lacking in manners, the driver pointed in the direction they were headed. "No station down there."

"I'm sorry," Tyler said, correcting him as courteously as possible, "but the Internet says there is, and it's open."

"The station is closed." Elder converted to partial English and said, "Continue per la route." He stared, apparently waiting for Tyler and Yuki to depart.

They moved on, as was their plan.

"Be careful with the dog," Elder added in a not-entirely-unfriendly tone. Then he and Son sped off, Son speaking into his phone—probably lodging a complaint about two vagrants.

Tyler and Yuki had progressed maybe thirty feet when Elder and Son careened up once more. "Alors!" Elder shouted over his honking horn. "Degage. Degage en haut."

Tyler's legs prickled as he turned to Yuki. "He's saying something like 'makes a clearance' or 'clears up,' but I get the feeling he's telling us to get the hell out of here." He slipped the leash to her and head-pointed to a bank of trees. "Better take Chiki over there."

Instead of moving away, Yuki planted her feet and stared at the truck.

Tyler was about to set down one of his five-kilo packs and escort Yuki to the trees when he stopped himself. Freeing a hand and turning his back could be construed as acts of aggression. "Just do as I ask," he said.

Yuki, who had begun to hum under her breath, hitched her hands on her hips and said. "'Get a piece of the rock.'" Then she practically shouted, "'Built Ford tough.'"

Must take a different tack. "Chiki's not safe here," Tyler said. "You need to get him away."

Yuki studied the leash in her hand and, at last, led Chiki toward the trees.

Tyler turned to Elder and framed his words to say *We get out of here down that way.* "On se dégage en bas." Unfortunately, the words must have missed their mark because Elder and Son jumped out of the truck and slammed its doors behind them. Tyler rechecked his expression. Uh oh. The literal French translation of this was "It emerges down." They may have mistaken his meaning. How to rephrase?

Before he could clarify, Son barked a curse word. He grabbed Tyler by the neck and started to shake him back and forth. Between Tyler's two overloaded hands and the thirty kilos on his back, he was about to tip over, so he let go of a bag. "Hey!" he said, and blurted out in English, "What the fuck are you doing?"

Screaming something in Corse, Son tightened his grip to a choke hold.

Fear and anger boiled up, immediate and hot. Tyler struck a tang soo do stance and rifled his palms upward, knocking loose Son's hands. He drew back to clip the exposed neck but stopped. Don't escalate. Too risky. Tyler caught a glimpse of the barking Chiki flailing against his leash.

Elder pinned his arms around Son to hold him in check.

Tyler squeezed his arms to his sides and stood firm, unwilling to flinch or step back. "What did you do?" he asked, so guttural his English sounded foreign even to himself. Seeing the confusion in their expressions, he attempted to ask what their problem was. "Qu'est ce que tu à fait?" Damn! That translated to "What are you quite?"

Son's face puckered in rage, and his head butted forward. Tyler saw a flash and heard a crack. A chunk of something lolled onto his tongue, and he tasted blood. He spat half a front tooth into his palm, and pain seared through his mouth. Liquid trickled down his chin. A red stream drizzled to the ground, and his mouth refilled at once.

A crimson streak was snaking down Son's forehead, traceable to a puncture the size of Tyler's broken tooth. All three were yelling at once, while Chiki was barking and tugging Yuki closer. Tyler could manage only English, but it was clear that the assholes got his drift.

A lull fell over the group, and Tyler gathered his wits. He touched his pulsing jaw, saying, "Tu a cassé ma dents." You broke my teeth.

Son spun on his heel and stormed off to the truck.

"Degage," Elder yelled, "or I'll call the gendarmes!"

"Appelez-les rapide, rapide," Tyler said. Call them quick, quick—or a close approximation. He held out his broken tooth for Elder to see. "What will they say about this?"

"They are going to say this is our land here." Elder swept his arm over the fields. "C'est comme ça." It is how it is.

Chiki, now at Tyler's side, was growling and lunging toward Elder. Yuki, a few steps behind, was pulling feverishly on the leash. On seeing her, Tyler feared the men might strike her, too. If so, he doubted he could contain himself. "Eh bon," he pressed. "Call. We'll see."

"Think about what you ask!" Yuki called out.

"Leave," Elder insisted.

"Call the police," Tyler pressed.

"Leave."

"Call them. Go on. Do it!"

One of the chess players across the street was hobbling toward them. He looked elderly, about Tyler's height and weight but frail. He fixed amused blue eyes on Elder. Yuki was humming her scared-to-death tune. "Monsieur," Tyler said in greeting. "You saw what happened. He broke my tooth."

Chessman nodded in a somewhat friendly manner. "Oui."

Tyler turned to Elder and demanded in French, "You are going to pay me a tooth."

Elder waved him off. "It's nothing, nothing at all."

"You are going to pay me a tooth."

Wham. The heel of a palm slammed into Tyler's jaw. "I'm going to kill you!" Elder bellowed

The world reeled, and Tyler saw stars. His ears were ringing from the impact, from Chiki's barking and from Yuki's full-throated aria. "Omoidasu haru no hi. Hitoribotchi no yoru." Remembering those spring days. But I am all alone tonight.

Son stood within striking distance of Yuki, so Tyler stepped in between them and alternated his gaze between Elder and Son. "Sir," he called to Chessman. "Do you see this?"

Chessman nodded and appeared calm, even amicable.

"Shiawase wa kumo no ue ni. Shiawase wa sora no ue ni." Happiness lies beyond the clouds. Happiness lies above the skies.

The attackers eyed Yuki as if marbles were spewing out of her ears. Then they returned to their car. Tyler might have felt relief if not for his throbbing jaw and the meaning of those lyrics. Yuki sang those words because she felt alone and defenseless. Her hapless wail sprang from hopelessness and despair.

The pickup engine roared to life. The assailants careened past and out of sight. Chess player shuffled back to his game. The two soccer players continued to stand and watch Tyler.

"He broke my tooth!" Tyler called to them. "I didn't do anything."

They exchanged looks, and the taller of the two called out, "Yes, we know." Then they resumed their game.

No. He had done nothing to aggravate the assault. Done nothing to defend himself. Nothing a real man with rights in a civil society would have done. Nothing. A look at Yuki and his heart sank. Her cheeks were streaming with tears, and Chiki's leash, though hanging slack, was lashed tight around her scraped and swollen hand. The tips of her puffed, blue-cast fingers might have belonged to a corpse. Oblivious to what had to be excruciating pain, she stood like a zombie and swayed side-to-side, peering down the road where the truck had disappeared.

Then it hit Tyler. He was contributing to Yuki's grief as much as those attackers were. She had lost her home, her college degree, her hopes for a future, and even her safety—all to be with him. No wonder he sometimes got the feeling that she couldn't stand the sight of him.

"C'est comme ça," he said, his mouth sour with the taste of blood and powerlessness and humiliation and guilt.

Later, after arriving in Porto, as Yuki lay sleeping under a canopy of pines, he pulled out his journal and wrote.

> I lost half a tooth and with it my naive admiration of toughness. Anger, however warranted, and thugness are no more than ways to manipulate, and I was letting myself be manipulated-for nothing, really. This experience taught an expensive lesson about as cheaply as possible. How many ways it could have ended worse. We are very lucky to be only this unlucky.

A THUNDER BOOM VIBRATED TYLER'S tooth as he immersed the last stack of dirty dishes in hot, sudsy water. Dr. Moreau had warned him that the resin crown might feel sensitive for a while, but for two months? Tyler put away the last of the clean dishes. It had been a long night. With luck, he might make it out of Le Degré before the tension that was brewing between Chef and Tony boiled over. Which was more uncomfortable, he wondered, work or another night of Yuki's silent treatment?

He swabbed the stainless-steel counters to the rhythm of the rain pulsing against the dining room's floor-length windows. Waitress Mel burst into the kitchen and picked up four *crème brûlées*. As if she sensed Tyler's distress at the two growling alpha males, she raised a black-dyed eyebrow at him that read *Let it go, Marco.* She disappeared into the dining room.

"Vous baiseur paresseux!" You stupid fucker! Chef drove his point home with the snap of a wet towel. Co-owner of the restaurant and too slender for a man who constantly sampled rich foods, Chef was six inches shorter than Tyler. Older, though. Probably in his early forties.

"Ouch!" Tony dodged and popped his knees as high as a stage puppet's. "Aye!"

Granted, a little Tony went a long way. The guy stood too close, jabbered too much, and went to great lengths to avoid any effort that resembled work. Small, unattended items tended to disappear in the rotund little man's presence. Tyler averted his eyes. Intercede, and he'd only get himself fired. He wiped his hands and hung the dishtowel out to dry.

Snap.

"Ouch!" Tony was shaking like a Chihuahua that had just wet the floor. The higher he hopped, the harder and faster Chef flicked the towel.

Snap. Snap.

"S'il te plaît, arrête!" Please stop, and Tony danced on.

Enough was enough. Tyler tossed his apron on the counter and stepped forward to intervene. Before he could reach out to snatch the towel from Chef's hand, Tony threw up his arms and screamed, "I quit!"

"Good!" Chef bellowed. "Now get out of town before I wring your thieving chicken neck."

Tony bolted through the dining room and disappeared out the front door. Tyler snagged a fatty ham bone from the trash and pushed open the backdoor. Working in the restaurant and drafting a petition for asylum in Venezuela were stressful enough. Yuki should have the courtesy to tell him what was pissing her off. No, there wasn't much he could do about Chef and Tony, but he could try harder to fix whatever was bugging her.

He turned left into the splat of cold rain. A buoy was clanging in the harbor out front. Five long strides through pitch-darkness, and his fingers found the wooden gate's hook. The postage-stamp-size backyard, which came with the bungalow, was mostly a patch of weeds to begin with, and Chiki's obsessive digging wasn't doing it any favors. Tyler stepped under the tile roof's overhang, and a cold, wet nose touched his hand.

"Hey, boy." He extended the ham bone, heard the clamp of teeth and felt a tug. Tyler released and listened to the tinkle of Chiki's dog tags as he trotted to his doghouse. He lifted the door latch and eased inside. A flash of lightning illuminated the black, pot-bellied stove, no longer necessary in May's heat. The two-room bungalow lacked plumbing, but an exterior spigot provided water. For showers and laundry, they had the campsite down the road. To its credit, the bungalow came equipped with an electrical outlet, a wood stove, electric range, bed, couch, table with two chairs, and a ceiling light. As far as he could tell, it had only one roof leak, albeit located at the foot of the bed.

Tyler snagged the light chain, and the bare, sixty-watt bulb cast a yellow haze over the floor. As usual, Yuki's hot teakettle awaited him on the two-burner range. Her biology book lay open next to the laptop on the two-person, drop-leaf table in the center of the room. Yuki's deep-sleep breathing drifted down from the upstairs loft, keeping time to Chiki's blissful chaws and yammers outside. Tyler poured himself a cup of tea and sat at the table. He turned on the laptop. Too exhausted to write full paragraphs, he tapped bullet points into *Tome*.

- Tony got smacked with a towel, and for once, he perhaps didn't deserve it. He quit and was told to leave town.
- Very busy night. Didn't get to eat until late. Arrived back at nearly 4:00 a.m.
- Yuki and Sosson not getting on too well, but not fighting either, just stressed out.

Hoping for insight into what might be troubling Yuki, he scrolled through his recent entries.

13 April 2006. Chemistry class terminated after twenty minutes. Yuki and I argued over whether her pre-answer to the homework was correct. She became angry, refused to accept fault with her solution or listen to me explain what could be better about the solution.

She dropped out of the class to take a nap. I returned to epsilons.

Then we started a most agreeable evening that abruptly turned for the worse. She held Chiki on the couch, teaching him to disobey me, already a trend that we need to work to diminish. Now we haven't talked for twelve hours. Both Yuki and I are too damned stubborn.

15 April 2006. Moved wood out of downstairs and continued to overhaul the epsilons. Yuki burned the rice and blamed me, then locked me in the attic. I requested to be set free, but she refused. I stomped my feet, and this threw her into a blind rage, throwing things around the house, then punching and kicking me.

Yuki had a temper, for sure, but she was hardly the first person he'd driven to distraction. Case in point: the Zenith incident. His apartment-mates Rob, Matt, and Phil had salvaged an analog television from Caltech's street-side trash. For more than a week, he had tolerated their calling out advice and questions to Captain Picard and Alex Trebek, but when they started to rail at reruns of *Robot Chicken*, he knew it was a cry for help.

Home alone one afternoon, he hauled the accursed TV back to the street from whence it had come. No sooner had he positioned the thing beside the curb than a chubby second-year geophysics major pulled up in a green hatchback. Tyler helped her load it, and off it rolled.

Returning to find the TV gone, Rob stabbed a finger at Tyler's nose. "What'd you do with it?"

"I'm helping you break your unhealthy addiction," he had offered by way of explanation.

Rob erupted with phrases like "pig-headed" and "pushy." Then Matt and Phil came home, and the conversation took a turn for the more colorful.

Yes, Present Tyler should work at being more flexible. He had to stop telling Yuki what to do unless she asked him for his opinion. This stomping business of his was uncalled for. Still, there was more behind Yuki's funk than simply over-exposure to him. For one thing, she always introduced him as her friend or boyfriend. Could she doubt his commitment to her and their relationship?

Tyler climbed the ladder to the loft. Yuki lay asleep on the bedroll, curled in a fetal position. He dropped to one knee and jiggled her shoulder.

She sat bolt upright. "What? What's wrong?"

He took her hand. "I don't say this often enough. I want you to know I love you."

"Uh huh." She blinked. "Love you, too."

"You're the love of my life, and I'd like us to get married."

She yawned and wiped a strand of stray hair off her face.

Granted, he hadn't expected giggles or happy tears, but a smile would have been nice. "Will you marry me, please, someday?"

"Really? This is your marriage proposal?" Her features darkened. "'When you care enough to send the very best?'"

He rolled onto his heels. "I didn't want to wait another minute. As soon as we can afford it, let's buy a ring. So will you marry me?"

"Fine." She climbed inside the sleeping bag and pulled it over her head.

The lump of her body lay motionless except for the rise and fall of her breathing. No whispers. No sigh of exasperation or fatigue. Just silence. Moments ticked past, marked by the *splat*, *splat*, *splat* of water into the stew pot. Tyler descended the ladder, turned off the light, and climbed back to lie beside her. A lightning flash illuminated a dripping knothole in the rough-hewn ceiling. *Splat. Plop. Splat.*

Storms continued through the night. Tyler woke around 9:30 a.m. to find Yuki gone, no doubt to her job from hell. He grinned to recall her return from her first day as a hotel housekeeper.

"'Guests are requested not to smoke or do other disgusting behaviors in bed,'" she had explained.

He washed down some leftover tuna tartare with strong tea. Not the most appetizing breakfast, but high in protein and nutrients. He patched a few bugs in his epsilons and stepped outside to refortify the garden's chicken-wire fence after Chiki's latest assault. He repaired what he could and had returned to broom sweep when Yuki rushed in.

"Boss yells a me all the time in French!" She braced her arms on the table and raised a contorted face. "She gets madder and madder, and I do not know why!"

He stepped forward to hug her, but she brushed him aside. "You need to quit that job," he told her for the umpteenth time.

She stomped a foot. "Don't be ridiculous. We barely get by with us both working. You know how hard I looked to find that job."

He headed for the door. Probably a simple issue of miscommunication.

"Where do you go?" Yuki's voice took on an edge. "Do not even think to talk to Madame Pruchard."

Tyler stepped outside. "Be right back." A few diplomatic words were sure to smooth out the situation.

"Stay away from that woman!" Yuki yelled from the doorway.

Tyler hopped on the bike and steered onto flat, bay-hugging D84. Sweet-smelling purple bougainvillea blanketed a stone wall to his left. Above, Le Degré clung to the terraced mountainside, and its blue wrought-iron balusters fanned past. Across the road to his right, calm waves sparkled in the morning sun.

He cruised through Porto and straight to the hotel. There, he followed a shrill stream of French to a thin, stoop-shouldered woman outside an aisle of first-floor rooms. Madame Pruchard, garbed in a faded gray-striped dress, stood with her back to him. She was wagging an arthritic index finger at the upturned nose of a twentyish, dishwater-blond housekeeper.

Tyler cleared his throat. "Excuse me."

The old woman spun and edged a wrinkled, horse-like face under his nose. "Oui?" she asked, her breath smelling of garlic and skunk.

The straight-haired girl—possibly Eastern European—took advantage of the reprieve to flip the bird to Madame P.'s back. *Merci*, she mouthed to Tyler before disappearing into an empty guest room.

Tyler put on his best French. "I wondered if I might have a word with you about Yuki. It appears there is a misunderstanding."

"That girl doesn't do a thing I tell her," the long-nosed woman snorted.

"She speaks very little French," Tyler explained, "and has trouble understanding what you're asking."

"Whose problem is that? Do I look like a damned interpreter?"

No, he wanted to say, *you look like the Wicked Witch of the West.* "If you demonstrate what you're asking," he said, "she'll be happy to oblige."

Madame P.'s frizzy gray ponytail, secured with a shoelace, waggled as if independent of her bobbling head. "Little Princess is too stupid to learn and too lazy to care."

"Yuki's very bright." He coaxed his tone back from the brink of condescension. "She's not the least bit lazy."

The woman cocked her head like a grackle about to peck a worm. "Well, she may have plenty of energy in the sack, but when it comes to tucking a proper bedsheet or cleaning a commode, she's slow as tar."

He counted to two. "She's trying to do things right, and you have her working twelve-hour shifts without a lunch break. You'd run low on steam, too."

Madame P. played a tiny, imaginary violin with her thumb and index finger. "I rest when the work's done, and so can she." Her jaw jutted forward. "Princess finds it necessary to bitch to you, does she?"

"If you're unhappy with her work, I'd like to help bridge the language barrier."

"Pfft." She crinkled her nose. "More like a work-ethic barrier."

He swallowed a swell of anger. "The law requires employers to provide breaks."

The crone hitched her hands on her bony hips and hissed into his face. "Does it, now? As I recall, it also requires employees to show documentation."

What had begun as a fishhook in his chest was now a grappling hook. "All employees are entitled to breaks."

A smirk. "I'll give Princess a break. Tell her she has next week off and the rest of the month. In fact, I'll give her June and July off, too."

Alarms buzzed in Tyler's head. "That's not what she wants or what I'm asking."

"It's what I want." She brushed him aside and gimped toward the lobby. "And I'm not asking."

He followed her. "Don't do this. Please."

Picking up steam, Madame rounded the registration desk and entered an office. She slammed the door in his face. "Get the hell out of here!" she yelled from inside. "I'm calling the police."

"But—" He raised his hand to knock, but the sound of her pressing key tones stopped him.

"Get lost!" she screeched. "I'll have you arrested."

"Yuki doesn't want trouble." Desperate, he pinned his arms against the door. "She asked me not to come here."

"Hello? Yes, I want to report a foreigner. He's assaulting me."

She was bluffing. Probably. No point sticking around to find out. Tyler backed away and chose a long route toward the bungalow. A metamorphic rock alongside the road caught his eye, so he needed to examine its grains of quartz and feldspar. A vine only took a few minutes to remove from a holly bush. The bike's lock required tending. Chiki was overdue for his daily dose of affection, and his water dish had to be cleaned.

Out of excuses, Tyler put on a bright smile and stepped into the bungalow. "Hey."

Yuki hopped to her feet. "Where did you go?"

"Just biking," he said, "and thinking."

"Biking where?" Her gaze cut laser beams through his skull. "Thinking about what?"

"Um, you don't need that stupid job."

Her palm snapped to her mouth. "You talked to Madame Pruchard, didn't you?"

He dug for a response. "I—I was trying to help."

"What did she say?"

He tried to sound upbeat. "Uh, well, she wants to give you some time off."

Yuki gasped. "You got me fired!" She grabbed her backpack and jammed in a blouse, underwear, and a pair of pants. She retrieved her zippered makeup bag and wiggled her feet into her canvas sneakers. "How dare you."

"What was I supposed to do, let that shrew rip my fiancée to pieces? You're totally right about her. She's demonic."

Yuki tore for the back door. "We are not engaged. You cannot just wake me up and pop the question and call us engaged. You think I do not know that all for show?"

Without documents, there was no way they could actually register a marriage. "Illegals can express their commitment to each other," he said. "There's nothing to stop us from conducting a ceremony."

"Yes, there is." She threw up an arm and turned away. "No half-assed proposal or pretend marriage is going to fix our problems."

"I thought it'd make you happy."

"You want to make me happy?" She edged up to his face, her voice rising to a pitch strikingly similar to that of Madame Pruchard's. "Respect I can take care of myself. Mind your own business."

"But this is a real Cinderella story."

"What is real is this is no fairy tale." She rolled the pack onto her back and strode out the door, signaling for Chiki to come along. "What is real is because of you we have no future, and I got to go beg for my shitty job back."

"Madame P. will come around," he said, wondering whether she was leaving to speak with her boss or leaving him forever. "You might want to give her a little time to cool down, though."

"We are out of here." Yuki stormed outside the backyard fence. Tyler and Chiki trailed close behind.

"Don't you go," Tyler said. "I'll leave."

She turned to face him, waving her hands as she spoke. "I don't care what you do, and I don't want to marry you anymore." She tromped away.

He followed her a few steps and then slowed to a halt. "Yuki."

Still walking, she raised her middle finger and shouted, "'This Bud's for you!'"

"Yuki, wait."

Chiki paused to see if his master was coming. Then he took a few steps to catch up with Yuki and turned again, his expression entreating. Yuki rounded the corner and disappeared from sight. Head low, Chiki trotted after her, and they were gone.

There was no point calling out or chasing after her. "I'm sorry," Tyler said to the barren scrap of yard and to the fresh thunderclouds rolling in from the west.

No way would he live here without Yuki. He climbed to the loft and stuffed his backpack full of clothes. He rolled up the bedroll, strapped it on, and climbed back downstairs. After wrapping Jaynes's *Probability Theory* in a plastic bag, he filled his Nalgene from the outside spigot and slid it into a loop on his pack. The patter of rain steadily accelerated as he made his way up the mountain's stone steps. A grove of pines offered a somewhat sheltered spot, so he unfurled the bedroll underneath and crawled inside. Unable to sleep, he tried without success to predict where drops of rain would hit his all-too-absorbent cocoon.

An hour or so passed, and the rain ended. Soaked to the bone and in zombie mode, he draped his bedding on a low-hanging limb to dry and migrated downhill. After following the road to the campground, he took a cold shower and put on damp clothes, then reported to work. He drifted through his afternoon shift, but as his daze wore off, the dink and scrape of pots and pans grew harsher and less bearable. He tried stuffing cotton in his ears and that took the edge off the noise, but the hyperstrong scents of braised beef and fish made him want to vomit. Every motion, no matter how routine, required concentration and sapped his energy. Customers eyed him as if they knew what he'd done and were judging him to be guilty.

The shift ground to a close at last, and Tyler's feet steered him out the door. He retrieved the laptop from the bungalow and plodded up the stone steps. Green eyes in bushes blinked at him in cold disregard. Peepers croaked *Yuki. Chiki. Lost them.* He shook his head to rid it of the refrain, but the chant persisted, more insistent than ever. *Yuki. Chiki. Lost them.*

On reaching camp, he ran through a troublesome segment of epsilon code. That kept the croaks at bay until his laptop battery died, and the chants resumed full force. He snugged into his cold, wet bedroll and closed his eyes—if only he could shut his ears. *Yuki. Chiki. Lost them.*

ON DAY TWO, A PIERCING WHINE jolted Tyler awake in early light. Yuki? No. Two tangled limbs were rubbing against each other in the wind. He dressed and shuffled downhill, unlocked his bike, and pedaled toward the hotel where Yuki worked—or used to work. Along the way, he thought of a poem:

<u>The Nod of the Sea</u>

Unregistered and unnoticed,
the land of a thousand unrecorded feats
passes in silence.

Hard breath hangs in cold air.
Questions, pushed by the bite of fatigue,
teeter on the edge.

Thoughts and hopes of every sort flurry,
descend into and rise out of insanity,
then melt into the morning calm.

The knowing nod of the sea
seems to forget.
But I was here,
and I, too, shall be forgotten.

A housekeeper's cart stood outside a room, halfway down the second floor. Tyler trotted up external stairs and along a white-railing walkway to an open door. No Yuki. Instead, the Eastern European girl looked up from a roaring vacuum cleaner and smiled. She turned off the machine and swayed her shapely hips toward him. Her employee badge read Mia.

"You come to rescue me again?" she asked with a tilt of her head.

"I was looking for Yuki," he said.

"She your girlfriend?"

Good question. Girlfriend…fiancée…wife…ex? "Does she still work here?"

Mia's expression registered disapproval. "Ya, boss bitch, she make her to clean toilet in office. It back up. Shit everywhere." She wrinkled her nose. "She on shit list. Get shit jobs."

Poor Yuki. "Tell her Mark stopped by, okay?"

She nodded and went back to vacuuming. He returned to Le Degré and fell into a routine: Clear the table. Reset. Wash the dishes. Empty the washer. Clear and reset. Wash and empty.

He planted his heavy legs in front of the sink and sank his arms in near-scalding water. The burn pulled his mind off the ache in his heart. Wash the pots and pans. Fill the dishwasher. With no reason to leave and masses of fish to clean, he stayed past 4:00 a.m. before disinfecting the sink area and making his way to the pine grove. *Yuki. Chiki. Lost them.*

Three days now without Yuki. Tyler lay on his bedroll and listened to an unusual birdcall. No, that was his cell phone ringing.

"So where are you?" Elise's fiery voice sounded more intense than usual. "Customers are waiting for their omelets and steaks."

Competent and ever in motion, co-owner Elise could be Jekyll or Hyde, and Tyler never knew who was at home. Like Chef, she looked to be in her forties, but that was where the similarities ended. Shapely in miniature, she cleared her path with a pen or clipboard extended outward like the prow of a ship. Her thick, loose-curled brown hair flagged behind her like a proud ensign. Sometimes cajoling, often shrill and on edge, Elise commanded a room, as well as Tyler's respect. This must be her way of telling him she wanted him to cook. A promotion!

"Be right there." He tore down the stone steps. How hard could it be to fry a few eggs and meat?

The potatoes took too long to soften. He charred a steak, ordered rare, to shoe leather. Then he crashed two loaded plates onto the kitchen floor. As he stooped over to sweep up the mess, Elise's footsteps sounded to his right.

She pushed him aside and stepped up to the griddle. "Table six needs busing," she said, tying an apron around her waist.

So much for the big promotion. Tyler cleared the table and reset it before busing and resetting two tables of four. The dining room was quiet, and dirty dishes were piling up in the kitchen, so he washed and rinsed a stack. But as he turned to refill the sink, Elise wagged soup ladle in his face and sprayed buttery white sauce across his cheeks.

"What's wrong with you?" She head-pointed toward the dining room. "You expect our patrons to stand around all day with their fingers up their butts while they wait for you to seat them?"

He probably ought to explain that he would gladly have seated people if he'd known they were there, but he was here washing dishes. Or he could point out that seating customers was the hostess's job, and Daki was in the pantry smoking a cigarette. But what good were excuses, and why land that poor girl in trouble, too? Besides, Elise had asked a good question. What *was* wrong with him?

"Sorry," Tyler said, but Elise was already halfway to the dining room. A fragrance of cloves and lilacs hovered in her wake. Stifling a sneeze, he went about resetting table six beside the front window. A figure outside caught his eye. Yuki! She was crossing the terrace and headed toward the bungalow. He would apologize for botching the marriage proposal, for almost costing her that job, for making her life miserable. Problem was customers were queued up. Two tables needed busing. No way could he break free.

Fewer than five minutes passed. Then Yuki strode in the opposite direction, her belongings heaped in her arms. She had come for her stuff, not to see him. He flushed with disappointment, then anger. Who needed her anyway? Good riddance. Peace out. That woman was the poster child for high maintenance. He scrubbed a damp cloth through a glob of grease. Daki walked past, in the process of seating a couple in sailing attire. Pretty, friendly, unattached Daki.

Tyler cleared the table in her trajectory. "Want to go to the Oasis after work?" he asked as she passed with a basket of rolls.

She brightened. "Sure."

Daki leaned toward Tyler from her seat at the black-lacquered bar and took a sip of her Oriou, a local, organic wine from the Domaine de Torraccia vineyard. She tucked a strand of silky, soft-curled blond hair behind an ear. "So where are you from?" she asked in lilting French.

"Canada," he said. "And you?"

"Switzerland." She smiled. "Ever been?"

"No."

"You would love the mountains." She took another sip. "But maybe not too much the cold winters."

"I know about cold." He took another slug of his bottle of Pietra beer, and his white-knuckled grip on its gold label relaxed, almost. "Canada is all about cold winters."

"What brings you to Corsica?" she asked.

"Just sightseeing. You?"

She nodded. "Me, too."

"You're a reader." She gestured toward the back of the barstool where his pack was slung. "You went to college, didn't you?"

Here they came, the personal probes. He supposed he couldn't disguise that he was educated. "Yeah," he said. "University of Toronto."

"You major in math?

"I guess."

She giggled. "You don't know?"

He shrugged.

"You have family?" she asked.

"An aunt in Montreal." Another lie. One more chink chiseled off his soul.

She tapped the top of his Jaynes book, which was poking out of his pack. "So where do you get your talent for math, from your mom or your dad?"

He flashed on Dad playing math games with him as a child, on a play grocery store Mom once constructed of egg cartons and empty tin cans. How he'd loved to ring the toy register and count change. He downed another gulp. "Yeah."

"I'll bet you're going to be a professor someday." She bumped her shoulder into his, and her little finger brushed his hand.

Tyler recoiled and somewhat recovered by raising his arm to finish his drink. He set the empty longneck on the bar. No, he didn't have time for this. He should be working on his epsilons. He studied a rack of liquor bottles that lined the mirrored wall behind the bartender and tried in vain to read the backward reflection of their labels. "Sorry, but I gotta go. Can I walk you home?"

Daki looked surprised, maybe even disappointed. A pretty girl like her was probably unaccustomed to having a date cut short. "No." She smiled, a little too large and frozen. "I'm good."

He paid for their drinks. Then he made his way out the door and up the mountainside. Damn those epsilons. Damn them for making him feel guilty for sacrificing a couple of hours of programming time.

> It was a rather unpleasant experience. I tried not to think about how this was a waste of my time, but my epsilons somehow inspired a guilt that I was sacrificing time that could be spent on my work. Furthermore, my socialization ability has deteriorated considerably from my youth. When combined with a language problem, it can really kill the conversation. But even as I genuinely evaded the typical awkwardness of this region, I still didn't really feel any desire for conversation. Just feeling old and out of place...

Okay, maybe he missed Yuki a little.

Wash. Rinse. Repeat.

• • •

9 May 2006. Tyler's heart skipped a beat at the appearance of a human form on the periphery of his vision. Probably another customer. He glanced sideways and spotted a pink jacket slung over a slim woman's back. Yuki! Work was slow, so he held up five fingers. He had his apron draped on a peg before Chef could nod his begrudging approval.

Tyler hustled next door and caught up with Yuki. She sat slumped at the kitchen table. Must have lost her job, or she'd be at work. "You quit the worst job you ever had?" he asked, cool yet friendly.

Fixing her eyes ahead and down, Yuki said, "No need to help irrational, stupid people's business anymore." She stretched out a hand that bulged with euros. "Almost six hundred. We can pay last month's rent."

Tyler fought an urge to wrap her in his arms, to explain how lonely life was without her, to tell her how dead he felt when she wasn't near. He wanted to explain that he had an inkling of what might be troubling her because the same angry shades from the past were tormenting him, too.

"Good for you," he said.

She locked him in her gaze. Now was his chance to pour out his heart, to tell her that he, too, felt the tidal push of emotions so powerful that they threatened to break free and force a fight to the finish. Instead, he let the moments tick past.

"Mind if I crash here for a while?" she asked.

He shrugged. "No problem. Maybe I'll stay, too, if that's all right with you?"

She winced a smile. "'I'd rather fight than switch.'"

He grinned. "How about not fighting at all?"

She nodded and began to gather their dirty clothes. He gave her a hand and then returned to work as she tramped on to the campground laundry.

TYLER COUNTED THE MINUTES until his shift ended. As part of his daily food allotment, he selected a large leftover pan of paella for Yuki. For Chiki, he dug through the slimy trash and rescued a half-eaten chunk of wheat-flour nut bread. On his return to the bungalow around midnight, he found Yuki awake and folding laundry.

"Want some paella?" He offered her the untouched dish of rice, saffron, chicken, and seafood.

Instead, she snatched the gross nut bread, saying, "I'll take this one." She took a bite before he could stop her.

"You don't want that." He reached for it, but she swung it away and chomped a supersize bite.

Maybe she hadn't heard him. "That's Chiki's," he repeated louder. "It came from the garbage."

"Don't yell at me," she mumbled through chipmunk cheeks. "You're not the boss of me."

He recalled the stench and slime of the rotten chicken skin he'd dug through to retrieve that half-eaten nut bread. "I'm telling you: you really don't want that."

A swallow. "Don't tell me what I want."

He wrested the butt out of her hands and flicked it outdoors to Chiki. A leap, and his little buddy caught it midflight. Tyler was turning toward Yuki just as she drew back and kicked full force at him. He blocked with his arm and sustained only minor irritation. Unfortunately, Yuki's thrust drove the tender part of her heel into the bony point of his elbow.

"Ouch!" She hopped on one foot. "Ooo ooo."

> Sosson was unhappy to see Yuki unhappy and also unhappy to be kicked. After returning from a soapless shower, Sosson found her in a better mood.

23 May 2006. Grateful to finish early, at 10:15 p.m., Tyler slipped outside and counted his pay, 225 euros. Unfortunately, that was exactly what he was owed. At this rate, he'd never make rent. Plus, Antoine had requested their revised petition for asylum by the end of the week, so he should turn down any extra hours, if offered. Answering the form's intricate questions was proving problematic. One wrong word and the Venezuelan authorities would reject the two of them as spies.

Tyler swung open the bungalow door to find Yuki slouched at the table and folding a white origami swan. Paper clippings that brought to mind bird droppings dotted the tabletop. To her right, eight legless fowl floated in formation like an armada of ghost ships.

"Hi." She snipped a wing of unfinished Bird Nine.

Tyler picked up a completed swan to examine it. Intricate. Elaborate. The thing probably consumed a half sheet of paper and one serious block of time. "We're not going to cover rent," he said.

Snip. Fold. "Guess we will have to move out."

Really? This from the woman who had twisted his arm into renting this dump? He could hardly care less about sleeping inside during the summer. But, no, Yuki had insisted they have a roof over their heads. "For protection from mosquitos," she had said. No matter that renting this crummy shack took every penny of their measly earnings. No matter that it was so pocked with holes that mosquitos flooded in constantly. He set down the bird and tried to bottle his irritation. "So what's your strategy for finding a job?"

Apparently, cutting useless paper toys required Yuki's full concentration. "Working on it," she said.

"Oh, yeah? Looks to me like you're just sitting here, not talking to anybody."

Her head jerked upright. "Just say it, why don't you?"

"Say what?"

"You don't want me here. I know you're dying to say it."

"Where do you come up with this crap?"

She flicked Bird Nine across the table, and it capsized two of its brothers. She rose and scooped up her bag, saying, "I'm going to the mountains. One month."

Tyler stared at her canvas bag. Bulging. Prepacked. Positioned to take wing. "Look." A rush of confusion swept away most of his annoyance. "I'm happy you're back. It's just that work's a pain, and we're short on rent. I'm stressed about writing the petition."

The birds sat in mute witness, holding her gaze. "That's what you say."

He grasped her shoulders and forced her to look at him. "It's true. I'm glad you're here."

Tears brimmed in her eyes. "I thought I was unwanted."

"No." He pulled her close and whispered in her ear. "You are wanted very much." He pried the bag from her fingers, and it plopped to the floor. Slipping a hand under her blouse, he ran a thumb under her soft, plump breast. He tingled all over. "Misunderstanding clarified?"

She pressed her hips to his, kissed his ear, and lilted, "'Something special's in the air.'"

"'Come fly with me,'" he whispered between kisses.

YUKI TOOK A SEAT at the bar toward the end of happy hour. She enveloped Tyler in a warm smile and mouthed, *Happy birthday.*

She was trying to make 2 June special—another sweet gesture in a long line of them. After two years and three months of exile—after twenty-seven years of existence—all he had to show for his time on this planet were the clothes on his back. Couldn't even pay rent. Yuki was a good sport to live outdoors, especially considering the constant stream of bloodthirsty tormentors that crept through their holey net. He put on a grin and crossed to her. Tonight, he had to find a way to show her how much she meant to him.

He elevated his pad in pretense of taking her order. "If you can hang out until I finish," he said, "we can walk up to camp together."

"Okay." She head-pointed to the chalkboard. "Give me special cocktail for ladies with nuts, please."

He let that slide.

The last customer left late, pushing cleanup past 11:30 p.m. Then, instead of leaving, Tyler insisted that Yuki check out a new video machine. "You gotta see this." He blasted an asteroid to demonstrate. "Isn't this neat?" He played again. "You counter with this." Points racked higher and higher. "Cool, eh?"

No reply. He glanced up to find Yuki gone. What a stupid, inattentive jerk he was, getting absorbed in meaningless shit and neglecting everything he cared about. It wouldn't be such a big deal if this were the first time. Why couldn't he learn? Maybe he'd find her at the campsite.

Tyler raced uphill, but Chiki greeted him with the enthusiasm of a lonesome dog. No Yuki. A patch of white on the bedroll caught his eye. As he lifted a handmade card from under a paperweight stone, his heart felt a pinch at the origami hearts and stars that dotted the card's cover. Inside, scribed in mind-blowing calligraphy were the words, *Happy Birthday.* Below them, in hurriedly scratched cursive, were the words, *See you on the ninth.* No explanation. No indication as to where she was going. Not even "Love, Yuki."

Maybe he should go in search of her, but where to look? No, probably better to give her space. He could apologize when she returned in a week. He dug into his pocket and found a piece of string he'd saved while carving a rump roast. He darned the damned rips in the mosquito netting before stretching out on his bedroll. Except that he was not alone. Wings whirred around his ears and whined a twisted intonation of the birthday song.

THERE WAS LITTLE THAT TYLER COULD DO about Yuki's disappearance, so he decided to direct his energy toward worming his way back into the good graces of Chef and Elise. He rose early and set to work rebuilding a section of the restaurant's patio. Two hours into the project, wear and tear from shoveling destroyed what was left of his shoes. Beside him, a full-size nude sculpture of a sea nymph danced a barefoot greeting to all who entered the restaurant. Inspired to abandon his shoes as well, he tied his laces and tossed the pair into the overhead branches of a shiny-leaved magnolia tree.

Two more hours of hard labor, and he finished up. By 4:30 he had the tools put away. If he hurried he could hit the campground showers and make it to work on time.

"What's this?" Elise was standing in the open doorway.

"How do you like it?" he asked, confident his good deed would score points.

She surveyed the patio, obviously impressed. Except when her gaze lifted to his shoes dangling from the tree, her expression turned sour. "Those aren't yours, are they?"

"Yeah." He rolled a board onto its edge and pulled it across the stones to demonstrate his meticulous leveling, a technique he'd learned from Dad when they'd built a patio around the pool back home in Glenmoore, P.A. "I filled the spaces with sand to lock the stones in place," he explained with pride, "and I graded it to slope a centimeter per meter, so rain will run away from the foundation."

Elise's eyes remained fixed on the discarded shoes, and her face was turning crimson. "Get those damned things down from there!" she barked. "Right now!"

Tyler overlooked her temporary distraction and, instead, waved his hand over the freshly laid patio. "I lined up the mineral patterns of the stones, so they all flow in the same direction to look like a river. Cool, eh?"

Elise was pacing back and forth, her hands on her hips. "Now!"

"Okay. Sure." He scooped up a handful of oversize pebbles and tossed one, managing only to twirl the rubber soles. Another toss and another, and the laces knotted like twine around the branch. A bad lob smacked the fieldstone wall, barely missing a plate-glass window and leaving a telltale brown splotch high on the restaurant wall.

"What the hell is the matter with you?" Elise roared.

"Sorry."

She slammed the door and disappeared inside. Tyler scaled the tree and shinnied out onto the shoe-bearing limb, except the farther he climbed, the lower the limb sagged. Any more, and the branch was sure to break. He inched backward and dropped to the ground.

Five minutes to five, and his clothes were smudged and grimy, his hands filthy. A sniff of his armpit about keeled him over. No way could he report late to work. Elise would can him for sure.

Tyler ducked inside to the restroom, slipped off his shirt, and washed his hands, face, hair and feet under the faucet. He was daubing away the worst of his body odor with wet paper towels when the new guy from Nigeria walked in.

Amine. Probably the toughest, softest guy Tyler had ever met. He looked even poorer than Tyler, and his background remained a mystery because he dodged questions about himself. But the poor guy's stub where a little finger should be and a scar that ran from his earlobe to the tip of his chin stood testament to a hard life. How he'd retained that gentle, earnest nature was anybody's guess.

"Hey," Amine said and stepped up to the urinal.

"Hey." Tyler swiped a blob of dirt off his pants and threw on his shirt. He was three-quarters buttoned before he realized the holes were misaligned. "I'll fix these later." He raked his fingers through his hair.

Amine nodded gravely and dug into his brown canvas pouch, producing a pair of flip-flops. "Put these on." He extended the worn but clean footwear toward Tyler.

"Thanks." Tyler slipped them onto his sore feet, and the two bolted through the door.

Maybe an hour passed. Tyler was busing in a load of dirty dishes, and Amine was rinsing plates and setting them in the dryer rack. "You okay, my friend?" Amine whispered.

He must have noticed that Tyler's hands were shaking with fatigue and hunger. "I'm fine," Tyler said. He gathered four clean place settings to reset table three and asked, "What's Elise got against shoes in trees, anyway?"

"Ha!" Amine snorted. "Those be gang symbols, don't you know? They mark territory."

Oh boy. On top of everything else, now Elise thought he was a gang member. At the next lull, Tyler hauled a ladder out of the backroom and took down his shoes. He chucked them in a trashcan. Hoping to redeem himself, he peeled more than three pounds of fresh garlic and sliced his fingers in the process. The wet cuts refused to clot, so he scotch-taped tissue tight around his fingers to finish the batch.

Elise tore through, more forward-tilted than usual. While she appeared not to see the enormous container of peeled garlic, she apparently had no difficulty noticing the bulbous wads on his fingers. "You will need to replace that tape." She scowled at him and dashed on.

A NEW DAY, AND YUKI WAS STILL MISSING. But this was only the fourth, and she had said she'd come back on the ninth. Business was slow, so Tyler asked Chef, "Anything you'd like me to do?"

Chef shook his head. "No."

Noon came around, and customers were sparse. "You sure you don't have anything for me to do?"

"No."

Twelve thirty. "I could take on a project."

"Nothing for you."

Amine hustled past, and Chef punched him in the arm.

Mel swished up to him and whispered, "Need to talk with you."

Tall and down-to-earth, Mel got along with customers, management, and employees alike—all seemed amused at her impudent attitude. She had this knack for saying whatever she pleased without causing offense. Even the devil-may-care sway to her hips when she walked seemed to telegraph that she could hardly care less about what people thought. To him and Yuki, she had become like a favorite aunt. He nodded toward a table of newly seated customers and began to mop in that direction.

Mel grabbed a handful of supplies and trooped over. As she handed out the menus, her winning smile lit up her customers' faces. A covert glance toward the kitchen, and she warned them in her cigarette-worn voice, "Stay away from our *blanquette de veau*, but today's *soupe à l'oignon* has a savory bread pudding that you'll be fighting to the death over." The two couples nodded in gratitude and buried their noses in their menus.

Mel sidled up to Tyler. "Saw Yuki," she rasped. "I invited her to stay with me, but she said there's not enough space."

Mel sometimes invited them over for drinks, and it was true. Though her one-room efficiency had amenities like running water, a kitchen sink, and carpeting, it was tinier than their bungalow. He swabbed a gummy substance off an adjacent table. "Where'd she go?"

Mel bobbed her thin shoulders and brushed her unnaturally black bangs off her forehead, exposing a second artfully painted eyebrow. "I'm leaving tomorrow for a few days on the mainland. Told her she's welcome to stay at my place while I'm gone. Will you remind her to come get my key if you see her?"

Tyler dunked the mop into the murky waters of the wheeled mop tank. "If I see her, sure, but that's a big *if*." Chef was giving him the stink eye, so he flopped the dripping mop head into the wringer and cranked the handle. The smell of bleach and soap burned his nose.

"Oh, honey." Mel hitched her hips and rested a foot. "You two just need space." A bell dinged.

"Thanks, Mel." He slopped the mop head on the floor, and she charged off to pick up an order.

9 June 2006. Tyler tucked his journal into a printout of a research paper on evolution and propped the pages upright behind the sink for easy reading. Chiki was tucked in for the night, and he had Yuki's welcome-home gift all planned. He double-checked his pocket, and the wad of cash was still there—enough, he hoped to persuade Elise to re-rent the bungalow to him. Yuki was sure to pass by on her way uphill. What he'd give to see her face when she saw the light on and realized he'd re-rented the place for her. He reached into the hot water to a mound of silverware and read the first page of the research as he washed.

Amine clunked a stack of dirty dishes next to Tyler's elbow and broke into a wide, toothy smile. "So far, so good, eh? Not too busy. Not too slow."

Tyler chuckled. "Just right." Now all he needed was a chance to present his offer to Elise.

Chef passed behind them, cursing something about a stupid bitch not knowing the difference between a perfectly grilled steak and shoe leather. "Vous baiseur paresseux," he said and scowled at Amine. Then he drew back and slammed the heel of his palm against Amine's ear.

Amine toppled sideways, and his arm dipped into Tyler's soapy water. Suds sloshed over the rim and splashed onto Chef's black leather shoes.

"Sorry. Sorry." Amine grabbed a towel and dropped onto all fours to pat at Chef's shoes.

But Chef plowed a set of tongs into Amine's back. "You idiot!"

"So sorry." He slopped the now-soaked towel over Chef's ankles.

Red-faced, Chef drew back and kicked Amine in the kidneys, rolling him into the puddle on the floor.

Tyler stepped between them and edged eyeball to eyeball with Chef. "That's enough," he said.

"Careful now." Chef's words came slow and guttural.

Amine bounded upright. "It's okay." He flagged the wet towel. "Everything be cool."

But Tyler continued to glare into Chef's squinted, veined eyes. He heard what sounded like a punctured tire—his own breath, seething through his gritted teeth.

At last, Chef turned away, muttering something about needing to prepare a fucking steak. Tyler took a bathroom break to pull himself together. After splashing water on his face, he stood upright, and a contorted, un-Tyler-like visage was staring back at him in the mirror. Inhale. Exhale. Now he'd done it: pulled the pin out of the grenade. Chef was sure to fire his ass.

He returned to his dishwashing and tried to focus on Yuki's return home that night. Oh, crap. He'd better get to Elise before Chef told her about his insubordination. He found her alone and taking inventory in the pantry. "I'd like to re-rent the bungalow, and here's half the money." Tyler pressed the wad of euros into her palm as he spoke. "I'll get the rest to you by end of month."

Elise rubbed her chin with her free hand, and a pained look crossed her face. "Hmm."

Chef must have spoken with her already. They were probably planning to sack him at shift's end. She looked to be weighing the pros and cons: Take half the money and fire him, and she'd be hard-pressed to collect the balance because unemployed renters never paid. But if she refused the money, then the bungalow would remain empty, and she'd get nothing. The place didn't come close to meeting code. She could never rent it to anyone legal.

Tyler kept quiet and let the euros do their work. He pictured Yuki's joyful expression at seeing the bungalow aglow and realizing he'd rented it for her.

"Okay." Elise sighed as if enduring great sacrifice. "But you better come up with the rest on July first."

"Deal." He grabbed her free hand and shook it.

Tyler's shift ticked to a close at nine o'clock. To celebrate Yuki's homecoming and his securing his job for another three weeks, he bought her a tart. Hurrying next door, he stepped inside the stale room and opened the window. While he waited for the bungalow to air out, he swept the floors, flipped the mattress, and made the bed.

Half past nine. He brewed hot tea before setting the table with a candle and the tart. No Yuki.

Eleven o'clock. He sat down to read. Midnight came and went. Yuki wasn't going to show. He ate the tart, locked the door, and trudged through heavy fog to rejoin Chiki at the campsite.

10 June 2006. What could have happened to that woman? Tyler exhaled slowly to quell another surge of worry. The steady flow of customers provided a welcomed interruption from the graphic images that kept running through his head. Elise, Amine, Daki, and even Chef seemed to be giving him wide berth. Okay, maybe he was a little on edge.

Not a moment too soon, the shift ground to an end. He strode outside, and his heart skipped a beat. A yellow glow was streaming through the cracks around the bungalow's door. Yes! Yuki must be home! He rushed next door only to find the place empty. Shit. He'd left the damned light on. What an idiot.

11 June 2006. Two days late and no sign of Yuki. Serious concerns. Elise strode through the restaurant with the zippered moneybag clasped under an arm. "Going to the bank," she called to Chef.

Tyler intercepted her at the door. "You know where Mel lives, right?"

"Sure. On the east side of town."

"Mind checking for lights in her apartment?"

"It's out of my way," Elise said with a shake of her head. "Don't drag me into your lovers' quarrel."

Tyler continued to block her exit.

"Fine," she said with a flap of her arms. "I'll drive by, but that's it." She swung her handbag forward like a battering ram and plowed her way out the door.

Hours passed. Elise returned and marched straight toward her office. "I saw something red in her window," she uttered as she passed by.

Tyler imagined blood drippings and flesh spatters. Bittersweet memories of life with Yuki in the desert flooded his thoughts. He finished work in bottled-up panic and sprinted uphill to the campsite. There, he pumped pushups until sweat trickled down his back and his arms shook with fatigue. He smoked a joint and wrote in his journal.

> Yuki is such an inconsiderate thing. I'm sick of worrying each time. If she wants to stay in the village, that's fine, but she should just fucking say so. Otherwise I worry that something happened, and I'm not doing anything to save her when she needs me. But she always does this, and it always turns out okay, so I'm just going to let her do her life. Even if it happens that she has a broken leg in the mountains...or has been attacked by some hooligans. Shit. Need to stop thinking like that.

ANOTHER LONG SHIFT DREW TO A CLOSE, and Tyler slipped out of Le Degré's back door. It was 12 June, three days past Yuki's return date. What could have befallen her? He couldn't bear the Pandora's box of horrors that a glance at the bungalow would uncap, so he steeled his gaze to the mountainside. But as he turned toward the stone steps, he couldn't resist a quick glance. He stopped dead in his tracks.

Light encircled the bungalow's door as if it were a black hole. Had he accidentally left the light on again? No, he didn't think so. He was caught in the event horizon and unable to turn away, so he let it pull him through the gate and up to the door. His knuckles rapped on the weathered wood. "Anybody home?" he asked.

"Come in."

Yuki's voice, and she sounded happy. He lifted the latch and stepped into the scent of lemons and tea. "Hey."

"Hey." She smiled over a steaming cup.

She looked relaxed and content, maybe even happy to see him. Stop biting the lower lip. What to say? "Hey." For Pete's sake. He slipped into the empty chair and sat facing her.

She gestured toward the teapot. "Want some?"

"Sure."

She retrieved his mug from the shelf, poured it full and added honey, just the way he liked. "Mel told me you rented the bungalow again." She set the mug in front of him and eased into her seat.

He took a sip of the hot, sweet tea, and his aching muscles relaxed from his shoulders to his toes. "I paid half the month's rent," he said. "Elise is all right with waiting for the rest." *Yes, she'll wait for eighteen days*, he thought, *and then she and Chef were planning to give him the boot.* Guess he could share that tidbit later.

"Nice surprise."

Yes. I intended it as a surprise, he wanted to say, *a gift to make you happy.* Instead, he went for nonchalant. "So where were you?"

She took a slow sip. "Camping."

"Your note said you'd come back three days ago."

She raised one shoulder in half a shrug. "I wanted to return in the morning, but I kept waking too late."

No crippling injury or illness had kept her away? No bruising attack or rape, just a silly whim? "You found it unthinkable to come back at any other hour?" His tone carried a bite.

Her smile vanished. "That's right."

He downed his tea and shoved the empty cup to the center of the table. He stood, inadvertently grating the legs of his chair across the wooden floorboards. "Pretty damned inconsiderate of you."

"Don't talk to me about inconsiderate."

They glared at each other until she turned away. She climbed to the loft, and he heard the rustle of her bedroll. All fell silent.

"Chiki's waiting for me," he called. Then he clicked off the light and pulled the door closed on his way out.

Chiki's enthusiastic bounds and wiggles made unclipping his leash impossible until a chunk of garlic bread quieted him. Tyler went through the motions of building a campfire. Then he sat on a log and stared into the flickering flames while he scratched Chiki's ears. Little buddy rested his muzzle on Tyler's lap as if he sensed his master's heartache. Chiki-san might have looked sorrowful if not for the stub of the loaf bobbling like a blunt cigar out of one side of his mouth.

What happened down there with Yuki? Tyler crawled into his bedroll. Chiki flopped close, providing unwanted body heat yet also the comfort of contact. Even so, Tyler tossed and turned, replaying the botched reunion. Yes, he was irritable. She had to know she'd worried him sick. Probably giving him a taste of his own medicine. Fair enough. How many hours had he worked on his epsilons and ignored her or played video games instead of spending time with her? Before she left, she'd complained that he didn't want her. Was it possible that she didn't know how he felt? Of course! How could she? She wasn't a mind reader.

He rose, threw kindling on the fire, and dug a pad of paper from his pack. In the fading light, he wrote her a letter.

Dear Yuki,

I can't sleep anymore because I'm overwhelmed with regret. You are the only thing that I love (other than Tiki [Chiki]) and the only thing I care about (other than Tiki), but somehow I lost precious moments with you-being distracted by things that I don't care about, like the computer. It makes me sad to treat you that way. I want to say that it hurts me more than anything to see you unhappy, and it hurts indescribably to know that I am the cause.

I'm sorry. I shouldn't be like this, and it's not the first time I've been inattentive. But I hope it's the last. It just confuses me: How can I be distracted by a video game when I could be spending time with you? I love you so much. I missed you every moment you were gone. I worried when you were late, and I held back how happy I was to see the bungalow light on. Even though I don't show it, this is the real Tyler beneath the mask that is becoming so thick and convincing that it even fools my dearest love. But it's just not real.

Before you left, we were good, close, and honest again. No mask-rather mask transparent only to each other (and to Tiki-san). Life can be too stressful. I get confused. Do stupid shit. I regret, and I'm sorry. Please believe me...I haven't really become who I sometimes seem like I've become. I don't understand why or how it's like this, but as soon as I can figure it out, I'll come back fully, all the time.

I love you. That's what I'm blathering about.

--You know who

Chiki led the way downhill in the silver-blue glow of a gibbous moon, and when they reached the bungalow, Tyler slid the letter under the door. He and Chiki shuffled back to camp. Little buddy seemed thirsty, so Tyler poured half his water into a bowl and listened to the vigorous laps. He slugged down what remained in his Nalgene and crawled into bed. He felt so tired his bones ached, but his shoulder blades settled onto one jagged stone after another, poking and prodding him to toss and turn.

Chiki's barking began as background noise in a dream before gradually seeping to the forefront of Tyler's semiconscious mind. Keeping his eyes closed, he shifted a bruised hip off a bump in the ground.

"Hey, You Know Who," Yuki's voice singsonged. "Wake up sleepy head."

Tyler cracked open an eye to her smiling oval face framed in soft-curled black hair. Heavenly. He bounded to his feet. "Sorry for being a jerk."

"Me, too." She cradled Chiki's muzzle between her hands and spoke in her schoolmarm voice. "We must be more patient with each other."

Tyler took her in his arms. They kissed, really kissed, like old times. He tossed the bedroll onto a thick cushion of pine needles, and it welcomed their eager bodies.

Tyler snuggled Yuki and indulged in a slow wake-up. The past few days in the bungalow had passed contentedly, but work was another matter. Chef was hitting Amine to obscene proportions, and more times than not when Tyler looked up, the man was shooting him the evil eye. Payday, just three days away, was ticking down like a doomsday clock.

"I checked into another dishwashing job," Yuki murmured, sounding half-asleep. "But the owner only wants to hire a guy. I know I just got back, but maybe I can leave today and enjoy nature in the forest, if that's okay with you. I'm still packed."

What good could come of unloading his fears about losing his job? Might as well let her enjoy a few worry-free days. "Sure," Tyler said. "I work the evening shift, so I can hike the first part of the trail with you. Then I'll come back, and you and Chiki can press on."

They skipped breakfast to trek to the trail and were soon hiking in the clouds. A cool breeze swished the limbs of towering evergreens, filling the air with pine scent. An upward-climbing stranger gazed into Chiki's panting mouth.

Tyler hikes among the towering pines.

"My!" he gasped. "He looks like a hyena."

Tyler chuckled. "So true!" They picked up their pace and proceeded deep into a solitary wilderness. Tyler shed his cover shirt, and as the sun rose to eleven o'clock, he peeled off the trail into a patch of ferns. Chucking his pack, he folded to sit cross-legged next to Chiki, now prone.

"Aahh." Yuki flopped onto her back beside them. "This should be every day normal."

Tyler dug out yesterday's newspaper, discarded from work, and puffed on an unlit, cigar-shaped twig. "Yes." He put on his Thurston Howell III voice as he scanned the front page. "A normal activity, yet a superior way of doing it."

Yuki kicked off her shoes and wiggled her feet. Tyler noticed a blister on the inside of her big toe. "Why do people buy shoes that hurt their feet?" he asked.

She cradled her head in her palms. "Gets back to attracting a mate," she said. "Peacocks fan bright feathers. Male baboons bare their shiny red butts. I like my shoes."

"Glad you don't prefer shiny red butts," he joked, and the conversation flowed to fashion as an agent in effecting species propagation and, hence, evolution. "Deterministic chaotic systems must arise as a limiting case of evolutionary systems," he concluded.

"Don't know about that," Yuki mumbled. "But people need to feel accepted, and they do things for reasons."

Chiki and Yuki drifted off to sleep, so Tyler pulled out his journal and wrote.

Ancient people made these walls, these trails, which now lie in neglect, abandoned to the pigs and cows.

> And such beautiful places these trails lead to. Will they be forgotten as well? I hope so. Then I can have them all to myself. There need to exist treasures for explorers to find. At the same time I also hope not, for it's such a loss. Neglect causes decay. So I have a contradiction...

His eyes fell on his prior entry:

> I feel sorry for Amine and am thinking of what I could do to modify the situation. Took a walk with Chiki and did a lot of stick throwing.

He sat thinking about fashion, about human motivations, about Amine and the likelihood of their losing their jobs. A glint of sunlight caused him to realize that the sun had slid well past vertical, so he rested his palm on Yuki's shoulder. "I have to go if I'm going to make it to work by five."

She blinked and sat up. "Miss you already."

A quick kiss, then he was moving fast. How to keep his job yet curtail Chef's abuse of Amine? Getting along with the man seemed unlikely. Maybe he could appeal to Elise's financial interests—convince her that even though she and Chef might not much like him or Amine, it was cheaper to keep them than to train their replacements.

Tyler reported to work early and interrupted a hushed confab between Elise and Chef. The two nodded grim hellos. Then Chef trailed him into the kitchen. One. Two. Tyler counted the seconds before the guillotine dropped. He emptied a carafe of stale coffee and poured in fresh water. Six. Seven. Out with the old grounds, in with the new. Chef cracked an egg with the force of a roofer whacking a nail.

Yuki had said, "People need to be accepted, and they do things for reasons." Could fear be what was really behind Chef's compulsion to fire him? Or the need for acceptance? "I was wondering." Tyler broke the silence. "Are there ways I can do my job better?"

Chef sized him up and down. "Spend more time in the kitchen and work faster." On that note, he filleted a tilapia.

Tyler took out the trash and returned to the rich scent of brewing Colombian dark roast. The coffee maker gurgled its final droplets, so he poured himself and Chef each a cup. A few sips and the caffeine kicked in. He mopped the floor and polished a sheen on the stainless steel *frigo* and stove.

"Look at that Marco!" Chef commented to Elise, loud enough for all to hear. "See how well he is doing his work." Throughout the shift, Chef touted Tyler's praises to Amine, to Daki, to everyone within earshot.

Late in the evening, Tyler asked, "Is there anything else I can do to improve?"

"No," Chef said, "just faster."

"I thought of a third." Tyler grinned. "I could be less disagreeable in the morning."

"Oh, ho!" Chef chortled. "Me, too."

Work in this positive ambience felt much lighter. More content, Chef even gave Amine an affectionate pat on the back. The shift ended almost before Tyler noticed, and he returned to the empty bungalow. On the table, nested under his orange bowl, he spied a letter from Yuki:

The outside of Yuki's letter to Tyler.

> I just realized how I was missing being in the nature, hiking around with you. It's sad to leave you. I'll be thinking about you throughout the trip. I know that. When you get a day off, we can go for a day hike somewhere.
>
> Chiki-san and I love you as much as you do! ...just zink about zat.
>
> Your future wife (hopefully...)

Happiness. Tyler polished off the draft petition to Venezuela and pulled out his journal.

> Found letter from Yuki. Made Sosson really really happy.

In order to deliver Antoine their petition information, Tyler and Yuki decided to combine business with pleasure and hike through the mountains to L'Abri. That night around the campfire he wrote.

What would life be without surprises? I keep the past as a surprise. This is opposite the usual situation of a fixed past and unpredictable future. Perhaps this is because I've always felt the future to be predictable enough that there's not enough room for surprise. That's what led me to this unpredictable past. Now there is a beautiful symmetry between past and present.

The meeting went well and inspired significant to-do lists. Then Antoine had to run, which was fine with them because they were hoping to return in time for Tyler to catch a good night's rest before his morning shift. They hiked right along, mulling their to-dos and the many possibilities before them. But on approach to the bungalow, a bright-white envelope came into view on the weathered wooden door. Secured with a red thumbtack, the legal-size envelope glared at them like an eviction notice.

Tyler extracted the single sheet and read its message aloud. "'Mark, don't be late for work. You'll be waiting tables as well as busing. Mel quit and left town. Be sure your apron is clean. Elise.'"

Yuki snatched it from his fingers. "What?"

Next to Antoine, Mel was their closest human friend. "This can't be right," Tyler said, as much to himself as to Yuki. "She wouldn't just pick up and leave without telling us. Would she?"

Yuki examined the paper. "No way."

He tried to recall something, anything that might have driven Mel away or that he might have done to cause her offense. The last time he'd seen her, she had fluffed her hair and chased a pen around a table, performing her best-ever Elise impersonation. They had nearly doubled over in laughter.

A dark thought squeezed Tyler's breath away. "What if Elise saw Mel impersonating her?"

"I can't believe this." Yuki's eyes flooded with tears. "Where would she go?"

They, more than most people, understood the value of goodbyes. Mel's disappearance without final farewells was more than disconcerting; it struck a raw nerve. This turn of events somehow made missing Dad's birthday later this week suck even worse. "Chef and Elise have to know what's going on." Tyler choked through what felt like a hot poker lodged in his throat. "I'm asking them tomorrow."

Yuki swung open the door, and its rusted hinges moaned. "We cannot just never see her again."

"No. No way." He fed and watered Chiki and left him out back. Then he went through the motions of helping put away the rest of their gear and supplies. He scrubbed most of the stains out of his dingy apron and tied it on the clothesline outside. Then he climbed into bed and lay on his back. Yuki tossed and turned as the hours ticked past.

Tyler eventually gave up on sleep and dressed in the dark. He wandered out back to pull his still-damp apron off the line. Chiki materialized at his side, so he stroked the dog's warm, furry head. Le Degré wouldn't open for another hour, but he had a key. Might as well go to work.

Tyler slipped inside the restaurant, switched on the lights, and draped his wet apron on a chair in front of a fan. He set an empty trashcan next to the stainless-steel refrigerator and busied himself cleaning out old food.

Yesterday's meeting with Antoine had gone well—encouraging, actually. Tyler filled a cooking pot with cold rinse water and another with hot, soapy water. He set all the fresh items from the top shelf onto the counter behind him.

"You have the details of your backgrounds down pat," Antoine had said with a nod of approval. "Now you need to write a cover letter that will convince the authorities that you'll contribute to Venezuela's growth. Show them how letting you immigrate will benefit their own careers." Tyler soaped the glass shelf and its sidewalls.

"Should I show how my computational genetics research could be applied to simulate the outcomes of geopolitical decisions?" Tyler had asked. "Or how quantum-computational physics may someday lead to the development of a quantum computer?" Rinse.

Antoine had looked perplexed. "Yes, well, you might need to explain those benefits in layman's terms. Yuki, I suggest you stress your aptitude as a Japanese-English translator."

Yuki had wagged an enthusiastic finger at Tyler. "We must pay attention to every detail," she had said. "Cross our *i*'s and not our *t*'s." Then, she had realized what she'd said and rolled her eyes. The three of them had laughed, really laughed. Resoap and rinse.

Tyler returned a box of baking soda, two tubs of sour cream, and a liter of whipping cream to the now-roomy and sparkling top shelf. He removed the second shelf's blocks of aged cheeses and set them on the counter. For two years, four months, and twenty-four days he'd lived as a fugitive, isolated from family with his dreams of a future on hold—more like unreachable on the other side of the looking glass. Wash. Rinse. Restock.

Venezuela had to accept them. Just had to. But what if it didn't? No way could he miss another birthday, another Memorial Day picnic, Thanksgiving…Christmas. Tyler emptied the bottom shelf and scrubbed it so hard that the refrigerator wobbled. Wash. Rinse. Restock.

Chef was the first to arrive. He flicked the lights on and greeted Tyler with a suspicious grunt. Tyler put coffee on to brew while Chef unlocked the front door and ignited the grill. He strode to the refrigerator, no doubt to take inventory of the day's vegetables and meats. He opened a door and reeled backward.

"What is this?" he asked, beaming approval. "You do this, Mark?"

The rest of the staff was due to arrive any minute, and Chef's mood was unlikely to get any better. Now was the time. "What's the deal with Mel?" Tyler asked. "Word is she left."

"Yes." Chef, still staring into the frigo, bobbed his head. "She is gone, yesterday, to Provence or some such place."

"What happened?"

Chef did that head-wobbling, puckered-lip gesture of his. "She quit is what happened. Just gone."

The front door tone sounded, so Tyler checked the dining room. Two men in suits had entered and were seating themselves near a window. Amine and Daki were chatting as they sauntered through the back door. "But why?" Tyler pressed Chef.

"How do I know?" Chef growled. "This is free country. People come and go as they please. Don't bother me with questions about that woman." He pointed his head toward the dining room. "Customers are waiting."

Tyler raised a palm in greeting to the businessmen, and the taller of the two lifted his cup. Probably Americans. Few Frenchmen would sully their taste buds with coffee before a meal. Tyler put on his almost-dry apron, stuffed an order pad and pencil into its pouch, and grabbed the fresh-brewed pot. The day was underway. No, he would probably never see Mel again, probably never learn what had happened to her. People and lives cycled through this twitchy, shadowy, empty-wash-rinse-repeat world that was now his life. He poured the customers' coffee, unable to fake a grin.

Lessons Learned

• • •

Tyler wrapped up his afternoon shift and turned from the sink to step into a crisp fall day, except the egg delivery caught his eye. Those open-faced cartons of twenty eggs each were going to sit on the counter all week if Chef had his way. What was it with Europeans that led them to think their eggs didn't need to be cleaned or refrigerated? Chef could complain all he wanted: these puppies were going to chill.

Tyler pulled open a door to make room in the *frigo*, and there was plenty of space—too much actually. He counted only one ham and four cubes of Chef's precious butter.

The battle of the beurre d'Echire had first begun when Elise waved a purchase order like a finish-line flag under Chef's nose. "You pay three times the going rate for this stupid butter!" she had complained. "We can't throw a stick without hitting a cow in Corsica. But no! You must import high-priced butter from a mainland village on the far west coast."

Chef had fanned his arms. "Our food is only as good as our butter, and its quality depends on the milk."

Elise jabbed a finger at the printout. "Tell that to our bottom line."

"Echire cream is pasteurized at a low temperature." Chef clutched his head with both hands, as if to keep it from exploding. "It is given time to culture with precise amounts of ferments, which must be exact. Without Echire we lose our sour, nutty flavor. Our sweet, sensuous melt. We lose our soul!"

"Pfft." Then Elise had stormed off to chastise Daki for a scuff on her shoe.

Chef had won that battle, so why was the butter drawer almost empty? Tyler swung around to grab the egg cartons. Only four instead of the usual ten. Better alert Chef.

Tyler found him scraping the grill, preparing to fry potatoes for his popular salt-cod *brandade.* Tyler picked up a peeler and rifled off a potato's thick brown skin. "Hey," he said. "We're running low on dairy and meat."

Chef looked at him as if he were hatching from an alien pod. "We close for the season on October first. How much food you want us to waste?"

This was 26 September. They were closing in four days? "Nobody told me." Tyler tensed to his bones.

Chef huffed. "Last I checked, we don't need your permission."

Amine couldn't know, either, or he would have said something. "You could have given us some notice," he said, surprised at the sourness of his tone.

Chef sniffed the cod in an obvious attempt to avoid Tyler's heated gaze. "And have you leave us shorthanded for another job, like Mel did?"

So that was why Mel had left: to take another job. Her putting in her notice had probably triggered a blowup, and Chef and Elise had driven her off to keep her from alerting the others about the impending closure. Tyler felt gut-punched. In four days, these people he'd come to care about—and who he thought cared about him, too—were plotting to turn on him and Amine and the rest of the staff. He and Yuki would have to find another place to live and another job. But how, this late in the season?

Tyler strode toward the back room, untying his apron as he walked. His toss missed the hook, and the apron rumpled on the floor. Who cared? He hit the door release and headed for the backyard.

Chiki must have sensed his distress because he wagged a cautious tail. "It's okay, boy." Tyler pushed up the kickstand and rolled his bike through the gate. Chiki didn't try to slip through. Such a good boy.

Tyler clenched his teeth and pumped his emotions deeper with each rotation of the pedal. He'd known this was a seasonal job, and this *was* fall now. Why in the world had he assumed that they would stay open as long as they had customers, maybe as late as November?

Half a mile from Porto, he glanced behind. A rooster tail of dust was approaching. Damn. It was Elise's Chevy truck. He veered right, stood on the brakes, and skidded like a third-base runner under a clump of bushes. He and his bike lay in a depression under a ceiling of brush as the white truck shot past.

The coast was clear. He should climb out. Instead, Tyler watched a grainy curtain of dust settle over his shrub's thickly coated leaves. Miniscule sand crystals ground between his molars and tasted of dirt and desolation. His eyelashes drooped with gray powder, framing the landscape as if he were peering through jail-cell bars. If only he could curl into a ball and sink into the dust.

No. No time for self-pity. If he and Yuki were to survive, then he had to find another job. Tyler pushed aside the brittle branches, picked up his bike, and pedaled on, one loop at a time.

Sunday, 1 October 2006. NO MORE WORK!

- Woke up at ten and couldn't really fall back asleep. Not feeling good at all. Didn't do anything until three, then ate some tortilla chips and slept until six.
- Rode bike to village and came back. Got a flat tire again!
- Thought a lot about how we don't want to be here anymore, but we just haven't got anywhere else to go. Sucks.
- A lot of hoping and idea searching about Venezuela...

8 November 2006. With no jobs and packs in hand, Yuki and Tyler stood outside Stone House. Its two stories of rounded stones looked more washed out and gray than he remembered. They'd spent too much time here. Their odds of detection and arrest increased with each tick of his pocket clock. But what choice did they have? Winter's blasts would soon be upon them.

Yuki wore a sad grin. "We're lucky to have a roof over our heads."

Tyler put on his cheery voice. "Very lucky. Absolutely." What he didn't say—what was weighing more heavily than the thought of another interminable winter here—was that he was having ephemeral anxieties about Thursday. In five days he was set to start his first job as an English tutor. Posting flyers with their cell phone number had been risky. Dumb, really. But they were desperate. Tyler quelled a surge of fear as he unlocked the door and held it open for Yuki. She shuffled inside like a death-row inmate treading her final steps along the Green Mile.

UNPACKING. MATH. THEN THURSDAY ARRIVED. Tyler slipped onto the bike and pedaled into a biting west wind, all too soon reaching 416 rue Pozzo. This was supposedly the Fraticelli's address, or so the woman's voice on the phone had claimed. No sirens. No suspicious vehicles parked within view. A few steps, and he was standing before an ornate Mediterranean-style door. He lifted a weighty brass knocker and rapped three times. No answer.

He turned to leave, but then the door swung open. A blend of baby powder and fresh-baked bread wafted over him, and a matronly woman in a beige apron over a purple-plaid housedress stepped from behind the door. "Bonjour," she said, breaking into a reserved smile. "You must be Marco."

The musical trill in her words matched the voice on the phone, so Tyler tried for calm and collected. "Oui. Here to tutor Jean Pierre and Carmine."

The woman turned, and a neatly braided ring of gray hair came into view on the back of her head. Six feet behind her, two boys slumped inward toward each other. The taller, auburn-haired teenager waved a half-eaten, chocolate-covered baguette and grinned through pursed lips and bulging cheeks. The shorter, thinner teen peered at Tyler with the same inquisitive expression as the woman who had answered the door, except his brown eyes bore a droopy, Stallone-like look. Definitely the grandson, JP.

Madame Fraticelli stepped aside and swept her arms inward. "Please to come in."

Tyler stole a final glimpse at the street. No authorities were slinking toward him with rifles trained on his heart. "Thanks," he said as he stepped through the doorway. He was here to teach English, so might as well start with an English greeting. Tyler stretched out an opened palm. "You must be JP."

JP gave his fingertips a confident squeeze and bopped backward.

Tyler reached out to shake eating boy's hand. "Hello, Carmine."

Carmine's eyes dropped to the baguette in his right hand, and he looked confused. Then he stuffed the chewed end into his mouth, and his newly freed hand pumped Tyler's. A rash of nonverbal communications ensued between the two boys, and Tyler thought he detected an approving glance. Probably buddies since childhood. He felt his face break into a smile. Ah, those innocent, carefree years. Rats. He'd neglected to offer a proper greeting to the matriarch of the house.

Unsure how to go about the process, Tyler gripped the grandmother's shoulders. "Nice to meet you, Madame Fraticelli." He moved in for a French two-cheeker, swinging first to the left before bobbing for the right cheek. Bam! His chin knocked her burgundy plastic frames across her nose.

Madame F. recoiled and, in the process, bumped the massive entry door backward on its hinges. A clunk. A twang. The brass knob jolted to a halt, an inch short of punching a hole in the ivory wall. Disaster averted, thanks to a prong doorstop.

The woman raised a wrinkled index finger and pushed her bifocals into place. She extended a hand as if nothing had happened. "Pleased to meet you," she said.

Tyler tried to compensate with a manly handshake, but his grip crunched the poor woman's metacarpals. He released at once, and though she neither flinched nor cried out, she cradled her hand to her waist. He knew he'd hurt her and winced on her behalf. Damn it!

Standing side by side and fidgeting, the olive-skinned boys looked on. A rococo grandfather clock tick-tocked. Madame F. broke the silence. "Come. I show you to the library."

Tyler intertwined his fingers over his belt and assumed his practiced teacher pose. "Great."

She led them across the hallway to a well-lit, book-lined room. A rectangular wooden table on an oval, hand-hooked rug dominated the space. A blue-and-white *SAT Subject Tests Preparation Booklet, 2006–07* topped the table, along with a gold-leafed porcelain tea set and a plate of sweet-smelling, chocolate-covered shortbread cookies. The sight set Tyler's mouth to watering. Should have found something to eat before coming here.

Madame F. poured them cups of hot tea and offered them cookies before excusing herself.

"Thank you," Tyler said as she disappeared through the doorway. The buttery, sugary crunch melted on his tongue and shot delicious energy into his veins. He took a sip and then devoured the cookie in two bites. Raging hunger took over, and he helped himself to another and another.

JP and Carmine studied him as he chewed and drank and restuffed his mouth until, gradually, he regained control. He thumbed through the SAT booklet and swallowed to empty his mouth. "How long before you take your college entrance exams?" he asked.

JP broke into a sheepish grin. "One year, and Nonna, she worry." He held up his thumb and index finger, nearly touching them. "Well, um, we worry, too, this much."

Carmine, who smelled of hormones and hair gel, pointed at himself and then at JP. "Our anglais, not so good."

Tyler turned to the English-language section as Nonna Fraticelli completed her second, not-so-subtle pass across the door opening. "Let's begin with verb tenses," he said, "simple present and present continuous."

JP AND CARMINE PROVED ATTENTIVE STUDENTS. All three were chuckling when Nonna F. materialized in the doorway. Tyler stood out of respect, and the boys followed his lead.

She limped toward them, her eyes taking in the empty cookie plate. "The hour is up," she said and extended a hand that sprouted with euros.

Tyler accepted payment. "Thank you for the opportunity to tutor JP and Carmine," he said, feeling his cheeks flush. "They're bright young men. And your tea and cookies were out of this world."

Peering over her bifocals, the grandmotherly woman fixed her blue eyes on the boys. "What do you say? Shall we continue next Thursday, same time, same place?"

"Yes!" JP and Carmine answered in tandem. Then JP added, "Marco's cool."

"I don't know." Madame F. looked stern. "He does not know how to kiss a decent greeting." She pruned a grin, and the teens giggled.

Tyler realized that he, too, was smiling. "Hope I didn't break your glasses or your nose—or your knuckles."

She flapped an exaggerated palm. "You Norse Americans never kiss on the cheek, no matter the situation. I see worse. From Ardèche, where I come, we kiss three times. Try to give a Corsican three kisses, and he evade you like you have the pox."

"And some people, they start off on the wrong cheek," JP said, bubbling. "That is the worst."

Carmine threw both arms in the air. "Just kill me. I want it to end."

Laughter.

Trying for tutor-like, Tyler asked, "Is there a map showing where which custom prevails?"

Madame F. made a face. "Of course not. I have this friend in Michigan where the handshake, it is the custom. Her sister from California, she catch me off guard and go in for the big hug. I wish to crawl out of my skin."

Michigan? California? The house turned airless and dark. Why would Madame F. reference those two states unless the details of his case were at the top of her mind? The probability of mentioning a particular state was one in fifty. To mention two states spiked the odds to one in twenty-five hundred: 0.04 percent. But wait, the odds of making reference to say California or New York—and maybe even Michigan—had to be higher than referencing, say, Arkansas or Delaware. Stop calculating! Get the hell out of here. Tyler beelined for the door. The woman didn't look like a government agent, but that was the perfect cover. Who would suspect Mrs. Claus?

He escaped outdoors and crossed the landing. But rather than bidding him good-bye at the door, the three trailed him down the steps. Tall, brown ornamental grass bent in a hiss of wind. The street was quiet, too quiet, like when he was in the woods and all the birds and tree frogs fell silent.

The woman's eyes torched through the metal that was Tyler's skull. "So you are a hand shaker?" she asked.

He tried to hold his face blank. "In Canada, where I'm from," he stammered, "we do handshakes and hugs."

She shook her head and rolled her eyes. "Too intimate."

Tyler tried to lick his lips, but his tongue was a swollen sponge. "More intimate than kissing?"

"Oh yes, a hug is much more personal than a few cheek pecks." She wrinkled her nose. "I have kissed greetings forever, but I would never hug anyone hello."

Was she trying to stall him until the authorities could make their move? He edged toward his bike. "I usually just nod. We Canadians aren't that physical."

She bobbed her head. "Ah, yes. The stiff, short nod."

He was coming undone. Had to get out of here. "See you next Thursday." He threw his leg over the bar and jammed down on the footpad. The bike shot forward. Too wracked with fear to look back, he turned at the first intersection and pedaled with all his strength. Streets turned to gravel. Farm fields unfolded ahead. Gasping for air and soaked with sweat, he chanced a glance behind.

No car was trailing in the distance. No helicopters were thudding overhead. He whipped onto a dirt lane and careened behind a bush. Dropping to his hands and knees, he crawled underneath bony branches and rammed his way to an alcove among the woody trunks. Lying on his stomach among the gray branches, he watched for helicopters, cop cars, soldiers—anything unusual.

An old lady in a rickety Renault putted south and parked in front of a farmhouse in need of paint. The sedan door crept open, and her stooped figure labored to carry a small sack inside.

What was he doing under this damned bush? This paranoia—no matter how justified—was corroding his mind. Tyler cupped his face in his hands and choked down memories of rolling his eyes at his hovering Grandmother J. He, too, once had a family who cared about him and made him cookies and tended to his education. Carefree Teen Tyler had slept long and late, safe and cozy in a bedroom all his own. He and Steve, like JP and Carmine, had played like puppies. Cam and Bryan and Dane--they had each read one another's thoughts in the glimmer of an eye.

Gradually, Tyler's breathing slowed. He reached into his pocket for a tissue, and instead, his fingers touched rag paper, the day's earnings. Rays of afternoon light dappled the leaf-covered ground, although at this angle the sun wasn't adding much heat. A shiver, and he shimmied backward to his bike. He cruised to the grocery store and wandered up one aisle and down the next.

What to buy? Too wrung out to focus, he placed familiar items in his basket as he meandered up one aisle and down the next. A liter of apple juice. A jar of Speculoos. A notepad. A bag of Spiritos. Feeling Tin Man–hollow, he paid the clerk, stuffed the items in his pack, and climbed onto the bike. Frosty gusts cut up the back of his hoodie as he pumped into the burn.

On reaching Stone House, Tyler stowed the bike in the shed and stepped through the back door. Yuki had fashioned a table centerpiece from evergreen sprigs, and its aroma blended with the scent of fireplace coals. He set his pack on the counter and gazed out the kitchen window, letting his bones absorb the peace and quiet.

Yuki glided downstairs. She looked thin and tired, though her face brightened at the sight of him. She slid the teakettle onto a burner and turned its knob to medium. "How was tutoring?"

He lifted the groceries out of his pack and set them on the Formica countertop. "Fine. Great, really."

Yuki gazed a long moment at the items before turning away to stare at her cup. Her dry, reused teabag rested inside, and he wondered how many times she had reused it. Did she even keep track? He always kept count, so he could judge how long to steep each cup.

Silence.

The kettle whispered, then whined to an ear-piercing whistle. Yuki stood as if deaf, engrossed in the shape of her cup or maybe its red and pink tulips. In slow motion, she turned off the burner and filled her cup three-quarter full. Tyler retrieved his teabag and ship's-anchor mug from the top of the sink. This was his bag's second use. He'd give it twenty seconds of steeping and three dabs. "If there's enough hot water," he said, sliding the mug and bag in her direction. "I'd like a cup, too."

Yuki's back became oddly rigid, and she poured his cup to the brim.

Tyler leaned over the sink and drained off a half inch. Then he slow-dipped his tea bag. One thousand one. One thousand two. Impossible to gauge seepage against the black ceramic of the cup, but he smelled black tea and chai, and he felt hungry. Starved. "What's for dinner?" he asked.

Yuki slammed down her cup, splashing the new notepad.

"Hey." He daubed it dry with the bottom of his T-shirt. "Be careful."

She stomped to the broom closet and wrested out her coat, her pack, and the green tarp. She flung open the back door and stomped into the orange late-afternoon sun.

The storm door thudded shut in a reminder that Tyler needed to replace its pneumatic closer. Puzzled, he opened the door and called, "Why are you mad? Where're you going?"

She swung an arm in the air. "Cèpes."

She must really want wild mushrooms, he decided. Girolles, better know as chanterelles, came into season twice a year in the mountains, and this was their prime time. Gourmet chefs treasured them like gold pieces and paid about as much per gram. Last spring on a hike up Cuccavera, he and Yuki had discovered remnants of what looked like a mushroom colony. Just yesterday, they had talked about returning to their secret site to hunt cèpes. Income from a windfall harvest could tide them through the winter. But why was she so ticked off and why leave unprepared at this late hour without him?

Mystified, he called, "You going to Cèpe Mountain?"

No answer.

He watched her and Chiki disappear down a side street. Then he eased the door shut and dug into the packet of Spiritos. As he savored a cookie's buttery flavor and tried to refrain from gobbling the rest of the pack, he opened the foodstuffs cabinet to put away the groceries. Bare, except for the free packets of salt, sugar, and pepper they'd taken from McDonald's. Below on the counter, the setting sun's golden beams were refracting through the apple juice bottle onto the blue notepad and turning its cover green. These scant supplies were a far cry from the makings of dinner.

Then it dawned on him why Yuki was ticked. She couldn't have eaten all day. Probably thought he was too lazy or too stupid to piece together a decent meal from his tutoring pay. Maybe he should chase after her and apologize. No. Better let her cool down. He'd go find her tomorrow, and they'd hunt girolles together. They'd have some fun.

Tyler poured a tall glass of juice and chugged it down. He set the bottle in the fridge, and its shelves, too, were starkly barren but for a box of baking soda. He trudged upstairs, sat at the desk, and stared out the front window while taking an occasional sip of his now lukewarm tea. The street stretched empty. Other than a lazy bank of cumulous clouds in the distance, the skies looked blue and clear. He opened the green cover of David Mackay's *Information Theory, Inference and Learning Algorithms* to his bookmark at chapter 24, "Exact Marginalization." Another sip and he dissolved into a world of cool-ass math.

Wow. With a little programming his epsilons could apply probabilities to draw these inferences. Reading and taking notes, Tyler worked his way to the chapter on neural networks. He paused to stretch and rub the chill out of his arms. Outside the window, darkness had fallen, and a crescent moon was breaking through the clouds. Then Tyler's breath caught in his throat. Those cumulous clouds were no longer distant or lazy. No, they were angry thunderheads, bearing southwest and closing fast on Stone House.

A flash of lightning jarred Tyler to unplug the computer and shut it off. A charged minute passed. Then both the screen and the house snapped dark. He fumbled downstairs to the kitchen, located a box of matches, and lit a candle.

The mountains during an electrical storm were no place for a person, and Yuki had only the green tarp for protection. No sleeping bag. No tent. Not even any food. Tyler sat in the candle's yellow haze and racked his brain for ways to find Yuki and Chiki and bring them to safety. One of his secret, backcountry cairns lay in the general direction of Cuccavera. Among other emergency supplies, it contained pouches of dehydrated meals. Yuki would never find the camouflaged pile of rocks on her own, and there was no way he could locate it in the dark. He would have to wait for morning.

Tyler carried the flickering candle upstairs and snuffed the flame. The odor of burned wick and wax filled his nostrils as he slid under the bedcovers. His toes wiggled and his heels bounced, eager to propel him into the mountains. Fine. Maybe their restless energy would warm him.

The lights clicked on, so he threw off the covers and stuffed a shirt and socks into his pack. A blink and darkness returned. "Damn." He climbed back into bed, and a flash of lightning startled him upright.

Five seconds passed. Then a peal of thunder rattled the house. Sheets of rain pelted the west windows. When the storm reached the mountains, that rain could turn to snow or ice. On top of electrocution, Yuki and Chiki were going to face slippery, frigid, extremely perilous conditions. Tyler relit the candle and checked the time: 2:05 a.m. He set the alarm for six thirty, blew out the candle, and flopped into bed.

Flash. He counted three seconds. Boom. Gradually, the interim from flash to boom narrowed to one second. The rain eased off the window and hammered straight down on the roof, so Tyler calculated the storm front to be moving at ten or fifteen miles per hour.

3:40 a.m. The raging tumult had to be hitting Cèpe Mountain and Yuki full force right now.

Lightning bolts gave way to torrential rain at 4:37 a.m. Then Stone House's electricity clicked on. Tyler gathered dry clothes and lost twenty-two minutes in a futile search for the tent and sleeping bag. Where could he have left them? Blankets and garbage bags would have to suffice.

5:35 a.m. First light. Tyler strapped two packs to his back, grabbed the umbrella, and set off. He struck a brisk pace up the narrow trail and readily found his secret cairn. After selecting bags of dehydrated potatoes au gratin, fettuccini, and chicken carbonara, he reconstructed the cairn and headed for Cuccavera.

7:20 a.m. Yes! Despite the detour, he reached the pass in a record one hour and forty-five minutes. Visibility poor. The ice droplets pattering his hood and the rain strafing the rocks would probably plug his ears to any response. Just the same, he stopped to call, "Wheeaay ho!"

The ascent angled more steeply, and the smell of wet weeds gave way to the sinus-cleansing scent of rushing water. With luck, the open umbrella could function as a transponder and sound catcher. "Wheeaay ho!" he called, listening so hard that his eardrums throbbed. He turned forty-five degrees, called and listened. Turned, called and listened. He completed the rotation and still heard only the sound of his own voice, plus hail and rain, always the rain.

11:45 a.m. Visibility zero. Slick rocks made the path treacherous, so he closed the umbrella and tapped along like a blind man using a cane. Gray boulders loomed like monsters out of the fog. Over and over he called, rotated, and called again. No answer.

"Where are you?" he bellowed into the soup. Nothing looked familiar. Where was the trail? Great. Now he was lost, too. He dug into his pocket and pulled out the clock. Still 11:45 a.m. Crap. Either he forgot to wind the thing, or moisture had damaged it. His fingers ached with cold as he cranked the metal key. No tick. No tock. He shook the timepiece and pressed it to his ear. Silence.

He hiked on. The rain eased to a sprinkle and allowed a gray blanket of fog to roll in. He shuffled forward, enveloped in a cloud and barely able to see his outstretched hands. Despite placing each foot with care, an unseen hazard snagged his toe, and he lurched forward. He stumbled past the point where he could right himself, but then, by chance, the umbrella's ferrule tip caught solid ground and stopped his fall. The foot-tripping rock rolled past and clacked down a bottomless abyss.

"Wheeaay ho!" Tyler called into the void, to no response. Desperate to spot movement or a fleck of green tarp, he inched to the edge of the cliff. A stiff north wind plastered his ice-soaked coat against his chest, and his teeth began to chatter. He willed his half-frozen fingers to tighten their grip on the umbrella shaft, but they lacked the strength. Still, he peered into the roiling fog. "Wheeaay ho!" he called again and again, until his chilled larynx sounded more goat than human.

A solitary lightning flash exposed a sixty-foot crag high to his right. The granite spike crooked upward like a witch's finger, its arthritic knuckle wrapped in the white ligament roots of scrub pines.

Tyler climbed to the crag's base. From there, he inched outward to the tip, testing each handgrip and foothold as he progressed. A sliver opened in the fog, revealing the cliffs across the canyon. Distant white streaks were curling down their stone slopes and spewing over their brinks: Flash floods. The thunderous cascades were likely to drown out Yuki's return call. Even so, he had to keep trying.

"Wheeaay ho!" he called.

Wheeaay ho drifted back to him. Probably just an echo. He called again, and once more, *Wheeaay ho* pealed up the canyon walls to him, its delay too long for an echo. Or was that just his wishful thinking? Tyler strained to hear past a whoosh of wind and angled outward until he risked toppling over. "Wheeaay ho!" he bellowed. One second. Two. Three. Four. Five.

"Wheeaay ho!" rode the wind like a blue whisper. Yuki was alive! He wanted to spring to her from his lofty perch. No, he forced himself to descend with painstaking care. On reaching the crag's base, he scrambled down three hundred feet or so over slick, jagged rocks. After slip-sliding to a ledge, he peered downward. Far below, a blurry creature was bolting along the canyon floor. It spun and barreled back. A wild boar? A hyena? No! Chiki must have heard his calls. Unable to negotiate the steep cliffs, he was tearing this way and that in search of his master.

"Wheeaay ho!" Tyler half ran, half slid down the mountainside and dropped onto the canyon floor. But instead of coming to greet him, Chiki charged toward a stretch of rocks and disappeared among them. Either his little buddy was showing the way to Yuki, or anticipation of his master's arrival was simply too much to bear.

Tyler decided to follow Chiki's lead, so he crossed flat, gravelly ground and rounded a bend to a forest of pines. Ahead, Yuki was kneeling under a drooping swag of evergreens. Her back was to him, and she looked stooped, as if she had broken a shoulder or maybe a leg. "Yuki?" he tried to call out, but her name came out a raw rasp.

She stood and turned, revealing a fledgling fire and no hint of injury. "You got here fast!"

He rushed to her and pulled her close. She felt warm and supple. Smoky hair had never smelled so enchanting. "I was worried," he said and allowed his fears to leak out. "That storm wouldn't quit, and I figured it was hitting you hard up here."

"No worries." She ran her fingers through his soggy hair. "What an amazing light show!"

A gust of wind whistled through the boughs, and water droplets tapped a sweet serenade on the needle-cushioned floor. Tyler touched a strand of Yuki's perfectly dry hair. "How come you're not wet?"

Her smudged cheeks lifted in a self-satisfied smile, and she gestured toward a stand of trees. Under a roof of low-hanging boughs, a bright-green tarp peaked to a pyramid. Beneath the tarp, the yellow tent mounded to a bump, kept safe and dry as an egg in its nest. "Easy peasy," she said.

Tyler thought he spotted the blue sleeping bag through the tent's open flap. "But you left with just the tarp?"

She wobbled her head. "I think, *This is crazy*, so back I come and find them next to the bike in the shed."

Feeling more foolish by the second, Tyler grinned. "I thought I'd lost them."

"I tied the tarp very tight, so Chiki and I could sleep. No more flap-flap to keep us awake."

"Smart."

Yuki's eyes clouded with worry. "Chiki, though, I think he did not get enough sleep."

So it wasn't the deadly lightning—wasn't the ravage of flash floods or wind sheer or slick ice or frigid conditions that aroused Yuki concern. No, what worried her most was whether Chiki had experienced a good night's rest. Tyler imagined nature's elements raging outside as Yuki and her charge snuggled warm and dry inside the tent.

"Any cèpes?" he asked.

Her pigtails wagged from side to side. "Not yet, and a day without cèpes is 'like a day without sunshine.'"

"That's an understatement." He pulled her to him.

The sun came out, but the cloud hung onto the forest. The rays of sunlight were unbelievable as were the circular, rainbow effects around the sun in the clean and crisp pine forest. Really, really the most beautiful thing I ever saw!

A Tree and a Bird

• • •

December 2006. Almost six months had passed with no word from Venezuela, and another of Mom's birthdays was coming around. This time, Tyler and Yuki were determined not to mope around Stone House. Instead, they would honor the day with a trip to Tree House. Rising early, they packed and headed for the door. The problem was Chiki. He lay like a lump of dough, too sick or tired to so much as wag his tail. Yuki tried to coax him to his feet with a bone, but he merely cracked open an eye and let it droop closed again.

Tyler touched Chiki's nose. No twitch. No flare. "Feels dry," he said. He went upstairs to retrieve Mackay and the laptop. On return, he sank onto the floor next to Chiki and ran a hand over the immobile dog's fur. "I'll keep an eye on our little guy for a while."

Yuki migrated to the kitchen where Tyler heard her dump their bag of wild, slightly wormy apples into the sink. Their adventure to Cèpe Mountain had yielded no girolles, but it had borne fruit. "I'll make apple pie. Recipe of Patrice," she said as a drawer opened and silverware clinked.

Chiki was twitching through a dream sequence, in no apparent discomfort, so Tyler worked his way through chapter 25. The smell of home-baked pie filled the house and poked at Tyler's stomach. At last, the oven door creaked, and what sounded like a pie plate scraped across a metal rack.

"Smells delicious," Tyler called. "When will it be ready?"

"'Sorry, Charlie,'" Yuki said, her voice firm. "Pie must cool."

Chiki's lips puffed in deep, healing sleep, so Tyler wrote.

Naturally, thought of an evolutionary implementation of decoding for error-correcting codes on trellises. This setup lends well to the chromosome partition of genetic material. Have one chromosome devoted to guessing the data bit by bit, another charged with constructing the trellis and perhaps yet another to determine which category of inputs to go for. More difficult inputs pay better, but include more risk.

He hammered out the math and was checking his work when a warm tongue licked the back of his hand. Chiki was standing beside him, fidgeting. "He's up and looks fine," Tyler announced.

Yuki came to check, carrying a plate with a giant wedge of warm pie for Tyler. "Poor baby," she cooed. But as she stooped to caress Chiki's back, the dog stretched forward. His jaws parted ever so slightly, and in an instant, the entire slice disappeared down his gullet.

"Hey!" Tyler objected.

Chiki romped to the door. He smacked his lips, and his eyes implored, *Get a move on, will you?*

"Guess the apple pie breakfast gave Chiki his bounce back," Tyler grumbled. He headed to the kitchen for a fresh plate.

They polished off what remained of the pie, and Tyler added extra containers of water to his already back-breaking pack. He took care to rebalance its weight. Chiki was tearing through the house like an unbanded balloon, so he let him outside. "Ready?"

"Almost." Yuki darted around the kitchen with her pack clinging to her back like a baby chimpanzee. She approached carrying a bag of garlic cloves, a container of olive oil, three large potatoes, a bottle of vodka, and a roll of aluminum foil.

"What's all that?" She ignored his question and unzipped his side pouch to stuff her items inside. "So much for my trying to balance this bad Larry," he groused.

She hustled to the kitchen and returned. "You will appreciate dinner later," she said as she wedged a baguette into his pack.

Tyler adjusted a shoulder strap. "Found a new, more vertical path," he said. "Want to take it?"

"No way. I saw you go last time, straight up and slip-sliding. It's too dangerous."

"It's faster."

She shook her head. "No, it isn't."

"I think it is."

She swung open the door. "Want to bet?"

"I could use another apple pie," he said.

She wobbled her head. "I could use a panini dinner."

"You're on." They made a quick stop at the shed to retrieve Shorty and Gandalf. Neither was much of a walking stick. Shorty was, well, short and brittle, while Gandalf bordered on sinister. When the barbs on its shaft weren't lancing Tyler's fingers, its angry slivers liked to impale his palms. But he and Gandalf had clocked untold miles together. Like him, Gandalf was lean and wiry. It flexed rather than broke, and it, too, had managed to grow and thrive in the impenetrable maquis. Well, not exactly thrive—more like survive. In that manner, too, they shared a common thread.

Yuki hit their regular trail with Chiki bounding ahead. Tyler faked a leisurely yawn and lounged against the shed door. He held up four fingers and a thumb. "I'll give you a five-minute head start."

Marching full steam away, Yuki stabbed Shorty skyward like a knight's pike. "We will wait for you."

"Wake me when you get there," Tyler called. Then he counted five slow sets of sixty and set out. The day was cool and sunny: perfect weather for hiking. He planted Gandalf between two stones, leaned into the steep incline, and hefted his weight plus the god-awful, heavy pack. Mountain air filled his lungs, and his muscles thanked him for the workout. A soft breeze wafted his bangs over his brow, and bird songs celebrated the day.

Three-quarters of a mile into his ascent, Tyler lost sight of Yuki on her less-taxing trail. Probably couldn't see her because she was so far behind. His thoughts turned to the chapter on Laplace's method, and contentment settled into the driving rhythm of his upward strides. With his T-shirt soaked and his muscles singing, he stepped, leaned, and heaved upward.

Then, without warning, his right foot slipped on a loose patch of scree. To counterbalance his weight, he pitched onto his secure foot. But he had neglected to take into account the hefty pack. It was catapulting hard left and gaining momentum, twisting him sideways and yanking him to the ground. He braced against its inertia.

Pop. A crack like a .22-caliber rifle fired off in his head. He recognized that sound: the snap of a torn muscle. Stars flashed. He slammed against the frozen mountainside and lay like a beetle on his back, but he felt no pain. Maybe he wasn't hurt after all? Then a branding iron seared through his lower back, down his legs, and up his spine.

"Aaaahooow!" A primal howl wrung Tyler's lungs empty, and he fell silent, unable to move or breathe. He fixed his eyes on the clouds and willed his lungs to open, to let in air. But they felt banded shut. He was on fire from the inside out, suffocating and swirling toward oblivion. The world darkened and went blank. Somewhere in the ether of his mind, he heard a gasp—his own—and cold, life-restoring oxygen rushed into his chest.

Gently, by one inch and then another, he lifted his right leg and let its weight roll him onto his side. Far ahead, with Chiki in the lead, he could see Yuki trekking up the mountain slope. Then, as if she felt his gaze or had heard his unearthly howl or sensed his pain, she stopped and turned in his direction. Tyler thought he saw her stiffen. Could she see him in the brush? Thank goodness! She'd come to his rescue. Then Tyler's insides tightened in fear. Residents barely noticed tourists moving along trails during the summer, but hikers were rare this time of year. For Yuki to stop midway and backtrack was bound to attract questioning eyes.

Gritting his teeth to keep from crying out, Tyler raised his arm and waved her on.

No response.

He waved again.

She hesitated and then signaled her acknowledgment. At last, she resumed her climb.

Pff pff pff. Tyler exhaled into a spasm, and gradually, the agony receded to bearable pain. The smell of damp earth offered solace yet little relief. A musical rhythm was tinging in the far recesses of his brain. A side effect of acute pain, perhaps? No, the ringing was coming from outside his head, and it was growing louder, drawing nearer. Prostrate and helpless, he stared in the direction of the noise.

Twigs snapped inside a thicket of brambles, and a scruffy-haired mastiff plowed through a gap, a bell jingling on its collar with every stride. At first, the beast appeared unaware of Tyler. Then their eyes met, and the creature froze in its tracks. Tan and muscled with its extremities tipped in black, the mastiff looked mean as a junkyard dog.

The creature's face was pitch black from its eyebrows to the base of its throat, giving the impression that it had dunked for apples in a tub of dirty motor oil. A sizable chunk was missing from a floppy, dark ear, so the animal looked as if it were being eaten one bite at a time. It sniffed, and its man-eating jowls mouthed the letter *O*.

Tyler tucked his chin to shield his neck, though judging from the way those monster jaws were jouncing up and down, his effort would prove futile. His fingers found Gandalf, and for once he felt grateful for its sinewy, briary shank. *Show no fear*, he thought. No fear. If Mastiff bared its teeth and lunged, he would club and kick with everything he had.

The world ground to a standstill as Tyler and Mastiff stared unblinking at each other. Tyler tried to look fearsome and big—hard to do while lying prone and defenseless as a chew hide. Even if he could move, the pack on his back was tethering him in place like a Judas goat, staked out as bait and unable to defend himself.

Mastiff gave a deep-throated rumble and lowered its body to the ground. It smacked its lips and belly-crawled within arm's reach of Tyler's exposed—and all too meaty—face. Then it dropped its muzzle onto its outstretched paws and puffed foul dog breath into Tyler's nose. Either Mastiff had gnawed on a decaying carcass or it was suffering one hell of an oral infection.

Tyler extended a slow hand and gently—firmly—patted its square head. "Hey, boy," he said, hoping to establish dominance.

Mastiff licked Tyler's hand and panted through what could only be described as a grin. *Fine, then*, its eyes read. *I'll keep you company while you recover.*

Relieved to have made a new friend, Tyler breathed through his mouth and commanded his back muscles to relax. He was too exhausted to keep his eyelids open and might have dozed, if not for the shivers that kept triggering excruciating muscle spasms—and each one was leaving him weaker. At the rate that the chill was seeping into his bones from the ground, he gave his extremities maybe ten minutes before they went numb, and he wouldn't be able to stand. Great. He couldn't move, yet he couldn't lie still, either.

Tyler drew a deep breath, blew into a shot of pain, and rolled onto his knees. Dizzy. Nauseated. He tried not to retch or pass out as he hand-climbed up Gandalf. Near upright now, he centered the pack over his screaming lower back and spat out a mouthful of apple-pie-flavored bile. A step upward. Then another. And another. Shaman Mastiff walked at his side, encouraging him up the incline.

Somewhere along the forced march, Mastiff went its own way. The sun eased low on the horizon, and Tree House came into view. Yuki trotted over to greet him.

"What happened?" She unstrapped his pack.

"Ahh! Go slow. Easy."

Gently, carefully, she lowered it to the ground. "You waved me on. I thought you were okay."

He held her arm and told her the story as they made their way to Patio. There he stretched on his side in the sleeping bag, and they watched the setting sun turn the sky blue with a hint of purple. Whip-cream clouds cradled two peaks and shared the mystical hues.

Darkness and cold were setting in, so Yuki lit a campfire. She wrapped the garlic bread in foil and set it on hot stones to toast. "Tomorrow it's roasted potatoes," she said as she poured vodka shots into two paper cups. She dropped an olive in each before handing Tyler a cup and raising hers in toast. "To Patrice."

"To Mom's health and happiness." Tyler downed his shot and let the olive's salty tartness blend with the bite of alcohol. "Thanks," he said. "Back feels better already."

Yuki opened a blue and white bag, and the scent of potato chips set Tyler's mouth to watering. She passed him a handful and bobbed a finger at him. "I'll take my panini extra crispy on ciabatta," she said. Then she added gently, "when you feel better."

> For the evening, we had vodka with green olives and chips for the opener, then garlic bread following the recipe of Mom, in honor of her birthday.
>
> 3 January 2007. Right now, a small stream trickles at my feet. The temp is cold with occasional gusts of wind. No stars are yet out, but they will be soon. My dog rests his chin, sometimes his whole neck, on my knees, keeping me warm despite the summer sleeping bag. The three of us are wrapped in a tarp. Yuki lies sleeping in my warm winter sleeping bag, a Christmas gift from my parents before The Fall. She tried to convince me to bring a flaky summer bag, too. But I said, "You bring what you want. I'm going to be warm."

He wrote a letter home.

> January 2007
> Mom & Dad,
>
> How are you guys doing? Sorry for my undue silence. I've been perhaps a little exaggerated in my precautions....Still not using the net much. There is so much potential there, but you really need to know what you're doing and make some assumptions about the adversary to achieve security. So that's why I still don't have an email address, and why I'm behind on things that you may very well have published on the net somewhere.

It's a constant worry that some terrible news awaits me on the web. I understand how you must feel without any news from me for so long. But I promise that if there was anything serious, you would hear about it right away. So no news is good news. Yeah, right. No news is just not undelivered bad news.

I'm doing well. Healthwise all is okay. I brush my teeth every night and eat enough protein. There were some pretty hard times for a couple of years there. I was feeling very alone and not even capable of admitting it. Naturally, this kind of problem wasn't going to resolve itself. Now that it's passed, I'm more comfortable talking about it. Otherwise I wouldn't have wanted to worry you!

It must be even harder for you guys since I don't disclose ANY information. Well, it's true that I don't need to be so cautious. It's probably safe to say that I've met a girl. It's been a long time since being with somebody felt so good. It looks like it's serious. I'm not promising any grandkids yet, but I'll keep you posted.

Of course, you know that I love you all enormously, and that I think of you every day. Not in such a painful way anymore, more something positive from the collection of our shared experiences. Positive for the possibility of picking up where we left off.

Lots of love,

Not a word on their appeal for asylum to Venezuela. Winter was crawling past like a slimy, gray slug.

It can be a cold world. With family and loved ones so far away, even warm days can feel chilly. And then there are the cold days, too.

There were nights when the stars served as a blanket and rocks did little to block the biting wind. The cold penetrates everything. Sleep just isn't possible. All you can do is curl up and wait. The time passes so heavily, especially when the nights are long.

It's another waiting contest, an endurance race, a battle where time is the only adversary and every moment passed is an insignificant victory. Then you reach a point where you don't want to go on anymore, where it doesn't even seem worth it. To continue, the cost of fighting exceeds the return on finishing. It's so much easier to just throw in the towel.

As you contemplate the beauty of the idea, a calm installs [itself]. It's so welcome, you stop shivering and stop thinking about the pain. It's so tempting to just fall into a worriless sleep, just for a few minutes...

But I stay awake. I rub my nose with my hands like every morning and keep shivering, because tranquility doesn't attract me. I have unfinished business. I have a family that I never even said good-bye to, because I never meant to leave, not for long. I still don't.

We all have our priorities in life, and mine are clearer than ever: To make right the wrong that I caused you. For all my flaws, one can't say I've lacked determination.

You've showered so much love upon me, and I've repaid you in quantity with worry.

Self portrait

February 2007. The wind howled outside. The day hung dark and dreary. Tyler worked on his epsilons while Yuki thumbed through vocabulary flash cards, quietly mouthing Spanish words. If *slow as molasses in January* was an apt description for last month, then February was a glacier inching down a slope.

Yuki drifted near and peered over his shoulder. "You always write math for yourself or *Tome* for others," she said. "But you never write anything for me."

"What would you like me to write?"

She tapped a fingernail on his computer screen and then moved away toward the kitchen. "A love letter would be nice."

"Fair enough." He gave the notion some thought and then began to type.

A Tree and a Bird

Once upon a time there lived a tree. The tree couldn't run. It couldn't even walk or move about at all. It had to stay and face whatever changes its environment presented. The tree wasn't sad though. It didn't want to go anywhere, and it didn't feel that it was missing out because all of the trees it knew, too, were fixed in their locations. Nobody dreamed of mobility. Nobody felt unsatisfied. Trees didn't evolve to move.

There lived in the branches of our heroic tree a small bird who had constructed a nest. The bird loved to fly, and not a single day passed without the bird venturing off on its bird business.

The two lived happily together, with the bird loving the tree and the tree more or less unaware of the bird. Mobility was everything for the bird. Even its nest was not really permanent. If the environment worsened, its wings could carry it off to another tree. However, the bird still needed the forest, and the forest still needed the trees.

Then the forest was cleared. The tree died, but [its species] didn't go extinct. The bird, however, could find no more trees in the ningen world and perished.

On reading the love letter, Yuki looked puzzled. “So am I the tree or the bird?”

“What do you think?” he asked, assuming the answer to be obvious.

She tilted her head left and then right as she studied the tale. “I am like the tree. Japanese roots run very deep, and our society is self-contained. I’m more grounded than you. You call me heroic. Thank you very much.”

“Go on.”

“You say the tree dies, but its species does not go extinct. Buddhists believe in *anatta*—no soul, no self, always rebirth.”

“So you think you’re the tree?”

“Hmm, the bird builds a nest wherever it goes. I do that, too, and I fly off sometimes while you do your math.”

“And you could always leave me for other ningens if things get too bad,” he added what was probably too uncomfortable for her to utter.

“You are flexible like a tree,” she said, looking puzzled. “You deal with changes to your environment. But you’re like a bird, too, because you venture off to explore and do your math business. And you are,” she gestured quotation marks, “‘more or less unaware’ of me a lot of the time.”

“So you say you’re the bird?”

“Ha!” she said with a laugh. “I am the bird and the tree; you are the bird and the tree!” She flipped her palm up and down. “We are two sides of the same hand, each yin and yang.”

He pressed his palms together under his chin and bowed his head. "Ah, Grasshopper."

THE MONTH WORE ON, and he wrote.

Co Loves

Covered in yielding defense,
filled with dreams
inspired by childhood stories,
the blade of grass dreams
of standing tall and firm,
of reaching proud
and strong for the sky.

Who whispers to the grass?
Dull thud pounding, again and again.
Such a violence under the shielded sky.
Skin wears from kneeling.

Knives and kicks leave sharp, red holes.
Again. Again.
The stains grow in size and number.
The grass weakens, yields.

Expressionless, the eyes that cannot cry,
whose tears dried away years ago,
search the clouds.
Who whispers?

The hands bleed.
Tears fall from the sky.
Rain streams off an icy face
and splashes against
the bloodstained grass.

Deaf from suffocation,
limp from fatigue,
lost in the confusion of being inversed,
the once-straight blade
lies tangled in the mud.

This poem, he kept to himself.

March Winds

• • •

March began with a disturbing rap on the front door. Tyler could see only the rounded top of a blue paisley head-scarf through the peephole, so he cracked open the door to the neighbor. Madame Degarmo hunched over her cane. The wrinkle-faced woman baked for the local *boulangerie* and, as usual, she smelled of yeast and flour. More than once, buttery emanations from her kitchen had awakened him to dreams of sinking his teeth into a piping-hot loaf of rye bread. He regretted that he and Yuki had rebuffed the woman's neighborly overtures, but her penetrating blue eyes seemed to probe his soul's secrets. Besides, making friends was asking for trouble. Case in point: Milos.

"Appel téléphonique," Madame D. panted. Phone call.

The blood in Tyler's veins turned to sludge. "For me?"

From the flurry of French that followed, he was able to make out, "It's Antoine, the youngest of the Prevot boys who own your house, uh huh." She leaned over and rubbed an imaginary mark halfway up her cane. "I know him since he was this high, uh huh. He loves my *ficelle*, don't you know."

Something was wrong, terribly wrong, and urgent. Tyler stepped onto the stoop and pulled the door closed behind him until he heard the latch go click.

Madame D. snapped her rickety fingers. "You must eat ficelle fresh, uh huh, or the inside dries out."

The slap of a chill March wind thinned the fog that was rolling into his mind. "Your *ficelle*, yes, it smells delicious."

"It's long distance," she warbled. "You run ahead. The phone is in the kitchen."

"Okay. Thanks." Tyler raced up the stoop into a living room thick with the scent of rising bread and a mustiness, traceable to a saggy-cushioned sofa. Her home was smaller and more worn than Stone House, but the layout looked the same. He passed through the living room into a kitchen that could have passed for an alien brood chamber. Trays of egg-like rolls lined countertops and a claw-footed oak table that filled the room. In the center of the table, a pitch-black handset lay keeled on its side like a dead crow among a clutch of alabaster eggs. Its ebony cord coiled upward to a black forties-style phone box on the wall that divided the kitchen from the living room.

Tyler fought an urge to ignore the call and, instead, to poke his finger into each roll and watch it deflate. Or maybe he should stuff one into his mouth to disguise his voice. He lifted the handset to his ear. "Antoine?"

"Mario?" Antoine's voice rang out. "I trust you are well?"

"Oh, uh, oui. And you?"

"Yes, yes, outstanding actually." Antoine's voice dropped to a whisper, as if that might thwart the NSA's listening ears. "I received a message from a Madame Lenoir at the Venezuelan embassy. She would like to meet with you and Yuki next Tuesday. She wants you to call her that morning and arrange the time."

Tyler's heart moonwalked into his throat. "Did she say if we've been accepted?"

"No, she wants you to call her for a meeting on Tuesday. I figure it's a screening interview."

Thinking out loud, Tyler murmured, "Tuesday's only three days away."

"I know it's short notice."

He swung the handset into view and ran his thumb over its smooth grip. Yes, this conversation was really happening. He vacuum-sealed the phone over his ear again and said, "We'll make it, for sure. You think we'll come back, or will we leave from there?"

"Hard to say." Antoine's words sounded drawn out and thoughtful.

"We'll see what happens." A tremor riffled through Tyler's voice, and he managed a shallow breath. "Thanks, Antoine. If this works out, we'll owe it all to you."

"You are most welcome. If you take the ferry to Marseille, maybe we can squeeze in a visit. My calendar is quite full, but call me, please. Let me know how things go."

"Sure. Of course." Three days. So much to do. "Thanks a million."

"You have a place to stay in Paris?"

"Oh, uh, yeah, I think so. We met this Parisian woman when we were on the mainland, and she invited us to stay with her. I'll give her a call."

"Sounds good. Let me know if you run into any difficulties, any at all."

"Will do. Thanks."

"Mario?"

"Yes?"

"Good luck."

Tyler's ribcage crimped. If the interview went well and their appeal was approved, then they could be whisked off to Venezuela and never see Antoine again. He drew a shaky breath. "You think this could be good-bye?"

A pause. "Just in case, tell Yuki bonjour for me. We must find a way to stay in touch."

"Absolutely, but this is just a meeting. We'll see you again." Tyler's Adam's apple spiked to a golf ball and blocked his windpipe. "Bon—" He swallowed. "Bonjour, my brother." He stood mute, listening to Antoine inhale.

"Bonjour," Antoine said, a crick in his voice. "Little brother."

Then click.

Tyler lowered the handset. His earlobe throbbed from pressing the rock-hard plastic against his head.

"You're going to Paris?" Madame Degarmo asked. She was standing in the doorway with her oven-mitts uplifted like a surgeon wearing sterile gloves. "Job interview or college?"

A flurry of panic. How much had she heard? "Sort of, ma'am," Tyler said.

She pulled a hot tray of baguettes from the oven and slid it onto a self-standing cooling rack beside the back door. "Antoine, he is a good boy." Her gaze bored through Tyler's skull, and she added, "He comes from good stock."

Where was she going with this? "As you probably heard, he's like a brother to me."

Lips puckered, she stuffed three delicious-smelling baguettes into a paper bag. "I don't care what people say. Any friend of the Prevots is a friend of mine." She pressed the hot sack of baguettes into his palm. "For you and Yuki. Now, you said something about having to make a call, so go right ahead."

What a generous, kind woman! He'd never noticed Madame Degarmo to have visitors, never heard her speak of family. Most people her age were retired, yet she labored each day to scrape out a living. Now she was letting him use her phone and sharing her only source of income. "Thank you for your generosity," he said from the heart.

She lumbered over to the front closet, reached inside, and pulled out a moth-holed wool coat. "I'll give you some privacy," she said as she buttoned the calf-length garment. "Just remember, it's long distance."

The door opened to a blast of cold air, and Madame D. was gone. Tyler dug out his pocket notepad and flipped through its pages. Yes, there was Lilou's number—beautiful, disarming Lilou who knew their dark secret. How he had railed at Yuki for blabbing to her, but in all fairness, he could understand why she'd trusted the woman. All this exposure to crusty Corsicans was probably tarnishing his perspective. Madame Degarmo certainly didn't deserve the cold shoulder he'd shown her all these months.

Pressing the handset to his non-aching ear, he dialed the holed metal ring upward from 0 until it stopped. He released, and the ring chirred back into place. Dialing 1, he completed the city code for Paris. Digit by digit, he dialed Lilou's number and waited for the smooth metal ring to curl back into place. Agonizingly inefficient, yet the antiquated mechanism felt oddly soothing, as if it held the power to slow the passage of time and was granting him space to recenter his emotions.

A throaty, cheerful voice answered on the third ring. Lilou. They exchanged greetings, and he explained that he and Yuki were coming to Paris. "We'd like to see you if you're going to be around," he said, opening a window for her to offer them a place to stay if she wished.

"Of course! You and dear Yuki absolutely must stay at my place. I'll not take no for an answer. Have you my address?"

He looked at the notepad: *Lilou Leroux, 12 rue Augereau, Paris*, written in Yuki's clear, artistic hand. "We do."

"Promise you'll ring me as soon as you arrive in town, any hour, day or night." She erupted in that sensual, carefree laugh of hers. "I have a gentleman caller, so I must go. But you'll call, won't you? Promise."

"Will do," he replied, and the connection went dead.

A meeting in Paris, lodging, and piping-hot baguettes—what a difference ten minutes could make. Tyler tore out a blank page and wrote, *Chère Madame Degarmo, merci pour l'utilisation de votre téléphone et pour les délicieuses baguettes.* Dear Madame Degarmo, thank you for the use of your phone and for the delicious baguettes. He anchored the note with a euro and locked the door on his way out.

No matter what, he and Yuki would find a way to stay together, but the situation was less certain with Chiki. If Tyler accepted that he and Yuki might emigrate to Venezuela and never see his little buddy again, then he wasn't sure he could depart for Paris. Yet if he operated under the assumption that they would return and then they weren't able to do so, things could be poorly arranged. He was facing two doors and needed to prepare for whatever might lie behind either one.

> Don't know if we'll ever come back. Can't imagine not coming back! How can we ever be ready to do both and neither?

Usually when they packed, Chiki acted like a gazelle, leaping here and there in anticipation. Not today.

"You think he knows?" Yuki whispered.

Ears drooping, Chiki stood outside in the rain. "Too much cleaning." Tyler tried to sound upbeat. "Or maybe he senses our stress." Regardless, Chiki's posture read of anxiety. Thank goodness JP and his grandmother had agreed to watch him.

> Walking in the rain with leopard bag was no fun. We were off to a very late start, too, and were likely to miss the bus. Hitchhiking worked, and we got there with an hour to spare. For the first time, Yuki met my student, JP, and his grandmother. They have been a rather big part of my life all winter, and I really liked seeing them meet her. JP was uncharacteristically shy because Yuki was so beautiful. He warmed up and accompanied us to the bus.

Tyler and Yuki joined a throng of passengers on Ajaccio's docks and waited to board the once-daily 7:00 p.m. ferry to Marseille. The twelve-hour cruise, scheduled to dock at seven o'clock the next morning, would allow ample time to catch a three-and-a-half-hour train to Paris. Few people in France scheduled morning meetings, so an 11:00 a.m. arrival should work fine.

It had been a long while since Tyler had navigated through high-pressure situations, and the extended wait compressed his stress levels to the point where nothing much mattered. Just as he was about to explode, the horde flooded forward across an expansive parking lot under threatening skies and, no doubt, in full view of all-seeing cameras.

As if in outward expression of his inner turmoil, the clouds unleashed thousands of BB-size pellets. Hail hammered his hoodie and splattered his boots. Yuki shielded her head under her jacket sleeve, and they scurried toward the ferry.

Three uniformed officers stopped them. "Have you been controlled?" a stiff-necked man asked.

Tyler's heart jumped into his throat. Then he recognized the man's partner, a former resident of L'Abri. "Tony!"

The lanky, red-haired chap looked puzzled and then brightened. "Marco!"

The officer waved off the ID check once he realized that Tony knew the two of them. "Just your tickets, please."

Tyler dug into his front pants pockets. Not there. Back pockets? No. Jacket pockets? No. Thigh? Shit. Trying to swallow a mounting panic, he checked his breast pocket. "Yeah, uh," he mumbled. "Tony's my neighbor." Jacket pockets. Pants front.

Back. Thigh. "Didn't know he worked here. Yeah, Tony's a good guy." He was babbling, acting more suspiciously with each failed search. "His dad has this really neat honey farm." Desperate, he reprobed his breast pocket, and the ticket found his fingertips. "Ah, here it is."

A quick glance, and the guard waved them up the gangplank. The ferry blasted its horn and eased away from the pier at eight o'clock.

Yuki's forehead creased with worry. "We're sixty minutes late already."

"We're good," Tyler assured her. "Marseille trains leave for Paris every hour. We'll still arrive before noon."

It was hard not to conjure up sentiments from the last time we took this route. Then I didn't give any thought to what would happen upon arrival. The experience was all very tightly centered about the present tense. This time it's different, but reminiscent of some common points. The future is so unpredictable, and it won't arrive until the boat lands. Distant, fixed, definite, like waking from a dream.

Tyler and Yuki located their berth and dropped their packs on the top and bottom mattresses of a bunk bed. The door swung open, and two fiftyish Germans plowed in, accompanied by two bubbly young women in tight leather skirts.

One look at Yuki, and Tyler picked up their bags. "Hungry?" he asked.

She rolled her eyes. "Oh, yeah."

They made their way to the dining hall and were comfortably ensconced when the ferry encountered heavy storms.

> The waves only intensified, and several times they threw the boat to such an angle that it emptied the shelves in the bar to the floor in a loud crash of broken glass and clanking metal. The mix then sloshed about. The trashcan freed itself from its box and roamed dangerously to the middle of the room. Most of the chairs tipped over, and so did a few tables. I forced myself to stagger across the room to re-imprison the trashcan. Otherwise it was sure to spill its colorful contents about the room. The night dragged on in bits and spurts.

THE CAPTAIN'S VOICE MADE TUESDAY MORNING'S PRESENCE KNOWN. "We apologize for the rough going," he announced. "Looks like we'll dock in Marseille a couple of hours late."

Bottles clanged behind the bar. Curtain hangers whooshed along their rails, and the TV blathered on unceasingly. Yuki rolled onto her stomach and covered her face with her hands. Trying to block the urge to vomit, Tyler fixed his gaze on the wall clock. "Crap," he said. "The soonest we can get to Paris is two o'clock in the afternoon."

An hour passed, and the PA clicked on. "My apologies," the captain's voice chimed, "but it looks as though we may arrive a little more than four hours behind schedule."

The ferry docked at 3:00 p.m., eight hours late. Tyler, frustrated and exhausted and with their food long gone, led the way down the gangplank. "The embassy closes at five thirty," he said as he helped Yuki with her bags. "There's no way we can catch the train and make it to Paris in time."

"Yes, way."

"Not possible."

Yuki charged onto the busy sidewalk and threaded through pedestrians toward the train station. "We have to try."

"No point in hurrying." Tyler maintained a long, leisurely stride and handily kept up with Yuki. "It's a fifteen-minute walk to the station. At best, we'll catch the four o'clock, so that puts us in Paris at seven thirty."

She marched ahead. "Madame Lenoir said she wants to see us today. Maybe she'll wait."

"We need to find a phone and give her a call to let her know we're trying."

She swept her arm through the air. "Fine. Where do we find a phone?"

No booth in sight. "Better step it up," Tyler said. "Best bet's the train station." They tore past a small grocery store, and his stomach ached with hunger. If memory served, there were no grocery stores near the train station. "We should stop and buy bread and sandwich meat."

"Call first." She continued without slowing. "Shop later."

They approached a second grocery store. "Look." He swung a bag-laden arm toward a plate-glass window. "Its checkout lanes are empty."

"Phone and tickets," she snapped. "Then food." They trooped on, scanning for a telephone booth to no avail.

Tyler's mouth was watering at a buttery aroma streaming from a street-side bakery as the massive pink roof of the Marseille Saint-Charles station loomed into view. "Um, fresh bread."

"Not now!"

They plodded up le Grand Escalier's tiered staircase into a cascade of downward-streaming businesspeople. Two, four, six green-patinaed street lamps on the right marked their endless ascent. At last, Tyler stepped up top to marble lions and ornate sculptures of French statesmen. Still no pay phone in sight.

He turned to check for a tail, and a breath-taking panorama of Marseilles stretched before him. A wide boulevard cut like a river through a canyon of tall, terraced buildings and disappeared into a distant sea of limestone structures. On the far horizon, stately mountains bumped skyward to overlook the city in all its glory. Tyler could almost taste the fresh air of the peaks. He felt the wind at his back, pushing him to join them.

Yuki nudged his elbow and pointed. "Phones." They stormed toward a bank of pay phones, but each cubbyhole was occupied and a dozen business travelers were standing in queue. The clock tower read ten minutes to four.

"We can't make a call and catch the four o'clock both," he said. "It's more important to call."

Yuki changed direction toward two giant open doors. Inside, Tyler spotted another phone bank. One cubby was available, so he grabbed the handset and punched in the numbers.

"Embajada de Venezuela," a hurried-sounding voice answered. "Oficina del consulado."

"Sí. I'd like to speak with Madame Lenoir, por favor."

"Sorry." The voice converted to English. "Madame has left for the day."

Tyler sensed the admin's hand was reaching for the disconnect button. "Well, we understand she wanted to meet with us today, but we ran into delays," he blurted out. "May we reschedule for tomorrow?"

"Whom shall I indicate is requesting a meeting?"

"Oh, uh, two interested parties. She has our letters of petition."

"Names, please."

"We'd rather not give those over the phone."

"Then give me the time you were supposed to meet with Madame today. I'll check her calendar and see if I can move you."

"Uh, well, we didn't actually have an appointment time. Her message said to call for a meeting today."

"I see. Well, how about telling me just your first name?"

"Mar...Mario. I mean Marco," he whispered. "But that's not exactly correct."

"What exactly is correct?"

"I'd rather not say like this."

A sigh. "Nationality?"

"Canadian—well, Japanese—well, that's another topic we'd like to discuss in person."

"So you two—who wish to remain nameless, from unspecified origins—are late for an appointment that does not appear on Madame's calendar, yet you claim she would like to see you, so I should make room in her busy schedule tomorrow. Is that correct?"

"Uh, yes, that's about the size of it. We're asking you to please find us a few minutes."

"Without basic information, I simply cannot schedule you to see Madame. Perhaps you should send her an e-mail or mail her a letter."

"We have. She has all our paperwork."

"Very well. What's the name on file? I'll check her desk for it."

Oh boy. "I'll have to get back with you."

Click.

Yuki shook her head. Apparently she'd overheard enough to get the drift.

Tyler sighed. "I'll go buy the tickets." The four o'clock had departed, so he booked them on the five fourteen, which included an additional delay and transfer at Avignon, wherever that was. Yuki was slumped on a smooth-worn bench, so he plopped his backpack next to hers. "Forty-five minutes to departure," he explained. "Okay if I get us some food now?" There it was, the irritated tone, borne of hunger and disappointment.

Yuki shot to her feet. "I will go."

"Fine." He slipped onto the bench's contoured wooden slats, still warm from Yuki's derriere. "I'll mind our bags." He watched her troop out the gaping entry and then found a vending machine and devoured a pack of stale cheese and crackers. Hungrier than ever now, he eyed chatting travelers as clench-jawed guards eyed him.

Five o'clock, and a line was forming at the boarding gate. Tyler's mouth watered at the aroma of a caramel latte that was wafting from a Starbucks cup in the two-fisted grip of a lanky brunette in black slacks. What if Yuki didn't return in time?

"All boarding TGV Duplex 5017 for Paris," the PA rang out in French. Where was she? "Last call for 5017 for Paris."

Tyler imagined searching the streets, overloaded with luggage and calling for Yuki. A figure, impossible to identify behind a bulging paper sack, glided through the entry doors and angled toward him. Yuki, maybe? Yes! He recognized a flick of black ponytail. Grabbing their baggage, he dashed onto the train and held open the persistently closing door until Yuki skirted inside. The doors sealed, the car rolled forward, and they were on their way.

> Upon arrival at our final destination, we had differing ideas of how to proceed. Yuki didn't want to bother our friend and preferred to take a hotel. I had promised to contact Lilou as soon as we arrived and thought it better to call before checking in. From my point of view, it would be better to stay with a friend than to have to show ID at a hotel. We called and found out that she wouldn't be there tonight, but nonetheless [she] offered us a place to stay. We decided to take the hotel and see her the next day.
>
> Selecting a hotel is like shopping. Something I'm not particularly fond of. We negotiated with a cool Chinese guy with bad teeth for a slight discount on an exorbitantly overpriced room. We had a shower in the room, and that was nice.

First thing Wednesday morning, Tyler made his way to a pay phone a few blocks from the hotel and called Madame Lenoir to reschedule. He was put through at once.

"My assistant tells me you gave the name Mark," Madame Lenoir said, "except that's not your real name."

"Yes." A colony of ants began to crawl up Tyler's legs. "That's correct."

"Well, I must have your real name if you wish to meet."

"Mark's the best I can do over the phone."

"Mark what?"

"Soss—" The word caught in his throat. How dumb to try to hold on to his real name by adopting an alias that sounded like Johnson. The NSA probably had software to scan for similar-sounding words. He leaned into the booth and braced for a lightning bolt. "Sosson."

"S-O-S-S-O-N?"

"Yes."

"Nationality?"

"Do we really have to do this?"

"Nationality, or this conversation ends here."

"American. I'm American, and my friend's Japanese."

"There. That wasn't so difficult, was it?"

He checked side to side. "Jury's out on that."

"What is the nature of your requested visit?"

He was a cornered mouse. "I'd like to go over all that when we meet. May we please come to see you?"

"No. My schedule is full. Besides, I'm restricted from exposing myself to unvetted individuals. I'm sure you can understand."

In all fairness, he *could* understand. An American guy with a fake name who refused to state the reason he wanted to meet was hardly someone for whom a diplomat should clear her schedule. But he was desperate. "Is there any way you can help us?"

A heavy sigh. "Ho-ld on."

Cars whizzed past, their drivers all appearing to eye him. Aircraft circled overhead like wasps buzzing over a fallen pear. Tailpipe exhaust was making Tyler's sinuses run, so he dug into his hoodie pocket for a tissue. When he looked up, a windowless van was parallel parking across the street. If police piled out, maybe he could commandeer a passing car? No way. French drivers would flatten him. A service alley halfway down the block might provide an escape route. Maybe.

A stoop-shouldered driver in overalls eased himself from the van and rolled open its side door. Tyler froze, every muscle on alert. The man leaned inward and pulled out a narrow, wooden-handle box. What looked like copper tubing and a sink trap bristled over one end. A plumber. Tyler managed to exhale as the man shambled into a dark-windowed restaurant.

"You still there?" Madame Lenoir's voice cut into his ears like razor wire.

"Yes. Yes, I'm here."

"I can have someone answer your questions, four weeks from this Friday."

Way too late. They had to get out of Paris. "Any chance we can meet sooner?"

"That's the best I can do."

No way they could hang around the City of Cameras and Cops that long. "We can't." He drooped in borderline despair. "But thank you for trying."

"Bonjour, then."

"Bonjour." He walked back to the hotel and related his failure to Yuki.

"Did you tell her we really, really need to see her?"

"Yes, I pressed hard."

Her lips pinched. "You were pushy, weren't you?"

"No, I was real polite." Her knitted brows conveyed her skepticism.

They lugged their bags to the dank hotel lobby and checked out to walk aimlessly down streets. The skies darkened and hung heavier, revealing the city's drab face. Then the clouds released, and icy, acid rain slapped the sidewalk, their shoes and legs, their heads and shoulders.

Yuki halted under a butcher shop awning and leaned against its stone facade. Wiping a trickle off her cheeks, she moaned. "This rain is washing away the hopes and plans we calculated in the shade of our forest."

He should probably explain that the rain bore them no ill will, that it consisted of water vapor in the atmosphere. If she observed a cloud on a clear day, then she'd see that parts of it grew and condensed as other parts evaporated and disappeared. Hardly any of this condensation fell to the ground because it lacked sufficient speed to overcome the powerful updrafts that supported the clouds. On occasion, tiny droplets condensed around particles of dust, salt, or smoke. Only when millions of these fortified droplets happened to collide and join together could they sometimes grow to a single raindrop with enough fall velocity to exceed the updraft. Then with luck, this extraordinary little raindrop might complete its journey to the ground, to the sea, and someday back to the clouds. Unless, of course, the more efficient Bergeron-Findeisen process came into play. In that case, frigid temperatures caused precipitation-size ice crystals to form from a cloud's water vapor. These crystals could fall as snow, or they melted partway to patter to earth as rain.

No. Rain couldn't possibly pass judgment on people, let alone plot to destroy their hopes and plans. A raindrop was a raindrop, just as a rose was a rose. None of them were small feats. All were products of amazing and awesome forces, but their existence carried no hidden motives toward humans in general or to him and Yuki in particular. Yes, he should probably tell her these things. But for reasons that escaped him, logical explanations ticked her off, especially when she felt blue. Besides, he doubted he'd feel like a flat tire right now if cold rain weren't spitting in his face and trickling down his neck.

He gave up trying to shield himself and Yuki from the frigid drizzle and trudged on. Probably ten blocks from Lilou's, he pulled Yuki into a phone booth. Pressed tight together, he felt her shiver. "We have one last card to play." He lifted the handset and tapped in the numbers before he could change his mind. "We need to call Antoine."

Yuki's index finger followed a raindrop that was wobbling down the glass. "Why bother? He's busy this time of day."

Tyler shrugged. "What've we got to lose?" One ring. Two. Three. Four rings. He should probably leave a message, but what was there to say?

"Oui?" Antoine's voice sounded muffled.

"Hi. We thought you'd be in court."

"I am," he whispered, a smile in his voice. "I saw the exchange was from Paris and hoped it was you. How are things going?"

Tyler recapped their appointment-making difficulties. He held the phone so Yuki could listen, too.

"That sounds like progress," Antoine said with a chuckle. "Madame Lenoir asked to see you, and you spoke with her. Now she knows you want to see her, too. I bet she's dying to learn your story."

An elephant lifted one cheek of its rump off Tyler's chest. "I suppose that's one way to look at it."

"Tell you what," Antoine said, all confidence. "You leave the task of arranging a meeting to me. In fact, I'll arrive this afternoon. We'll talk strategy over dinner tonight."

"But—"

"We have much to cover."

Once again, Antoine was swooping in to the rescue. Tyler glanced into Yuki's wide eyes and tried to bottle a flicker of hope. She smelled earthy and wet, like chicken dumplings and over-ripe berries. "Okay," he said. "Great."

"Must run. Call me at five."

Click.

Tyler lowered the handset onto its hook.

"You think he can change Madame Lenoir's mind?" Yuki asked.

Tyler shrugged. "If anybody can, it's Antoine."

She angled her face at his. "Is he driving all the way here just to help us?"

Marseille to Paris was a seven-hour drive. "Knowing Antoine, he'll arrange other business while he's here, but I get the feeling he's doing this for us."

Mystified and reenergized, they reached Lilou's apartment building around noon and took the stairs to a second-story hallway. They nearly bumped into Lilou as she stepped out of her door. She smelled of Easter lilies and wore a tight-fitting red silk suit. Her face looked thinner, which accentuated her long, mascara-laden lashes.

Lilou threw her arms around them, "Yuki! Marco!" she cried, all kisses and hugs, and they all began to talk at once.

Yuki tucked a truant strand of wet hair into her ponytail, exposing a lipstick-smudged cheek. "We're lucky we caught you before you left," she said, looking like a kid whose experiment with her mother's makeup had gone awry. Tyler did his best to rub his cheeks clean before handing the tissue to Yuki.

Lilou's crimson designer shoes danced under a clasp of shimmering rhinestones. "Please, please do join Léandre and me. We'll make it a double date."

Yuki took Lilou's hand. "We'll come back tomorrow and catch up."

Instead of crashing her date, we headed off to the Louvre and passed the day looking at ancient Roman statues and relics from Egypt; of course, the Mona Lisa; and enough paintings of Jesus to satisfy my needs.

Tyler in front of the Louvre

Friends and Strangers: Forces of Nature

• • •

Five o'clock came, and Antoine answered on the fourth ring. "You were right." He blew a discouraged sigh. "This was more difficult than I anticipated. I couldn't get us in to see Madame Lenoir."

"Thanks for trying," Tyler said, doing his best to mask his disappointment.

"Then everything fell together at the last minute." Antoine chuckled. "Interview's tomorrow, nine o'clock. Our appointment's with an Iris Garcia. They assure me she's a decision-maker, and she can accomplish what we need. We can all attend."

"I can't believe it!" Tyler realized he was yelling into the phone, so he lowered his voice. "You're incredible."

"Oui, a force of nature," Antoine said, sounding amused. "Eight o'clock for dinner tonight work for you, Olio Pane Vino, 44 rue Coquillière?"

Tyler fixed the address in his memory. "Eight o'clock's great."

"See you then." The line went dead.

High fives. Tyler and Yuki exited the payphone, and he grinned to watch her march her square step. They found an Internet café and searched the web for a place to spend the night. Trendy Hostel, only six blocks away, was available at twenty dollars US—more than a bidon, but it looked clean and included free Wi-Fi plus breakfast.

A TENT-BOARD SIGN OUTSIDE THE CREAMY-WHITE, two-story building read TRENDY HOSTEL BEDS AVAILABLE in French, German, Swiss, and English. A glass door glided open, so Tyler and Yuki stepped into a brightly colored, apparently unattended lobby. Tyler migrated to a rack of travel brochures—or "travel literature" as Grandma J. called them—and selected a pamphlet featuring the Cathedral of Notre Dame.

A pleasant male keeper wearing a badge that read AIMERIC materialized behind a stainless-steel counter and asked, "May I help you?" He guided them through the registration process and issued them each black-and-white-checkered comforters and sheets that smelled of detergent and bleach. Hampered by a severe limp, Aimeric showed them upstairs to a fifteen-by-fifteen-foot room packed with bunk beds. All but one bunk's top and bottom mattress lay covered in black-and-white comforters, giving Tyler the impression that he had stepped through the looking glass into an Alice in Wonderland world of race-car flags. Almost before he could calm the vertigo-like sensation, Yuki had unfurled her comforter on the lower mattress.

He threw together his upper bunk and held out the brochure for Yuki to view its cover, a close-up of the cathedral. "Want to go?" he asked. "It's close."

"Sure."

Soon they were ambling north through commercial neighborhoods. They crossed the Seine and hopped onto a low wall to sit and marvel at the man-made wonder. "'Generations of stonemasons,'" Tyler read, "'labored to create the cathedral's ingenious architecture and flying buttresses.'"

Darkness was falling, so street artists were dropping canvas flaps over their booth windows. The chill, humid scent of the Seine filled the air, and a lone riverboat floated past them below. Tyler and Yuki ducked into a secondhand bookstore to warm their toes and browse its shelves.

When a thick-lensed staffer switched off their section's lights, Tyler felt pressured to make a purchase. He overpaid for a coffee-table book about South America—not specific to Venezuela, but it contained a lot of photos, cultural history and factoids about the country.

"You know the name *Venezuela* derives from Spanish?" he read aloud. "It means *little Venice*."

Yuki bobbed her head, obviously considering the new information. "So when we leave, we take some of our Europe with us."

"That's right," he said, feeling a wave of nostalgia at the thought.

Lacking a watch and afraid to risk arriving late, they hustled along rue du Louvre before turning left onto rue Coquillièr. Vertical steel bars lined the first-floor windows of four- and five-story buildings along both sides of the street. A garlicky aroma of pesto and cheesy bread wafted over them, and they spotted a nondescript doorway labeled Olio Pane Vino. They found no Antoine inside, so they exited.

As luck would have it, the temperatures on this first day of spring had dropped lower than at any time during the winter. Tyler and Yuki rubbed their arms as they paced under a sign that read Optical House. At a quarter past eight, Antoine's blue Audi pulled up and parked across the street.

Eating in a restaurant felt strangely reminiscent of what was once normal. Depending on tomorrow's meeting, maybe dining out would someday become normal again. Tonight, though, Tyler felt like a poser, and judging from Yuki's stiff posture, she was feeling the same way. "Wonder what our waiter would think," he whispered to her, "if he knew he was serving two fugitive vagabonds?"

Yuki's chin jutted forward, and her shoulders eased into her chair back. "We have as much right to be here as anyone."

Bolstered at her spunk, Tyler inhaled the buttery scents and let the drone of ambient conversations wash over him.

Antoine raised his glass. "To your successful, free lives. May Venezuela be good to you."

"From your lips to Iris Garcia's brain," Tyler added, and they clinked.

"Then let's share our aspirations," Antoine said and leaned in. "See if we can make them come true."

Another sip, and Tyler ventured, "I'd like to reconnect with my family and maybe be a quantum physicist again."

Yuki flushed and added, "We would like to get married."

"Who knows?" Antoine said with a bob of his brows. "I may run for office."

"Salud!"

As their glasses emptied and refilled, the possibilities poured out. "We could save to buy a house in the country. Chiki would love that."

"Maybe I could design women's clothing, Venezuelan-Japanese-American style."

"Can you picture me in a judge's robe?"

"Sure can." Tyler raised his glass again. "To each of us making the world a better place in our own ways."

Yuki's cheeks were rosy, and she looked content. Then, she began to sing, softly at first, as if sharing a secret. "'I'd like to buy the world a home and furnish it with love.'"

When Yuki felt over-the-top terrified, she broke into her heart-breaking lullaby. For her to sing aloud in front of others, well, she had to feel over-the-top ecstatic. Tyler rarely enjoyed the pleasure of her perfect pitch these days, and he even recognized the tune: a Coca-Cola commercial from before he was born. He joined her in quietly singing, "'Grow apple trees and honey bees and snow-white turtle doves.'"

Antoine refilled their goblets, a puzzled look on his face. Then he began to sing, too, "'I'd like to teach the world to sing in perfect harmony.'"

Gentle as an evening breeze, they serenaded one another.

I'd like to buy the world a Coke
And keep it company.
That's the real thing.

Tears were streaming down Yuki's cheeks, and Tyler detected a glisten in Antoine's eyes. Trying to collect himself, he realized that not only had he lost his American birth family, but if all went as planned, he was about to lose his French family, too: Antoine and his brothers and their dear father, and Lilou, Dino, Amine, Mel, George, and Rosine. A procession of Europeans who had brought hope and light to his life wound through his memory.

Antoine and Yuki were studying their plates in quiet contemplation, wrestling with perhaps the same or similar ghosts of impending hope and loss. Patrons at the other tables were peering at them, and Tyler realized his cheeks were wet.

To his relief, the waitress broke the silence with the check. Antoine snatched it and ran his fingers through his hair. "Might be our farewell dinner," he rasped.

Tyler resolved for the millionth time to somehow, someday repay this generous man who was the brother he never had. "I hope so," he said, "and yet I hope not."

Antoine pushed away from the table. "Guess we better get going."

They walked him to his car. "You know," Tyler said, "we spoke of everything that matters, but we didn't discuss what will matter most in a few short hours."

"Ah, yes." Antoine dug out his keys. "Just tell the truth. You will do fine."

Tyler reached for Yuki's hand and felt the squeeze of her fingers. "We'll follow your lead."

Antoine grinned. "Very well then, meet you at nine sharp. May I drop you off at the hostel?"

Trendy Hostel, only a few minutes south by car, was an hour and a half away on foot. But Antoine was staying at the Ritz, seven minutes north and in the opposite direction. One look at Yuki and Tyler saw that she agreed. No way would they impose further on their cherished friend. "No thanks," he said. "We feel like walking."

> We made it back to the hostel, and all the residents were in bed-though not quite asleep. We fell asleep quickly, dreaming about the significance of tomorrow.

TYLER AND YUKI WAITED FOR ANTOINE outside a corner restaurant on the opposite side of the street from the Venezuelan embassy. The doorjamb above their heads read *DAB* __ *BAR* __ *DAB*. To their right along rue Lauriston, a fifteen-foot-high stone wall encased nearly the whole block. A prison perhaps? Across the street, a white-aproned grocer was setting out cartons of fresh vegetables under a blue-striped awning. But what captivated Tyler's attention—and what he was struggling to avoid staring at—was the Venezuelan sovereign territory a few doors to the left of the grocery store.

Other than the flap of a yellow, blue, and red flag and an inauspicious oval plaque on a stone column that bore the words EMBAJADA VENEZUELA, the five-story stone edifice might have blended in with the pallid battery of smudged stone buildings along rue Copernic. Black filigreed grates over second-floor balconies kept the embassy's occupants from falling out, and a wrought-iron fence along the sidewalk kept intruders—or fugitive asylum-seekers—from climbing in. Two reliefs of a female face, framed in leaves or feathers, gazed down on all who passed under a portico entry. The Madonna perhaps? Ninety percent of Venezuelans were Roman Catholic.

A pistol-like pop startled Tyler from his observations. A silencer? No, just the snap of that flag in a gust. He blew into his palms. "What could have happened to Antoine?" he asked.

"Who knows?" Yuki jogged in place, hugging herself. "We are going to get arrested for loitering." She rubbed her forehead, cueing Tyler to the approach of a stranger. As in sync as two swallows in flight, they turned from a trench-coated passerby who was rounding the corner. The lanky man hustled across the intersection and disappeared into the now-open grocery store.

The metro station down the street offered the best chance of a working pay phone, but to reach it, Tyler would have to pass the embassy. "I'm going to call Antoine," he said.

Yuki blew a stream of frost into the air. "Watch. Now he will show up, and we will have to wait for you."

"I'll be quick." Tyler locked his eyes straight ahead and strode along the far side of the street opposite the embassy. As hoped, a phone booth topped the metro's stairwell. The buzz of its dial tone confirmed a live line. He slipped in his card and called.

"Just behind schedule," Antoine explained. "Parking near a lighting shop now."

Tyler glanced toward the embassy. Across from a storefront ablaze in light fixtures, a blue Audi was kissing the bumper of a red Ferrari. Only Antoine would attempt to squeeze that station wagon into a snippet of gravel next to a construction fence—or dare try to park in a tight spot behind a Ferrari. Yuki was making her way to the car, so Tyler took off at a jog to join them.

Together, they walked to the portico and passed under the watchful eyes of the Madonna. On second thought, that headdress looked too regal for the Virgin Mary. No, this figure probably represented María Lionza. Tyler pictured his newly purchased book's illustration of Alejandro Colina's sculpture of Venezuela's revered goddess of nature, love, peace, and harmony. The bare-chested woman, often pictured on a horse-size tapir, played a central role in a widespread religion that blended African, indigenous, and Catholic beliefs. In her raised left arm she brandished a female pelvis, symbolizing fertility. A wise choice on the embassy's part to portray only her face, Tyler decided.

Inside the portico, a black eight-armed chandelier hung from the ceiling like a spider poised to drop on their heads. Antoine pulled open an iron-grate door, and they entered an atrium adorned with gold-leafed murals. High up in three corners, with no pretense of concealment, dark-eyed cameras peered down at them. Tyler pressed a call button, and the minutes ticked past.

At last a deadbolt clicked, and a short, dark-haired woman in a snug purple suit and a sunflower-covered shoulder scarf stepped through a door. Her rich mahogany complexion seemed to defy age, and in one dancing sweep, her chocolate-brown eyes appeared to x-ray their skeletal systems. She smelled of coconut.

"Buenos dias. You must be Counselor Prevot." She greeted Antoine with a firm handshake and direct eye contact, Venezuela style. "Yo soy Iris Garcia. Please call me Iris."

Antoine gestured toward Tyler and Yuki. "Iris, I'd like you to meet Marco and Yuki Sosson."

She shook their hands, saying, "Buenos dias." Then she motioned for them to follow her down a hallway. They trailed her past a room that bustled with colorfully dressed staffers talking into headsets. They passed six closed doors and entered a room with open-slatted venetian blinds on two sides. A pulled-down screen dominated the third wall, and a mirrored wall, probably two-way, occupied the majority of wall four. In the far-right corner a coffee service filled the air with the aroma of coffee, its polished silver reflecting the crystal chandelier that hung over the table.

Impressive. But what gripped Tyler's attention was the oval conference table. Inlaid blocks of lacquered wood and mother of pearl spiraled outward from the tabletop's center to its edges: the Fibonacci sequence at its finest. As Tyler gazed downward into the seemingly infinite pattern, he felt as if he were peering into a spiral staircase. Mystical and dizzying.

Iris flicked her wrist as if brushing off a picnic table, and Tyler could almost hear the scatter of leaves from Venezuela's national tree, the araguaney. "Please, take a seat," she said.

Antoine pulled out a high-backed chair on his left for Yuki. Tyler selected one to Antoine's right. All gingerly set their notepads and file folders on the exquisite tabletop. A smiling assistant served them espresso with cream and sugar. Tyler helped himself to extra napkins, so he could slip two underneath his saucer, just in case. Yuki and Antoine followed suit.

"A little background seems in order." Iris spoke slow, studied English. "I am in charge of this embassy. I am not Ambassador Chaderton's aide, nor am I his administrative assistant. Neither of us has seen your application."

Not possible. Tyler opened his manila folder to show her the signed and stamped proof of receipt. Then he let his fingers rest. No good could come of challenging this woman. Besides, her excuse provided the most positive of all possible explanations for her country's belated response. He riffled past the card to a printout of their application. "We brought more signed originals," he said, "in case you and others might like them."

She granted him a stiff, miniature nod. "Gracias."

He stood and handed the twenty-two pages across the table's swirling expanse.

Iris glanced at the cover letter before interlocking her fingers on the stack and fixing her eyes on him. "I am completely unfamiliar with your case. Please explain from the beginning."

A glance at Antoine triggered an encouraging nod. "Could take a while," Tyler said. "It goes back to college."

"Please." Iris slow-blinked. "Use all the time you need and spare no detail."

"All right," Tyler said. "I was a theoretical-physics major at the California Institute of Technology. Yuki was going to a university in Irvine when we met in Los Angeles."

"Mark scored a perfect eight hundred on the math sections of both the SAT and GRE tests," Antoine added, sounding like a proud sibling. "And Yuki was majoring in international studies. Correct?" He looked at Yuki, who bobbed her head.

"One story at a time, por favor." Iris fixed her gaze on Tyler. "Yours first."

With Antoine adding explanatory details and answering legal questions, Tyler and Yuki unfolded their stories. Whenever appropriate, they incorporated examples of ways in which they could contribute to Venezuela's welfare.

> It was good to have Antoine there. Iris warmed up and was very nice. We left with the mission of chopping our application into two separate ones and translating them and their references into Spanish.

TYLER PUSHED AWAY FROM HIS OPEN LAPTOP on Lilou's kitchen counter as Lilou sidled barefoot to the stove and lit a burner. She filled a copper kettle and slid it over the flame.

"The good news," Tyler continued, "is that we didn't have to bid you or Antoine adieu, and separating our applications into Yuki's and mine isn't a problem. Bad news is that with only a couple of years of high-school Spanish and the help of online translation services, I'm afraid our docs might sometimes use the wrong words and sound stilted."

Lilou tightened the belt of her white silk robe and leaned forward to read his screen. The wrap draped loose and low, exposing her plump breast almost to the nipple. The hem of her calf-length robe washed like a warm tide over Tyler's knee, and her cherry perfume made his nose tingle. Between the cascade of her uncombed auburn hair and the way her crimson-polished fingers splayed around an ultrathin cigarette, Lilou looked a model of French beauty. Was she coming on to him? Unlikely, with Yuki asleep on the sofa six feet away. Just Lilou being Lilou.

She lifted her arm, and the red fleur-de-lis on her cuff slid up her pale forearm. "Last night while you sleep, Yuki and I, we have a little chat." She edged close. "You see how I live? You like my apartment?"

He raised his guard. "Yeah, it's nice."

"You and Yuki could live like this." A sweep of Lilou's hand encompassed the room. "I could teach her my trade, and we could be partners. Split her revenues fifty-fifty."

So that explained Lilou's unbridled interest in Yuki and why she had opened her home to them. She wanted to become Yuki's madam. Tyler felt hurt yet somehow also relieved. At least now he understood Lilou's motivations.

"What did Yuki say?" he asked.

Lilou removed the lid of a white porcelain canister and sniffed its contents. Tyler caught a whiff of freshly ground coffee. "I put the offer to you," she said. "What do you say?"

Yuki must have declined, so now Lilou was approaching him. Careful. This was her chosen profession, and she was no doubt good at it—perhaps the best. She meant the offer as a high compliment to Yuki, and he could appreciate the attraction: wealth and glamor, flexible hours and independence, a magnetic power over others. But he had seen what prostitution could do to people, how it chipped away at their self esteem—and Yuki had so little to begin with. Yes, he played a lot of roles with her: partner, lover, provider, protector, and he was undoubtedly her greatest annoyance. But he would sooner die than serve as her pimp.

"That's a generous offer," he said. "I can see this life works for you, but our dream is to emigrate to Venezuela. Yuki wants to apply her skills in language, law, and design. I need to do math, maybe even physics."

"Are you sure?" She looked hard at him. "You could have good lives here. Take the spare bedroom while you become established."

From now on, when he complimented Yuki on her beauty and she replied that it was a curse, he would understand that she wasn't entirely joking. Her looks and build, while a blessing, were also a burden that carried risk. "No," he said, "but thanks."

Now the rubber was going to hit the road. Lilou would either tell them to get the hell out, or they'd move forward as friends. Tyler waited for her to decide. The teakettle whistled as she scooped ground coffee into a French press. She poured the glass container full with bubbling water, and while it steeped, she took a pull on her cigarette and blew a cloud of smoke toward the ceiling.

"Well, then." She brushed her hair off her neck. "I shall help you follow your dreams and assist with introductions to Madame Richard."

Yes! Lilou had chosen friendship. But who was this Madame Richard? When Lilou said "Madame," was she using the French equivalent of Mrs. or saying madam, as in the woman in charge of a brothel?

"Who's Madame Richard?" he asked.

Lilou's contoured brows arced to half-moons, and she crossed her cigarette-free hand over her chest as if preparing to sing France's national anthem. "Surely, the good people at the embassy told you about the Circle, and the woman who beats at its heart?"

He rolled his shoulders. "No."

"Those imbéciles!" She stubbed out her cigarette. "Do they really think they can keep the Circle from you and doom you to failure? Without the Circle you have as much chance of gaining asylum as I have of becoming the pope."

Tyler recalled his first encounter with Lilou. She had introduced herself, saying, "I know everyone who is anyone in Paris." At the time, he had admired her charm and hubris, maybe even sensed her decency, but he had assumed she was joking. Never imagined her proclamation to hold any truth. He studied her for clues that she was messing with him.

"There's an organization that helps fugitives apply for asylum in Venezuela and determines whether they're approved?"

She lifted a blue embroidered silk throw off the back of the sofa and spread it tenderly over Yuki. "Oh, mon cher," she whispered. "You would be surprised at how many souls wish to flee one country or another and how few places offer sanctuary from the mighty US of A." She cupped Tyler's face between her warm palms. "Most are perverts or drug lords or war criminals, of course." She puckered her painted lips and made a kissing sound. "Someone has to screen them from entering Venezuela." She swayed to the French press and squeezed its handle downward.

Tyler watched the simple but effective mechanism separate the coffee grounds from hot water to create a luscious, caramel-colored fluid. If this Madame Richard and her mysterious Circle actually existed, then this clinched it: Lilou really did know everyone who was anyone in Paris. "Any idea how we can reach her?"

Lilou set an etched cream and sugar set on a gold-inlaid table. "I may," she said, clinking three leaded-crystal cups into their matching saucers. Tyler caught a glimpse of a label, Baccarat. Everything about Lilou was pure French. "The *flics*," she continued, "they arrest Madame now and again to try to squeeze information out of her. She tells them nothing, of course, but she has become—how do you say?—wary of entrapment. I shall call on your behalf after we have had our café and are ready for the day."

"That's very kind of you." Sunlight glistened through the cut crystal, and white light separated into its spectral colors. Rainbows of violet, blue, green, yellow, orange, and red shimmered across the table, and Tyler traced an orange ray to its originating prism. Yuki sat up and stretched, so Tyler filled the three cups a quarter full of cream and sugar. Lilou topped them off with an intoxicating stream from the French press.

The Test

• • •

Connecting with Madame Richard, even over the phone, proved to be a challenge. When at last Lilou succeeded, she flagged Tyler and Yuki over to listen.

"Perhaps you would feel more comfortable to schedule an appointment," Lilou asked the woman, "if I met with you first?"

"What good would that do?" The shrill voice barked. "I know you. It's these strangers you're trying to foist on me I know not."

"Now, now, I foist no one on you." Lilou's lower jaw inched forward. "I thought perhaps you would like a refreshing change of pace from the scoundrels you usually aid and abet."

This set off a flurry of unintelligible French expletives.

"Trust me, la chérie," Lilou said with a wink at Yuki and her voice turning to honey. "This couple is truly deserving, and you know better than I that Venezuelans are all about relationships. Without your endorsement, they stand no breath of a chance."

A pause. "How long have you known these so-called friends of yours?"

Lilou sighed. "Only a year, but in my line of work, a person learns to read people. I'm telling you, they are ideal candidates. Have I ever steered you wrong?"

The question triggered another flurry, and Tyler detected phrases that translated to "the fat Nazi" and "that half-blind assassin." Then the voice became low and calculating, which provided him with an opportunity to decipher a whole sentence. "And have you forgotten that little knife-swallowing art thief you sent me?"

Lilou wobbled her head. "Two or three bad apples of how many?"

A heavy sigh. "You say he's twenty-eight, and she's twenty-six? That's recruitment age for MI6 and CIA. For all you know, they could be agents from anywhere."

"Tsh-tsh." Lilou propped a bare foot on a chair and examined her bright-red pedicure. "They work for no government."

"Okay, so maybe they are Hamas or al-Qaeda or…I do not do Middle Eastern."

Lilou rolled her eyes at Yuki and then Tyler. "Ça craint! Must you be so suspicious?"

"Do you have any idea how many times the *poulets* have hauled me in this year alone? Twice, and it's only March. Twice, I tell you. One day I will not be so lucky as to walk free."

Gaining Madame R's support was a tough business, and more vital to their success than Tyler had imagined. "Tell her we appreciate her caution," he whispered, "and we can meet her anywhere she likes, any time—just soon, please."

"I heard that!" Madame Richard screeched. "Does he think I am deaf or that I do not speak the English?"

Oh boy.

"I invited them to listen to our conversation," Lilou countered. "They stay with me like family, and they need your assistance. S'il vous plaît."

Another pause. "Say I meet with them. Don't expect me to organize scrap papers from a shoebox or write their applications for them. Do I have your personal assurance that they will bring me a polished, final draft?"

Yuki squeezed Lilou's forearm and nodded. Tyler signaled the Boy Scout pledge.

"Oui," Lilou said. "You have my word and theirs."

"I make no promise to vouch for them. Are we clear on that?"

"Absolutely. I only ask that you meet with them."

The voice dropped to growly mutterings before saying, "Very well. Five o'clock. My office."

"Merci. Adieu." Lilou ended the call with a tap of her French-tipped nail. Glowing with satisfaction, she glanced at her watch, "Oh, mes chers amis, you go and prepare." She shooed Tyler and Yuki out with the back of her hand. "Come back no later than four thirty." Then she added, "and no sooner."

Tyler and Yuki shared a street vendor's cheese soufflé and then signed into an Internet café. They finished drafting their applications into two separate letters around one o'clock. Reference articles were inserted by one forty-five. Auto-translating took until two thirty, and final revisions consumed a god-awful long time. It was almost four thirty before they scrambled through heavy rain to Lilou's door.

At Tyler's knock, a gray-haired bureaucrat-looking fellow made a hasty exit. The three made a mad dash to the metro, arriving at their stop five minutes behind schedule. Not good. Venezuelans, especially those who worked in business and international situations, were known for their punctuality. If Madame R.'s phone voice was any indication, she would be prompt to the point of fanatical.

The three of them took long strides down a gentle slope and hurried past an abandoned office building with broken windows. A row of shops. A chic neighborhood. Lilou snapped to a halt outside a commercial building with ground-level parking and pointed down the block. "The Circle leases the upstairs of that building on the corner."

The building, constructed of interlocking russet-and-cream sandstone, had a timeless, classical look that spoke of strength and security. Dormers on a slate-covered gambrel roof suggested a third story but were probably decorative, and Grecian half columns bordered a middle window that protruded to a balcony.

Lilou must have read Tyler's discomfort because she said, "I'll go in first and check it out."

He gestured toward a crowded outdoor market across the street from the Circle's building. "We'll hide there and watch for your signal."

A nod. Lilou beelined for the building's giant double doors. Tyler and Yuki proceeded down the cobblestone street and crossed into an odiferous blend of cheeses, smoked pork, and caged chickens. He was about to remark on the site's perfect camouflage and view of the Circle's headquarters when Lilou reemerged in front of the carved, glossy-white entrance. She appeared to be trying to placate a tiny, hand-waving woman. Probably Madame Richard. Yuki was stooped over a massive chunk of Roquefort cheese with her back to the scene.

"Don't look." Tyler kept his voice steady. "Just follow me."

Yuki clamped her arms to her side, visibly restraining herself from turning around. "What's going on?"

"Laugh." He pasted on a smile. "And talk."

She bared all but her wisdom teeth and took on a Julia Roberts—or Chucky—sort of expression. "'Look, Ma. No cavities!'" She was gesturing wildly. "'Smile! You're on *Candid Camera*.'"

He grabbed her hand and said, "Ease up."

But as he led her across the street, she bellowed, "'Pardon me, would you have any Grey Poupon?'"

"Shhh." He pulled up in front of an electronics shop with a video game playing *Animal Crossing: Wild World* in its window. Fifty feet distant, Lilou and the stranger continued their animated discussion. With any luck, she would see them and signal that the situation was clear—or to run. "'Silly rabbit.'" Tyler choked down a peal of nervous laughter. "'Trix are for kids.'" Great. Now he was losing it, too.

Sure enough, halfway through the second video game demonstration, Lilou motioned them over. The walk toward the two women felt endless and scrutinized, as if he and Yuki were crossing a neutral zone from South to North Korea.

"Madame Richard," Lilou said as they drew near, "please to meet my dear friends, Yuki and Marco Sosson."

Not a dwarf, but close. Fifties. Wispy gray hair. Skin slightly wrinkled. Madame Richard stood board stiff and shoulders back.

"Buenos tardes," she said, her royal-blue eyes cutting from Tyler to Yuki to Lilou and back to him as she emphasized *tardes*, or *late* in Spanish.

Tyler hoped she was simply using the appropriate afternoon greeting but sensed she was making a point.

Lilou giggled, appearing uncharacteristically ruffled. "Don't you know? Madame was waiting in the stairwell when I walk inside. We shoot right back out here. Boom."

The woman exposed straight white teeth in what might have passed for a smile but was not. "It's not that I do not trust you." She leaned in and lowered her already-soft voice. "Pero—but—I do not trust you."

Tyler looked to Lilou and Yuki for guidance. They appeared equally perplexed, so he met her gaze and dipped his head. "Uh, your humble servants." Great. Just what Venezuela needed, a kiss-ass throwback to the Middle Ages.

Madame Richard gestured down the street and murmured something. Tyler thought he heard *vamos* and *café*. Okay. She wanted to talk over coffee. They walked four across with Yuki and Lilou flanking the slight woman on each side and Tyler streetside to Yuki's right. Madame R. angled forward and said something to him: "Iris Garcia cuando?"

He slowed to match the group's pace. "Iris? We met her yesterday at the embassy."

Fire flooded Madame Richard's eyes. "So she send you a mí para hacer su interpretación? How dare she treat me como traductor!"

This time Tyler heard her all too clearly, but what in the world was she saying? *Interpretation. A translator.* His cheeks burned. Crap. She was offended at being treated like a translator. "Oh no," he said. "Iris didn't send us. Yuki and I just learned of you and the Circle this morning."

Madame Richard redirected her glare to Lilou. "So it is you who informs on me?"

Showing the good sense to pretend that she didn't hear, Lilou lengthened her stride to the beat of a bongo drum pulsing from a café three doors ahead. The scent of fresh-brewed espresso and pastries enriched the breeze.

"So it is you two," Madame R. asked Yuki, "not Iris, who begs this service?"

"Sí." Yuki cleared her throat. "I mean s'il vous plait. I mean por favor."

They entered the narrow café and wormed their way between cramped tables to the back of the room. A silk-throated chorus was crooning complex Afro-Cuban harmonies above the hollow thrum of the bongo. Amid the big-band sound, Tyler recognized elements of American jazz. He made out the phrase *Bruca maniguá.*

The four squeezed into bistro chairs around a two-person cast-iron table. Lilou's warm thigh pressed against Tyler's right leg, so he shifted left and closer to Yuki. A longhaired, round-faced waitress approached to take their orders. Madame R.'s flying fingers appeared to be signaling a complex order for espressos all around, so Tyler allowed himself a deep breath. He sat back and let the lyrics wash over him. "Yo soy cí, negro de nación. Sin la libertad, no pue'o viví." First-person Spanish. Yes, Amine had talked about the C region of Nigeria and about having relatives in Cuba. *Negro de nación* must refer to black slaves. The refrain repeated, providing another chance to translate: I am black of nation. Without freedom, I cannot live.

A jab of Lilou's elbow brought Tyler back to the conversation. Madame R.'s lips were moving at him, and she looked miffed.

He pointed to a speaker above their heads and nodded. "Mucho gusto la música."

Lilou shook her head. "She wants to know what your problem is. Your situation."

He'd have to yell for Madame R. to hear—not exactly a safe place to air details of their fugitive status. "Well, uh." He looked to Lilou for rescue.

She turned toward Madame Richard. "It's like this."

Tyler caught bits and pieces of Lilou's explanation. The problem was the balding, rotund man and his emaciated female companion seated behind Madame R. As Lilou spoke, the pair's dialogue trailed off and they sat upright, attentive as two meerkats.

Madame crossed her arms and leaned back, ever closer to the snoopy couple. "So you two are felons wanted by the FBI?" she asked, plenty loud for Tyler and Yuki—as well as the whole restaurant—to hear.

The gaunt woman listener tucked a strand of gray hair behind her earlobe, no doubt to clear her auditory canal. Tyler covered his mouth and coughed. "I am. I think. Yes."

"No one was harmed," Lilou blasted out, "other than a few gas-guzzling autos and a tumbledown outbuilding."

Lips moving and brows raised in question, Madame R. flicked her thumb and index finger as if igniting a lighter.

Oh boy. "It was a huge mistake," Tyler shouted. "I was young and drunk, and things spun out of control."

"Mark is not an arsonist, if that's what you're asking." Lilou's tone carried an edge. "He and Yuki may be fugitives, but they are decent, highly skilled people. They will contribute years of significant benefit to your homeland if you will please help them gain asylum."

Arsonist. Fugitives. Asylum. At the drop of each word-bomb, Tyler could almost see the couple's ears grow and cup toward them.

The waitress squeezed past the sharp-eared duo and set out napkins with spoons, condiments, and four steaming espressos. Madame R. left her drink black and appeared annoyed as Tyler, Yuki, and Lilou enriched theirs to creamy caramel. She raised her little finger and lifted her coffee in toast. "Salud."

"Salud."

Madame R. took a sip before launching into a barrage of incomprehensible syllables, probably questions.

Tyler jerked a shaky nod. Rats. Now he was overloaded on caffeine. Add in the woman's inaudible voice, the loud music, and the blatant eavesdropping of their neighbors, and this meeting was going just great. He turned to Yuki and shot her an electric grin. "Enjoying my coffee."

She replied with a wide-eyed blink.

The song accelerated to a snappy tango-conga rhythm, and the chorus repeated, "Yényere bruca maniguá." In the mountains lies the answer. What he wouldn't give to be sitting on a quiet, solitary peak right now, blue skies above and a snowcapped mountain range stretching outward. Madame R. murmured something that sounded like Navajo. Then she threw both hands into the air as if miming the letter *Y* in the "YMCA" song. She must have decided not to help them and was now terminating the meeting. At least the torture would end.

Tyler slugged down the last of his espresso. Then he snagged the passing waitress and pressed the check and twenty euros into her palm. He gathered his documents, but then Madame R. extended her palm. Did she want him to hand them over? A waste of time, but what harm could come of sharing? He slid the papers across the table, and Madame R. held the stack up as she read the cover letter. The couple behind her leaned forward and practically rested their chins on her shoulder.

"Excuse us," Tyler blasted at the precise moment when the café happened to fall silent.

The couple looked offended but backed off, and the music and conversations resumed. Hoping to pique Madame R's interest, Tyler wrote down the file names and paths and handed her his backup USB drive. "In case you'd like the electronic format," he said on the off chance that she could hear him, or cared to.

Madame R. sprang to her feet and shoved the documents at Yuki, who clutched them like a shield to her chest. Madame began to wag the USB at Tyler as if it were a firecracker about to explode. Then she smacked the device into his palm.

"What'd she say?" Tyler asked. "What's going on?"

Lilou's hands spun like propellers. "Just stand and nod."

He did as instructed, and the four made their way to the exit. Outside, Lilou lowered her head and her voice. "She is inviting us to her flat."

Yuki brightened. "That's so nice of her."

Lilou raised a shoulder. "Maybe."

Tyler's danger barometer shot to the red zone. "What's wrong?"

"It is just that I have never known her to do this before. I don't have any idea where she lives or what she has in mind."

"You think this is a trap?" Here came the angry ants again, biting a path up his spine. "Like maybe she needs somebody to hand over to the cops, so they'll get off her back?" he asked.

Lilou pursed her lips and extended her arm to hail a cab. "I cannot go with you. I have a date." The taxi rolled to a stop at the curb. "This is your decision."

Madame Richard braced her hands on her hips, awaiting an answer. Impossible to read. The feisty little character was tough and cantankerous and seemed almost as paranoid as he was. But she was plugged in. Without her assistance and blessing, Venezuela would never accept them. Tyler looked at Yuki. "I think we'd better go."

She covered her mouth and said, "No choice."

"We'll have to watch out," he whispered before turning to Madame Richard. "Muchas gracias por la invitación. Un momento, por favor."

The woman crossed her arms in reply.

Lilou slid into the taxi's back seat. "Good luck," she said. "See you later, God willing."

The cab sped away, and street lamps flared yellow, as if warning him to use caution. Madame R. led Tyler and Yuki down the block to a nondescript two-story apartment building. Their shoes scuffed up a flight of poorly lit concrete stairs that smelled of insecticide. A steel door opened to worn brown carpet. The scent of stale marijuana filled the hallway. Odd numbers to the left, evens to the right. Madame R. stopped at room 217 and inserted a key into a lock on a plain gray door with a peephole. The hinges creaked, and they stepped into a dark hallway.

"Bienvenida." She slammed the door, and pitch-darkness engulfed them. "Mí casa es…mí casa," she said.

The sound of a twisting deadbolt brought to mind a scene from a Hitchcock movie, yet Tyler also felt a surge of relief. At least now he could hear the woman speak. Something thumped. Then a series of bumps and grunts filled him with terror. He gripped Yuki's arm, and they backed toward the locked door.

The footfalls drew nearer, thudding closer and closer. Something rammed into Tyler's calves, and he spun for the knob. But a heavy object now entwined his legs and nearly toppled him over. A light flicked on, and he could see enough to right himself.

"Ha!" he exclaimed. "A cat!" And not just any cat, a long-haired, morbidly obese tabby with moon-shaped ears and eyes. Spots, not stripes, dappled a thick, grayish coat that was rubbing on Tyler's khakis.

Yuki giggled. "Here, kitty kitty." She reached down to a second cat, this one fluffy and white and purring like a well pump. It touched a pink nose to the back of Yuki's hand before pushing upward and compelling her to caress its head.

"Plumoso. El Tigre. You two behave yourselves." Madame Richard glared at the cats as she jabbed a flat palm toward Tyler and Yuki. "Coats, por favor."

They slid out from their jackets, and Madame hung them on a row of pegs below a life-size poster of Hugo Chavez. Dressed in a red jacket and cap, looking as serious as a drill sergeant, Venezuela's president stood with one arm jabbed out at them. He was rumored to be a man who didn't take well to—and seldom heard—the word *no*. Madame R. took off her coat and draped it on a smooth-worn peg at Chavez's feet.

Tyler scanned the antiques. None bore a tuft of fur. No scent of kitty litter. "We have a dog that goes nuts at the smell of cats," he said, trying to buy time to assess the situation.

"This way." Madame R. led them down the hallway and through a parlor.

Yuki ran a finger over a camel-backed chair with an upholstered seat. "Nice antiques."

If Madame R. heard, she gave no indication. Instead, she ushered them into a small, windowless room with a desk and computer bearing the manufacturer's label SIRAGON. File cabinets and shelves loaded with notebooks lined the walls. She dabbed a finger at the desktop. "Upload your files, por favor."

They'd come this far. Why not? Tyler slid into a seat and inserted the USB. A few keystrokes, and Yuki's letter flashed onto the screen. "There we go," he said.

Madame R. rolled two office chairs next to Tyler, though she and Yuki remained standing. "As you know," she said, "Venezuela has some of the largest proven oil reserves outside the Middle East. But we have a weakening democracy and a politicized military."

"We've been studying your country's history." Tyler scrolled slowly down the page in case Madame R. was reading it. "But we have a lot to learn." Out of nowhere, El Tigre rifled onto Tyler's lap and curled into a ball. Deep, resonant purrs vibrated through Tyler's body and perhaps the whole room.

Madame R. plopped down in a chair next to Tyler and patted the empty seat to her right. "You remind me of Venezuela's Alexandra Braun," she said as Yuki sat next to her. "She was voted Miss World last year, you know."

Yuki flushed. "Gracias."

They sat in silence, all three staring at the slow-scrolling screen. Then Plumoso hurled itself onto Yuki's lap, and its front paws kneaded her upper thighs.

"Bueno," Madame R. said with a sigh of exasperation, or possibly acquiescence. "Considering how my boys like you, I suppose I might translate. But you must promise not to tell Iris I did the work. I don't want that woman thinking she can dump more of her workload on me."

Tyler and Yuki nodded in unison. "Sure." "No problem."

"Mis queridos," she said, probably to her cats but maybe to them. "Perhaps we should do a quick read-through. I give you a few pointers, if you like."

What a kind and energetic woman she was! She filled us with stories about names from Venezuelan politics, familiar and unknown, about local protests, about the misrepresentation in the press. We finished by watching a Barbara Walters interview with Chavez. It was a very positive experience, and we shared a lot of smiles on the walk home.

Tyler relaxed into an unstoppable grin as he and Yuki passed under a streaming streetlight. "The café. The cats. I'm thinking they were some sort of test," he said, "and it appears we passed."

Yuki goose-stepped forward from his side. "Com-pose and re-fine los doc-u-men-tes," she said, marking time as she recited their instructions.

He heard himself chuckle. "That's right."

She spun ninety degrees on her heel before turning another right angle and heading back toward him. "Sub-mit the draft to Ma-dame R."

One last turn and Yuki was again walking beside him. He tucked a hand around her waist and snugged her close. "You got it."

She kissed his cheek. "Then what?"

"Well, assuming she gives us the go, she'll either take it to Madame Garcia at the embassy, or we will."

"Then what?" Yuki sounded like a kid turning a storybook page.

He had been pondering the same question with mixed feelings. "Then we wait," he said. "We go back to Corsica, fetch Chiki, and hope for good news."

"I miss Chiki-san," she said, her voice dreamy, "and I cannot wait to lead a regular, normal, boring old life."

He missed the little guy, too, and could barely remember earlier days when he'd awakened without fear: Fear of arrest, fear of never making it home, fear of Yuki or Chiki taking ill, fear of hooligans attacking them. And there were the recurring nightmares of harm coming to his family back home. Yes, Venezuela must accept them. Just had to. For now, though, going back to

Corsica was their best and only option. Besides, Chiki needed them, and they needed him. Spring was in the air. The season of rebirth and fresh starts was upon them. Hikes and living in the wilderness, working for cash, and busing tables awaited. He stopped and took her face in his hands.

"Me, too," he said. "We'll find a way to bring Chiki with us, or we'll have him shipped over later."

"How long do you think we will need to wait?" She wrapped her fingers tight around his. "One week? Maybe a month?"

He regretted that he lacked a valid answer to give her. "More than a week. These things take time."

They walked on, swinging clasped hands.

"How much time?" Yuki raised their arms to a peak and held them skyward. "I crave the wave—of Venezuela."

Waiting was going to be torture. "We don't have to be there to make changes in our lives," he said. "From now on, I intend to listen better and pay more attention to your feelings."

"And I will be more patient, less cranky pants with Sosson."

"We'll take it one day at a time," he said, and a strange mixture of hope, relief, and anticipation settled over him. "We'll get through this together." Who knew what the future would bring? One thing was certain: trying to predict too far in advance would put chaos theory into play. The best laid plans….

Whatever dangers and disappointments lay ahead, he would find a way to make a better life for Yuki and communicate with his family back home. Just had to.

—The End—

A portion of
the royalties for
The Fall and Rise of Tyler Johnson
will be donated to

LCJP
LONGMONT
COMMUNITY JUSTICE
PARTNERSHIP

No young person should feel his or her life is over, no matter how serious the mistake. The Longmont Community Justice Partnership collaborates with the Longmont, Colorado police, schools, and municipal court to provide restorative justice as an alternative to the traditional criminal justice system. Adult and juvenile offenders with pending criminal charges may be referred to LCJP if they are willing to take responsibility for their choices and make repairs to relationships that have been impacted by their actions. Volunteer facilitators trained by LCJP lead group dialogues in which offenders, victims, and community representatives identify how involved parties have been harmed and discuss how the offender can make things right. Ninety percent of offenders referred to LCJP complete their contracts to repair harm and avoid having criminal charges on their records.

LCJP is a 501(c)(3) nonprofit organization. To learn more, please visit www.lcjp.org.

ABOUT THE AUTHOR

• • •

PATRICE JOHNSON IS PUBLISHING HER account of the life of her son, Tyler, to tell the true story.

Patrice graduated *summa cum laude* from Alma College and received her master's degree in English literature from Michigan State University. When her children were young, she taught high school English and community college writing. She also spent sixteen years in the computer industry and was a weekly columnist for the industry's largest trade publication. Patrice served as vice president of marketing and communications with a Fortune 500 company and has founded three successful technology companies.

Patrice has been quoted in *USA Today* and *Business Week*. She has authored a chapter on corporate quality in a college textbook, and her writings have received six first-place awards from the Michigan Press Women.

She and her husband live on their eighty-acre family farm in the Midwest.

70549940R00306

Made in the USA
Columbia, SC
09 May 2017